Talking Animals

University of Pennsylvania Press
MIDDLE AGES SERIES
Edited by
Edward Peters
Henry Charles Lea Professor
of Medieval History
University of Pennsylvania

A listing of the available books in the series appears at the back of this
volume

Talking Animals

Medieval Latin Beast Poetry, 750–1150

Jan M. Ziolkowski

University of Pennsylvania Press

Philadelphia

Cover stamp: Illustration of the Tityrus from John Vinycomb, *Fictitious and Symbolic Creatures in Art* (London, 1906).

Copyright © 1993 by the University of Pennsylvania Press
All rights reserved
Printed in the United States of America

Library of Congress Cataloging-in-Publication Data

Ziolkowski, Jan M.
    Talking animals: medieval Latin beast poetry, 750–1150 / Jan M. Ziolkowski.
        p.   cm—(Middle Ages series)
    Includes bibliographical references and index.
    ISBN 0-8122-3161-9
    1. Latin poetry, Medieval and modern—History and criticism.
    2. Animals in literature.   I. Title.   II. Series.
    PA8065.A54Z55   1993
    871'.030936—dc20   92-46709
                                                                              CIP

TO SASKIA, ADA, AND YETTA,
three little girls who were born
while this big bad wolf lurked at the door

Contents

Acknowledgments

This book has occupied my thoughts intermittently for more than a decade. For the financial support that enabled me first to explore medieval Latin beast poetry in my dissertation, I feel an abiding gratitude to the Marshall Aid Commemoration Commission. For intellectual inspiration during three years at Cambridge University I owe the greatest debt to Peter Dronke, who pointed me toward poems and perceptions that otherwise would have eluded me. At the same time I thank Jill Mann, who supervised me for one term.

For the time years later to recast the dissertation I am indebted to the Guggenheim Foundation. For permission to incorporate parts of articles into small sections of the present book I am grateful to *Bestia, Denver Quarterly, Mediaevalia, Mittellateinisches Jahrbuch, Poetica,* and *Res Publica Litterarum.* Unless otherwise specified, translations of texts throughout the book are my own. To the Loeb Classical Library Foundation of the Harvard University Department of the Classics I am indebted for a publication subvention.

The happiest continuity for more than the past dozen years has been my family. My wife has offered me so much support that dedicating a volume about talking animals to her would seem insufficiently earnest recompense. Instead, I dedicate the book to the three loquacious creatures for which she and I share responsibility. Perhaps when older, our daughters will enjoy the beast fictions with which their father spent countless hours away from them. At least they will understand my frequent moments of distraction in reading to them: the animals in their bedtime stories made my thoughts turn from play to work. I hope that the reverse has also occurred: if the sportiveness of their stories has leavened this book, so much the better.

Introduction

Car sur Regnart poeult on gloser,
penser, estudïer, muser
plus que sur toute rien qui soit.

One can gloss, think, study,
and muse upon Renart more than upon
anything else there is.
        (*Le Roman de Renart le Contrefait*, lines 105–7)

Not all stories about animals are fables, but in English the only common
term to designate fiction in which animals are important characters is *beast
fable*, often reduced crudely to *fable*. Although beast fables have been and
probably always will be preeminent among the different types of literature
about animals, the term should not be stretched beyond the limitations of
form that lend fable its specificity: a fable has a rigid structure that requires
the story part to be brief and the meaning (or at least one meaning) of the
story to be communicated overtly in the moral.

A more inclusive label for fiction about animals would be *beast literature*. As used in this book, beast literature is not a genre on the order of
the epic, romance, or novel. Rather, it comprehends texts from many
genres—texts in which the principal actors are animals, usually talking
animals. Yet despite their generic diversity, such texts merit being examined together since many authors who produce beast literature perceive as
soon as they begin to write that they are competing with, and benefiting
from, not just other works in the genre in which they write but also all
other stories about animals that they have read since childhood. When
authors or readers are confronted with an animal protagonist, they are
inclined automatically to think of other types of literature about animals,
regardless of whether those other types are in the same genre. The moral
of the story is that beasts override genre.

Medieval Latin beast poetry is a subclass of beast literature, delimited
by both the chronological and formal indications that *medieval Latin* and
poetry entail. The words "beast poetry" translate the German *Tierdichtung*,

an old word that has been guaranteed currency in the second half of the twentieth century through the title of a book by Hans Robert Jauss: *Untersuchungen zur mittelalterlichen Tierdichtung* (1959). A panoply of other terms has been created by German critics and theorists to designate literary genres in which animals figure prominently, such as *Tiermärchen, Tiersage, Tierfabel, Tierschwank*, and *Tierepos* (Knapp 1979a, 102–14; Knapp 1979b), but *Tierdichtung* has the advantage of being the least rigid and most comprehensive. As I employ the phrase in this book, "beast poetry" indicates poems in which the central character is a talking animal or bird.

Animals and birds are especially salient in three types of medieval literature: one is beast fable, often called Aesopic fable; another is the *Physiologus* and its close relative, the bestiary; and a third is the cycle of stories that turns around Renard the Fox. The extent to which these three sorts of literature were known in the Middle Ages and continue to be known today has hindered more than helped proper appreciation and appraisal of medieval Latin beast poems. When the beast poems have not been ignored altogether, they have often been lumped with one of the three better-known genres. Because the medieval Latin poems lie chronologically between ancient fable and the *Physiologus*, on the one hand, and the Renard cycle, on the other, they are presented as either the degenerate descendants of fable and the *Physiologus* or as the rude predecessors of the Renard cycle. Both of these schemata blur the strong differences in spirit and form between the medieval Latin poems and other types of literature in which animals appear, especially the three major genres. Above all, they do an injustice to the variety and complexity of the medieval Latin poems.

According to a conveniently clear modern definition, a beast fable is an account of a single fictional event in which at least one character is an animal and which is preceded or followed by an explicit moral exposition (Perry 1952, ix). This definition allows for overlapping between beast fable and beast poetry: not every beast poem meets the criteria of beast fable, but many verse beast fables qualify as beast poems. Yet although in theory beast fable and beast poetry could have overlapped, few medieval Latin writers of the twelfth and earlier centuries simply versified prose fables, even when they wrote school exercises (Voigt 1894). Even when poets reworked the story parts of fables in compositions of their own, they introduced special twists in the framing and style that distinguished their poems from the fables. Most important, the beast poets tended to modify the usual fabular structure of a short narrative followed by a moral. Although a beast poem such as the *Ecbasis captivi* is sometimes called a fable, it is not a fable in the strict sense since it lacks the outright moral essential to beast fable (Schaller 1970a, 93–95). Even a poem such as Alcuin's "The Cock and Wolf" departs from the most typical form of fable by concluding with two morals, one delivered by a character within the narrative and another pronounced by the narrator.

Medieval Latin beast poetry also differs fundamentally from the animal sections of the *Physiologus* and bestiary. Whereas the beast poems are expressly fictitious narratives, the *Physiologus* and bestiary first purport to describe the behavior of real animals and then derive lessons of religious significance from this behavior. Whereas the main characters in the beast poems are talking animals, the animals in the *Physiologus* and bestiary do not talk.

Beast fables and the core material of the *Physiologus* were already circulating in antiquity. In contrast, the *Roman de Renart* is a conglomeration of Old French poems about the fox which took shape only in the late twelfth century, but which went on to inspire imitations in most vernacular literatures of Western Europe (Flinn; Best). Although a few medieval Latin beast poems share with the Renard cycle the general theme of the fox-wolf feud as well as specific points of detail, there are many disparities between the Latin and the vernacular poems. Whereas the Renard poems were written within vernacular traditions (since the very word *roman* implies a Romance language, the notion of a Latin *roman* is inherently oxymoronic!), the medieval Latin poems responded to Classical Latin poetry in both structure and style. In spite of their occasional similarities, such poems as Leo of Vercelli's "Meter," the *Ecbasis captivi*, and the *Ysengrimus* are certainly more than coarse prototypes of the *Roman de Renart*. All occupy very special places in medieval Latin literature, and the *Ysengrimus* is arguably a masterpiece within medieval European literature as a whole.

The title of the *Roman de Renart* suggests a second difference between the medieval Latin beast poems and later vernacular beast poems. The proper noun *Renart/Renard*, which commemorates the fox who is the central figure of the corpus, signals that the animals in the *roman* are so highly individualized that they have names, like human beings. In contrast, only two twelfth-century medieval Latin beast poems introduce animals with names (*Ysengrimus* and *Speculum stultorum*), only one of them the fox called Renard (*Ysengrimus*).

Seeking a single source or blend of sources for all of the medieval Latin beast poems is futile. Nineteenth-century scholars tended toward two extremes in explaining the origins of medieval Latin beast poetry

(Flinn 20–27; Yates 1979, 14–17). One group viewed the poems as learned, monastic, and derived from written fables or jests (Paulin Paris; Lucien Foulet). Another group regarded the poems as Latin records of folklore and stories that had been popular in vernacular languages, especially Germanic languages, long before the twelfth-century *branches* of the *Roman de Renart* (Jacob Grimm, Léopold Sudre, Karl Voretzsch, Gaston Paris). As was suggested long ago (Adolf Graf), there is no need to squeeze the medieval Latin beast poems into such discrete categories as Aesopic beast poems or Renard-cycle beast poems. Such pigeonholing obscures the fact that Latin poets would have known both learned fables from their basic schooling in Latin and vernacular animal tales from oral literature in their native cultures.

Oversimplistic classification cheapens the quality of the medieval Latin poems because it leaves one of two false impressions: either that the poems are the epigones of classical fable or that their supreme achievement was to prepare the way for the *Roman de Renart*. Seen through the distorting lenses of fable and of the *Roman de Renart*, the medieval Latin beast poems lose their sharp edges. They are inspected from one point of view for how they meet or fail to meet the requirements of classical beast fable, from another for how they presage the vernacular poems. Their most unusual, and most characteristically medieval Latin, features pass unnoticed for the very reason that they mark the medieval Latin poems apart from other genres in which animals appear.

There have been fine essays and monographs on individual medieval Latin beast poems, particularly the three longest poems (for an overview of the scholarship, see Knapp 1979a), and there have been brief but stimulating surveys of the early poems in two articles (Ross; Schaller 1970a). In addition, there have been enlightening chapters on selected Latin poems within books on medieval beast literature as a whole (Jauss; Best). Finally, there has been a fine new edition and translation of the *Ysengrimus*, with an introductory monograph (Mann 1987). Yet in spite of these partial efforts, there has never been an interpretative book wholly devoted to medieval Latin beast poems.

The beast poems to be examined here were written between A.D. 750 and 1150—between the beginning of the Carolingian renaissance and the middle of the twelfth-century renaissance. How many beast poems were composed during this span of nearly half a millennium but have not survived can only be conjectured. A full history of medieval Latin and vernacular literature that has been lost has yet to be written (Wilson). The fact is that fewer than a dozen brief poems of this type are extant from the eighth through the eleventh century. Especially important are Alcuin's "The Cock and Wolf"; "The Sick Lion" and "The Sad Calf," formerly attributed to Paul the Deacon; the anonymous ninth-century "Nanny Goat"; Sedulius Scottus's "The Ram"; the anonymous ninth-century "Swan Sequence"; Eugenius Vulgarius's "Comic Visions"; Leo of Vercelli's "Meter"; and two eleventh-century poems of unknown authorship, "The Cock and Fox" and "The Wolf." In addition, there are a few short dialogic beast poems from the early period, which culminate in the eleventh-century *Ecbasis captivi*, the first beast poem of more than a thousand lines. From the twelfth century are two much longer narrative poems, the *Ysengrimus* and the *Speculum stultorum*.

The medieval Latin poems have few immediately discernible traits in common with one another. They were not the products of the same time or region. They range greatly in length, from under fifty lines to over six thousand, and also in meter. Indeed, the individual pieces are as difficult to characterize as the class of poetry was simple to define. In structure a beast poem can be as humble as one speech by a bird struggling to fly home safely (in "The Swan Sequence"), but then again it can intertwine a dozen main stories and another dozen visions, reminiscences, and divagations (as in the *Speculum stultorum*). In style the poetry encompasses the cryptic allusiveness of Eugenius Vulgarius's "Comic Visions," the deft quotation of classical verse in Sedulius Scottus's "The Ram" and the *Ecbasis captivi*, and the lush vocabulary of the *Ysengrimus*.

The beast poems were created for many occasions and audiences. Not all of them were written by bookish pedants and intended solely to be pored over in the library. Some of them were composed to be read aloud, sung, and staged. Their audiences were sometimes as grand as imperial and episcopal courts. But even when a beast poem was designed mainly for the brethren of a single monastery, it could have had a very lively mise-en-scène: some were perhaps scripts for schoolroom performances in which pupils donned animal masks, others for recitation in the refectory.

If the beast poems are so very heterogeneous, it may be asked what justification there is for considering them together. One response to this question is that despite their many differences the poems are nonetheless subtly interconnected. For instance, identical narrative motifs crop up in several poems. Thus the same tale of the ailing lion king lies at the heart of "The Sick Lion," *Ecbasis captivi*, and *Ysengrimus* and is mentioned obliquely in Leo of Vercelli's "Meter." To take another example, the tale of the cock and the fox that is the topic of "The Cock and Fox" recurs in one story in the *Ysengrimus*. Finally, the fable of the ass in the lion's skin appears in both Leo of Vercelli's "Meter" and the *Speculum stultorum*.

Another response is best conveyed through an analogy. A person who visited a museum of early experiments in aviation would see flying machines that bear little resemblance to one another. Some would have the pilot reclining, some upright. Some would have fixed wings and propellers, others movable ones that flapped. Some would have four wings, some six, others two. Some would be made of canvas, some of wood, others of metal. In short, no two of these prototypes would look exactly like each other, and many of them would have no major features in common with any of the others except that their fabricators shared the dream of flying in them. The medieval Latin beast poems are like these early efforts to create flying machines. For all their superficial differences, they are all produced by poets who shared an unusual poetic language and similar inspirations: while the schooling of these poets familiarized them with written beast fables and the *Physiologus*, their native cultures gave them oral beast fables and tales. Many of the medieval Latin poets held two broad goals in common: they aimed to fuse this material into longer literature and to retain its amusing qualities while overcoming its reputation for childishness. But they had no predetermined sense of the genre in which they wrote.

Whether composing in Latin or a vernacular language, whether living in the ancient, medieval, or modern world, authors who center their fictions upon talking animals share special opportunities. For instance, one capacity of animals is to make a fiction accessible to a broad audience: although the particular associations attached to a given animal vary from culture to culture, taken as a group animals are a language common to all people. This universal currency is what Orwell had in mind when he wrote *Animal Farm*. As he stated in the preface to the Ukrainian edition of the book (405), "On my return from Spain I thought of exposing the Soviet myth in a story that could be easily understood by almost anyone and which could be easily translated into other languages." Animals have earned this universal status not because they are so much the same the world over but because people are so much the same; for most animals in fiction are not portrayed realistically but instead are anthropomorphized: that is, human motivation, characteristics, and behavior are attributed to them.

Although in the hands of a propagandist animals can be used to inculcate the values of an existing regime, they can also help the literary subversive to attack the status quo. Apart from being meaningful and approachable to all sorts of people, animals permit authors to take risks that they cannot take in stories explicitly about human beings. In particular, beast fables and beast folktales provide underdogs (the pun is purposeful)— whether oppressed classes or endangered individuals—with the means to express their viewpoint and to pass on advice to enable those like them to survive. Through beasts they can comment upon the powerful, express their resentments and frustrations, and fulfill in fantasy dreams that they could not realize in life (Hausrath 1937; La Penna; Luria; Pugliarello).

How does beast fable make all this possible? To caricature enemies or oppressors as animals is a relatively safe form of humor, since often the targets of such mockery will refuse to make themselves ridiculous by acknowledging that any resemblance exists. As anyone who has observed the social interaction of children can testify, no one willingly admits to being a pigface. Partly for this reason, the related practices of humanizing animals and animalizing human beings have long been the mainstay of many adult insults and jokes, especially ones concerned with class and ethnic struggles.

Phaedrus (ca. 15 B.C. to ca. A.D. 50) summed up the close relationship between animal fiction and class oppression in explaining the origins of fable:

Nunc, fabularum cur sit inventum genus,
brevi docebo. Servitus obnoxia,
quia quae volebat non audebat dicere,
affectus proprios in fabellas transtulit,
calumniamque fictis elusit iocis.

Now I will explain briefly why the type of thing called fable was invented. The slave, being liable to punishment for any offence, since he dared not say outright what he wished to say, projected his personal sentiments into fables and eluded censure under the guise of jesting with made-up stories. (Book 3, Prologue 33–37, ed. and trans. Perry 254–55)

Was he right? It is a revealing coincidence that Phaedrus, as well as his predecessor, Aesop, the legendary Greek fabulist of the early sixth century B.C., and Uncle Remus, the fictitious teller of the Brer Rabbit stories collected by Joel Chandler Harris (1848–1908) in the United States in the second half of the nineteenth century, were all slaves who later became freedmen. Indeed, the Uncle Remus stories have been interpreted convincingly as draping animal hides over expressions of the animosity that enslaved people felt toward masters, over information about survival techniques, over portrayals of the harsh violence and hunger of plantation life, and over the wish-fulfillment of stories in which weak and oppressed creatures overcome cruel, more powerful opponents (Bone; Flusche; Wolfe).

Ancient fabulists professed to believe that fable as a genre allowed a person of humble origins to succeed. Phaedrus minced no words in the epilogue to his second book of fables (Book 2, no. 9, lines 1–4, ed. and trans. Perry 247–49): "The Athenians set up a statue in honour of the gifted Aesop, and by so doing placed a slave on a pedestal of everlasting fame, that all men might know that the path of honour lies open and that glory is awarded not according to birth, but according to merit." In modern-day terms, Phaedrus saw fable-writing as one career in which meritocracy prevailed, even for a person as socially disadvantaged as a freedman.

Many of Phaedrus's fables have social implications, even though their morals are explicitly ethical. For example, of the first five in Book 1, only one has a purely ethical moral without any social implications (Book 1, no. 4, ed. Perry 196–97). But just what are the social messages of Phaedrus's fables? The fable of "The Frogs Asked for a King" (Book 1, no. 2, ed. Perry 193–95) brings home the dangers of tyranny. "The Frog Who Burst Herself and the Cow" (Book 1, no. 24, ed. Perry 218–21) is paired with the moral that one should keep to one's station. "The Two Mules and the Robbers" (Book 2, no. 7, ed. Perry 242–45) ends with the truism that "the little man is safe." The moral of "The Meeting of the Wolf and the Dog" (Book 3, no. 7, ed. Perry 266–69) is "how sweet liberty is."

Of course, beast stories have never been the exclusive province of underclasses. Individuals of any class can resort to fables and tales about animals when they believe that they would run risks in speaking out more directly in another medium. In one of the earliest surviving ancient Greek poems (written around 700 B.C.), Hesiod cast his grievances about a vexatious tyrant in a tale about a hawk and a nightingale (*Works and Days* 203–12; Puelma). Three centuries later Socrates (who lived from 469 to 399 B.C.) was reputed to have busied himself while in prison with the versification of Aesop's fables (Plato, *Phaedo* 61b, trans. Tredennick 44). The philosopher's choice of activity fits well with the theory that ancient fable was a weapon of the small and weak against the mighty (Meuli 1975). In *Animal Farm* George Orwell presented his views of the former Soviet system in what he calls a "fairy tale" about pigs and other farm animals in part because overt criticism of the Soviet Union was impossible in 1944 in the face of the strong allegiance to the Soviets in England at the time (Armstrong 14). As these examples suggest, animal stories can be used as tools for education or even propaganda.

The idea of using different types of animals to represent different classes in human society and thereby to express social criticism was not lost upon medieval fabulists (Henderson 1973, 1978, 1981, 1982). For example, Odo of Cheriton, probably the best-known of thirteenth-century Latin fabulists, sometimes used fables as a vehicle for social criticism, particularly of the church. Marie de France, who wrote fables in Old French verse at roughly the same time as Odo, was even more persistent a critic of her society, from the highest reaches of the nobility through the lowest of the peasants. In many instances she replaces *moral* terms of the earlier fable collections—words such as strong, weak, malicious, or innocent—with social terms such as rich, poor, lord, or serf. Coincidentally, animals represent kings, secular lords, peasants, and ecclesiastics. These tendencies pervade her collection of about a hundred fables, of which more than two dozen have clearly stated social applications. To look at a medieval writer coming from a very different background, the Hebrew fable-writer Berechiah Ha-Nakdan expressed a specially Jewish viewpoint in his collection of fox fables, but he still showed a characteristically medieval proclivity to establishing explicit identifications between animals and social classes.

All three of these authors single out specific social classes in their morals rather than leave the connection to the reader's imagination. The moral in Odo's version of "The Puffed-Up Frog" is indicative. Whereas Phaedrus (Book 1, no. 24, ed. Perry 218–21) offered the simple prefatory moral that "When a man without resources tries to imitate the powerful he comes to grief," Odo spells out precisely who the powerful and resourceless are, in his opinion:

> Thus there are many men who see bishops, abbots, archdeacons—officials who, so to speak, approximate cows—ambling along with a show of great ostentation. Such onlookers wonder to themselves just how they may become as great as these officials. And at length they make the attempt. In consequence they come—spiritually and physically—to their deaths. (no. 92, trans. Jacobs 140)

Apart from the social criticism and meritocratic career possibilities that the fable genre enabled, writing about talking animals also brings sheerly literary liberty: it often gives authors more license to experiment with styles and registers than they would find in writing about human characters. Rhetoricians such as Nicolaus of Myra (fifth century A.D.) urged writers of fables to make their language humble to match the animal characters. He wrote:

> It is necessary that the language of fable be very simple, straightforward, and free from all rhetorical complexity and periodic order, so that the meaning is clear and the words do not seem greater than the characters in question, especially when the fable is composed of brute animals. (*Progymnasmata*, ed. Spengel 3: 454, "Mythos," lines 22–28; my translation)

Yet even though writers sometimes followed such directives without wavering, more often they could not resist playing off traits of the most serious literature (such as epic) against a plain-and-simple style. They have taken pleasure in demonstrating that the power of speech corrupts, that no sooner can an animal talk than it yields to the impulse to talk too much, to lie, and to boast. From the beginning, poems in which talking animals are the protagonists—for example, *The Battle of the Frogs and Mice* (*Batrachomyomachia*) in ancient Greek—have often created a humorous incongruity in juxtaposing seemingly childish or frivolous animals with both verbal and formal echoes of epic. Like all sorts of mock-epic compositions, such poems attain much of their humor through deliberately violating such directives: a mock epic achieves its effect through making much of little and little of much.

Medieval Latin examples of such mock epics would be "The Wrangle of the Dwarf and Hare" and "The Lombard and Snail." In "The Wrangle of the Dwarf and Hare" (ninth century?) the unknown poet evokes Aeneas and Turnus; Achilles; and Adrastus, Cadmus, and Tydeus before sinking bathetically to a struggle in which a hare has the better of a dwarf and a dog. Like the proverbial dwarf on the shoulders of a giant, "The Wrangle of the Dwarf and Hare" was placed by its scribe immediately after the works of Vergil (ed. Dümmler 354). In "The Lombard and Snail" (probably twelfth century) the poet calls to mind Hector, Achilles, and Hercules in depicting a Lombard as he readies himself to do battle with a snail, which he believes to be a heavily armed monster. "The Lombard and Snail" has an artistic analogue, since a motif of a man combating a snail appears in the margins of North French illuminated manuscripts from the end of the thirteenth century (Randall).

Loosely related to the mock epics are such parodies and imitations of

Ovid as "The Flea" and "The Louse." Although the former belongs to the long line of parodies in which poets profess to long for the freedom of the louse to wander over the bodies of their beloved, it begins not with an allusion to Ovid's "ring poem" (*Amores* 2.15) but to "The Gnat." Yet none of these medieval mock epics and parodies exploits the possibilities for humor in personifying the animals to the point where they can speak. Instead, "The Wrangle of the Dwarf and Hare" and "The Lombard and the Snail" concentrate upon ridiculing the human actors in their down-scaled epics.

This propensity to make much of little and little of much, rather than being restricted to thoroughgoing mock epics, is also evident in other types of literature in which talking animals appear. Horace, who employs fables more freely than any other classical Latin poet, now writes them in a laughably overwrought bombast, now slips into homely colloquialisms (e.g., the fables of the Frog and Calf in *Satires* 2.3.314–20 and of the City Mouse and Country Mouse in *Satires* 2.6.79–117: Archibald 1902, lxxxix, and 1910, xvi–xix; Witke 72–75). Like many later fabulists, Avian creates incongruities between his furry or scaly characters on the one hand and his style on the other by quoting Vergil (Gaide 24, passim).

The most tangible evidence of the comic potential in animalizing Vergil comes not in literature but in ancient vase painting. The painter took one of the most solemn moments in Roman legend, the flight of Aeneas from Troy: as the city burns and Greek invaders are everywhere, Aeneas takes flight with his father upon his back and his son holding his hand. The scene was charged with symbolism: the founder of Rome leads the future by the hand while he hefts the burden of the past upon his shoulder. But the vase painter, finding the solemnity too much to endure, rendered the scene ludicrous by substituting dog- or ape-headed creatures for Aeneas and his family, while arranging them in their standard postures (Wright 19–22).

The literary freedoms that beast stories offer their authors are not restricted to style. Both the authors and the readers of beast stories tend naturally to concentrate upon the beasts so much that they insist less upon adherence to rules of genre than they would do normally. In other words, authors who write animal satires, dream-visions, novels, or epics have only half their minds upon the customary mechanics of those genres; the other half turns willy-nilly to memories of literature in which animals are prominent, regardless of whether or not such literature is in the genre in which they are writing.

A few concrete examples are in order. One is *The Battle of the Frogs and Mice*. In genre this poem is unquestionably a mock epic. It falls into two distinct sections. The first, which covers the first ninety-nine lines, relates the events that begin with the encounter between the mouse Crumb-Snatcher and the frog Puff-Jaw. After the mouse and frog meet at the water's edge, the two boast of their homes and foods. Eventually the frog persuades the mouse to ride on his back to the home of the frogs. All goes well until a watersnake frightens the frog into diving, whereupon the mouse drowns. The second section of the mock epic, which stretches from line 100 to the end of the poem at line 303, tells of the battle between the mice and the frogs that fills the remainder of the day upon which Crumb-Snatcher expires.

The text of *The Battle of the Frogs and Mice* contains several indications that the first part is based upon a fable. For one thing, as in most fables the story is not localized geographically. For another, it begins in a "once upon a time" style typical of fable. In the third place, the story-type has a precise parallel in fable (Perry 1965, 490–91, Appendix no. 384). The fable and the corresponding section of *The Battle of the Frogs and Mice* differ most obviously in length: the *Battle* is much longer because it incorporates many elements of heroic epic (an invocation of Muses, statement of theme, ceremonial greetings and exposition of genealogies, and mythological similes).

Apuleius's *Golden Ass* is a more famous ancient text about an animal that unites both fabular and nonfabular stories and lore about animals. Apuleius alludes to beast fable and uses animal folklore (Scobie 1983) as well as animal lore drawn from the cult of Isis. In addition, he includes such etiological trivia as the anecdote about the beaver that appeared in Phaedrus. In the tale of Aristomenes, Socrates describes the witchcraft of his lover: "A lover of her who had rashly ravished another woman, she changed with a single word into a beaver—because when that beast fears captivity, he frees himself from his pursuers by self-castration, and she wished that penalty to slash the man for his enjoyment of another than herself" (37).

The conglomerative tendency of ancient literature about animals holds strong in the Middle Ages. For instance, the poet of the Middle English *The Owl and the Nightingale* brings up beast fables as well as bird folklore and bestiary lore in his dialogue (Hume). In particular, of the many examples he cites, some are fables. The Nightingale tells fables of the Falcon and the Owl (lines 99–138) and of the Cat and the Fox (lines 809–36), both of which are familiar from the fables of Marie de France. The owl makes references to a story of a nightingale (lines 1049–62, 1076–1104), which includes the execution of the bird.

To extend my argument a few centuries further, the syndrome that I am describing was not peculiarly ancient or medieval. In one of the *Exemplary Novels* (*Novelas ejemplares*), the "Dogs' Colloquy" ("El coloquio de los perros"), Cervantes mentions Aesopic fable and Apuleius's *Golden Ass* explicitly and may be indebted indirectly to Lucian's "The Dream, or the Cock" (Pierce 103–4; Scobie 1973, 46). One literary animal seems inevitably to lead to another.

Because beast literature cuts across genres, this study of medieval Latin beast poetry will open with a chapter on literary sources and analogues in several genres. As their cultural and literary settings demonstrate, the medieval Latin beast poems are more than the rough drafts of tales that constitute the *Roman de Renart*. They had a literary past and present as well as a future. In fact, because they incorporate the responses of their authors to many earlier sorts of beast literature, the poems cannot be evaluated intelligently until their most likely inspirations have been identified and described.

The remainder of the present study attempts to chart the irregular contours of medieval Latin beast poetry. In subsequent chapters I survey what is known and can be hazarded about each of the beast poems written between A.D. 750 and 1150. These four centuries saw experimentation with beast poetry begin among the poets around Charlemagne, continue in other parts of Europe, and reach a crescendo with the long poems of the eleventh and twelfth century. The terminus of 1150 brings the book to a close with the *Ysengrimus*. Although Latin beast literature continued to be written after the *Ysengrimus*, the momentum passed to the vernacular poets who fashioned stories of Renard the Fox and his companions. Furthermore, Nigel of Canterbury's *Speculum stultorum*, although by no means unrelated to earlier beast literature, represents a departure from the trickster stories that form an ever more important ingredient in earlier Latin beast poetry.

In reading each medieval Latin beast poem, I pay special attention to uniquely medieval Latin narrative arrangements and poetic techniques, such as sustained quotation of classical poetry and parody of liturgy. To convey the breadth and variety of medieval Latin literature, I include in this survey discussions of many poems which have rarely, or never, been considered in conjunction with the narrative beast poems: debates and flytings between two animals or insects, riddles about animals, epitaphs for animals, and last testaments dictated by animals. So that both the narrative and nonnarrative material can reach a greater audience than it has in the past (especially but by no means solely in the English-speaking world), I supply appendices with my own translations of all the pieces from the tenth century or earlier and all but the longest pieces from the eleventh and twelfth centuries. In the hope of further increasing the accessibility of the material, I have followed a system of parenthetical documentation that refers to bibliographies of primary and secondary sources at the end of the book.

Although the primary emphasis rests on close interpretation of each poem, the readings are expected to reveal a literary-historical development in medieval Latin beast poetry between A.D. 750 and 1150. To highlight the changes that took place, the separate readings are arranged chronologically and are punctuated with suggestions about how the poems interrelate. Whereas the appreciations of the single beast poems will elicit what is fresh and heterogeneous in them, I hope that the remarks at the end of the chapters and in the conclusion will establish that these singular poems deserve to be studied together. There are few reasons to consider beast poetry a genre but many grounds to deal with the poems as one group (Wehrli 113).

Last but not least, the variety and vitality of the beast poems offer an excellent means of dispelling the commonly held misconception that medieval Latin poetry is staid or dull in comparison with the vernacular writings of the Middle Ages. Like many other medieval Latin writings, the beast poems were poised at the intersection of three sometimes overlapping, sometimes divergent cultures: the native cultures that prospered in vernacular languages, the Christian culture that was spread through ecclesiastic institutions (Servaes), and the classical culture that was preserved through the Latin educational system. The medieval Latin beast poems have points of contact with each of these three cultures, for medieval Latin culture was an ever-changing composite of all three. Although this culture rested in the hands—in the pens—of people who were, with rare exceptions, male clerics, it was anything but monolithic. A shared language, educational experience, and religion provided these authors with the common ground on which to communicate and, knowingly or not, to celebrate the rich multiplicity that Europe is and has been since it was first conceived.

1. Inspirations and Analogues

The medieval Latin beast poems were not merely the rudiments of what later became the *Roman de Renart*. Although little has been written about their sources (Ross 2; Jauss 84; Schaller 1970a, 91), the beast poems can be shown to have profited from a heritage of literature about animals. Indeed, they drew from such a large reservoir of inspiration for their stories and descriptions of animals that the difficulty in studying sources and analogues lies not in detecting them, but in grouping them in manageable and meaningful categories. In this chapter I seek out genres of ancient and early medieval literature in which animals play a major part and which could have inspired medieval Latin poets. For simplicity's sake I divide the forms of literature into three classes: beast fables and tales; the *Physiologus* and bestiary; and such genres of classical and early medieval Latin literature as *voces animantium*, animal epitaphs and wills, and beast riddles. Although this listing cannot be exhaustive, it is meant to determine the most important of the literary models that medieval Latin beast poets were likely to have recalled as they composed poems about animals.

Fables and Tales

The idea of telling fables seems universal, almost innate in the human imagination. As William Thackeray stated evocatively (*The Newcomes*, chap. 1, as cited by Jacobs 229): "the tales were told ages before Aesop; and the asses under lion's manes roared in Hebrew; and the sly foxes flattered in Etruscan; and the wolves in sheep's clothing gnashed their teeth in Sanskrit, no doubt." But is the fable form so widespread as Thackeray would have it? If we assume with him that the genre encompasses any and every tale about animals with human traits, then the answer would have to be affirmative. But is such a loose definition acceptable or useful? Surely we can catch tighter hold of the elusive terms *Aesopic* and *fable*.

At first blush the task of defining *Aesopic fable* seems ludicrously simple. After all, almost every child has seen or heard versions of Aesop's fables, and knows what they are even without being able to articulate it. But there are intransigent problems with both words in the expression. Take the element *Aesopic*. Despite the ubiquity and vitality of traditions about Aesop (Schirokauer), it is not certain that any so-called Aesopic fables record even approximately fables told by a man named Aesop (Perry 1965, xxxv–xxxvi). As a consequence, the term refers not to fables *by* Aesop but to fables that are felt to be *in the manner of* Aesop. Thus Aesopic fables exist not just from the period in which the largely legendary Aesop lived but from all periods, and editors and collectors of Aesopic fables must set arbitrary chronological limits of their own.

If we abandon the adjective *Aesopic*, we must pay all the more attention to *fable*. And yet even by itself the word poses difficulties. Before defining it, we must dispel the hazy preconceptions about *fable* that our language induces in us; for *fable* belongs to a lexical family that has members spread throughout English: from Latin we have inherited such words as *fairy, fame, fate, confess, ineffable*, and *preface*, and from Greek, *aphasia, blaspheme, euphemism, phone*, and *prophet* (Watkins 5, "bha-²").

The basic connotations of *fable* and its closest relatives in English can be subsumed under three headings. First, fable is associated with talking. This meaning is intrinsic in the Latin *fabulor, -ari (fabulo, -are)* "to chat, to make up a story" (*Thesaurus Linguae Latinae* 6/1: columns 34.79–36.70), from which such Romance languages as Spanish and Portuguese derive their basic verbs for speaking *hablar* and *falar* (Meyer-Lübke 271). The most obvious cognates in English are *confab, confabulate*, and *confabulation*. The connotation of talking creates an interesting parallel between fable and parable, which has contributed to French and Italian the basic verbs for speaking *parler* and *parlare* (< *parabolo, -are* < *parabola*; Meyer-Lübke 512).

A second connotation of fable is of lying, where a possible derivative is the word *fib*. (The *Oxford English Dictionary* states that the noun is "of obscure origin; possibly shortened from FIBLE-FABLE.") The fibbing nature of beast fable is presumed in the expression "cock and bull": although the expression cannot be traced to a specific fable, it probably refers to a fable or tale in which a cock and a bull are portrayed anthropomorphically (Hendrickson 53–54; Lyman 25). Because many fables feature animals which act and talk like human beings, opponents of fable (e.g., Augustine, *Contra mendacium* 1.13.28) have often charged that the genre is inherently untruthful, and the word *fable* can mean "a falsehood, a lie" (*The American Heritage Dictionary* "fable 3").

Finally, fable is connected with fiction and fantasy. The word *fabulous* in English (like the German *fabelhaft*, French *fabuleux*, or Italian *favoloso*) suggests that something is legendary, barely credible, or astonishing (*The American Heritage Dictionary*, "fabulous"); and the word *fabled* is used to describe what is legendary or fictitious—what does not exist, but what has been made known through stories (*The American Heritage Dictionary*, "fabled").

Although each of these three sets undoubtedly contains a grain of truth about the nature and spirit of fable, defining fable as literature demands a more secure footing than is offered by the popular connotations of the word *fable*. The word *fable* is construed in many ways today, just as the words *fabula* and *fabella* were in antiquity and during the Middle Ages (de Boor; Knapp 1975b, 78–83; Knapp 1979b, 53–68). It also requires abandoning the habit of regarding fable as both a general spirit or tone and a specific literary form (contrast Blackham ix; Drabble 335; Holman 217).

For our purposes, the meaning of *beast fable* must be sufficiently broad to describe the stories about animals that form the core of classical and medieval fable collections, but the term must be narrowed to exclude many unrelated sorts of material (such as historical anecdotes and natural history) which insinuated themselves into fable collections. Adopting twentieth-century criteria for determining what is and is not a fable poses obvious hazards. An ancient, a medieval, or even a modern writer who gathers or composes fables need not work with stringent conceptions of genre as literary critics or theorists would do. Because fabulists were indiscriminate about their material, adopting modern principles puts us in the awkward position of rejecting from the corpus of genuine fables items that seem chronologically close to Aesop himself and that were deemed by ancient fabulists to have been fables. Nonetheless, the risks of such exclusion seem less hazardous than the confusion of leaving fable amorphous.

A fable is a short tale, in prose or verse (Perry 1952, ix). Expressly fictional, it must recount either one action or a progression of actions that is supposed to have taken place once in the past. The fable is distinguished from other short tales by the moral: the fable must be told not just to entertain, but also to impart a moral.

Although the idea of outfitting a story with a moral seems natural or universal, in fact the moral as we know it was slow in evolving. Where the fable form originated and where it passed in its transmission are large and embroiled questions. The earliest stories with structures similar to fables come from the ancient Middle East (Perry 1959, 26–28; Kramer 124–31):

the only difference between the Greco-Roman fables and the fables in such ancient wisdom books as the fifth-century B.C. *Ahikar* is that in the latter the morals are never pithy statements separate from the stories but instead lines delivered by speakers within the stories (internal morals). The fable format with which we are most familiar—a story part followed by a separate moral (epimythium)—evolved only after a transitional phase, in which the story parts were indexed by a separate moral (promythium) that preceded them (Perry 1940).

Thus the moral may take any of several forms. It may be stated within the tale by one of the characters. Alternatively, it may be summarized separately. When it precedes the narration, it is designated a promythium; when it follows, it is an epimythium (Perry 1940). The moral may be a strained addition or a natural adjunct to the tale. It may be directed at a single person or at an unspecified group of people. But however it fits with the story, the moral is an essential and indispensable ingredient of the fable.

The presence of a moral protects the story part of a fable from the charge of being an out-and-out lie, since the moral gives the fabulist a meaning, at once deep and explicit, that goes beyond the fiction; and the presence of a moral distinguishes fable formally from other types of short narrative such as riddles, allegory, parables, and animal folktales. Although even the simplest kinds of folktale (including animal stories) are often fraught with philosophical significance (whether profound or worldly), the storyteller is interested in this meaning only secondarily. His primary concern is to relate a story—to move along the action or the drama or the explanation. In contrast, the most distinctive feature of the fable form is that this philosophical import is divulged openly in the moral.

Although fables do not have to contain animals, animals have always bulked large in fable collections and in fable theory. In ancient Greece fables were divided into two categories: Aesopic, in which the characters are animals, and Sybaritic, in which they are human beings (Chambry xxiv). Isidore of Seville draws a similar distinction in the two types of fables he describes (*Etymologiae* 1.40.2):

> Sunt autem fabulae aut Aesopicae, aut Libysticae. Aesopicae sunt, cum animalia muta inter se sermocinasse finguntur, vel quae animam non habent, ut urbes, arbores, montes, petrae, flumina. Libysticae autem, dum hominum cum bestiis, aut bestiarum cum hominibus fingitur vocis esse conmercium.

> Fables are either Aesopic or Libystic. Aesopic fables are those in which dumb animals are imagined to have spoken with each other, or in which the speakers are things which have no soul, as cities, trees, mountains, rocks, and rivers.

In contrast, Libystic fables are those in which there is verbal interchange of
men with animals or animals with men.

In the thirteenth century John of Garland defines fable differently, but he
shares with Isidore the conviction that animals are paramount in fable
(*Parisiana Poetria*, chap. 5, lines 392–97, ed. and trans. Lawler 104–5):

> Si narratio fuerit obscura, per fabulam appositam uel per appologum clari-
> ficetur, per integumentum quod est veritas in specie fabule palliata. Et no-
> tandum quod omnis appologus est fabula, sed non conuertitur. Est enim
> apologus sermo brutorum animalium ad nostram instructionem, ut in Auiano
> et in Esopo.

> If a whole narrative is obscure, it may be made plain by means of a suitable
> story or fable, through the device known as Integument, which is truth
> cloaked in the outward form of a story. And notice that every fable is a story,
> but not vice versa. For in a fable dumb animals are made to speak for our
> edification, as in Avian and Aesop.

Even today the importance of animals in fable causes the terms fable, Aesopic fable, and beast fable to be used interchangeably. For our purposes,
the term *beast fable* will be reserved to designate those fables in which
an animal or bird is a major character, but not necessarily a speaking
character.

Despite their number and variety, medieval Latin fables, like much of
medieval Latin literature, have usually been examined not as manifestations
of independent cultures but either as the outgrowths of ancient literature
(Nøjgaard 1964–67) or as the precursors of later literary phenomena in
individual European countries (Filosa) or languages (Grubmüller 1977).
Only recently have they been considered within an international, dia-
chronic framework (Adrados 1979). Because medieval Latin fables remain
relatively unfamiliar territory, a short description of the corpus and its
most salient characteristics seems in order.

Many fables that originated in antiquity are still widely known and
have left their mark in everyday speech—as when we use the expressions
"the lion's share" or "sour grapes." These same fables were also dissemi-
nated throughout western Europe in the Middle Ages, primarily in two
families of Latin anthologies (a convenient edition remains Hervieux; a
smaller sampling is in Schnur). Both families abound in beast fables: of the
ninety-eight fables in the *Romulus*, eighty-eight are beast fables; of Avian's
forty-two fables, twenty-nine qualify as beast fables.

One family comprised prose recastings of the Latin verse fables that had been written by Phaedrus in the first half of the first century B.C. Of the three extant members in this family two had extremely limited circulation: the collection transcribed by Ademar of Chabannes (ca. 988–1034) around 1025 and the collection preserved in a Wissembourg manuscript (written in the tenth century or at the end of the ninth), now Wolfenbüttel, MS. Gudianus Latinus 148 (Gatti; *Romulus* ed. Thiele lvi–lvii, clxxxi–clxxxv, cc–ccxix). The third, and by far the most influential, member in the family of prose reworkings of Phaedrus was the so-called *Romulus*. The *Romulus* is extant in two recensions, the *Recensio gallicana* (*Romulus* ed. Thiele clxii) and the *Recensio vetus* (*Romulus* ed. Thiele clxii, clxvii–clxxii). This collection takes its name from the dedicatory letter, which purports to have been sent from a certain Romulus to his son Tiberius or Tiberinus. The heart of this collection probably took shape in the fifth century in Gaul (*Romulus* ed. Thiele cxvii–cxviii). Although the collection is deeply indebted either directly or indirectly to the fables of Phaedrus, it contains many other fables from different sources.

The *Romulus* circulated later in various reworkings. Probably in the eleventh century it was recast with a fresh Christian emphasis on good and evil, rather than on gain and loss (Grubmüller 1977, 70–72; Jauss 24–55). This version is known as the *Romulus Nilantinus*, after its early eighteenth-century editor, Johann Friedrich Nilant (Grubmüller 1977, 70). In other reworkings of the *Romulus* selected fables were versified. One such collection, known alternatively as the *Anonymus Neveleti* (after Isaac Nevelet, who printed it for the first time in 1610) and mistakenly as the fables of Walter the Englishman (Grubmüller 1977, 78), was probably compiled at the end of the twelfth century. It enjoyed extraordinary popularity and survives in more than a hundred manuscripts (Grubmüller 1977, 81: ed. Foerster; ed. Hervieux 2: 316–51). Another collection, the *Novus Aesopus*, was put together at the end of the twelfth century by Alexander Neckham.

The other main family of fables was the poetry attributed to Avian (although the name was originally perhaps Avienus), most of it translated from a Latin prose paraphrase of Greek verse fables of Babrius (Küpplers 3–64; Grubmüller 1977, 59 n. 69). The poems of Avian, who flourished around A.D. 400, were in their turn adapted by later poets: around 1100 two poets (the *Novus Avianus* poet and the Poeta Astensis), one of them from Asti, reworked Avian in leonines and elegiac distichs (Bertini 1975, 31; Manitius 3: 773–75). But Avian's fables had their greatest influence in their unadapted form (Gaide 1980, 52–57); they were a standard component of many medieval textbooks, even before the *Liber Catonianus* and *Auctores octo morales* took shape (Boas; Clogan; Voigt 1891).

Both families of fables owe their survival to the schools. The use of anthropomorphic animals continues to be salient in basic education, both formal and informal (Provenzo): many children have their first systematic brush with the alphabet through Big Bird and Sesame Street, while such creatures as the Cat in the Hat and Winnie the Pooh are entrenched in early childhood readings. The especial appeal of animals to children was recognized already in antiquity by teachers, who used beast fables to smooth the transition to grammatical or rhetorical training from nursery rhymes, animal folktales, and bedtime stories—all of which went under the name of "old wives' tales" (*fabulae aniles*) in Classical Latin. Of the many grammarians and rhetoricians who commented in passing about the importance of fables in elementary education (Beudel 34–37, 51–56; Hausrath 1898, 312–14), Quintilian gave the most explicit picture:

> Igitur Aesopi fabellas, quae fabulis nutricularum proxime succedunt, narrare sermone puro et nihil se supra modum extollente, deinde eandem gracilitatem stilo exigere condiscant: uersus primo soluere, mox mutatis uerbis interpretari, tum paraphrasi audacius uertere, qua et breuiare quaedam et exornare saluo modo poetae sensu permittitur. Quod opus, etiam consummatis professoribus difficile, qui commode tractauerit cuicumque discendo sufficiet.

> Therefore let pupils learn to paraphrase fables of the Aesopic sort, which follow closely upon the stories of the nursery, in plain and unexcessive language; and thereafter to effect the same simplicity of style in writing. [Let them learn] to resolve metrical verses [into prose], next to convey its meaning while changing the words, and then to reshape it more freely in a paraphrase; in this it is permitted both to abridge and to elaborate, so long as the poet's meaning remains intact. This task is difficult even for polished instructors, and the person who handles it well will be qualified to learn anything. (*Institutio oratoria* 1.9.2–3, ed. Winterbottom 1: 58.1–9; my translation, adapted from Colson 116–17)

The exercises in resolving verse and paraphrasing that Quintilian prescribed may not have been restricted to Aesopic fables (Roberts 15), but they certainly never excluded them. In fact, a broad range of archaeological evidence attests to the diversity of exercises in which fables were used in ancient schools. For instance, there are fragments of pottery on which fables were copied as exercises in handwriting (Spiegelberg 7–8, 17) and wax tablets which contain the text of fourteen fables, some of Babrian origin but written from memory, replete with schoolboyish errors, omissions, and additions (the A.D. third-century *Tabulae ceratae Assendelftianae* found in the ruins of Palmyra: Hesseling 293–314; Crusius 228–53; Beudel). Finally, there is reason to believe that fables were used as material for translation exercises. Eighteen fables are included in the third book of the bilingual schoolbook that is now known as the *Pseudo-Dositheana Herme-neumata* (written ca. A.D. 207) and that was employed in teaching Greek to Latin speakers and Latin to Greek speakers. The impression given by the *Pseudo-Dositheana Hermeneumata* is borne out by papyri of Latin versions of Greek fables: of the different exercises prescribed in the *Hermeneumata*, those concerned with fable were the most often practiced (Bertini 1975, 18–19; Della Corte). How much influence the *Pseudo-Dositheana Herme-neumata* exerted upon medieval Latin beast poetry remains open to question (*Romulus* ed. Thiele lxv–lxix; Kaczynski and Westra 1982, 33–35), but we do know that such use of fables in translation exercises is also attested at the other end of the Middle Ages:

> Cause them to make a good and pithy report of the Fable; first in English, then in Latine: and that either in the words of the Author, or of themselves as they can; and as they did in English. For, this practice in English to make a good report of a Fable, is of singular use, to cause them to utter their mindes well in English; and would never be omitted for that and like purposes. (Brinsley 145)

The chances are good that there was an unbroken continuity in the use of progymnasmatic exercises, such as the *Hermeneumata* (Murphy).

Fables continued to be used in the Middle Ages both as texts for elementary reading (Voigt 1891, 42–53; Glauche 98) and as material for exercises in recapitulation and composition. One possible model of such an exercise survives in three poems in elegiac couplets attributed to Alexander Neckham; all three relate the fable of the eagle and the tortoise, the first "profusely" (*copiose*) in thirty-two lines, the second "succinctly" (*compendiose*) in ten lines, and the third "compactly" (*subcincte*) in four lines (ed. Hervieux, 3: 463–64; see Bertini 1975, 33–34; Mann 1986, 197). A more unusual alternative is presented by a fragmentary eleventh-century *Romulus*, in which each promythium is composed in a different meter and is provided with an elucidation in verse (Voigt 1894, 149–58). The practice of retelling fables as a school exercise would have had at least two important side effects: pupils would have produced occasional variations or innovations upon old fables and would have become comfortable with building compositions around animals. As far as attitudes are concerned, such exercises would have encouraged everyone who received an education to view fable as common property.

The privileged status of fables in elementary instruction may seem odd, in view of the many doubts that have been expressed about fable from antiquity onward. For instance, fables were received skeptically on account of their levity. Seneca, writing around A.D. 43, suggested that Aesopic fables were a frivolous sort of literature, not appropriate to occupy the attention of a serious person ("Consolatio ad Polybium" 11.8.3, in *Dialogorum libri duodecim*, ed. Reynolds 275.7–19). Fables were also questioned on account of their very fictiveness. In a commentary on Macrobius the twelfth-century philosopher William of Conches concluded:

> Per fabulas enim, quas ille composuit, ad aliquam morum instructionem exortamur, et tamen per eas nichil veri significatur. . . . (Dronke 1974, ed. 69, trans. 18)

> By the fables that he [Aesop] composed we are encouraged to a certain improvement of morals, and yet nothing true is signified by them. . . . (my translation)

Despite the discomfort that some thinkers expressed about fiction, collections of fables continued to be seen in the medieval centuries as ideal schooltexts. As Conrad of Hirsau (ca. 1070–1150) declared in the *Dialogus super auctores* (lines 455–58, ed. Huygens 86), the simplicity of fables made them well-suited to the cognitive capacities of developing children:

> Sequitur Avianus in ascensu parvulorum et velut in gradu lactentis infantiae positus eorum, qui solidum cibum nondum possunt capere nec adhuc disciplinis validioribus auctorum maiorum operam dare.

> Avian follows in the development of children and represents, as it were, the nursing infancy of those who cannot yet take solid food and cannot yet apply themselves to the stronger disciplines of major writers.

More important, fables couple the pleasure of an imaginative little story with the edification of its moral unfolding. They provide a means of luring ignorant people into learning (Boccaccio, *Genealogie deorum gentilium libri* 14.9, ed. Romano 2: 709.3–9; trans. Osgood 51). By their very form fables embodied the Horatian ideal of *delectatio* and *utilitas*. As the fables of Avian were characterized in a twelfth-century *accessus*, "intentio eius est delectare nos in fabulis et prodesse in correctione morum" ("his intention is to delight us in fables and to be of benefit in moral correction" [lines 13–14, ed. Huygens 22]). Fable was felt to have an inherently moral or ethical purpose: "Ethicae subponitur, quia tractat de correctione morum" ("[the fable] is subsumed under ethics, because it deals with moral correction" [line 15, ed. Huygens; compare Hervieux 1: 580]). Because of its power to train pupils in differentiating between virtue and vice (Hervieux 1: 559), fable came close to attaining the stature of theology. Indeed, in a translation of Aesop's fables (1477) Heinrich Steinhöwel draws a parallel between fable and theology: "Every fable is invented to show men what they ought to follow and what they ought to flee. For fable means as much in poetry as words in theology. And so I shall write fables to show the ways of good men" (quoted in Lenaghan 18).

Thus schoolteachers were not alone in recognizing the utility of beast fables in bringing home messages to mixed audiences. Orators and preachers, among others, also knew a good thing when they saw it. Consequently, we should not be surprised to find that the first assemblages of fables in antiquity were published for orators to use in exemplifying points as they composed their speeches; nor should we be astonished to learn that beast fables represent a major constituent in the exempla literature of medieval preachers.

With morals to justify stories, fables were certified as acceptable by the arbiters who decided which literature Christians should read. Augustine observed approvingly that fable, although fictive, is truthful in its signification (*Ad Consentium contra mendacium* 12.28, ed. Zycha 508–9). Fables retained this mark of approbation through the Reformation. Thus Martin Luther, who translated an anthology of Aesopic fables, put fables on a par with the Bible:

> faciemus Sion ex ista Sinai aedificabimusque ibi tria tabernacula, Psalterio unum, Prophetis unum et Aesopo unum. (Doberstein 70)
>
> We will make a Zion out of this Sinai and we will build there three tabernacles, one for the Psalms, one for the Prophets, and one for Aesop.

Elsewhere he premised: "Surely there is more learning in Aesop than in all of Jerome" (Doberstein 72).

The extent to which fables were welcomed into the bosom of medieval Christianity can be seen in André of Fleury's biography of Gauzlin, abbot (1005–1030) of the monastery of Fleury at St. Benoît-sur-Loire. Writing in 1041, André records that Gauzlin's successor Arnold (1030–1032) had the dark refectory brightened with wall paintings of Aesop's fables (Goldschmidt 44–47). Each side wall was decorated with seven fables (and each painting included a *titulus* or caption with a corresponding verse moral), whereas the wall facing the entrance to the room was covered with depictions of Christ, the four and twenty elders, and choirs of saints. This juxtaposition of fable, which need be only perfunctorily ethical, and of purely Christian doctrine is a visual correlative to the two morals, the first ethical and the second Christian, with which Alcuin's "The Cock and Wolf" concludes (see also Bauer in Bertini 1985, 1053). The description of the dininghall sheds light on the *Ecbasis captivi*, which was written to be read to monks as they broke the Lenten fast on Easter Sunday: beast fiction and Christian verity complemented each other.

The homogeneity of fable through the millennia is more apparent than real. Although in form the fable is relatively fixed, in content it demonstrates remarkable flexibility. During the Middle Ages it changed in response not only to Christianity, but also to the new social frameworks. Whereas in the eleventh and earlier centuries fables had served general ethical or religious ends, in the twelfth and later centuries they became a vehicle for the expression of social criticism (Henderson 1973, 51–136; Henderson 1978, 1981; Schütze).

The high standing of fable had several consequences on beast poetry. Beast fable was the first and most important form of narrative about talking animals that the Latin poets met in school. The beast poets suggest that fable influenced them more than any other literary form, because they often described their own compositions as *fabulae* (although the word as used in medieval Latin can be notoriously difficult to translate: Dronke 1974, 3–5; Knapp 1975b, 78–82). In the first line of the moral to the "The Cock and Wolf" (line 29), Alcuin called the story a *fabula*. The anonymous author of "The Sick Lion" named the tale of the ailing lion-king a *fabula* (line 68). By designating their verse as *fabulae*, the two poets were not binding themselves hand and foot to the conventions of beast fable. Alcuin supplemented an old-fashioned fabular moral with a new Christian one, whereas "The Sick Lion" poet omitted a moral altogether. Two eleventh-century beast poets showed that they too found the beast fable worthy of their efforts, although in need of modification and justification. The author of "The Cock and Fox" belittled the whimsical little fable that he related, but vindicated the poem as a whole by appending a moralization (strophes 35–72) that runs longer than the narration itself (strophes 1–34). The *Ecbasis captivi* poet, while disparaging his *fabella* as a "page of lies" (40, "mendosam . . . cartam"), contended that nevertheless it was instructive.

The structure of fable (story and moral) gave beast poets a distinctive, albeit very constrictive, model that they were obliged either to accept, modify, or reject. Quite possibly, fables also influenced medieval beast poets in the characterization of individual animals, since the animals in both beast poems and beast fables tend to conform to similar stereotypes. More certainly, fabulists and beast poets provided each other with a wealth of narrative elements. Already in ancient times individual fables shared their narrative structures with an entire mock-epic about animals, *The Battle of the Frogs and Mice* (Perry 1965, appendix no. 384; Wölke 91–98; Ziegler and Sontheimer 1: 842), and with sections of prose novels about an ass-man, the Greek "Lucius, or the Ass" and Apuleius's *Golden Ass* (Thiel 1: 184–86). Similar interchanges of stories and language took place between fables and medieval Latin beast poems. Even though fragmentary, Leo of Vercelli's "Meter" confesses a debt to the fable of the ass clothed in the lion's skin, which was Avian's much-loved fifth fable (on its influence on medieval Latin poetry, see Egbert of Liège, *Fecunda Ratis*, ed. Voigt 143). Two centuries later Nigel of Canterbury—whose thoroughgoing familiarity with Avian's poetry shows in repeated quotations and reminiscences—made the same fable the starting point of his satire, the *Speculum stultorum* (Nigel's line 58 quotes the last line of Avian's fable, which his lines 57–80 paraphrase). The fox-and-cock fable that Alcuin, the poet of "The Cock and Fox," and the author of the *Ysengrimus* modified to suit their special purposes is a doublet of the ancient fox-and-partridge fable (cf. Perry 1952, nos. 562–562a). The *Ysengrimus* and many of the long vernacular beast poems in the Renard cycle are replete with versions of fables that are found in medieval fable collections (Best; *Ysengrimus* ed. Voigt).

Apart from such clear-cut examples of direct and indirect borrowing from written Latin fables, no one can say how many other stories in the beast poems are transformed fables (Knapp 1979a, 113). Precisely because the beast poets and their audiences knew Avian's poems and *Romulus* well, the poets avoided heavy-handed imitation. They did not simply replicate stories and techniques familiar to them from the classroom. Indeed, the school associations of fable forced beast poets to innovate for fear that otherwise their compositions would seem childish. Even such artful and aristocratic fables as La Fontaine's run the risk of being relegated to children.

The one collection of Aesopic fables known to have been written before the Christian era, that of Demetrius of Phalerum in the late fourth century, was intended as a handbook of materials for writers and orators (Perry 1962; Perry 1965, xiii). Phaedrus, who lived in the first fifty years of the Christian era, is the first Latin or Greek author who gathered fables to be read as literature in their own right. Until his time, fables had been regarded only as illustrative tales and, instead of appearing for their own sake, surfaced only incidentally—and usually singly—in tragedy, comedy, history, philosophy, and other genres (Perry 1965, xi–xiii).

For this reason, beast fables came down to the Middle Ages not just in the *Romulus* and in Avian's poems, but in the gamut of classical literature. They attracted the particular attention of both ancient and medieval readers when they appeared in the poems of an important poet, such as Horace (Archibald 1902, 1910). Quintilian remarked commendingly that Horace had not found fable too humble a form to use in his poetry (*Institutio oratoria* 5.11.19). Later fabulists acknowledged their debts to Horace in various fashions. Phaedrus made a number of allusions to Horace (De Lorenzi 1955, 119–32; Nøjgaard 1967, 2: 152–53). Avian, in a prose prologue to his fables, commented upon the prominence of fables in Horace's poetry:

> Verum has pro exemplo fabulas et Socrates divinis operibus indidit et poemati suo Flaccus aptavit, quod in se sub iocorum communium specie vitae argumenta contineant. (Lines 10–13, ed. and trans. Duff 680–83)

> Such fables by way of example have been introduced by Socrates into his inspired works and fitted by Horace into his poetry, because under the guise of jests of general application they contain illustrations of life.

In Horace's fables Avian perceived compelling insights into life behind a frivolous façade. In fact, the few fables Horace relates in their entirety are laden with commonsensical wisdom. Such are the two beast fables that come up in the second book of the *Satires*. One of them (*Satires* 2.3.314–20) is a variation upon the Aesopic fable of the ox and the frogs, with the moral that a person should not strive beyond the limits of his natural talents; the second (*Satires* 2.6.77–117), in the satire contrasting city life and rural life, is the fable of the town and the country mouse.

Besides the fables to which Horace himself alludes or which he relates, several beast fables occur in early glosses on Horace's poetry. Two of these (one about a fox and a raven, the other about a vain crow) have no apparent connection with fables in Phaedrus or, for that matter, in the whole ancient corpus (*Pseudacronis Scholia* 2: 173, 225; *Pomponii Porfyrionis Commentum* 312). Their incorporation into the scholia implies that at a very early date the works of Horace became a magnet for hitherto unrecorded oral fables or newly invented written fables. Horace's reputation as both beast fabulist and moralist, in the era that has been dubbed the *aetas horatiana* (Traube 2: 113), made his poetry an obvious quarry for medieval Latin beast poets. Verbal recollections of Horace are salient in two crucial beast poems: Leo of Vercelli's "Meter" and the anonymous *Ecbasis captivi*.

The store of fables increased rapidly. In antiquity theoreticians attempted with little success to distinguish between the fables of Aesop and the fables of Aesop's successors. Quintilian alluded to the problem only in passing (*Institutio oratoria* 5.11.19, ed. Winterbottom 1: 283.6–9); Phaedrus used the term *Aesop's fables* to designate the former group, *Aesopian fables* the latter (4 Prologue 11–13). In the Middle Ages wholly new groupings, as well as new redactions of established compilations, brought about the transformation of old fables and the annexation of previously unrecorded ones. The fables recounted in the Horace glosses were two such additions. Where these new fables originated and how they were transmitted until they were committed to writing are troublesome issues and require consideration of the audiences that fable had outside grammar schools.

According to Quintilian (*Institutio oratoria* 5.11.19, ed. Winterbottom 1: 283.6–12), fable was well suited not only to uneducated children but also to uneducated peasants:

> Illae quoque fabellae quae, etiam si originem non ab Aesopo acceperunt (nam uidetur earum primus auctor Hesiodus), nomine tamen Aesopi maxime celebrantur, ducere animos solent praecipue rusticorum et imperitorum, qui et simplicius quae ficta sunt audiunt, et capti uoluptate facile iis quibus delectantur consentiunt.

> Those fables, even if they did not originate with Aesop (for Hesiod seems to have been their first author), nevertheless are known especially by the name of Aesop. They usually beguile the minds of the rustic and unlearned, who both lend an ear more naïvely to fiction and also, for desire of pleasure, show favor readily to those things which bring gratification.

There is reason to believe that peasants were not just the audience of fables, but themselves created fables or at least the story parts of fables. If so, then in the Middle Ages fable retained the associations with low social classes—"low culture"—that it had acquired thanks to the slave / freedman status of Aesop and Phaedrus (Wehrli 114). A chronicler of the seventh century, Fredegar, tells two fables, neither of them indisputably from written tradition. One fable is termed a nonliterary "peasant tale," a *rustica fabula*. This fable is concerned with a wolf who guides his young to a hilltop, points out the panorama, and warns them that in the entire purview there is no one who will be friendly to them; the wolf draws the lesson that, in consequence, his whelps must either stand united or perish:

> While Theuderic was in pursuit, the holy and blessed Bishop Leudegasius of Mainz, who loved Theuderic's valour as much as he despised Theudebert's folly, approached Theuderic and said: "Finish what you have begun and exploit to the full the outcome of your action. There is a countryman's tale that tells how a wolf went up into the hills with her cubs, and when they had started to hunt she called them round her and said: 'As far as your eyes can see, and in whatever direction, you have no friends, except a few of your own kind.' So finish what you have begun." (*Chronicorum liber quartus*, year 612, ed. and trans. Wallace-Hadrill 31; ed. Krusch 139)

Aimoin, who continued the *Chronica*, relied upon Fredegar's telling when he related the fable (*Chronica*, ed. Krusch 213). Four hundred years after Fredegar wrote down the "peasant tale," Egbert of Liège included it in his verse *Fecunda ratis*, a farrago of proverbs and fables envisioned as a textbook (ed. Voigt 181–82). Although Egbert cites no authority for his version, it seems more probable that he had heard the fable than that he had culled it from Fredegar's historical writings. After all, in his prologue (ed. Voigt 1) he freely admits having used unwritten material, and the alternative title of his work, *De aenigmatibus rusticanis*, also presupposes that some of his anecdotes and sayings sprang from folk traditions or oral literature (ed. Voigt xix–xxii).

Fredegar's other fable (*Chronica*, ed. Krusch 81), a garbling of one found first in Babrius (no. 95, ed. Perry 116–22: see Ehrismann 1918, 1: 367; Keidel), lends weight to the notion that written Aesopic fables sometimes passed through oral intermediaries before reentering literature. Such transformations warn us not to be too quick to infer that written classical beast fables were the direct sources of similar medieval Latin beast stories. The medieval poets could have been working from oral fables: as Isidore pointed out in the *Etymologiae* (1.40.1), the very etymology of the word *fabula* (*for, fari* "to speak, talk") indicates that fable is rooted in orality (contrast Thompson 1946, 218).

The ocean of beast fables and folktales, which would have been extensive even if it had comprised only ancient Greco-Roman fables and subsequent medieval contributions to the corpus, grew vaster as oriental fables became known in Europe. The great Sanskrit *Pañcatantra*, dating from the second century B.C., was translated into many non-European languages, notably Arabic as *Kalila wa Dimna* (Brockelmann; Keith-Falconer 1885, lxxv–lxxix, lxxxvi). It reached Europe as a whole only in the twelfth or thirteenth century (Benfey; Chauvin). Around 1280 a converted Jew named John of Capua produced the *Directorium humanae vitae*, a Latin prose rendering of a Hebrew version of the *Kalila wa Dimna*. In the twelfth or thirteenth century another Italian, Baldo, wrote the Latin verse *Novus Aesopus*, based perhaps indirectly on a lost Latin translation from the Arabic, but perhaps directly on an Arabic or Hebrew version (ed. Hilka 2–3). Then in the fourteenth century an anonymous author put into Latin a Greek version of the *Kalila wa Dimna* (ed. Hilka). Despite the lateness of these Latin translations (and the scant interest that they seem to have aroused), parts of the *Pañcatantra/Kalila wa Dimna* corpus seeped into Western beast fables and beast poetry before the whole became widely known: for instance, the story of the man and the grateful animals toward the end of Nigel's *Speculum stultorum* derives ultimately from the *Pañcatantra* (Chauvin no. 71; Baldo, ed. Hilka 13–14). But there is no conclusive evidence that such seepage was ever extensive before the end of the twelfth century.

Because Latin fabulists were receptive to new material and because fables passed readily back and forth between oral and written circulation, beast fables and beast folktales interacted constantly during the Middle Ages: "Aus den Klöstern wanderten die Tierschwänke oft unter das Volk, um in verjüngter Form wieder von den Klöstern aufgenommen zu werden" ("Comic tales about animals often traveled out of the monasteries among common people, only to be appropriated again in rejuvenated form by the monasteries") (Graf 1920, 21: quoted by Knapp 1979a, 23; Kaczynski and Westra 1988, 117). So intense was the interaction and so hazy the line between them that the two forms were mistaken for each other, as they still tend to be. Thus the first prologue to the Low German *Reynke de Vos*, composed in the late fifteenth century, opens with the reasonable statement that some pre-Christian poet-sages expressed their wisdom in the form of fables but proceeds to the preposterous conclusion that *Reinaerts Historie*—part of the Renard cycle—is such an ancient collection (Best 135)! Like many medieval poets, the author of *Reynke de Vos* draws no distinction between fables about animals and tales about animal tricksters.

Except as reworked in fables, very few beast folktales survive from antiquity or the early Middle Ages. For want of evidence, it is impossible to estimate even roughly how many beast tales were in circulation at a given time. To take but one example of how little we know about beast tales in antiquity, there is the story of the mice and the weasels/cats. Although the story may be connected with *The Battle of the Frogs and Mice* (Morenz), the only firm literary evidence for the existence of such a story is a statement at the beginning of one of Phaedrus's fables: "Cum victi mures mustelarum exercitu / (historia, quot sunt, in tabernis pingitur)" (4.6, ed. and trans. Perry 310–11: "When the mice, overcome by the army of weasels— / a story pictured in all the taverns"). In this case, the pictorial evidence is fortunately extensive: in addition to ancient shards and papyri, there are Coptic wall paintings that illustrate scenes in the story (Brunner-Traut). But in many other cases oral stories of animals doubtless perished without leaving a trace in either literature or art.

The situation is similar in the early Middle Ages. It surely indicates the popularity of oral beast poetry that when Bishop Julian of Toledo writes in a letter (A.D. 680–691) about different types of verse and encourages his correspondent to avoid the "songs of vernacular poets" (*cantica vulgarium poetarum*), he cites by way of example the line: "Lupus dum ambularet viam, incontravit asinum" ("As the wolf was walking along the road, he met an ass" Bischoff 1959, 247–56; repr. Bischoff 1966, 1: 296). In other words, the first example of a popular composition that comes to the mind of the bishop is a song telling of a wolf and an ass (Dronke in Bertini 1985, 1054)! Yet this line, the earliest extant medieval Latin fragment of beast poetry, survives purely by chance: in most cases the very popularity of such poetry dissuaded the literate from recording it.

The loss of medieval beast poetry in the vernacular languages was even greater than of that in Latin. For instance, by far the earliest tatter of Middle English beast poetry that has come down to us appears in a fable of Isegrim turned monk in the Latin prose collection of Odo of Cheriton (Wilson 125); at the end of the fable Odo quotes an English proverb that seems to sum up a tale about a wolf: "If all that the Wolf unto a preest worthe, / and be set unto book psalmes to lere, / yit his eye is evere to the wodeward" (Fable 22, ed. Hervieux 4: 195–96: "Although the wolf should become a priest and should be set to learning the Psalms from a book, still his eye is always turned toward the wood"). Like the quotations in both Julian of Toledo and Odo of Cheriton, the variety of fables represented in the Old French collection of Marie de France proves that there was interplay between the Latin and the vernacular beast traditions (Warnke).

In tracing parallels between beast poems and fables written in Latin we should not underestimate the importance of unwritten fables and unwritten folktales. Although Latin beast poets would have known written fables through Avian's poems and the *Romulus* collections employed in basic education, they would have been acquainted with beast stories first through tales told in their native languages. If these tales resembled those in most oral traditions, they would have fallen into two major categories: etiological tales (represented in medieval Latin beast poetry in episodes in which animals lose their tails) and trickster tales (Thompson 1946, 319; Radin); for like most cultures, medieval Europe had its equivalent of the Uncle Remus and Anansi-type stories told by African Americans and the Coyote stories of Native Americans.

Christian Animal Symbolism

There was no single medieval Christian view of animals, any more than there is one today. On the contrary, medieval Christianity encompassed many different, sometimes conflicting thoughts about animals. A fable by Odo of Cheriton (Fable 30–30a, ed. Hervieux 4: 205–6) typifies the inconsistency of attitudes toward animals in the Middle Ages: to convince a knight that there are no animals in heaven, a scholar-clerk relates a beast fable! *The Owl and the Nightingale* provides evidence of similar inconsistency. The poet has one of the two talking birds argue that animals have no power of reason, but later he relates a fable that suggests animals are sufficiently reasonable to be held accountable for their conduct: it describes the execution of a nightingale. Bernard of Clairvaux (ca. 1090–1153) was guilty of similar contradictions: although in one text he rails against carvings of animals and grotesques in cloisters (*Apologia ad Guillelmum Sancti Theoderici Abbatem*, chap. 12, sections 28–29, PL 182.915D–16A; Rudolph), he owned a Bible heavily illustrated with animals and he employed the fox to symbolize heresy in another of his writings (Klingender 335).

The erratic or inconsistent outlooks expressed by individuals reflect the confusion that existed on the doctrinal level. Two distinct views of animals come through, the one either theocentric or anthropocentric and dismissive of animals, the other anthropomorphic and inclined to humanize animals. According to the first view, animals are absolutely inferior to God and human beings because animals have no power of reason. For instance, Augustine states:

> Magna enim quaedam res est homo, *factus ad imaginem et similitudinem dei*, non in quantum mortali corpore includitur, sed in quantum bestias rationalis

animae honore praecedit. (*De doctrina christiana* 1.22.20, lines 5−8, ed. Martin 16, trans. Robertson 18)

> A great thing is man, made in the image and likeness of God, not in that he is encased in a mortal body, but in that he excels the beasts in the dignity of a rational soul.

This view derives from the Bible. The few individual animals in the Old Testament are interesting not on their own account but rather because they indicate God's disposition toward man (Bernhart 34−44). Balaam's ass, the only talking beast in the Bible (unless one counts the serpent that approached Eve), is no more than a tool of God's will (Numbers 22.28; 2 Peter 2.16). Similarly, when Aaron's rod changes into a serpent, the snake has no volition or significance of its own; it is simply an implement in a miracle (Exodus 7.10−12). No substantial revision of thinking takes place between the Old and the New Testament: the viper that bites Paul (Acts 28.3−5) is as devoid of personality as Aaron's magic serpent.

Yet although theologians saw animals as altogether inferior to human beings, other people tended to humanize animals by treating them as if they had the power of reason. This proclivity had both unhappy and happy consequences. The unhappy consequence was that animals were held responsible for any injurious acts they committed. Whole species of insects and rodents were excommunicated if they caused damage to crops. By roughly the same principle, individual animals were sentenced to death when they committed homicide, especially infanticide (Amira; Berkenhoff; Evans; Hyde; Ménabréa). This conception of animals as reasonable and therefore responsible for their sins may have played a part in the beast literature of the era, just as Darwinism has contributed to the formation of beast literature in the nineteenth and twentieth centuries (Allen 8−10, 78−79; Gose 17−28; Norris); for it is a curious coincidence that the Middle Ages, when beast trials were common in real life, produced much literature in which fictitious beast trials take place (Graven).

The happy consequences are evident most often in the lives of the saints, where we see animals treated as the equals of human beings (Boglioni; Donatus; Falsett; Mullin; Toldo; Waddell). St. Francis's preaching to the birds or taming of the wolf of Gubbio, far from beginning, actually culminated a long hagiographic tradition. In the lives of the saints animals are portrayed as being capable of performing acts of charity and as having sufficient understanding to respond to preaching. Animals are often presented as being the special companions of saints, providing them companionship and supplying them with food. The interdependence between animals and saints is captured in medieval art: many saints were as easily recognized by their associated beasts (for example, St. Mark the Evangelist by the winged lion, St. Luke the Evangelist by the winged ox, St. John the Evangelist by the eagle, St. Agnes by the lamb, St. Giles by the doe, or St. Hugh of Lincoln by the swan) as knights in the lists could be identified by their blazons.

The saints had good reason to pay close attention to animals, since many of the saints regarded—or professed to regard—animals as their equals. But even those medieval thinkers who believed that human beings alone possess reason and virtue recognized that human beings can learn from observation of animals. Like plants or precious stones, animals are vocabulary in the language of creation by which God communicates in material form what exists immaterially; they are words in the book of nature (Curtius 319–26).

The language of creation could be studied in many writings. Most likely to have affected medieval Latin beast poets were the Latin translations of the *Physiologus* ("The Naturalist") and the commentaries on the hexaemeron with which the *Physiologus* was closely related (Rowland). Although the poets would have been exposed first to Latin fables (especially in the poems of Avian and the prose of the *Romulus*), they could not have proceeded far in their schooling before encountering the *Physiologus*. They would have associated the *Physiologus* and fable because of their general similarity in structure: fable consists of a narrative with a moral, *Physiologus* of nature observation with moralization.

The *Physiologus*, from which the bestiaries later evolved, probably took shape in the second century A.D. in Egypt or Syria. It presents animals, birds, plants, and stones, first analyzing their habits and properties and then relating these pseudoscientific findings to aspects of Christian life, especially to the fundamental mysteries of the Incarnation and Redemption (Grubmüller 1978). Rather than picturing the imaginary exploits of supposedly real individual animals (as Henry Williamson, Ernest Thompson Seton, and Jack London would later do), each entry in the *Physiologus* purports to record the behavior and traits typical of an entire species. Rather than encoding an ethical or social message for the reader to decipher, each entry concludes with an explicit religious interpretation (for three entries, see Appendix 8, *Physiologus Latinus*).

At some point between the fourth and ninth century, the Greek *Physiologus* was translated into Latin: the earliest extant manuscript of the Latin version is ninth-century (Henkel 21–24). It may have been the book condemned in the sixth-century forgery, the *Decretum Gelasianum*: "Liber Physiologus, qui ab haereticis conscriptus est, et beati Ambrosii nomine praesignatus, apocryphus" ("The book known as the *Physiologus*, which was written by heretics and goes under the name of Ambrose, is an apocryphon"; ed. Dobschütz 348), but even if banned, it continued to be read and copied (Lauchert 95–96; Henkel). The Latin *Physiologus* survives in at least four distinct families of redactions before the twelfth century (Sbordone; Orlandi 1985; editions by Carmody).

The *Physiologus* reached true ascendancy after the eleventh century, when an otherwise unknown Theobald reworked twelve extracts in poetry (Henkel 39–41; Orlandi 1973). Theobald's version of the *Physiologus*, the only one to have retained a stable shape through the centuries, was much perused in the Middle Ages. It figured in the holdings of many libraries and, as a standard schoolbook, was explicated in forewords and in glosses (Glauche 124; Henkel 53–58; ed. and trans. Eden 4, 81–82). Out of the *Physiologus*, biblical and patristic sources, and ancient naturalist traditions arose the bestiaries, the subject matter of which is largely restricted to animals, with an admixture of lapidary and aviary lore. Like the *Physiologus* the bestiaries sought relentlessly to find transcendent meanings in the behavior of animals, but the meanings extended beyond the purely theological to embrace the broadly metaphysical and even courtly: the bestiari of love takes its place alongside bestiaries more closely imitative of the *Physiologus* (for an anthology, see Peter of Beauvais).

As was the case with Avian and the *Romulus*, the popularity of the *Physiologus* and Theobald's versified extracts did not leave a corresponding imprint on medieval Latin beast poetry. Apart from the clear-cut influence of the *Physiologus* on Aldhelm's riddles (Lauchert 96), which in turn affected several beast poems, there are no verbal echoes of the *Physiologus*. The one poem to cite the *Physiologus* and to appropriate its lore is the *Ecbasis captivi* (Voigt 1875, 58–62; Brinkmann 119). Yet the *Physiologus* may have affected beast poetry indirectly, through the allegorical approach to animals that it embodied.

Classical Poetry

In fables and folktales medieval Latin beast poets had a treasure house of stories about animals, in the *Physiologus* a supply of lore about animals. In addition, they received from both fables and *Physiologus* a predisposition to view stories or anecdotes about animals as the pleasure that precedes a dose of moralization. What the beast poets gained from nonfabular classical poetry was different: elements that they could include in their compositions. Three forms of Latin poetry stand out for the frequency with which they were incorporated into medieval Latin beast poems: catalogues of words describing animal sounds (*voces animantium*), animal epitaphs and wills, and beast riddles.

Among the many sorts of catalogues that occur in classical and medieval poetry, lists of birds are amply represented. Ovid envisaged a dead parrot received in Elysium by swans, doves, the phoenix, and a peahen (*Amores* 2.6.53–56); and medieval poets enumerated the birds conquered by the nightingale in song competitions (Jarcho 574, 579). Not limiting themselves to birds, Latin poets catalogued animals and fishes as well. In addition to Ovid's *Halieuticon* there are Ausonius's *Mosella* (lines 75–149) and fourth *Epistle*.

Often catalogues reflect a desire to versify animal lore and technical vocabulary. For example, a poem by Eugenius of Toledo versifies a section of Isidore of Seville's *Etymologiae* which lists hybrids and the species which mate to engender them.

De animantibus ambigenis

Haec sunt ambigena, quae nuptu dispare constant:
burdonem sonipes generat conmixtus asellae,
mulus ab Arcadicis et equina matre creatur,
tityrus ex ovibus oritur hircoque parente,
musmonem capra verveno semine gignit,
apris atque sue saetosus nascitur ibris,
at lupus et catula formant coeundo lyciscam.

(Eugenius of Toledo, *Carmen* 42, lines 1–7)

Mongrel Animals

These are mongrels, which come into existence when two breeds wed: when a horse couples with a she-ass it begets a hinny; a mule is produced by Arcadian asses and a mare; a tityrus is born of sheep and a he-goat; a nanny-goat pregnant by sheep semen gives birth to a moufflon; a shaggy hybrid is born of wild boars and a sow; and a wolf and a bitch produce through their union a greyhound bitch.

In animantibus bigenera dicuntur quae ex diversis nascuntur, ut mulus ex equa et asino; burdo ex equo et asina; hybridae ex apris et porcis; tityrus ex ove et hirco; musmo ex capra et ariete. Est autem dux gregis.

(Isidore of Seville, Etymologiae 12.1.60)

Among animals those are called mongrels which are begotten by different species, as a mule by a mare and an ass, a hinny by a stallion and a she-ass, hybrids by boars and sows, a tityrus by a ewe and a he-goat, and a moufflon from a nanny-goat and a ram. He is the leader of the flock.

Eugenius's poem survives in more manuscripts than most of his other works (ed. Vollmer 258; Bernt 145), but the theme was apparently left untouched by subsequent poets (although the hero of one poem is a "leader of the flock" named Tityros). In contrast, the *voces animantium* influenced medieval Latin beast poets before becoming a staple of lyric poetry (Jarcho 574, 579).

The term *voces animantium* designates lists of birds and quadrupeds which paired the names of the creatures with the verbs for their distinctive cries (Klenner; Marcovich; Díaz y Díaz). Like fables, the *voces animantium* apparently owe their survival to their usefulness in the schools, for they appear often in handbooks on grammar. They challenged, developed, and tested the abilities of pupils at remembering animal names and calls (Lawler 36–39, 237–39). When in verse they added the further challenge of accommodating unusual words to the rigors of meter (Díaz y Díaz 154–55). The didactic potential of the *voces animantium* can be demonstrated by a very short, but untranslatable quotation from the chapter entitled *De ionico minori* in Aldhelm's *De metris et enigmatibus ac pedum regulis* 131 (ed. Ehwald 179, lines 18–21): "Pande exempla vocis confusae de diversis rerum naturis congesta! Haec sunt species vocis confusae, ut maiorum auctoritas tradidit. Nam apes ambizant vel bombizant, aquilae clangunt, anseres crinciunt vel trinsiunt, aves minuriunt vel vernant vel vernicant, accipitres pipiant vel plipiant, anates tertisant." The various *voces animantium* written in hexameters are, in effect, glossaries in verse of verbs that indicate the characteristic sounds and calls of different birds and animals.

The earliest such compendia date to late antiquity. There were numerous prose versions, one of which has often been mistakenly attributed to Suetonius (Finch; Marcovich), but the most influential *voces animantium* were in verse. One strain leads from Ausonius (*Carmen* 72) in the fourth century through Eugenius of Toledo (*Carmen* 41) in the seventh, who was imitated in turn by Paulus Albarus (*Carmen* 4) in the eighth century. The most succesful imitation was the *Carmen de philomela* (of unknown authorship and uncertain date), which appends a vast *voces ani-mantium* to a brief praise of the nightingale (Klopsch).

Another form of classical Latin poetry which influenced medieval Latin beast poets includes animal epitaphs and wills. This type of poetry seems to have been more venerable and varied than the *voces animantium*. As far as is known, Catullus was the first Latin poet to write a dirge for a dead animal (Herrlinger). His lament for Lesbia's *passer* (usually translated as "sparrow," *Carmen* 3) was of no direct importance for medieval Latin poetry, because Catullus's poems were scarcely known in the Middle Ages (Manitius 1: 63, 65, 176, 261, 708; 2: 35, 45, 720; 3: 269, 963), but his lament left traces on other more widely available classical poems. After Catullus Latin laments for dead animals tended to stylize sincerity or to exaggerate parody but never to fuse them as he had done (Herrlinger 81–91). In one group, Martial (4.32, 11.69) and Ausonius (*Carmen* 33) reduce grief to an epigrammatic platitude (Herrlinger 100–105, "Anhang" nos. 47–53). Moving in the opposite direction, Ovid made parody the hallmark of his lament and epitaph for Corinna's parrot (*Amores* 2.6). Ovid's captivating poem found a ready imitator in Statius, who wrote a similar lament for a parrot (*Silvae* 2.4).

In a class by itself is "The Gnat" (*Culex*), a pseudo-Vergilian poem that describes the tragic death and afterlife of a gnat. The insect is killed after stinging a shepherd to alert him to the approach of a serpent. On the following night the gnat appears in a vision, reproves the shepherd for ingratitude, and describes the underworld. As a consequence the shepherd erects a tumulus with the epitaph: "Parve Culex, pecudum custos tibi tale merenti / funeris officium vitae pro munere reddit" ("Little Gnat, to thee so well deserving, the guardian of the flock pays this service of death in return for the boon of life," 413–14). Although tedious to the taste of many readers, the *Culex* was long accorded grudging respect because it was believed to be part of Vergil's juvenilia.

After laments for dead animals became a fashion in poetry, at least one parodic last testament for an animal won a niche in prose: "The Testament of the Piglet" (*Testamentum porcelli*), a pig's labored account of how his epitaph should read (see Appendix 30). Jerome made two very informative statements about the circles in which "The Testament of the Piglet" enjoyed a vogue:

Nullus tam imperitus scriptor est, qui lectorem non inveniat similem sui; multoque pars maior est Milesias fabellas revolventium quam Platonis libros.

In altero enim ludus et oblectatio est, in altero difficultas et sudor mixtus labori. Denique Timaeum de mundi harmonia, astrorum cursu et numeris disputantem, ipse qui interpretatus est Tullius, se non intellegere confitetur. Testamentum autem Grunnii Corocottae Porcelli decantant in scholis puerorum agmina cachinnantium. (*In Isaiam* Book 12, PL 24.425A1)

No writer is so maladept that he cannot find a reader suited to him; and far greater is the camp of those who ponder Milesian tales than the books of Plato. In the one sort of reading is play and delight, in the other difficulty and sweaty toil. Indeed, Cicero confesses that he does not understand the *Timaeus*, which discusses the harmony of the universe as well as the course and number of the stars—even though he himself translated the *Timaeus*! Yet troops of guffawing boys in the schools reel off the testament of the pig Grunnius Corocotta.

Quasi non cirratorum turba Milesiarum in scholis figmenta decantet: et testamentum Suis, Bessorum cachinno membra concutiat, atque inter scurrarum epulas, nugae istiusmodi frequententur. (*Adversus Rufinum* 1.17, PL 23.412AB)

As if the throng of curly-headed boys in the schools did not reel off the fantasies of Milesian tales and as if the testament of the pig did not make their limbs quake with guffaws, and as if at the banquets of men about town trifles of this sort did not enjoy constant repetition.

Both passages suggest that "The Testament of the Piglet," if not a product of the schools of late antiquity, at least was a form of entertainment among schoolboys—and among bons vivants outside the schools. They put "The Testament of the Piglet" on a par with the often erotic adventure stories known as Milesian tales (with which Apuleius's *The Golden Ass* proclaims an affinity), and they imply that "The Testament of the Piglet" was memorized and circulated orally.

"The Testament of the Piglet" captures the pleasure of young students in parodying the form and language genuine testaments which they were obliged to study and in bringing expressions and constructions from popular speech into a usually learned style of Latin and thereby producing "kitchen Latin." It is filled with names that allude to pigs and related species, porcine noises, pork products and spices used in producing them (Tardel 75). Finally, it enables pupils to make teasing and even offensive remarks about different occupations through the body parts that the pig bequeathes. A related motif of "distribution of body parts" appears in a *Romulus* fable (no. 68, ed. Thiele 226–27): here the irony is that the donkey, after choosing death as an escape from the drudgery of its life, is worked as hard dead as alive: its corpse is made into musical instruments.

To conclude, the Roman predilection for animal laments, wills, and epitaphs could have reached medieval Latin poets through many channels, but especially through grammar schools (where some of the classical poems were likely to be read and where other compositions could have circulated orally among the pupils). Of course, there is no need in every instance to insist upon an immediate connection between the medieval and the classical poems, because the idea of writing animal wills and laments has occurred independently to poets at many times and places in the history of the world. The humor of such compositions is universal (Pérez Vidal).

The sincere animal dirge thrived in medieval Latin poetry, from Alcuin's poem about a nightingale in the eighth century (*Carmen* 61) through Thierry (Theodorich) of St. Trond's lyric on his dead dog in the twelfth (on Thierry, see Préaux 1947; for a translation, see Appendix 13). Although the paternity of Alcuin's poem is unclear, Thierry's poem reveals an incontestable debt to the pseudo-Vergilian "The Gnat," to which it refers in its closing lines (Préaux 1978), and to Ovid's poem for Corinna's parrot. As the influence of the parodic "The Gnat" would encourage us to suspect, the parodic lament is also represented in medieval Latin: a lament for a hare ("The Little Hare Wept") enjoyed a considerable vogue in the later Middle Ages (compare Tubach, no. 376). Probably through the inspiration of both "The Testament of the Piglet" (Lehmann 1963, 172) and carnivalesque rituals connected with the Feast of the Ass (see Appendix 24), the parodic will survived abundantly in the twelfth and later centuries in the heterogeneous versions of "The Testament of the Ass" (*Testamentum asini*; see Appendix 29; Rice 37–75). The *Testamentum asini* was still a topic of discussion in the days of Erasmus and Luther (Tardel 80–81). In beast poetry, the animal epitaph led a charmed existence. Four prominent beast poems incorporate animal epitaphs: Sedulius Scottus's "Ram," lines 133–40; the *Ecbasis captivi*, lines 1079–93 and 1166–70; the *Ysengrimus* 7.417–22; and Nigel of Canterbury's *Speculum stultorum*, lines 593–94.

Another important genre of Latin poetry in which animals, even talking animals, are paramount is the riddle. Although the theory that riddles influenced the beast poets has never been documented (Ross 275, n. 19; Jauss 84), in the final pages of this chapter I hope not only to prove that riddles influenced beast poets, but in addition to detail the nature of their influence.

For the early Middle Ages, Symphosius (fourth to fifth century) was the enigmatist par excellence, a poet taught and emulated in the schools

(Bernt 117–18, 151–52). His collection of riddles, a hundred three-line poems, was copied repeatedly at a time when other forms of epigram were not being composed or copied, and his good fortune prompted several poets of the British Isles to follow in his footsteps: Aldhelm in the late seventh century and Tatwine, Eusebius, and Boniface in the eighth.

The number of extant manuscripts and the prominence of riddles in medieval curricula guarantees that riddle collections would have caught the attention of beast poets. The riddles must have appealed to them on several accounts. For a start, riddles and fables had interacted with each other from a very early period. Symphosius set the standard for this feature of the Latin riddle collections. He devotes a full fourth of his collection to riddles on animals, birds, and insects (nos. 14–38). In his riddles about the ant and the fly Symphosius draws upon a fable of the ant and the fly which he would have known from Phaedrus (4.25, ed. Perry 340–43) or a prototype of the *Romulus* (nos. 22–23, ed. Thiele cxxx). Symphosius's two pieces (*Aenigmata* 22–23) constitute an interdependent pair, the first riddle being the ant's declaration of her virtue and the second the fly's confession of her wickedness (Jauss 84):

Formica

Prouida sum uitae, duro non pigra labore,
Ipsa ferense umeris securae praemia brumae.
Nec gero magna simul, sed congero multa uicissim.

Musca

Improba sum, fateor; quid enim gula turpe ueretur?
Frigora uitabam, quae nunc aestate reuertor;
Sed cito submoueor falso conterrita uento.

Ant

I am foresighted about my life. Not a sluggard when it comes to hard work, I carry on my shoulders the reward of a carefree winter. I do not heave great loads all at once, but I heap up many loads one at a time.

Fly

I am wicked, I confess; for what vileness does my gullet fear? I who avoided the cold return now that it is summer. But I am dislodged quickly when terrified by a deceptive wind.

At another point in the collection (*Aenigmata* 33–34) Symphosius juxtaposes the wolf and the fox, a fact which suggests that he knew of their
enmity from either fables or folktales.

Aldhelm, who imitated Symphosius in publishing a volume of exactly
one hundred riddles, was as fond of animals and as willing to garner themes
from books of animal lore as the fourth-century riddler had been. Over
one-third of his riddles deal with animals (nos. 10, 12, 14–18, 20, 22, 26, 31,
34–39, 42–43, 47, 56–57, 60, 63–65, 71, 75, 82–84, 86, 88, 96, 99), and
certain ones contain hints that he knew the *Physiologus* (Lauchert 96; Manitius 1: 137, n. 5). Another enigmatist, Eusebius, concluded his sixty riddles
with a score of zoological puzzles, largely based on lore recorded in Isidore
and Solinus (Taylor 63).

Even if riddlers borrowed freely from treatises on beasts and from
fables, what proof is there that beast poets took from *aenigmata*? One
indication that medieval manuscript compilers and poets sensed an association between riddles and beast poetry is that they so often grouped them
side by side in the manuscripts. Both manuscripts of the *Ecbasis captivi* were
bound with Aldhelm's riddles (ed. Ehwald 44). The beast flytings in Berlin,
Deutsche Staatsbibliothek, MS. Phillips 1825, are included among riddles
by Symphosius (Strecker, *MGH Poetae* 4: 793, 4: 1081–83). The unique
text of "The Sick Lion" is in a manuscript with riddles (Dümmler 1878,
107–8). On at least one occasion Eugenius of Toledo's *voces animantium*
and nightingale poems were collected with Symphosius's riddles (Paris,
Bibliothèque Nationale, MS. latin 8440). As regular school fare, Symphosius's enigmas and Avian's fables were often collocated in teaching collections (Glauche 25, 27, 30), and the familiarity of this arrangement might
explain the proximity of the *Physiologus* poems to the riddles in the Anglo-
Saxon *Exeter Book* (ed. Krapp and Dobbie xlix–li, lxv–lxvii): *The Panther*,
The Whale, and *The Partridge* run from folio 95b to 98a, while *The Riddles*
begin near the top of folio 101a.

Another confirmation of the special relationship between enigmatists
and beast poets is that they made similar use of titles. Both Symphosius
and the medieval Latin riddlers diverged from their classical forebears in
that, rather than taxing the reader's ingenuity, they routinely gave away
the solutions to their conundrums in the titles (Bernt 40–41, 115). Because
of the titles, a riddle can hardly be distinguished from a descriptive epigram; and a reader could easily have mistaken a riddle for a short narrative
poem. For this reason, Aldhelm's riddles could have inspired Egbert of
Liège to give titles to his gallimaufry of proverbs, fables, fairytales, and

anecdotes, many of which focus upon animals; in fact, Aldhelm's example could have moved either Egbert himself or one of his copyists to entitle the *Fecunda ratis* the *De aenigmatibus rusticanis* (Manitius 2: 537, n. 1; *Fecunda ratis*, ed. Voigt xix–xxii). Evidently either Egbert or the copyist considered any short, entitled narratives (especially those with talking animals) the same as *aenigmata*.

Medieval Latin beast poets, just as they gleaned the Bible and the poems of Vergil for phrases and line-endings relating to animals, made free with language used in portraits of animals in the riddles of Symphosius and Aldhelm. Alcuin, who had studied Symphosius's style and technique with a practiced eye, relied on both in his own poems about animals (Bernt 117, 201). The first beast poet was familiar with another enigmatist as well. In his nightingale lament he reveals a hitherto unremarked debt to Aldhelm's vignette of the same bird in a riddle (cf. Alcuin, *Carmen* 61.7 "Spreta colore tamen fueras non spreta canendo" with Aldhelm, *Aenigma* 22.3 "Spurca colore tamen, sed non sum spreta canendo").

Aldhelm came to the mind of a second beast poet, too. Two lines in Sedulius Scottus's *De quodam verbece* are modeled on verses in one of Aldhelm's riddles. Both parallels derive from Aldhelm's riddle about the *muriceps*, "the mouse-catching cat." In the riddle, they occur in a passage where the cat explains its reluctance to hunt with packs of dogs, since the hounds might turn on it: "Nec volo cum canibus turmas agitare fugaces, / Qui mihi latrantes crudelia bella ciebunt" (Aldhelm, *Aenigma* 65.7–8: "Yet will I not pursue the fleeing bands with baying hounds, for dogs would turn on me, and bark at me their threat of cruel war"). These two lines were an appropriate choice for Sedulius (71–80) as he recounted the wrangles of a ram with overzealous dogs:

> "But if, on the contrary, your rage and hoarse barking should incite you to gory wars against peaceful little me [72: "in me tranquillum bella cruenta ciet"], then I swear by this head, by these horns, and by this proud forehead that I will give you the rewards you deserve."
>
> Having made this statement, he managed suddenly to soothe the hearts of the beasts; a peace began to dawn and the two sides leapt back. But there was one dog which was just like the barking god Anubis, which had as grandfather the dark-spirited hellhound known as Cerberus, and which was accustomed to hunt fleet stags and hideous bears in the manner of its grandfather: with a threefold throat [79: "gutture qui triplici cervos agitare fugaces"].

The choice is all the more apt, since both scenes revolve around cases of mistaken identity: in Aldhelm's riddle dogs are said to confuse a fellow hunter (i.e., the cat) for quarry, while in Sedulius's poem they punish the ram who is a victim of a crime and let its perpetrator run scot-free.

The *Ecbasis captivi* contains two quotations from Symphosius. One of them resembles the reminiscences in the poems of Alcuin and Sedulius Scottus, in that the *Ecbasis captivi* poet characterizes the fox with a turn of phrase from Symphosius's riddle about the same animal: compare the line openings of *Ecbasis captivi* (1002–3), "Tunc versuta dolis . . . tristatur facie" ("Then the fox, versed in trickery, grows sad in her countenance"), and *Aenigma* (34.118), "Sum versuta dolis" ("I am versed in trickery"). The other elevates quotation to a more intricate art. A pompous little hedgehog, baulking at an assignment, objects that collecting apples is below his station. After all, his background is superior to that of his taskmaster: "Quis tibi vel qualis? Magni sum gente Catonis" (661: "Who or of what sort do I seem to you? I am from the clan of great Cato"). In this case, the reader cannot appreciate the new line unless he remembers an allusion contained in the original one in Symphosius (*Aenigma* 86). In the fourth-century poem the jest is a pun that hinges upon the reader's knowing the full name of the Cato in question:

PERNA
Nobile duco genus magni de gente Catonis.
Vna mihi soror est, plures licet esse putentur.
De fumo facies, de muria mihi sapor inhaesit.

HAM
I trace my descent from the clan of great Cato.
I have one sister, though more are thought to be so.
My complexion is of smoke, my taste is of brine.

The ham, which is made from the meat of the pig (*porcus*), belongs to the *gens* of M. Porcius Cato—who was reputed to be a braggart himself (Livy, *Ab urbe condita* 34.8–12). Aldhelm uses the same sort of humor in his riddle on the camel (*Aenigma* 99.1).

The recollection of Symphosius in the *Ecbasis cativi* remains, for all its complexity and humor, a quotation. The time has come to venture to rougher ground, by attempting to delineate the effects of enigmatic poetry on the poetic methods of the medieval Latin beast poets. One technique shared by poets writing about animals and riddlers is that of not naming a creature or of naming it only obliquely, through an etymology. In his first poem on the nightingale, Eugenius of Toledo turned this device to the advantage of terseness by playing on two etymological interpretations of the word *philomela*, the one "dark-loving" and the other "song-loving": "Sum noctis socia, sum cantus dulcis amica, / nomen ab ambiguo sic philomena gero" (*Carmen* 30: "I am a companion of the night, a companion of sweet song; thus from these two elements I have the name nightingale"). Although Eugenius's poem is an epigram and not a riddle, it scarcely differs from later riddles such as Aldhelm's on the night-raven (*Aenigma* 35), which also plays on the elements in a Greek noun (*nycticorax*: Howe 49, lines 1–7):

> Duplicat ars geminis mihi nomen rite figuris;
> Nam partem tenebrae retinent partemque volucres.
> Raro me quisquam cernet sub luce serena,
> Quin magis astriferas ego nocte fovebo latebras.
> Raucisono medium crepitare per aethera suescens
> Romuleis scribor biblis, sed voce pelasga,
> Nomine nocturnas dum semper servo tenebras.

> My nature appropriately reproduces my name in two aspects, for the "shadows" have part of me, and the "birds" the other part. Only rarely does anyone see me in the clear light, particularly since at night-time I frequent hiding-places beneath the stars. It is my custom to chatter in mid-air in a harsh voice. I am recorded in Romulean [i.e., Latin] books, although my name is Greek, while I inhabit nocturnal shadows through my name (trans. Lapidge 77).

In their etymologizing technique, both poems anticipate Egbert of Liège's verses on the owl, "uolucris de nocte uocata" ("the bird named after the night": lines 1669–74, *Fecunda Ratis*, ed. Voigt 201).

The couplet by Eugenius of Toledo, although not intended as a riddle, resorts to another ploy of riddling: letting the beast speak a monologue about itself. Seeing that animal monologues were not a custom in the classical fables transmitted in the *Romulus* and in the poems of Avian, the chances are strong that poets who gave long speeches to their animals were inspired to do so by animal riddles. This is especially true for poems that make indisputable allusions to riddles, such as Sedulius Scottus's "Ram."

A third characteristic of riddles likely to have affected beast poets is that they close with an injunction to the reader or listener to solve the poem. Similarly, the last couplet of "The Sick Lion" exhorts the dedicatee to search for the meaning of the poem: "Servulus ecce tuus depromit hos tibi versus. / Fabula quid possit ista, require valens" (67–68: "Lo, your humble servant offers these verses to you. Seek out with vigor what this fable can mean"). Theodulf of Orléans ends his rehearsal of bird portents (*Carmen* 72.223–24) with the same kind of challenge: "Singula quis referat: quae, quo, cur, quando, vel unde? / Monstrata haec crebro tempore signa patent" ("Who would relate every single detail: what, whereby, why, when, or for what reason? These portents shown on repeated occasions are plain"). Although the first line echoes a construction that Ovid uses in *Amores* 1.5.23 and *Tristia* 3.7.43, as a whole Theodulf's couplet comes closer to riddles than to love poetry. Leo of Vercelli also may have had in mind the process of solving a riddle when he labeled his poem a "nut for the schools," as if the poem needed to be "cracked" (7.55–56: "Ergo relicta / Iam nuce scolis").

As the manuscript traditions of the riddles and the reminiscences of them in the beast poems suggest, the beast poets had to have known riddles. The beast poets would have learned much from riddles, since many of the riddles ascribed to animals human emotions, human virtues and vices, and especially a human propensity to talkativeness. As a result, the beast poets allowed, or even intended, the enigmatic tone of the animal riddles to permeate their beast fictions.

If this examination of the sundry inspirations and analogues to beast poetry leads to any one sure conclusion, it is that medieval Latin beast poets were not writing in a cultural vacuum. On the contrary, they were aware of many treatments of animals in both oral and written literature. In fable and folktale, in Christian literature such as the *Physiologus* and lives of the saints, and in classical poetry they came upon animals and means of representing animals which helped them to breathe distinctive life and character into their own poems. Their knowledge, not their ignorance, of previous animal literature explains much of the novelty in their poems.

2. Beast Narrative and the Court of Charlemagne

> It was an abiding problem, in classical and medieval times (and still today?), how to amalgamate narrative and moral, and we can think of the antique fable as a form which represents a never-ending search for an integration of moral and structure within the framework of the didactic animal tale. (Nøjgaard 1979, 3)

The canon of narrative beast poems that survives from the eighth, ninth, and tenth centuries is very small: not even a dozen such poems can be located. In any case, *canon* is a misleadingly dogmatic word to apply to the early beast poems, which vary greatly in their times and places of origin, as well as in their intended audiences, verse forms, and techniques. In this chapter, I set my sights on narrative poems that have been connected with the court of Charlemagne. In so doing, I seek to evaluate the features that distinguish the earliest of these poems as well as to uncover the tendencies that they share, tendencies that will cast light on the eleventh-century *Ecbasis captivi* and the twelfth-century *Ysengrimus*.

Alcuin and Other Carolingian Poets

Were there animals in the myths, trickster tales, and fables told by the neolithic people who painted bison and deer on cave walls? Whatever the answer, there can be no doubt that animals have appeared in literature from the ages before Aesop through the decades after Orwell—with no end in sight today or tomorrow. Of the many ways in which this beast literature can be classified, one helpful distinction can be drawn between, on the one hand, those writings in which animals are anthropomorphized so much that they speak and, on the other, those in which the animals are not so thoroughly humanized.

Writings of both sorts exist from many periods: for instance, in the late nineteenth and early twentieth centuries the animals of Joel Chandler

Harris's *Uncle Remus* and Rudyard Kipling's *Jungle Books* could be contrasted to those of Ernest Thompson Seton and Jack London, in the late Middle Ages the animals of the Renard the Fox cycle to those of the bestiaries. Two Latin poems composed during the reign of Charlemagne are especially interesting because, although closely related to each other, they already embody these same extremes in the literary depiction of animals.

Although the verse quoted by Julian of Toledo—"Lupus dum ambularet viam, incontravit asinum" (Bischoff 1959, 247–56; repr. Bischoff 1966, 1: 296, "As the wolf was walking along the road, he met an ass")—demonstrates that rhythmic beast poetry existed as early as the sixth century, the earliest complete medieval Latin beast poem comes two centuries later from the cosmopolitan culture of Charlemagne's court. Various poets who were satellites of the Emperor explored new ways of using animals in poetry.

One of the two indisputably Carolingian poems about animals was written by Alcuin, the scholar and churchman from northern England who was persuaded by Charlemagne to superintend the educational revival in his realm. In thirty-one dactylic hexameters Alcuin's "The Cock and Wolf" relates a story (Appendix 1) that anticipates loosely the events of Chaucer's *Nun's Priest's Tale*: a cock, after being caught by a wolf, escapes through the ruse of convincing the wolf to sing for it. The poem opens with a praise of the cock:

> Dicta vocatur avis proprio cognomine gallus.
> Nuntiat haec lucem, terrarum decutit umbras,
> Tempora discernit, lumbis succingitur, huius
> Subditus imperio gallinarum regitur grex.
> Hunc laudans deus intellectum dicit habere:
> Quippe sub obscuro dirimat qui tempora peplo. (Lines 1–6)

> There is a bird called by the special surname "cock." This bird announces daybreak, dispels shadows from the earth, marks the times of the day, and is girded about his loins. The flock of chickens is ruled subject to his authority. God praises the cock by saying that he has understanding: to be sure, he brings the times of the day from beneath an obscure cloak.

Since Alcuin and many members of his audience were steeped in the Bible—the Latin Bible—it is not surprising that this six-line vignette contains two prominent allusions to cocks mentioned in the Bible: in the third line to Proverbs 30.31, "gallus succinctus lumbos" ("A cock girded about the loins"), and in the fifth to Job 38.36, "Quis posuit in visceribus hominis sapientiam? vel quis dedit gallo intellegentiam?" ("Who hath put wisdom in the heart of man? or who gave the cock understanding?").

The biblical allusions put the poem on a solid Christian footing, and they alert the reader that the subsequent events in the poem are not to be interpreted literally, but allegorically. As one later interpreter of Proverbs 30.31 commented wittily, "I have never seen a cock with girded loins and, unless I am mistaken, it would walk more easily without any girdle than girded about the loins" (Julian of Vézelay, *Sermon* 19, ed. Vorreux 2: 398, lines 12–14).

After the description of the cock the action unfolds swiftly. The cock, pecking for food, dares to go outside his fixed territory and, as punishment for this brazenness, is snatched by the wolf (10–11). In an artful bid to escape, the cock flatters his captor on his voice and ultimately persuades him to demonstrate his talent (13–18):

"Sepe meas tua fama, lupe praefortis, ad aures
Venit et ignoto monuit rumore, quod altum
Vox tibi magna sonum claris concentibus edat.
Nec tantum doleo, inviso quod devoror ore,
Quantum, quod fraudor, liceat ne discere de te
Credere quod licuit."

"Often your fame, O wolf of exceeding strength, has come to my ears and has told in a strange rumor that your great voice can produce a deep sound with sonorous harmonies. I do not grieve so much to be devoured by a hated mouth as to be cheated of being allowed to learn from you what to believe about your voice."

As soon as the wolf bows to his vanity (19) and opens his mouth, the cock takes flight to a nearby tree branch. In triumph, the bird admonishes the wolf below (26–28): "Decipitur merito, frustra quicumque superbit. / Et capitur falsis cariturus laudibus escis, / Ante cibos voces dum spargere temptat inanes" ("Whoever grows proud without reason is deservedly deceived, and whoever is taken in by false praise will go without food, so long as he tries to spread about empty words before eating").

In its basic outlines Alcuin's poem parallels the fable of partridge and fox that appears first in the corpus of surviving fables in the eleventh-century collection of Ademar of Chabannes:

Perdix dum in loco eminentiori sederet, advenit vulpis et dixit ei, quam formosa est facies tua? crura tua ut <ostrum>, os tuum sicut corallum. nam si dormires, pulchrior esses. credens ei perdix clausit oculos; atque eam ilico vulpis rapuit. at perdix fletu permixta locuta est, per artium tuarum virtutes te quaeso, ut antea nomen meum dicas, et sic me devorabis. at ubi vulpis perdicem voluit nominare, aperuit os et evasit perdix. dolens vulpis ait, heu me quid opus fuerat loqui? respondit perdix, heu me dormire quid necesse erat, cui somnus non venerat?—qui ubi eis necessarium non est, loquuntur, et ubi eos vigilare oportet, dormiunt. (*Romulus* 35, ed. Thiele 110–11; Ademar 30, ed. Bertini 1975, 159–61)

As the partridge was sitting on an elevated spot, the fox came up and said to her: "How beautiful your face is! Your legs are like the finest purple, your mouth like coral. Yet if you were asleep, you would be still more beautiful." Believing the fox, the partridge closed her eyes; and the fox at once seized her. But the partridge spoke the following words, intermingled with weeping: "I entreat you by the powers of your cunning to say my name beforehand, and then to devour me." But when the fox wanted to name the partridge and opened her mouth, the partridge escaped. Lamenting, the fox said, "Alas! What need was there for me to speak?" The partridge responded, "Alas! Why was it necessary for me to sleep, when sleep had not come to me?"—There are people who speak when it is unnecessary for them to do so and who sleep when they ought to be vigilant.

Because neither Alcuin's poem nor Ademar's fable has a clear analogue in ancient fable, attempts have been made to trace the origins of both pieces to fable traditions in ancient and medieval cultures throughout Eurasia—in the ancient Indic, Greco-Roman, Germanic, and Byzantine traditions (Graf 25–47; Knapp 1979a, 71–72; Yates 1983, 116, 123).

Whether Alcuin created or adapted the story of the wolf and cock, his handling of the material is original. His version stands apart from Ademar's prose fable and all other versions in many respects (Dargan 6, 13). In its *dramatis personae* Alcuin's poem features a cock instead of a partridge, a wolf instead of a fox. In style the biblical reminiscences with which Alcuin studs the opening of his poem are a world apart from Ademar's spare prose. In theme Alcuin emphasizes the perils of pride, whereas Ademar stresses the need for choosing carefully the times to speak and to sleep. The most forceful contrast between the two compositions emerges in their conclusions: whereas Ademar follows a typically fabular structure of telling a short story and providing a concluding moral (an epimythium), the Carolingian poet not only has the cock pronounce a straightforward moral, but even frames the fable between two profoundly religious statements.

The description of the cock in the first six lines of Alcuin's poem establishes the bird as a type of the good Christian. Since this emphasis recedes in the central portion of the poem and in the commonsensical moral pronounced by the cock (26–28), the appearance of an explicitly Christian meaning in the last three lines (29–31) gives the poem an unexpected symmetry: "Respicit haec illos, qui cum sint, fabula, nacti / Iure salutis opus, privantur fraudibus atris, / Attendendo cavis falsas rumoribus auras" ("This fable applies to those people, whoever they are, who have obtained salvation rightly, but are then deprived of it by black deceits, in paying heed to false breezes with their empty rumors"). The combination of the Christian exordium and peroration endows Alcuin's poem with a level of Christian meaning absent from Ademar's version.

In his handling of the fable Alcuin actuates a tension between a conventional fabular moral and an additional Christian one. Throughout most of the poem Alcuin makes clear that his sympathies lie not with the infernal wolf (20), but with the exemplary Christian cock. The bird, he implies, transgressed only once against the faith. Because its single instant of pride is a transitory sin outweighed by its countless virtues, the cock (conventionally the announcer of salvation) is entitled to have the last word, a mini-homily on pride (26–28). Then, after taking pains to highlight the cock's positive features, Alcuin creates an ambiguity in the closing moral. Although the final lines could be taken as referring to the cock's loss of salvation through listening to the wolf, there are strong reasons to prefer the opposite interpretation: the wolf is equated with those persons who have obtained "salvation" ("salutis opus": 30) only to lose it, the cock with those who wrest away this salvation through their dark deception. If the latter interpretation is correct, then the poet forces the hero and villain of the fable as it is usually constructed to change places so that he may give the fable a Christian moralization.

The matching of one story with two different morals occurred occasionally in both ancient and medieval fables. For example, the thirteenth-century Latin writer Odo of Cheriton relates a fable that has a prefatory moral (a promythium) of general ethical import and a concluding moral (an epimythium) with a specific social application:

THE FALCON AND THE KITE

This one applies to everyone whose forcefulness and audacity are merely physical.

Once upon a time a falcon seized a kite and clamped down hard, using only one of his two claws. "You wretch," taunted the falcon, "aren't your body, head, and beak as massive as mine? Aren't your claws and talons as strong?

I've got you in my grasp and, soon, will kill you. Why are you letting this go on?" The kite replied: "I know perfectly well that I'm as strong as you, and that the parts of my body have just as much force as yours—but it's my heart that fails me."

Thus many men are as forceful as others, as powerful as others, and as richly endowed when it comes to laying out expenditures. But what they don't have is heart. Again, there are many who can fast and hold to the rigors of religious life just as well as others. But they too don't have heart. (*Fabula* 54, ed. Hervieux 4: 225; no. 79, trans. Jacobs 129)

The twelfth-century Old French poet Marie de France once takes the opposite tack: she relates a fable that is overtly Christian in the doctrine enunciated in the story part but that is simply ethical in the epimythium (*Fables* 53, ed. and trans. Martin 148–51).

Alcuin reaffirms his sophisticated reversal of meaning with a masterstroke of quotation: the first line of the Christian moralization echoes verses from Boethius's *Consolation of Philosophy* (3, meter 12.52–54) which describe how Orpheus lost Eurydice when he looked back toward hell:

Heu noctis prope terminos
Orpheus Eurydicen suam
vidit, perdidit, occidit.
Vos haec fabula respicit,
quicumque in superum diem
mentem ducere quaeritis;
nam qui Tartareum in specus
victus lumina flexerit,
quicquid praecipuum trahit,
perdit, dum videt inferos.

As they approached the edge of night,
Orpheus looked back at Eurydice,
lost her, and died.
This fables applies to all you
who seek to raise your minds
to sovereign day.
For whoever is conquered
and turns his eyes to the pit of hell,
looking into the inferno,
loses all the excellence he has gained.
(Trans. Green 74, lines 49–58)

Just as Orpheus lost Eurydice when he looked back, the wolf lost his booty when he succumbed to the blandishments of the cock; and just as Orpheus returned from death, the cock escaped from the lethal bite of the wolf. Thus Alcuin gives a special beastly twist to a myth that fascinated the Middle Ages.

The concluding moral and allusion explain why Alcuin replaced the usual characters in the fable with a different bird and animal. To suit his Christian moralization, he features instead of the partridge the pious cock, instead of the fox the infernal wolf. But Alcuin's reasons for choosing the cock and wolf need not have been solely stern and moral: it is also possible that he could not resist an implicit contrast between the cacophonous howling of the wolf and the melodious singing of Orpheus. For this wry juxtaposition the fox would not have served nearly so well.

The delightful combination of mirth and earnestness in Alcuin's poem would have made it an attractive candidate for recitation before Charlemagne's court. In fact, this piece by Alcuin and another by Theodulf of Orléans probably constitute a recitative pair, one of them a poetic riposte to the other, both designed to be read aloud before the rival scholars at the court. That other poems were recited under such conditions has been proven conclusively (Schaller 1970b, 1971a, 1971b).

Theodulf's poem is forty-six lines in elegiac distichs (see Appendix 11). The events in his poem take place on the grounds of a monastery at Charroux—a monastery about which his poem provides the most notable early evidence (Oexla 193–94). In the opening eighteen lines Theodulf lauds the monastery for its saints, monks, patron, books, vestments, and other holdings. According to Theodulf's account, the Christ-given tranquillity of Charroux was broken in only one way: a fox which had been raiding the supplies of the monks once seized a hen. But the beast was not allowed to cause this disturbance with impunity, for as it attempted to escape, it became trapped in a bush and was killed as it hung by its paw. This incident could reflect medieval lore about animals, since foxes were believed to hang from trees to escape dogs (Atkins lxvii), but Theodulf does not breathe a word to suggest that he regards the episode in his poem as a folklore motif rather than a real occurrence. To conclude the poem, Theodulf expresses the hope that Christ will continue to ward off "demonic error" and cherish the monks of Charroux.

As the foregoing interpretations indicate, Alcuin's and Theodulf's poems differ fundamentally. Whereas Alcuin's poem is a fiction based upon a fable and includes a talking bird, Theodulf's contains no talking animals and relates an event that is supposed to have actually taken place. From Theodulf's perspective the fox and hen are not fictional: they are tokens from a benign God to a favored monastery (40). Receiving these signs are the monks themselves, the "faithful throng" (6, 39) whose presence frames and justifies the incident with the fox. In portraying animals sensitively and individually, but with an eye toward their significance in the divine scheme, Theodulf resembles hagiographers rather than fabulists; for miracles of foxes which are compelled first to return stolen hens and then to die appear routinely in the lives of saints (Diez and Bauer 177).

Yet although unlike in terms of their genres, although completely opposed in the degree to which they anthropomorphize animals, the poems of Alcuin and Theodulf are otherwise closely related. The mere presence of animal protagonists would have sufficed to make an audience familiar with one of the poems think of the other, especially since both tell of devilish animal predators foiled in efforts to carry off poultry, but the two poems are also connected in other ways. Both commence with lines ending in the same Latin phrase ("cognomine galli"), a coincidence that would have struck anyone who heard the poems read aloud in close succession, and both urge a Christian understanding of the events related within them. The poems are monuments to the sophistication of literature about animals, both talking and mute, both humanized and unhumanized, in the reign of Charlemagne.

The warm interest in animals that Alcuin and Theodulf felt was not confined to these two poems, though only Alcuin's may be termed a beast poem. Many of the scholars who stayed with Charlemagne gave one another animal nicknames. This practice was cultivated with especial fondness within Alcuin's contingent. Sometimes the appellations were Latin approximations to the Germanic roots of the men's real names in their vernacular languages. Thus Alcuin called his friend Arno "eagle" (*aquila Epistola* no. 59, ed. Dümmler 4: 102; no. 146, ed. 235–36; no. 150, ed. 245; no. 157, ed. 255; no. 158, ed. 256; no. 159, ed. 257; no. 169, ed. 278; no. 185, ed. 310–11; no. 186, ed. 311); Arno himself used the same byname (no. 66, ed. Dümmler 4: 109–10); and Theodulf styled himself "clan-wolf" (*gentilupus: Carmen* 27.64, ed. Dümmler 1: 492). Often the names were devised for other, now obscure motives: in correspondence Alcuin termed himself "swan," "goose," and "swallow" (*cignus: Epistola* no. 59, ed. Dümmler 4: 102; *anser*: no. 159, ed. 257; and *hirundo*: no. 146, ed. 235). Both Alcuin and Arno assigned the sobriquet "cuckoo" to their young protégé, Dodo (*cuculus: Epistola* no. 66, ed. Dümmler 4: 109–10; no. 226, ed. 370; no. 233, ed. 378).

The whimsy of using animal codenames or nicknames may have been transported to the Continent in the seventh century from Ireland, since Columban once referred to himself as "ring dove" (*palumbus: Epistola* no. 5, ed. 3: 170), or from England, since Aethelwulf called himself "noble wolf" (*lupus clarus: Carmen* 23.1 *De abbatibus*, ed. Dümmler 1: 603). But no one took the practice to such great lengths as the Carolingian scholars. The most extreme example is a prose letter in which Alcuin reports on intrigues at the papal court (see Appendix 2). As a brief selection will demonstrate, the letter is a bewildering cryptogram of animal names substituted for the names of real people:

> Whom should I believe, if he said anything about the eagle [Pope Leo III (795–816)]? He who recently left the peaks of the Roman citadel so that he could drink the fonts of the Saxon countryside [Paderborn] and see the lion [Charlemagne], who rules over all living creatures and wild beasts; or what our blackbird, flitting among them, handed over to the monastic cock [Adalhard], who is accustomed to wake the brothers for their morning vigils; so that through him the solitary sparrow on the roof [Alcuin] should know what was being agreed between the lion and the eagle.

Under such conditions animal nicknames were ultimately assimilated into the Latin verse of Carolingian poets. In an eclogue of twenty-six elegiac couplets, Alcuin bemoans the heavy drinking of his unruly pupil, Dodo, by recounting the sad plight of a cuckoo-bird which is lost at sea and in danger of drowning (*Carmen* 57, ed. Dümmler 1: 269–70). Dodo's (or, rather, the cuckoo's) story is rehearsed fitfully, in an amoebean exchange between two shepherds (Bulst; Scott 1965). Two short quotations will convey the flavor of this eclogue:

Menalcas:	Plangamus cuculum, Dafnin dulcissime, nostrum,
	Quem subito rapuit saeva noverca suis.
Dafnis:	Plangamus pariter querulosis vocibus illum,
	Incipe tu senior, quaeso, Menalca prior.
Menalcas:	Heu, cuculus nobis fuerat cantare suetus,
	Quae te nunc rapuit hora nefanda tuis? . . .
Dafnis:	Quis scit, si veniat; timeo, est summersus in undis,
	Vorticibus raptus atque necatus aquis.
Menalcas:	Heu mihi, si cuculum Bachus dimersit in undis,
	Qui rapiet iuuenes vortice pestifero.
Dafnis:	Si vivat, redeat, nidosque recurrat ad almos,
	Nec corvus cuculum dissecet ungue fero.

Menalcas: Weep for our cuckoo, O beloved Daphnis
          Whom the cruel stepdame seized from his own.
Daphnis: With querulous voice, let us weep for him together;
          As old man, Menalcas, pray begin.
Menalcas: Cuckoo, alas, once wont to sing to us,
          What hour has now snatched you from your own? . . .
Daphnis: He may not come, I fear he is plunged in a maelstrom,
          Snatched by its vortex and now dead by drowning.
Menalcas: Woe to me, if Bacchus has drowned my cuckoo,
          Who loves to snatch young men in his poisonous gyre.
Daphnis: If he lives, let him return, run back to the fostering
          nest, let not the raven slash him with savage claw.

(Trans. Scott 1965, 515)

Why Alcuin referred to his pupil by the codename "cuckoo" (*cuculus*) and not by the name of another bird is a question that has never been posed, even though this case differs sharply from those in which an animal element in an Old English or Germanic name is simply translated into Latin (e.g., Arno to "eagle" *aquila*). Possibly Alcuin used the nickname because the word *cuculus* at that time carried connotations of slothfulness (on these connotations in the writings of other authors, see Brugnoli 1959a, 66–67) or possibly because it denoted, in early medieval monastic parlance, a foolish young monk. The cuckoo appears in this light (and not, as is usual in a later period, as the bird of spring or cuckoldry) twice in the poems of Froumund of Tegernsee (*Carmen* 19.1, 35.4). Whatever Alcuin's motives, in his eclogue he likens the activities of Dodo in real life to the vicissitudes of an imaginary cuckoo: Dodo runs off to drink, the cuckoo flies away and nearly drowns in the ocean.

Whereas Alcuin's poem employs only one codename, Theodulf's "What Do the Swans Do?" (see Appendix 12) cites a long roll call of animal nicknames and thus, even more than Alcuin's piece, demands knowledge of the animal bynames current at the court of Charlemagne (A. Hauck 2: 171; Collins 217; Schaller 1971a). Its fifty-six elegiac couplets begin with a catalogue of birds and their doings, leading into a seeming pastoral. Gradually, one senses that the landscape is not unequivocally bucolic. The David is Charlemagne, the Delia his wife. Alcuin, Einhard, Riculf, and many others are also designated by nicknames. The beasts which stand for people and those which are truly animals are often impossible to keep apart. Largely as a result of this confusion, there has been argument over the identity of the addressee: do the words *corvus, corvulus,* and *corvinianus* refer to Hrabanus Maurus, whose Old High German name would be translated literally as *corvus* in Latin (Ebert 1878, 98–100; Schaller 1971a; Schaller 1971b, 154–56)?

In massing human alongside animal names and in its aptness for recitation before a group of insiders, "What Do the Swans Do?" bears a likeness to the prose "Cyprian's Supper" (*Cena Cypriani*) and even more to the versification by John the Deacon (ca. 825–ca. 880). The original "Cyprian's Supper" was composed in late antiquity to be read aloud or conceivably even to be performed to the accompaniment of miming. Although a person named Cyprian may have written it, the famous third-century Church Father Cyprian was certainly not the author. "Cyprian's Supper" plays with the lore of the Bible, perhaps in part to parody the biblical exegesis of Zeno of Verona (second half of the fourth century), but mainly to achieve laughter. The procedure of "Cyprian's Supper" is straightforward. After a cursory setting of the stage ("A certain king, Johel by name, was preparing a wedding feast in the Orient, in Cana in Galilee. He invited many people to attend his banquet") there follow numerous lists that describe the appearance and conduct of the guests. All the banqueters are characters from the Bible, and "Cyprian's Supper" alludes to details of the passages in which these characters come up: for example, Eve sits on a leaf, Cain on a plough, Abel on a milk pail, Noah on the ark, and so forth. Like the "Monkish Pranks" (*Ioca monarchorum*) "Cyprian's Supper" is meant to entertain and edify through testing the biblical knowledge of the audience.

The humor of "Cyprian's Supper" secured an enthusiastic response in the Carolingian era (Wattenbach and Levison 468–69; Bakhtin 286–89). Around 855 Hrabanus Maurus prepared an abridgment, which he dedicated to King Lothar II. When Charles the Bald came to Rome to be crowned on Christmas day in 875, another version was performed at his table. The performance was repeated in Rome on Easter in 876. Shortly afterward, John, a deacon of Rome, recast the prose "Cyprian's Supper" in 375 rhythmic verses of 15 syllables. As in the original, there are many lines in the poem in which biblical characters are paired with animals. For instance,

> Ecce partes quisque suas   tenebat in dextera,
> Quas ex variis conviva   venatibus ceperat.
> Esau tenet cervinas,   vitulinas Abraham,

Abel Agninas tenebat,   Noe arietinas,
Samson tenet leoninam,   Heliseus ursinam.
           (117–24, ed. Strecker 4: 882)

Look! Each guest held in his right hand his portions,
which he caught in hunting.
Esau holds portions of stags, Abraham of calves,
Abel held portions of lambs, Noah of rams,
Samson holds a portion of lion, Elisha of bear.

Although the explanation for the juxtaposition of Noah and the ram is not immediately evident, the reasons for the other pairings can be discovered easily in the Bible: Esau was known as a skilled hunter (Genesis 25.27); Abraham served the angels with a boiled calf (Genesis 18.7); Abel was a shepherd (Genesis 4.2); Samson tore a lion into pieces (Judges 14.6); and Elisha caused the Lord to send two bears to kill forty-two boys (4 Kings 2.24).

John the Deacon outfitted his version with a dedicatory letter to Pope John VIII, as well as with a prologue and an epilogue (ed. Strecker 4: 857–69; Lehmann 1963, 14–16). In the prologue John offers an interesting tidbit of information: that his poem was to be recited on Cornomannia (Lapôtre 346–49), a holiday of role reversal which continued to be celebrated until after the middle of the eleventh century (Liver 1971). A detailed account of Cornomannia is provided in the *Liber Politicus* written by a twelfth-century Roman canon, Benedict (ed. Fabre 18–23). According to Benedict, Cornomannia took place on the Saturday after Easter (*Sabbato in Albis*). The sacristan of each diaconate was costumed as a fool, carrying a staff covered with bells, and wearing a garland of flowers in the shape of horns. The sacristans went to the Lateran Palace with the archpriests and lower orders. One of the archpriests took a seat facing backward on an ass. When the pope appeared, the archpriests laid garlands at his feet. Three arch-priests supplied additional gifts, one a live fox, one a rooster, and one a fallow deer or a weasel. In payment the pope gave coins to each of the three and offered a blessing, whereupon everyone returned home. The sacristans went from door to door, blessing houses, sprinkling holy water, laying leaves on the hearths, and distributing wafers to the children. At the end the sacristans sang Hebrew verses, after which they were paid.

As will be seen, John the Deacon's version of "Cyprian's Supper" probably influenced Eugenius Vulgarius's "Comic Visions," a beast poem written a few decades later. "Cyprian's Supper" has been offered as a parallel to the *Ecbasis captivi*, a beast poem of the eleventh century which was similarly designed to regale a circle of colleagues upon the feast day (Ross 280) and which resorts to the same brand of biblical humor; the author of the *Ecbasis captivi* includes Esau's retriever as a tracking dog in his poem (332) and makes Jonah's whale one dish on the lion-king's banquet table (547). In view of the vogue that "Cyprian's Supper" enjoyed in Carolingian circles, it is tempting to detect its influence in Theodulf's "What Do the Swans Do?" After all, Theodulf's poem shares several features with John the Deacon's poem. Both would have amused courtiers who knew the persons intended by the animal names and other codenames; both could have been delivered with accompanying mimicry of people in the audiences.

Yet the similarities between John the Deacon's version of "Cyprian's Supper" and Theodulf of Orléans' "What Do the Swans Do?" are only superficial, since the two poems leave markedly different impressions. Whereas John's poem delights with a parade of biblical erudition and is undilutedly jovial and festive, Theodulf's gives a barbed account of court life. To amuse the members of the court and at the same time to avoid the consequences of being explicitly abusive, Theodulf presents the courtiers under bynames that often involve animals and evokes the atmosphere of the classical eclogue.

Partly because of his sharp tongue Theodulf was cast out of the court from 817 until his death (Manitius 1: 538–39). While exiled, Theodulf learned of many unusual natural events. In his opinion, these events indicated that God disapproved of the harsh treatment Theodulf had received. In a verse letter that Theodulf wrote during exile, rivers run dry and birds slaughter one another (see Appendix 10): the reader is to infer that this chaos in nature parallels the internecine strife—and the unjust banning of Theodulf—in the world of human beings. The poet drives home this analogy in three passages in which he identifies the birds with people who participated in battles made famous through classical Latin epic (157–59; 175–76; 213–14). The part of the poetic epistle that deals with birds was designated "The Battle of the Birds" (*De pugna avium*) in three of the manuscripts. Theodulf could have derived the inspiration for the classicizing similes either from Vergil (*Georgics* 1.381–82) or from the use of the word *agmen* by Christian writers such as Ambrose (*Hexaemeron*, book 5, chap. 23.81–82, ed. Schenkl 198.13–24) and Hrabanus Maurus (*De universo*, book 8, chap. 6, PL 111.245A).

Near the end of the poem Theodulf, in a final grandiose simile, likens the ground covered with the corpses of birds to the battlefield at Cannae after Hannibal's massacre of the Romans in 216 B.C. After this comparison he poses a row of questions about the signification of the carnage:

> Ut furor Annibalis complevit funere Cannas,
>   funere sic avium haec rura repleta manent.
> Singula quis referat: quae, quo, cur, quando, vel unde?
>   Monstrata haec crebro tempore signa patent.
>
> (Lines 221–24)

As the rage of Hannibal filled Cannae with death, so the countryside becomes filled with the death of birds. Who would relate every single detail: what, whereby, why, when, or for what reason? These portents shown on repeated occasions are plain.

The epic allusions have prompted modern interpreters of the poem to raise several questions. Are the allusions parodic (Kratz, "An Epic Parody"), or are they not (Jauss 70)? If they are parodic, do they parody Germanic heroic epics (Ross 276)? Or do they parody Latin epics (Kratz, "An Epic Parody")? The notion that the epic trappings allude to Germanic epic has been rejected soundly (Kratz, "An Epic Parody"). What remains is the network of metaphors, similes, and quotations that connects the events in Theodulf's poem to scenes in classical Latin epic and to events in classical history. Through this network Theodulf does more than achieve a stylistic effect; he also magnifies the importance of the avian conflicts in human terms. In asking the questions at the end of the poem he intends to disclose a disorder among human beings just as calamitous as that among birds. Simultaneously, he echoes the words of Ovid (*Amores* 1.5.23), the poet whom he took as his model during his exile (Brugnoli 1959b; Smolak).

With his verse letter, Theodulf can be numbered among the first of various medieval poets who cloaked their complaints of political troubles in stories about animals. A similar need for discretion persuaded Alcuin to convey information in the form of an animal story in the enigmatic prose letter that he wrote to Adalhard of Corbie to report on papal politics in September 799 (see Appendix 2). But the impulse to make animals the vehicle for political commentary did not originate with Alcuin or Theodulf, for such an impulse knows no boundaries of time or place: writers in politically vulnerable positions from before Aesop until after Orwell have chosen to express in the guise of stories about animals thoughts they would not risk stating outright.

"The Sick Lion" and "The Sad Calf"

St. Gall, Stiftsbibliothek, MS. 899 was produced in the late ninth or early tenth century (Bruckner 122). Its contents include Alcuin's poem about the cuckoo (*Carmen* 57, ed. Dümmler 1: 269–70) and a selection of poems by Paul the Deacon. Amid Paul's poems are three fable-like pieces, all concerned with animals. One leaf containing the first forty lines of the longer beast poem was detached from the St. Gall MS in the early sixteenth century and now resides in Vatican City, Biblioteca Apostolica Vaticana, MS. Reg. Lat. 421 (Neff xv; Kaczynski and Westra 1982, 32).

Initially, the three poems were ascribed to Paul the Deacon, a Lombard who spent some years at Charlemagne's court. This ascription is supported by the inclusion of the poems among Paul's poems in the manuscript and by the slight similarity in content between the poems and Paul's verse riddles (Müllenhoff 3). Yet because they differ stylistically from Paul's poems, the idea of Paul's authorship was soon rejected (Neff 190–92).

At the beginning of the twentieth century one scholar attributed the poems to Notker Balbulus, "Notker the Stammerer" (Winterfeld 1904). Although this attribution has been rejected twice (Neff 191–92; Schaller 1970a, 92–93), two scholars have recently resuscitated it (Kaczynski and Westra 1982). In view of the disputed authorship, it will be necessary to consider each of the three hypothetical points of contact between "The Sick Lion" and the writings or life of Notker Balbulus.

In the first place, the pattern of events in the poem is supposed to correspond roughly to a pattern that recurs in Notker's *The Deeds of Emperor Charlemagne (Gesta Karoli Magni Imperatoris)*: an unworthy bishop commits an outrage, Charlemagne judges the bishop immediately, and the bishop is punished with public humiliation (Kaczynski and Westra 1982, 36). To find the same pattern in "The Sick Lion" requires making two major assumptions: that in the beast poem that bear represents a bishop, the lion-king Charlemagne. If these assumptions are rejected, the only pattern that is common to both "The Sick Lion" and Notker's *Gesta* is simply the progression of crime, judgment, and punishment with public humiliation. Surely such a general paradigm is not unique to the incident described by Notker!

The second presumed point of contact between the two works is the adjective *invictus*. This adjective, which appears twice in the "The Sick Lion," is held to be an idiosyncrasy derived from Notker (Kaczynski and Westra 1982, 36–37). But could the poet of "The Sick Lion" not have known the adjective from classical Latin literature, where it is applied routinely to emperors and other leaders (*Thesaurus Linguae Latinae* 7.2.186.15–84)?

Third, the motif of worn shoes in the poem is interpreted as poking fun at Notker's friend Ratpert, who was purported to have led "such a sedentary life that he wore out only *duos calceos* per year" (Kaczynski and Westra 1982, 37). Here again, the explanation presupposes the presence of a historical reference when none is needed; for other explanations are possible. The humor of the worn shoes could be derived from the likelihood that medieval mime players sometimes wore worn shoes slung about their shoulders as a prop (Froumund of Tegernsee, *Carmen* 19.14–22, ed. Strecker 54) or from the fact that medieval pilgrims measured the length of their travels in pairs of worn-out shoes (Voigt 1884, 143, n. on *Ysengrimus* 3.379–80). Alternatively, the shoes could be humorous because the fox had a reputation—perhaps earned through its real-life behavior—for stealing shoes (*Vita sancti Ciarani episcopi de Saigir*, 5–6, ed. Plummer 219). Probably the most obvious explanation is that the motif alludes to a ruse by which the Gabaonites duped Joshua into believing that they had traveled from afar when instead they had come from nearby: "Cunningly devising [they] took for themselves provisions, laying old sacks upon their asses, and wine bottles rent and sewed up again, / And very old shoes, which for a show of age were clouted with patches, and old garments upon them: the loaves also, which they carried for provisions by the way, were hard, and broken into pieces: / And they went to Josue . . . and said to him, and to all Israel with him: We are come from a far country, desiring to make peace with you" (Joshua 9.4–6: Neff 195 n.).

For want of evidence, the attribution of the poems in St. Gall, Stiftsbibliothek, MS. 899 to Notker Balbulus must be discarded, and there is no reason to reintroduce the ascription of the poems to Paul the Deacon. Until new evidence is brought forward, the poems should be considered the work of an anonymous poet at St. Gall.

"The Sad Calf" is an uncomplicated story in five elegiac couplets (see Appendix 25). A calf, wandering in search of his mother, meets a stork who asks him why he is lowing. The calf relates that he is hungry, having gone without milk for three days. The bird retorts that he has not had milk for three years and that the calf is a fool to fret over such a trifle. Insulted, the calf quips that the stork's skinny legs prove how poorly he has eaten. This story has no bearing on later beast poetry, except that it takes up the subject of calf-cow attachment (*Ecbasis captivi* 80, 85, 87, 1159–60; Nigel of Canterbury, *Speculum stultorum* 265–68).

"The Sad Calf" is followed by "Gout and the Flea," a poem in seven elegiac distichs (see Appendix 20). To paraphrase, this poem relates that in bygone days gout afflicted the poor, the flea the rich. Both were miserable: gout, lodged in the feet of the hardworking pauper, had no peace because its host was in constant motion, while the flea was threatened constantly with death because the rich man was well rested. After the two changed places, gout had ample rest and the flea was never troubled by a victim too tired to battle it at night. There is no dialogue in this poem, which has the air of a straightforward fable.

Preceding these two poems is a third that occupies a memorable place in the history of medieval Latin beast poetry. Like the cock fable that Alcuin wrote, "The Sick Lion" (see Appendix 26) presents a story that recurred in many subsequent Latin fables (Hervieux 2: 282–83, 308–09, 561–62, 604–6) and beast poems, including the *Ecbasis captivi* and *Ysengrimus*. The story type, which may be entitled "The Sick Lion, Fox, and Flayed Courtier" (Perry 1965, Appendix nos. 258, 585, 698; Thompson 1955–58, no. K961.1.1; Curletto), centers upon the lion king and his court (Hélin 1951; Bartelink; Kaczynski and Westra 1982). When the lion falls ill, all the animals, except the fox, assemble to make public their grief and to suggest remedies. One of the king's lackeys—here a bear but elsewhere a wolf (*Ysengrimus, Ecbasis captivi*)—denounces the fox for treason and arranges to have her condemned to death. (In both "The Sick Lion" and the later *Ecbasis captivi* [417, 436, 491, 757, 998, 1165], the fox is female, in accordance with the feminine gender of the Latin word *vulpes*.) Alerted of this verdict, the fox piles worn-out shoes on her shoulders to convince the animals, especially the ailing lion, that she has traversed a vast distance. She persuades the court that she has scoured the globe in search of a cure—and that she has found one. Pressed to reveal the remedy, the fox tells with feigned reluctance that the monarch should be wrapped in the hide of her detractor, the bear (Foulet 371–73; Kaczynski and Westra 1982). As soon as the cure is put into effect, the fox taunts the flayed beast.

Parts of the story related in "The Sick Lion" have loose analogues in earlier literature. In fact, an ancient Babylonian tale about a fox comes close to anticipating the central narrative of both "The Sick Lion" and later

Latin fox-and-wolf poems (Ebeling 1927, 20–23, 48–49; Ebeling 1957, 1; Johnston 83–84). The fox makes a pact with the wolf, against the dog who serves the herdsman. When dragged to judgment for this crime, the fox and wolf besmirch each other. Through clever eloquence the fox bests the wolf. Like Renard in the medieval European cycle or Brer Rabbit in the nineteenth- and twentieth-century North American Uncle Remus stories, the fox is an archetypal trickster, feigning piety while bamboozling opponents (Ebeling 1927, 17; Johnston 84).

More specifically, there has been speculation over the relationship between "The Sick Lion" and a similar Greek prose fable about "The Lion, Wolf, and Fox" (Adrados 1984, 259). At first the Latin poem was assumed to be a verse reworking of an ancient fable in the Aesopic corpus. Then, when it was realized that the Greek fable was attested nowhere earlier than a ninth- or tenth-century Byzantine recension of the Aesopic corpus, "The Sick Lion" was posited to be a Latin version of a Germanic fable that reached Byzantium orally (compare Hausrath 1937; Hélin 1951, 418; Schaller 1970a, 93–95; Knapp 1979a, 21–23). Most recently, the Latin has been presented as a reworking of a fable found in a bilingual teaching collection (Kaczynski and Westra 1982, 31–34).

Whether the poet of "The Sick Lion" learned the story through reading a Latin version of a Greek fable, through hearing an oral version of a beast folktale in his native language, or through being exposed to both oral and written versions cannot be known (Schaller 1960–61, 71). But whatever the traditions upon which the poet drew, he was not responsible for introducing into the story from his own historical context as many new elements as has been sometimes proposed (Kaczynski and Westra 1982, 35–36). In particular, he was not innovating upon his source or sources of inspiration when he cast the bear as the victim of the excoriation: the bear plays this role both in oral versions of the tale collected in modern times by folklorists (Krohn) and in a thirteenth- or fourteenth-century Armenian written version presumably translated from an earlier Greek original (Perry 1960, 158–59). The interchangeability of the bear and the wolf in such stories may have begun at a very early period among Indoeuropean peoples (Carpenter 131).

In the last couplet the poet of "The Sick Lion" implies that the story has a higher application, perhaps to political affairs in which the addressee is involved: "Servulus ecce tuus depromit hos tibi versus, / Fabula quid possit ista, require valens" (67–68: "Look, your humble servant offers these verses to you. Seek out with vigor what this fable can mean"). There is no justification for assuming that the "humble servant" here is Paul the Deacon and the addressee the Emperor (Neff 192). The only notable feature that the poem shares with the riddles that Paul and Charlemagne exchanged in their correspondence (Manitius 1: 258, 270) is one quite common in fable and fable-like poetry: it demands to be solved by the reader or listener.

Other authors of fable-like poems allowed an enigmatic tone to permeate their fictions. For instance, Leo of Vercelli may have had in mind the process of solving a riddle when he labeled his poem a "nut for the schools" ("Meter," 7.55–56: "Ergo relicta / Iam nuce scolis"), as if the poem needed to be "cracked." As this phrase suggests, not the least reason why beast poems and riddles influenced each other was that both were associated with play, festivals, and childishness. Then as now, cracking a joke and cracking a riddle were related activities.

Perhaps the puerile associations of fable and riddle enabled the poet of "The Sick Lion" to risk broaching an otherwise dangerous political topic. Such a reading requires finding a political solution to which the characters and events of "The Sick Lion" could plausibly have referred.

One hypothesis is that the story of the bear refers to the fate of a real-life courtier whose name ended in the Germanic onomastic element *bero* (Ross 275; Schaller 1970a, 93–95), but this hypothesis is based on the false premise that the poet of "The Sick Lion" deliberately substituted the bear for the wolf as the antagonist of the fox.

Another idea is that the treatment of the bear refers to vicissitudes in the career of an actual bishop (Kaczynski and Westra 1982, 36). The justification for this approach is that when the fox mocks the flayed bear for the appearance of its hands and head, the terms are ones that were used to describe the costume of a bishop: "Quis dedit, urse pater, capite hanc gestare tyaram, / Et manicas vestris quis dedit has manibus?" (65–66: "Who gave you, father bear, this fancy headdress to wear on your head? And who gave you these gloves for your hands?"). Centuries later, Bruin the bear is mocked by Renard the fox in a similar fashion: "De quele ordre volez vos estre, / qui rouge chaperon avez?" (*Roman de Renart* 1.698–700, ed. Roques 25; trans. Terry 113: "But tell me, are you aspiring to a monastic order? What's this red hood-like thing that's on your head?"). The flayed wolf in Marie de France's version of the fable (no. 68, trans. Martin) is taunted in the same way. Yet the reference to a bishop in "The Sick Lion" is not unequivocal. For instance, the types of clothing described by the terms *tyara* and *manicae* were worn first by the ruling classes in late

Roman antiquity and only later by religious powers (Eisenhofer and Lechner 153–55; Klauser 17–23). In fact, when the wolf in the *Ysengrimus* (3.991–1131) is flayed like the bear in "The Sick Lion," he is accused of arrogating to himself kingly attire. Elsewhere the scraps of fur left on the paws and head are understood to be gloves and cap, plain and simple (Perry 1965, Appendix no. 698; compare Appendix 4 below). Finally, even if we brush aside the ambiguity of the words *tyara* and *manicae* and accept that they are meant to describe a bishop (Mann 1987, 25, n. 79), we do not know the specific bishop to whom they refer.

As long as historical explanations remain at the worst wholly ungrounded and at the best inconclusively speculative, the only certainties about "The Sick Lion" are literary: that it is the earliest extant version in Latin of a story which later won renown, and that the poet judged the moral too obvious or too dangerous to bear direct statement. Like Alcuin's fable of the cock and wolf, "The Sick Lion" is not content merely to tell a straightforward fable and to tack onto it the usual sort of moral. Like Theodulf's verse letter, it approaches being a riddle because it rests its claim to value and attention on a hidden meaning. But a poem that begins with the "once upon a time" quality of a fairy tale ("Aegrum fama fruit quondam . . .") should not be racked to fit a Procrustean bed of historical allegory.

3. Further Beyond Fable

The beast poets affiliated with the palace of Charlemagne and his successors were still conditioned by their schooling in beast fable, even though they took measures to mould the standard story-and-moral arrangement to suit their special needs. Alcuin added Christian allegory, while "The Sick Lion" poet left out the moral and ended his poem instead with a riddle-like challenge. But other ninth-century writers seem to have gone beyond fable and to have responded to a wider range of beast literature and beast traditions. "The Nanny Goat," Sedulius Scottus's "The Ram," and "The Swan Sequence" are as unlike in structure and function as three poems can be.

"The Nanny Goat"

Of the three ninth-century beast poems just mentioned, the anonymous "The Nanny Goat" most closely resembles a conventional prose beast fable. In fact, the exchange that it relates in five elegiac couplets is a version of the fable of the shepherd and the she-goat in "Perotti's Appendix," a collection of thirty fables preserved solely in a transcription by Niccolò Perotti (1430–1480) from a manuscript of Phaedrus that was subsequently lost (Perry 1965, xcvii–xcviii, 406, no. 24). "The Nanny Goat" itself is in a miscellany of seven poems that was copied at the end of the ninth century, perhaps in Milan, between Horace's *Carmen saeculare* and *Epistles*. The manuscript is now Paris, Bibliothèque Nationale, MS. lat. 7972.

As "The Nanny Goat" begins, a she-goat is bleating because one of her horns has been knocked off. The herdsman comes to her and asks her to tell the owner of the herd, when he arrives, that she has both horns intact. The goat retorts that words will not conceal the obvious state of affairs. As the poet rephrases the moral in the final couplet of the ten-line poem, he presents the anecdote as an object-lesson to a particular person, whom he leaves nameless:

DE CAPRA

Ecussum cornu gemeret dum forte capella,
    Pastor eam gregis talibus orsus adit:
"Oro, gregis dominus cum te prospexerit, ambo
    Esse tibi dicas cornua fronte tua."
Trunca capella dehinc: "Quid narras, pastor inepte?
    Nonne duo feret ipse deesse mihi?
Verba queunt istud certe celare nequaquam,
    Apparet, factum, res manifesta satis."
Hoc tibi de parvo possim narrare nepote:
    Te sine quod fertur, non opus ipse feras.

THE NANNY GOAT

Just as a she-goat was moaning that her horn had been struck off,
the herdsman of the flock came up and addressed her in the following words: "I beg of you, when the owner of the flock looks at you,
say that both your horns are on your forehead." The [5] mutilated
she-goat retorted: "What are you saying, you foolish herdsman?
Won't he see for himself that I don't have two? Words, you should
be sure, can't conceal this matter: the evidence speaks for itself." I
could relate this to you about your little kinsman: what is suffered
without your involvement, you need not suffer [10] yourself.

With the exception of the fable in "Perotti's Appendix," the witty
heroine of "The Nanny Goat" finds her closest relative in a section of the
Aramaic *Ahikar* (fifth or fourth century B.C.):

> The leopard met the goat when she was cold. The leopard answered and said
> to the goat, "Come, I will cover thee with my hide." The goat [answered]
> and said to the leopard, "What need have I for it, my lord? Take not my skin
> from me." For he does not greet the gazelle except to suck its blood. (*Ahikar*
> 118–20, trans. McKane 168)

This section of the *Ahikar* has been described as "a contest fable in which
the goat fences skilfully with the leopard, evades him with a clever feint
and earns the plaudits of the reader for her canniness. The moral, if there
is one, would be that it is better to be cold than to be dead" (McKane
168). Such "contest fables" appear to have entered the corpus of classical
Aesopic fables under the influence of Mesopotamian fables and disputations (Gordon 1958, 1).

Although a beast fable in verse, "The Nanny Goat" differs from "The Cock and Wolf," "The Sick Lion," and "The Sad Calf" in its outlook on animals. Whereas in the Carolingian poems animals are sequestered from human beings in a universe of their own, in the ninth-century verses a goat and a man meet and converse as equals. Indeed, if one of the two characters proves to be superior, it is the talking animal: she makes a fool of the shepherd.

With this fresh perspective, "The Nanny Goat" fortuitously counterbalances "The Ass Brought Before the Bishop," another piece extant in Paris, Bibliothèque Nationale, MS. lat. 7972—and also in a Stuttgart manuscript. "The Ass Brought Before the Bishop" (see Appendix 17) depicts a bishop who agrees to consecrate an ass as a priest, only once he has noticed the bribe (a bar of gold) that the sponsor of the ass has attached beneath its tail. The ass is a dumb beast, incapable of dialogue, no more the principal actor in this poem than the ox in the later poem *Unibos*. In contrast, the goat in "The Nanny Goat" has a sharp tongue and a quick wit. Her combativeness and repartee are typical of other animals in ninth-century Latin poetry, particularly of the animals in the beast flytings.

Sedulius Scottus's "The Ram"

By including facts and phrases from the Bible, Alcuin's "The Cock and Wolf" and the anonymous *Ecbasis captivi* give their animals a high, sometimes comically disproportionate, prestige, but the mid–ninth-century "Ram" of Sedulius Scottus (see Appendix 9) was the first beast poem to be based on an event related in the Bible.

"The Ram" is one of the most exciting Latin poems to survive from the ninth century; it is an impressive piece of seriocomic writing, one that draws daring parallels between the death of a ram and the Passion of Christ. Although the second longest of Sedulius's many poems (only *Carmen* 2.7 is longer), "The Ram" achieves its varied effects within an economical plot: a ram given to Sedulius by Hartgar, his patron, is first stolen, then released intact, and finally mauled to death by dogs which take it to be a henchman of the thief, who escapes unscathed.

Sedulius claims that the incident around which he fabricates his poem happened in actuality. Whatever the reality may have been, Sedulius altered it to accommodate numerous allusions to the Bible and to classical

Latin poetry. Among the biblical reminiscences, the poet's comparison of his ram, Tityros, with the ram immolated by Abraham bears special note (cf. 121–22 and Genesis 22). Like Tityros, the biblical ram was caught by its horns in a thicket (Genesis 22.13) and sacrificed in place of a human, and like Tityros, the ram of Genesis was considered by exegetes as an ovine precursor of Christ (on the exegesis, see Nikolasch). Although the story of Tityros may have been inspired by a true occurrence (rams do get trapped by their horns) or by a fable, neither fable nor fact could have accounted for the elaborate theological constructs of "The Ram," the creation of a mind steeped in Bible study. Sedulius, who took pains to draw the reader's gaze to Abraham and Isaac, probably devised his poem on the basis of the episode in Genesis.

Despite its length "The Ram" contains fewer topical allusions than many of his other poems. Still, the mention that the ram had been given to Sedulius by Hartgar, Bishop of Liège, fixes the composition of the poem within a span of seven years: it must have been written between 848, when Seduluis came to Liège from his native Ireland, and 855, when the Bishop died (Manitius 1: 315–23; Düchting 1970, 122).

Whereas Sedulius's other poems have been largely ignored in scholarship, "The Ram" has won many admirers. Readers concur that "The Ram" is "the most original" of Sedulius's poems (Bieler 123; Düchting 1968, 139; Meyers 185, 196). This unanimity evaporates, however, once the discussion shifts from the poem's originality to its genre. According to one scholar, the poem is a repository of Germanic beast lore, a chance survival of oral "beast fairy tales" (Mierlo [1943a] uses the term *Tiermärchen*; contrast Jauss 59–65). According to others, it is a "beast short story" (Jarcho writes of *Tiernovelle*, 566, 579), an epicedium (Herrlinger 122), a mock-necrology (Bieler 123), a mock-epic narrative with *planctus* and epitaph (Kratz 1976, 319), "an elegant and sophisticated little piece of mock-heroic" (Cooper 17–18), an epyllion (Düchting 1970, 122, 127), verses on an Aesopic theme (Kaczynski and Westra 1982, 33), or a masterpiece of parody (Meyers 197). From each new consideration of the poem, a new name for its genre has resulted. Paradoxically, the lack of consensus about the genre of "The Ram" pays the highest conceivable compliment to its originality. Sedulius tapped so many poetic resources and emulated or simulated so many types of poetry that "The Ram" defies quick pigeonholing.

In the rush to associate "The Ram" with a given genre, no one took the trouble to place Sedulius's beast poem in the context of the other poems he wrote (see Ratkowitsch). Perhaps in his other compositions we will find landmarks that will enable us to move through "The Ram" without straying.

The only two of Sedulius's poems that are known to have been copied in more than one manuscript, "The Ram" and "Our Glory Returns," were both written in elegiacs, directed to the bishop, and concerned with sheep. "The Ram" survives in Brussels, MS. 10615–729 (twelfth century), folios 219ᵛ–220ʳ and Freiburg im Breisgau, Domkapitelsbibliothek, MS. D 1442 (the manuscript is ninth century, but the poem is copied in a tenth-century hand), folios 31ᵛ–32ʳ (Düchting 1970, 14). The copy of the "Gloria nostra redit" in Metz, MS. 500 was destroyed in 1944, but another is extant in Brussels, MS. 10615–729 (twelfth century) (Düchting 1970, 14).

"Our Glory Returns" opens with four merry couplets celebrating, in the manner of an eclogue, the safe return of a shepherd:

> Gloria nostra redit, clementia luxque serena;
>   Cuncti laetemur: gloria nostra redit.
> Cedite vos, tenebrae; frontis nubecula cedat;
>   Dum iubar est praesens, cedite vos, tenebrae.
> Daphnis amoenus adest pastor bonus atque beatus;
>   Tytire, plaude manu: Daphnis amoenus adest.
> Fistola nostra sonet ternoque foramine terni
>   Multones veniant; fistola nostra sonet.
>
>   (Lines 1–8)

Our glory returns, serene mercy and light; let us all rejoice: our glory returns. Depart, darkness; let the cloud of a frown depart from the brow; so long as our radiance is present, depart, darkness. [5] Our pleasant Daphnis is present, a good and fortunate shepherd; applaud with your hand, Tityros: our pleasant Daphnis is present. Let our pipe sound and, at the sound of its three stops, let three sheep come; let our pipe sound.

"Daphnis" (as the poem charmingly styles Hartgar) is a *pastor* both in the strict Christian sense, because he is a bishop, and in the classical and literal meaning of the word, because he controls the sheep which Sedulius desires so passionately (*Carmen* 2.36.17–18). In a special Sedulian sense (*Carmen* 2.3.26), Hartgar is the *pastor* of the Irish, since he provided hospice for Sedulius and his compatriots.

In the remaining eight distichs of the poem, Sedulius glides deftly

from extolling sheep to averring that both sheep and Daphnis will earn immortality, provided that Sedulius receives the sheepskin to use for parchment; for sheepskin was very important as a writing material (Wattenbach
1896, 121–23).

Scandito, multo, fores naso cornuque superbo,
10   Gaudia multa ferens scandito, multo, fores
Vellere deque tuo pellantur frigora multa,
      Nos defende, precor, vellere deque tuo,
Pellis et exuviis sit kartula famaque perpes,
      Nomen sparge polo pellis et exuviis.
15   Despice sic miseram, meliorem delige vitam,
      Multo, brevem vitam despice sic miseram.
Fors eris astrigeri praefulgens sidus Olimpi,
      Mox Aries caeli fors eris astrigeri.
Multo venito triplex, tu multo corpore multus;
20   Cornua sena levans multo venito triplex.
Sublevet altithronus sic nostrum Daphnin ad astra,
      Felici cornu sublevet altithronus.—
Scribere non valeo nec multas ferre Camenas:
      Te sine, multo, fleo, scribere non valeo.
                                                                (Lines 9–24)

Climb outside, sheep with proud nose and horn; [10] bringing
many joys come outside, sheep, and may many chills be dispelled
by your fleece, and defend us, I entreat you, with your fleece, and
may there be from the remains of your hide parchment and everlasting fame, and spread your name throughout heaven with the
remains of your hide. [15] Thus despise this wretched life, choose
a better one, mutton, thus despise this brief, wretched life. Perhaps
you will be a shining constellation in the star-studded heavens,
perhaps soon you will be the Aries of the star-studded heavens.
Come, threefold mutton, you mutton with much body; [20] come,
threefold mutton, raising your six horns. Thus may God throned
on high raise our Daphnis to the stars, may God throned on high
raise him up with his blessed horn. —I am unable to write or to
bring forth many poetic Muses: without you, mutton, I weep, I
am unable to write.

To complement the whimsy that a sheep may outlast death, Sedulius puns incessantly on the adjective *multus* ("great": lines 10, 11, 19, 23) and the noun *multo* ("wether": 8, 9, 10, 16, 19, 20, 24).

The gaiety of "Our Glory Returns" may have pleased Hartgar's entourage and encouraged Sedulius later to attempt a more ambitious poem about sheep. Whatever the reason, the ninth-century poet made "The Ram" much longer and more involved than the "Our Glory Returns." For example, even before narrating the tragic tale of how Tityros was stolen and died, Sedulius allows himself to strike a special tone in three preliminary sections. In the first one, he depicts God's creation of sheep; in the second, he elaborates upon his personal infatuation with mutton; and in the third, he singles out for praise the extraordinary ram, Tityros.

This preamble initiates the three forces that govern the rest of the poem. The biblical typology inherent in the "sheep genesis" (Jauss 65) resurfaces again and again, finally to predominate in an analogy between Tityros and the ram immolated in lieu of Isaac (Genesis 22.13). In contrast to the scriptural references, the autobiographical details at first seem incidental, brought up only because Sedulius happens by chance to have owned the hero of the poem, but these details become paramount at the close of the poem, in an epitaph that eternalizes Sedulius's craving for mutton. Most pervasive of the three forces that regulate the poem is the classical language, mainly from Vergil's *Aeneid* (Meyers 187–88), that Sedulius cultivates. Pagan antiquity also supplies the gods, historical figures, and literary personages whom the poet invokes. Thus in the opening portion of the poem Sedulius refers to Lethe, the river of forgetfulness in Hades (17); to the constellation Aries (31), which was illustrated vividly in manuscripts (Rawson 67, plates 94–95: British Library, MS. Harley 647, folio 2b and British Library, MS. Tiberius BV, part 1, folio 32b); to Lucina as a byname for the lunar goddess Diana (33: Ratkowitsch 254, n. 9); and to the myth of Pan and Luna (35–36: Vergil, *Georgics* 3.391–93; Ratkowitsch 254, n.9).

At times the classical coloring blends with the biblical one to produce unusual blends: a robber who traces his lineage from Goliath is characterized as a Cacus (43–44), whereas the ram called Tityros dies at the teeth of a dog named Cerberus (97) but is compared with the sacrificial ram—one is tempted to say "scapegoat"—in the Abraham and Isaac episode. The mention of Tityros is complicated by the fact that this name would have called to mind not only the herdsman of Vergilian renown—a herdsman whose name Sedulius appropriated in two of his other poems (Rat-kowitsch 257)—but also a formidable creature which was supposedly the cross between a she-goat and a ram (Düchting 1970, 280; for illustration, see Vinycomb 217).

The biblical and classical tones mingle most often and forcefully in the central narrative, which commences after the enumeration of gods who are enamored of Sedulius's ram and after the tactful announcement that the ram was a present from Hartgar. As the story shows, the ram's demise results not from a flaw in his character or comportment, but from an un-provoked act of crime: a robber asconds with Tityros. For this nefarious deed, the miscreant receives a train of names that associates him with the devil. He is a swarthy Ethiop (Kratz 1976, 321), a Cacus (Lehmann 1959, 2: 230), and a spawn of Goliath (*Carmina* 1.16.11, 2.8.25). As the scoundrel carries the ram through the undergrowth, a pack of dogs sights them and gives such vigorous pursuit that the robber drops his woolly booty and takes to his heels. The ram, mistaken for the culprit, is attacked, but he puts up valiant resistance and persuades the dogs that he is innocent. All the dogs relent except the bellicose Cerberus, who accuses Tityros of be-ing a fox in sheep's clothing (83–84). This Cerberus is a grandson of the mythical Cerberus (78), a character whose unsavory reputation rivaled that of Cacus and Goliath (Savage 1949–51).

Sedulius adds to the foreboding atmosphere of this scene through two pointed allusions to Aldhelm's Latin riddle about a cat set upon by dogs (cf. 72 and 79 with *Aenigma* 65.7–8), but Tityros is not yet ready to surrender like a cat to a pack of dogs. Unable to tolerate the calumny which Cerberus has pronounced against him, Tityros butts the dog in the face, breaking two of the beast's teeth with his horns. Far from giving up, Tityros has all but won the skirmish when, inexplicably, he turns tail. If only he had stood his ground! As he flees, his horns catch in a thicket and he is held helpless as he is slain from behind by the cursed Cerberus. Like the stag in the famous fable, Tityros dies as a result of the physical attrib-ute which makes him most proud: his set of horns. The fable, found in the verse of both Phaedrus (1.12) and Babrius (43), was current in the Middle Ages in the prose of the *Romulus* collections (Hervieux 2: 764).

Although not a cento, "The Ram" rests on a bedrock of classical expres-sions absorbed from Ovid, Persius, and Vergil (Meyers; Ziolkowski 1983b, 20–24). Whereas in some lines the phrases are adopted casually, as if only in passing, in other verses they are crowded together to achieve a deliber-ately mock-epic, Vergilian effect (cf. 54–56 with *Aeneid* 1.725, 9.749, 8.305).

Yet the playful tone coalesces with, rather than excludes, the underlying Christian meaning. The couplet describing the ram's demise demonstrates this cohesion amply: "Labitur exanimis multo, miserabile visu, / irrorans vepres sanguine purpureo" (99–100: Düchting 1970, 124; Kratz 1976, 320). While the original context of the words *labitur exanimis* and *purpureo* (the death of Camilla in *Aeneid* 11.818–19: contrast Kratz 1976, 320) contributes nothing precise to the reader's vision of the ram's downfall, the language imbues the scene with the gravity of a classical Latin epic. The same observation holds true for the cliché *miserabile visu* and for the first three words of the second line (cf. *Aeneid* 8.645). The Christian significance of this couplet, still veiled at this moment, is emphasized at the end of the poem, where Sedulius likens the death of the ram to that of the lamb of God, Christ (both died to save a *latro*: 117–20), and to that of the ram substituted for Isaac (121–22). It is also possible that Sedulius brings into play the parable of the Good Samaritan (Luke 10.29–37, especially 30: Düchting 1968, 141; Düchting 1970, 125).

Sedulius's equation of Tityros to the Old Testament ram and, by extension, to Christ is not a last-minute solemnification of the poem. Rather, it is carefully anticipated through a verbal allusion to Genesis. The terse account in the Bible tells that the ram, like Tityros, met death because it was entangled (*haerentem*) in a thicket (*vepres*) (Genesis 22.13: Düchting 1970, 124; Meyers 45–46). Like Tityros, the biblical ram was sacrificed in place of a human being. We are entitled to conclude that the scene which Sedulius portrays is patterned in its language on Vergil but in its meaning on the Bible, and it rests on the word *vepres*, charged with this dual importance.

Because so many words in the text carry a double weight, it is a tribute to Sedulius's finesse that the poem never seems to oscillate between two opposed extremes. The word *pius* serves in one appearance as a ludicrous claim to epic dignity, when the ram intones "sum multo pius" (68) as unabashedly as his Vergilian forebear declared "sum pius Aeneas" (*Aeneid* 1.378; see Schaller 1960–61, 71, and Kratz 1976, 320, in opposition to Jauss 64–64). In a later instance, *pius* functions as an epithet of a pious Christian martyred for his faith ("Aspris inhaesit heu pius ille locis": "Alas, the pious ram became stuck in those rough places," 96).

Still more words gain resonance from the special connotations which Sedulius gave them in his other poems. When the poet calls the ram the *custos* of the flock (4, 25, 68, 133) and names it after Vergil's most famous shepherd, the ram assumes the air of a pastor who lays down his own life in order to shield his flock against the wolf. This metaphor of shepherd, sheep, and wolf, which recurs in Sedulius's other poems (*Carmina* 2.1.18– 20, 2.21–22, 3.26, 5.12, 6.17–18 and passim, 7.5–6 and 124, 21.8, 68.24, 71.25, 72.18–20), accords perfectly with the figurative construction implied at the curtain-fall of "The Ram": Christ, the leader of the flock (who happens to be a ram), surrenders his life in an attack by the wolf (in this instance, a hell-hound descended from Cerberus). Sedulius's scene gains in Christian symbolism if we assume that his audience, which was familiar with typological readings of the Psalms (127–32), interpreted Psalm 21.17, "many dogs have encompassed me" ("circumdederunt me canes multi") as referring to Christ's tormentors (Kratz 1980, 9; Marrow).

The dog's most heinous offense against the virtuous ram is his "untruthfulness" ("falsidici": 89) to which the ram, untainted by any mendacity (115), reacts by making the assault that culminates in his death. Falsehood was the sin that most preoccupied Sedulius in his other poetry: he wrote one poem against liars (*Carmina* 2.55) and another two against false witnesses (*Carmina* 2.56–57). In all three poems the liars are satanic beasts—wolves, foxes, and asps—who harry the faithful sheep (55.7; 56.12; 57.7). These false men merit the same unflattering epithets as the namesake of Cerberus received in "The Ram": they are pitch-black Ethiops (55.17). Their "threefold tongues" ("lingua trisulca": 55.17) correspond to the "three throats" of Tityros's killer ("gutture triplice": line 79). In both cases, the number symbolism can be explained on the same basis as in the Midrash Rabbah, Deuteronomy (Shofetim) 5.10 (trans. Freedman and Simon 111): "Why is the evil tongue named 'the threefold tongue'? Because it slays three people, him who speaks evil, him who listens to it, and the victim of the slander." In sum, Sedulius's poems against liars and false witnesses share with "The Ram" too many expressions for the common theme to have been fortuitous (cf. *Carmina* 2.55.3 with 41.73, 2.57.4 with 41.84), but it is impossible to determine whether the falsehood poems or "The Ram" came first.

In both the falsehood poems and the ram poem, the liars use animal metaphors to insult their opponents (cf. "The Ram" 83–84 with *Carmina* 2.55.7–8). They have the effrontery to accuse the truthful of having lied. In neither case, does the slandered party fail to notice and to respond to the evil. In the falsehood poems God perceives "false figments" ("figmina falsa") with "flashing eyes" ("vibratis oculis": 57.14), while in "The Ram" the hero lunges with "brandished horns" ("vibratis cornibus") to smash the mouth of the "false-speaking" beast ("os falsidici" 89). Not accidentally, the falsehood poem conjures up the image of horned Moses taking action (57.21). Elsewhere in Sedulius's poetry, God enlists the faithful to raise the "ecclesiae cornua clara" (67.37–38, 77.13: cf. *Apocalypse of Golias* stanza 33 and notes, ed. Strecker 23). In one poem, the faithful warrior is a sheep capable of becoming a lion when confronted with wickedness (67.30–32); the ram undergoes the same leonizing metamorphosis (61–62).

By the earlier-mentioned Vergilian allusions and perhaps by judicious inclusion of self-quotations from his falseness poems, Sedulius manages in the main narrative of "The Ram" to strike a subtle balance between the classical and Christian forces that he counterpoised in the first three sections. He is equally adept in the final three parts. The fifth segment (100–104), two taut couplets, memorializes the reactions of figures from classical mythology to the death of the heroic ram. A sixth section (105–16) discards this mock-epic hyperbole for a rehearsal of the ram's good points. In a form of drollery which anticipates later beast poetry, Sedulius lauds natural traits of his ram as commendable human attainments (cf. Nigel, *Speculum stultorum* 1185–90). The ram drank neither beer nor wine (Meyers 192–93) and eschewed sumptuous food. In addition, he dressed in a humble suit of wool and walked rather than rode a horse (in contrast to the animals in the later Renard cycle: Bianciotto 27–42). To cap his virtues, he spoke no lies but only the *mystica verba* of *baa* and *bee* (Ziolkowski 1983a, 287–90).

The seventh section of "The Ram" (117–32) makes explicit, almost in the fashion of an exegetic gloss, the somber religiosity that informed the action of the narrative. Without faltering, Sedulius draws analogies between Tityros and Christ, between the sheep thief and the robber crucified beside Christ (Luke 23.39–43), and between Tityros and the ram in Genesis, which was itself a prefiguration of Christ (Ambrose, *De Abraham* 1.8; Düchting 1970, 124–25; Schwab 1981):

> Agnus ut altithronus pro peccatoribus acrem
>   gustavit mortem filius ipse dei,
> carpens mortis iter canibus laceratus iniquis
> 120   pro latrone malo sic, pie multo, peris.
> Quomodo pro Isaac aries sacer hostia factus,
>   sic tu pro misero victima grata manes.
> O pietas domini clemens ac larga potestas,
>   qui non vult homines morte perire mala!
> 125   Dextra superna dei latronem salvat iniquum,
>   olim quae cuidam mox cruce praestat opem.
>   (Lines 117–126)

Just as the lamb who sits enthroned on high—the Son of God himself—tasted biting death for the sake of sinners, in the same way
you, pious mutton, taking the route of death, ripped apart by the
unfair dogs, [120] perish for the sake of a wicked bandit. Just as the
holy ram became a sacrifice in Isaac's stead, so you remain a welcome victim in the place of a wretch. O how merciful is the piety
and broad the power of the Lord, who does not wish men to pass
away in a bad death! [125] The celestial right hand of God, which
once promised to bring help soon to a certain man on a cross, now
saves the shameful robber.

At this juncture the ram has the air of a martyr, rather than of an epic hero,
but even in the course of his *passio* (Jauss 63; Düchting 1970, 122, 126) the
classical atmosphere lingers, as is evident in Sedulius's choice of the word
Olympus to describe the Christian heaven and God, "the Lord of Olympus" (129).

Just when the poem heads toward a devout close with a paraphrase
of a Psalm, Sedulius brings humor, and his own personality, once more
to the fore. He expresses his willingness to give any sheep a hot bath
(135–40), from head to foot. These lines were first interpreted as alluding
to pious bishops or abbots who washed the feet of their guests (Jarcho
561–62). Similarly, they were later explained as referring to the monastic
practice of washing the feet of wayfarers (Düchting 1970, 280, n. 17).
They have also been considered a bold travesty of ritual footwashing on
Maundy Thursday (Schaller 1960–61, 71–72), and therefore an allusion to
John 13.9 (Meyers 194) "dicit ei Simon Petrus: 'Domine, non tantum pedes
meos, sed et manus et caput'" ("Simon Peter saith to him: Lord, not only
my feet, but also my hands and my head"). If Sedulius had had parody in
mind, he could also have been thinking of Exodus 12.9, which specifies
that the paschal lamb be roasted "his head with his feet" ("caput cum
pedibus eius"). In fact, the poem could be interpreted as expressing Sedulius's desire to partake of Christ the lamb on Easter, a day when lambs,
eggs, and other foodstuffs were brought to churches to be hallowed. But
such elaborate and chronologically specific constructions would fail to appreciate the simpler and likelier possibility: Sedulius is joking that he will
make mutton stew—a true Irish stew (Schaller 1959–60, 72)—whenever
the opportunity presents itself.

An evenhanded appraisal of "The Ram" should not underplay the
autobiographical force because the strain between epic language and religious spirit that pervades "The Ram" is, in a sense, dissipated into laugh-

ter by Sedulius's mania for mutton. His infatuation with the ram helps to make his poem as gentle and unblasphemous a burlesque of the Passion as *The Second Shepherds' Play* is of the Nativity. The Wakefield pageant establishes a daring network of correspondences: the supposed birth on Christmas of a child, who is in fact a stolen sheep disguised as a child, is linked by implication with the Nativity of the *agnus Dei* who saved humanity. "The Ram" traces similarly audacious connections between the death of a ram and the Passion of Christ.

"The Ram" is all that it has been called—a parody, a mock-epic, an epyllion, and more—but above all, it is the highly individual creation of Sedulius Scottus. The poem has refused to be categorized generically for the simple reason that it was not designed to satisfy the requirements of any one literary form. On the contrary, in it Sedulius reveled in the distinctive artistic possibilities that he had won when he had decided to write about talking animals. Like other medieval Latin poets who wrote about loquacious beasts, Sedulius vied with the weightiest models he could find—in his case, Vergil and the Bible—and pinned his hopes for success on an extensive use of parody and on a sophisticated narrative structure with several levels of meaning; like some of his followers in the composition of beast poetry, he succeeded in creating a masterpiece.

Walahfrid Strabo's Man and Eagle

Religious concerns have a high profile in both Sedulius Scottus's "The Ram" and Alcuin's "The Cock and Wolf." In many parts of Sedulius's poem, the actions of animals are significant because they are related to the Crucifixion or to Old Testament scenes associated typologically with the Crucifixion. In Alcuin's poem, the interaction between the cock and wolf is presented tropologically, as the loss of salvation that can befall any Christian who fails to be vigilant. The two ninth-century poems with talking birds lack the biblical dimensions of Sedulius's and Alcuin's poems, but they reveal a penchant for eschatological matters. Both the anonymous "Swan Sequence" and Walahfrid Strabo's "To Erluin, about a Certain Dream" (*De quodam somnio ad Erluinum*) tell of birds that journey beyond the present world, one en route to heaven and another in search of salvation.

Walahfrid Strabo, despite the tragic brevity of his life, played a major role in ninth-century intellectual activity. In forty years he made an enduring mark, not solely at Reichenau, where he served as abbot after being a monk, but even throughout Western Europe thanks to his accomplishments as a theologian, liturgist, naturalist, royal tutor, and, last but not least, poet (Beyerle 1925b, 92–93; Hartig 629).

As a child Walahfrid, who was born in 809, studied at the cloister of Reichenau (Brunhölzl 1975, 345–58). After 825 he went to Fulda, where he continued his education under Hrabanus Maurus. In 829 he was sent to the court of Louis the Pious to instruct the future Charles the Bald. In 838 he returned to Reichenau as abbot. He was accidentally drowned on 18 August 849, after a decade in which he had to leave his monastery occasionally for political reasons.

The cognomen *Strabo* (*Strabus* was the form he preferred) refers to a cast in Walahfrid's eye. By coincidence, the nickname puts Walahfrid in a class with great seeing-impaired bards such as one-eyed Odin and blind Homer. Both references, although unintended by Walahfrid, are appropriate in view of Walahfrid's oeuvre, which includes four visionary poems in Latin: "Wetti's Vision" (*Carmen 3: Visio Wettini*), "Verses to Empress Judith about a Certain Dream" (*Carmen 24: Ad eandem* [=*Iudith imperatricem*] *de quodam somnio*), "On the Statue of Theodoric" (*Carmen 23: De imagine Tetrici*); and "To Erluin, about a Certain Dream" (*Carmen 19: De quodam somnio ad Erluinum*).

The most substantial of these poems is "Wetti's Vision," a poem of nearly one thousand hexameter lines that Walahfrid composed at Reichenau in 826 when he was an eighteen-year-old. This long poem, although it hews closely to a prose account by Walahfrid's fellow monk and abbot Heito, is based partly on Walahfrid's eyewitness experiences; for despite being only fifteen years of age at the time, Walahfrid was already at Reichenau in 824, when his teacher Wetti experienced visions of heaven and hell on his deathbed in the monastery.

"Wetti's Vision" has been characterized as "the first account of a vision in verse. One might even say that it is the first *literary* vision in the sense that it represents the first conscious attempt to cast a vision in a literary form" (*Visio Wettini*, ed. Traill 16). Of all the visions produced in late antiquity and the early Middle Ages, Walahfrid's "Wetti's Vision" comes closest to Dante's *Commedia* in two ways: its emphasis on purgation in the other world and its placement of purgatory on a mountain.

In comparison with Walahfrid's three other vision poems, "To Erluin" has been shunned by scholars. One explanation is prudery; for although Walahfrid deals with the seemingly earnest subject of heaven seen by a dreamer, the vision he relates almost transmogrifies Wetti's pious vision. Another reason is that "To Erluin" refuses to comply with expectations of medieval visions. More than one scholar has remarked upon the monotony of early medieval visions, owing to the repetitiveness with which they employ various motifs, images, and concepts (Patch 320; Gurevich 123). Unlike its contemporary visions, Walahfrid's poem has no part of such conformism. Like many other medieval Latin beast poems, it sits provocatively at the juncture between learned and popular traditions.

Walahfrid's poem comprises only 14 1/2 elegiac couplets in its present state (see Appendix 14). According to its title, the poem was addressed to a person named Erluin, but it is concerned neither with Erluin nor with Walahfrid. Rather, it relates how a dreamer named Pollachar is wafted by an eagle to the outskirts of heaven. During the journey the man grows fearful and suffers from a combination of stage fright and motion sickness. Accordingly, he seeks permission to purge himself so that he will not bring human vileness within the precincts of heaven. The eagle allows the dreamer his request, but then commands him to return and to wait for his foulnesses to come to earth, on the principle that anyone willing to sully the heights of heaven does not merit the privilege of approaching God. The poor man awakens in a bed saturated with the all-too-real results of his dreamed release. What began as a most promising anabasis ends in a crassly catastrophic catabasis.

A few words about the transmission of the poem are in order, since the form in which it survived has a bearing on both its constitution and its interpretation. "To Erluin" is extant only in the late ninth-century St. Gall, Stiftsbibliothek, MS. 869. This manuscript, not just the property of St. Gall but, in fact, a product of the scriptorium there, also preserves a copy of Walahfrid's "Wetti's Vision." The text of "To Erluin" breaks off at the bottom of a folio. Its conclusion, perhaps only a missing pentameter, would have come on the following folio, but a few folios have been lost. Interestingly, although a few of Walahfrid's poems have erasures where names were mentioned (e.g., *Carmen* 51.13, ed. Dümmler 399; *Carmen* 56.2, ed. Dümmler 401), this is one of only two incomplete poems in the whole of Walahfrid's oeuvre (the other is *Carmen* 87, ed. Dümmler 420–21), and none of Walahfrid's other poems in distichs ends with a hexameter instead of a pentameter—but the mutilation seems more likely the result of accident than of censorship. Although the poem lacks its ending, the course of events is probably no clearer than it would be if it had a complete conclusion.

Because Walahfrid's poem deals with bodily evacuation, "To Erluin" has been interpreted as having a "strong parodic touch" and representing "an irreverent reaction to the abuses of the burgeoning belief in dreams" (Kamphausen 199–200). According to this view, Walahfrid deliberately creates an absurd contrast between the solemnly classicizing form and bluntly scatological content of the vision (Kamphausen 201). Thus the poem is seen as "a drastic example of medieval cloister humor" (Kamphausen 201–2). Like many poems written in medieval monasteries, this one could have been intended for a close circle of friends who knew and teased each other—the target of their humor in this case being a person who suffered from the sort of incontinence described.

There is undoubtedly wit in the poem, building toward the bathetic moment when the dreamer strains with all his might to relieve himself. The eagle controls this humor verbally. By directing the dreamer to hold onto its tail it has the foresight to distance itself from the crucial event. The bird brings out the incongruity between the dreamer's destination and behavior through the contrast between two of his imperatives, "Perge" (7) and "Expurga" (20). Its hissing speech, which culminates in a stream of sibilants (26), mimics mockingly the sounds that presumably emitted from the dreamer as he performed his duties. The eagle even remarks explicitly upon the absurdity of the dreamer's aspirations for heaven (23).

Beyond the play of words and sounds in the eagle's speeches, the poem contains elements similar to the broad humor of some folktales. For instance, the conduct of Walahfrid's dreamer is reminiscent of a common etiological tale that explains why dogs sniff one another under the tails (Thompson 1955–58, no. A2232.8; cf. Q 433.3; Dähnhardt 129–42; M. Leach 217–20). In the version related by Phaedrus (*Fable* 4.19), an embassy of dogs is despatched to petition Jupiter for a better lot in life, but the dogs are dismissed from the heavens after their fear causes them to let loose their dung. As in Walahfrid's poem, an inability to control the mundane operations of the body leads to the loss of heaven. The involuntary defecation of the dogs signifies their impurity and unworthiness before the leader of the gods, just as the dreamer's release in "To Erluin" indicates his unfitness before God's eagle. But the most obvious lesson to draw from both the ancient and medieval poems is not theological but practical and moral: people should not seek a lot above their station, since they may find themselves unworthy and humiliated.

The humor of Walahfrid's poem probably seems more drastic to people today than it would have to a person with a medieval sense of decorum, which accepted freer discussion of bodily functions than is presently the case (Curtius 434–35; Bakhtin 303–67). One example of the liberty with which Walahfrid could deal with apparently scatological matters even in a serious context occurs when Scintilla delivers her first speech in his poem "On the Statue of Theodoric" (*Carmen* 23.20–27). She describes all manner of filth, including black dung and feces. Walahfrid's candor about bodily functions means that, while there can be no question that "To Erluin" has its light moments, the mere occurrence of defecation does not make the poem irreverent, parodic, or devoid of serious ramifications. The comment at the end of the poem that the dreamer had been "deceived by wrongful visions" was not necessarily an indictment of attributing too much importance to any and every vision, and the presentation of nocturnal incontinence need not have been simply humorous.

In Walahfrid's "To Erluin" the dreamer forfeits heaven as his penalty for the absurdity of taking literally the notion of purgation. Similarly, readers of the poem run the risk of being punished with incomprehension if they take the events narrated too literally. With a complexity inversely proportionate to its length, this vision poem calls for more than one form of analysis. To do it justice, I propose to examine first the literary backgrounds of the eagle, of the passage to heaven, and of the classical references and allusions; next, the place of the poem among visions of the ninth century; then, the relevance to the poem of medieval and modern oneirocriticism; and finally the socioreligious context of medieval monastic views toward nocturnal emission.

Both composers and audiences of Latin poetry in the Middle Ages treasured repetitions, alterations, and recombinations of stock elements from the literary tradition they shared (Curtius). Consequently, one useful approach to medieval Latin literature entails studying the relations between a given text and its predecessors. In the case of Walahfrid's poem such connections are found in characters and narrative motifs, as well as in literary references and allusions.

The avian element in "To Erluin" is self-evident. After all, the eagle is the first and last character to speak. The prestige of the eagle in literature and its visibility in real life made it a natural choice for this conspicuous role. Because it dominated the upper air, the eagle was the foremost of birds in ancient Latin poetry and fable (Sauvage 161–75; Pugliarello 97–110). In the *Physiologus* (chap. 8, ed. Carmody 1939; trans. Curley) it is extolled for being able to renew its sight, an ability to be emulated by Christians when the eyes of their hearts grow dim. As the bird with the spiritual vigor to rise to God it became the emblem of St. John, whence its use in church lecterns to support the Gospels.

In Walahfrid's poem the eagle is needed for more than its prestige; it must transport a character into the upper air. In so doing it takes a place in a long and rich lineage of birds that carry persons aloft in myths, fables, and folktales (Thompson 1955–58, nos. F62, F62.1; cf. B542.1, B542.1.1, B552). Of these fowl, eagles were the best known for ferrying people to safety—and especially to heaven. Yet despite their heavenly connections, eagles suffered from the equivocality that accompanies most mythological instances of human flight; for the yearning to fly has been attended by an equally powerful fear of flying.

Birds in general and eagles in particular were associated closely with the soul, especially as it ascends from the body at death. First came the idea that the human soul takes flight from the body in the form of a bird, especially that of a bird of prey (Cumont 293). In the next stage the bird no longer represented the soul itself but rather it fulfilled the function of psychopomp, a conductor of souls. Thus during the Roman period people held that the soul was borne aloft by an eagle, which was the bird of the sun.

From ancient times the eagle had been regarded as the servant or incarnation of the astral king (Cumont 294–95), whence its standing as Jove's squire in Latin literature (Sauvage). It carried on its back mortals judged worthy of mounting to heaven (Cumont 295). Thus in ancient sculpture the apotheosis of Homer sometimes depicts the poet being borne aloft by an eagle (Cumont 295–96, fig. 7, 324).

The divine associations help to explain not only the assertive manner of Walahfrid's eagle but, even more important, its prescience, which borders on omniscience. The status of the eagle as God's proxy casts a particularly interesting light upon the bird's role in subverting the dreamer: the eagle first entices the dreamer into making the ascent with promises of "great rewards," then encourages him to rid himself of his waste, and finally castigates him for both the ascent and the emission of waste.

Most directly relevant of ancient associations between the eagle and matters divine to Walahfrid's poem is the myth of Jupiter and Ganymede. According to a widespread version, the father of the gods himself assumed the guise of the eagle in order to transport to Olympus the young man he desired (Thompson 1955–58, no. R13.3: Ovid, *Metamorphoses* 10.155–61). One phrase in Walahfrid probably alludes to Vergil's account of the myth (*Aeneid* 5.255–57), where Jupiter directs his winged servant to abduct Ganymede in its talons: Walahfrid uses the words *Iovis armiger* in the same metrical position as Vergil does in recounting the seizure of Ganymede (*Aeneid* 5.255: compare *Aeneid* 9.564). The scene was often illustrated in ancient art, sometimes as an apotheosis on funerary art (Schauenburg; Forsyth; Weisbach 145–47, 215–17). But whereas Ganymede assumed a role as catamite to his god, Pollachar aspires to a different expression of love to his deity; and whereas Ganymede poured nectar in his capacity as cupbearer to the gods, Pollachar makes an altogether different offering in his heaven.

Many of the attributes and myths associated with the eagle in antiquity remained common knowledge throughout the Middle Ages. To take a memorable example that was recorded a half millennium after Walahfrid, Dante tells in *Purgatorio* 9.19–33 (ed. and trans. Singleton 88–89) of a dream in which an eagle in the classical mold came and carried him aloft. Imitating and transforming Dante, Chaucer also related in *The House of Fame* a dream in which he was transported by an eagle. One noteworthy point of coincidence between Dante's aquiline passage and Walahfrid's is that, like the eagle in Dante's dream but unlike the eagle in the usual myth of Ganymede, the eagle in "To Erluin" fails to bring a man permanently to heaven. This failure has many literary antecedents (Provenzo 6–7), of which five are especially significant.

First, one section of the Babylonian myth about Etana relates how King Etana is carried heavenward at his own request by an eagle, but after losing heart he implores the eagle to turn around. The eagle responds by dropping Etana three times, in the first instance letting him fall for two hours but catching him, in the second doing the same again, and in the third . . . the extant text breaks off, just as the eagle has released the King from the height of three ells above the ground (Röllig 494–99). Apparently illustrating the myth of Etana are more than a dozen cylinder seals, picturing a man who sits between the wings of a bird that is flying up to heaven (Röllig 497–98). The myth is mentioned fleetingly in *The Epic of Gilgamesh* by Enkidu, who relates that in a dream he had one night not long before his death he was transported to another world where "there was Etana, that king of Kish whom the eagle carried to heaven in the days of old" (trans. Sandars 92). Although not all reports of heavenly flights can be traced to Etana, it is likely that many stories of men carried to heaven by raptors such as eagles descend ultimately from this one (Röllig 496–97).

Second, there is an episode in the Alexander romance in which Alexander has two griffins—not eagles—yoked to a basket. After starving the birds for three days, Alexander steps into the basket and holds up a spear, upon the point of which he has attached a piece of liver. The famished birds fly toward the liver until Alexander meets a flying creature high in the air. At this moment Alexander looks down, grows frightened, and points the spear down, so that he can return to earth (Hägg 144–45, figs. 40–41).

Third, in a fable that circulated in both ancient and medieval Latin collections, an eagle, having agreed to teach a tortoise or another creature to fly, carries it high into the heavens but then lets it crash and die (Alexander Neckham, *Fable*, no. 2, ed. Hervieux 3: 463–64; Avian, no. 2; Babrius, no. 115). In all versions of the fable the moral is that uncontrolled ambition will be punished (Thompson 1955–58, nos. L420, "Overweening ambition punished," and L421, "Attempt to fly to heaven punished. Car supported by eagles"). To cite a case in point, Odo of Cheriton's version from the early thirteenth century gives a long mystical interpretation in which he equates the eagle with the devil, but in summing up he reverts to the conventional moral: "So it goes for fools winging nimbly toward the firmament: They fall from places prominent, to the depth of evils' torment" (*Fable*, no. 5, ed. Hervieux, 4: 182; no. 12, trans. Jacobs 76–77).

Fourth, there is a parallel in animal tales that tell of a tortoise who, after being carried aloft by fastening his beak to a stick that two birds suspend, either is dropped or else loses hold when he opens his mouth to talk (Thompson 1955–58, no. J2357; Aarne and Thompson no. 225A; Hunger; Puntoni). The manner of the tortoise's demise is particularly pertinent to Walahfrid's poem, since we are not told how the fall of the dreamer actually occurs. Although the eagle is pointedly designated by the unusual compound word *unguirapus* (not listed in any major dictionary except Blaise 1975, 939), the dreamer is not dropped from its talons. Rather, he has hold of the bird's tail in his mouth. Do the tailfeathers work loose spontaneously? Do the tailfeathers remain in place, but the dreamer loses hold at the bidding of the eagle or God? Or did Walahfrid transfer a motif from a story he had heard to a vision he invented without thinking through the consistency of his narrative?

A final antecedent for the failure of the eagle in "To Erluin" to bring the dreamer permanently to heaven appears in one of the *Letters of Parasites* (no. 23, ed. and trans. Benner and Fobes 204–9) by Alciphron, a Greek rhetorician and sophist of the second century A.D. (I thank Rebecca Nagel for drawing this letter to my attention.) The letter deserves to be quoted in full because of its various resemblances to Walahfrid's poem:

LIMENTERUS TO AMASETUS

I want to go to one of the men who put up their cards by the temple of Iacchus and who profess to interpret dreams; and there, after paying them down these two drachmas that you know I have in my hands, I want to describe the dream which appeared to me. But there is no harm in communicating to you also, since you are my friend, this strange and utterly incredible vision.

It seemed to me in my dream that I was a good-looking young fellow, no ordinary person, but that Ilian lad, the very smooth-bodied and very lovely Ganymede, the son of Tros, and that I had a shepherd's crook and a Pan's pipe, and a Phrygian cap covering my head, and that I was shepherding my flock and was on Mount Ida. Suddenly a great eagle with crooked claws, his gaze fierce and his beak hooked, swooped down upon me, lifted me by his talons from the rock where I was sitting, carried me high into the air, and, speeding swiftly on his course, brought me to the heavenly regions; then, just as I was on the point of touching the gates at which the Hours stand their guard, I was struck by a thunderbolt and fell, and the bird was no longer the great eagle from heaven but a vile-smelling vulture, and I was my own self, Limenterus, without a rag on me, as though I were ready to take a bath or to wrestle.

As you may well believe, I was terrified by such a fall as that and awoke; and now I am worried about this incredible vision, and I want to learn, from the experts in such matters, what the dream portends—if there can be anybody who really knows and who truthfully tells what he knows.

Here, as in Walahfrid's poem, we find overtly fanciful names (*Limenterus* means "hunger-gut," *Amasetus* "never-chews"—both apt for parasites) and, more important, a dreamer who is carried by an eagle to the very gates of heaven but who is stricken and falls—to the accompaniment of vile smells—into naked vulnerability.

Walahfrid does not advert explicitly to any earlier stories, but this lack of reference is not surprising when one considers how his message differs from that of his analogues. In Walahfrid's poem the dreamer is ejected from heaven and falls from grace *not* for overweening ambition but instead for the inappropriateness of performing bodily functions. Thus the motivation of the dreamer in Walahfrid's poem would appear to have no connection with the evil pride that was sometimes attributed to human attempts at flight, most scandalously in the legend of Simon Magus ("Acts of Peter," 31–32, trans. James 331–32). Nor would the message of "To Erluin" seem related to Walahfrid's expression of modesty in the epilogue to "Wetti's Vision," where the poet seeks exoneration for the imperfections of his verse; using the image of a bird, he protests that he was forced to write the poem in spite of his inabilities: "For any bird that is forced

to outfly its wings falls from its lofty flight and plummets to the ground"
(trans. Traill 74; cf. Dante, *On Eloquence in the Vernacular*, book 2, chap. 4,
para. ii, trans. Haller 40).

Walahfrid does not invoke the examples of Icarus and Phaëthon, over-
ambitious youths who were cast down for flying too high and for not
accepting their limits as mortals. Indeed, his only overt reference to any
mythological or literary work involving flight is to Daedalus (13). This slice
of mythology can be cut two ways. On the one hand, the myth of Daedalus escaping from the labyrinth of Crete by way of the air was interpreted even by Christians as an image of the soul escaping earth and
gaining the heights of heaven (Courcelle 1944, 66–69; Cumont 294). The
special parallel between Daedalus and Pollachar would be their shared desire to end an exile. On the other hand, Daedalus was perceived, as was
Icarus, as an embodiment of overreaching pride. Although unlike his reck-
less son, Daedalus saw the hazards of leaving the place assigned him by
fortune (Ovid, *Tristia* 3.4.21–26) and the advantages of not mounting too
high (Ovid, *Metamorphoses* 8.183–235, esp. 203–6), he did not comprehend
the intrinsic rashness of defying the laws of gods and attempting to alter
his nature as a man. To this way of thinking, Daedalus should have known
that aspiring to fly was an act of unnatural presumption (Horace, *Odes*
1.3.34–40). Which of the two interpretations sheds more light on "To
Erluin?" Since the words that describe Pollachar's emotions bespeak fear
rather than presumption (ii *timidum*, 12 *terrorem*, 13 *timore*, 14 *horret*), the
Daedalus in Walahfrid's poem can be taken more convincingly as representing the soul than as embodying pride. If Pollachar is presumptuous,
his presumption is implied only subtly as an overeager pursuit of "great
rewards" (8).

Despite the mention of Daedalus, the classical style of "To Erluin"
results not so much from such overt references to literary description of
men and eagles as from less overt allusions and phraseology. Thus Pollachar does not simply fall asleep but instead enjoys "sleep infused with
Lethe's gift" (3). He is carried aloft not by an angel but by an eagle (Jupiter's armor-bearer), not to God's but to Jupiter's realm.

Against the generally classicizing backdrop projects a specifically Ovidian foreground. For instance, the poem opens with the words *nox erat et*
("it was night, and"), a phrase that recurs time and again in Latin hexa-
metric poetry (Schumann 3: 569–70). But here the words allude specifically to poems in the Ovidian corpus (*Amores* 3.5, *Ex Ponto* 3.3.5: Lehmann
1927, 8–9). The fifth line in Walahfrid's poem also echoes one in Ovid,

Ex Ponto 3.3.9. Likewise, the sixth in "To Erluin" plays upon Ovid, *Ex Ponto* 3.3.18.

The network of thoughts connecting Walahfrid's poem and Ovid's *Ex Ponto* 3.3 is even denser than the words. In the early part of the poem (3.3.3−4) Ovid draws attention to the difficulty of differentiating dream from reality—a difficulty all too pertinent to the dreamer in Walahfrid's poem! Moreover, the web of Ovidian allusions in Walahfrid's "To Erluin" is not restricted to *Ex Ponto* 3.3. The words *praemia magna* in line 8 probably call attention to *Amores* 2.9.40. The most humorous allusion is in line 15, which describes the bloated body of Walahfrid's dreamer in terms drawn from the letter addressed by Canace to Macareus about her pregnancy: "Iamque tumescebant vitiati pondera ventris, / aegraque furtivum membra gravabat onus" (*Heroides* 11.37−38: "And already the burden of my vice-filled belly was swelling, and the secret load weighed down my sickened limbs"). Among the other Ovidian touches in Walahfrid's poem are "purior aethra" in 12 (*Ars amatoria* 3.55) and *longum mundus duraret in aevum* in 21 (compare *Ex Ponto* 4.8.7 "impetus iste tuus longum modo duret in aevum").

In combination with phrases common to Classical Latin and early medieval Latin poets, the allusions to Ovid create an exuberantly classical effect. Whether or not readers will find a disjunction between the classicizing elegance of the style and the crudity of the content depends, to some extent, upon their awareness of medieval views on visions, on dreams, and on nocturnal emission.

Like their counterparts in many eras, people in the Middle Ages believed in an afterlife and were filled with fears and hopes about the migration from this world to the hereafter. They articulated their feelings and beliefs in an outpouring of texts about the otherworld as seen in visions. These visions can be classified in various ways (D'Ancona 70−82; Dinzelbacher). For example, they can be divided on the grounds of various internal traits: whether an apparition comes to the visionary (as in Boethius's *Consolation of Philosophy*) or whether the visionary journeys into another place (as in Dante's *Divine Comedy*); what the visionary sees if he or she leaves this world (torments of hell, chastisements of purgatory, and joys of heaven, or a combination of the three); and what the visionary's physical condition is (ecstatically awake, entranced, or sleeping). Despite its oddities, Walahfrid's poem can be categorized according to these standards as a journey to heaven that takes place while the visionary is asleep.

Visions can also be subsumed under headings determined by external evidence. For instance, they can be classified on the basis of the geographic location in which the visionary was situated or the vision was recorded. Thus early medieval visions can be grouped under such headings as central European, Anglo-Saxon or Irish, and north German (Dinzelbacher 126). Such geographic considerations are important, because the authors of literary visions are often inspired by local interest in both visionary texts and visionary experiences. In the lovely agricultural image of one Italian writer on visions, "Le visioni sono come le ciliegie: una tira l'altra" (Ciccarese 9): "Visions are like cherries: one attracts another." To state the principle more banally, visions come in clusters.

The monastery of Reichenau in the ninth century saw the fruition of one such cherry cluster. Indeed, Wetti's visions occurred under the direct influence of a visionary text: the last book that the monk requested was Gregory the Great's *Dialogues*, from which he had selections read aloud to him as he slipped toward death (Heito, "Wetti's Vision" 4, ed. Dümmler 269). Furthermore, Heito may have been moved to compose the prose "Wetti's Vision" by his acquaintance with the *Visio cuiusdam clerici de poenis Fulradi in purgatorio*, which an unknown cleric dedicated to him (Künstle 704; Dolbeau 404), for like "Wetti's Vision," the vision of Abbot Fulrad of St. Denis portrays purgatory and its torments. The vision of Fulrad suggests the likelihood that Heito had a special interest in visions long before Wetti died (Beyerle 1925b, 90). Another text which may have been recorded at Heito's instigation is the *Visio cuiusdam pauperculae mulieris*, which was copied together with "Wetti's Vision" in the oldest manuscript in Reichenau toward the end of the 830s. Whatever the precise sequence of these various works, they are evidence that the monks of Reichenau were exceptionally interested in visions and active in recording and transmitting them.

It is conceivable that the rash of visions experienced and recorded at Reichenau in the 820s and 830s, after first filling Walahfrid with enthusiasm, eventually left him with reservations about the vision genre as a whole. Once again, we must evaluate the hypothesis that "To Erluin" is "an irreverent reaction to the abuses of the burgeoning belief in dreams," an attempt to ridicule excessive credulity in experiences that can be anything but sublime (Kamphausen 200).

If this hypothesis should hold true, then Walahfrid's "To Erluin" would be the earliest literary expression of such skepticism to survive from the Middle Ages—a parody of a vision that was created more than a century before the poem about Heriger, Archbishop of Mainz (913–927) (*Cambridge Songs*, no. 24). The poem can be summarized as follows: a false prophet is interrogated by an archbishop about his otherworldly adventures, first in hell and then in heaven. In the end he is dragged off at the archbishop's behest to be beaten because he admitted filching food while in heaven. Like two other poems which also are contained in the anthology known as the *Cambridge Songs*, the poem about Heriger relates a comic tale of deceit and lying that resembles a fabliau (Dronke 1973, 284). Since the poem about Heriger is itself very much a "lying" fiction, it cannot be viewed too soberly as "an exemplum for the intervention of the Church against *Lügenmärchen*" (contrast Ehrismann 1918, 1: 360; 1932, 1: 371 with Beyer 79). Yet the poem does have a serious dimension, in that it depicts an ecclesiastic leader defending basic tenets of Christian belief against a buffoonish false prophet.

The similarities between "To Erluin" and the poem about Heriger are outweighed by the differences, especially in atmosphere. The poem about Heriger, with its teasing references to hell and heaven and with its repeated references to feasting and fasting, has been related in texts in the lineage of "Cyprian's Supper" (Lehmann 1963, 18; Bakhtin 289–90). Most prominent among the descendants of "Cyprian's Supper" is Rabelais, whose *La vie très horrificque du grand Gargantua* (book 2, chap. 30) contains an entertaining parody of an otherworld vision. Walahfrid's poem reveals no comparable concern with food and drink, or with festivals and "popular-festive forms and images."

Even if Walahfrid's poem *is* a parody, the parody lies in the manner in which the dreamer fails to attain heaven, not in the mere fact of his failure; for the New Testament (John 3.13) states unambiguously that heaven is off limits to mere mortals: "nemo ascendit in caelum nisi qui descendit de caelo, Filius hominis qui est in caelo" ("no man hath ascended into heaven, but he that descended from heaven, the Son of man who is in heaven"). Like the pseudoprophet in the poem about Heriger, and like Pollachar, most medieval visionaries who reach heaven in their visions cannot remain there indefinitely. This inability is self-explanatory: the visions are spiritual events, at the end of which the souls must rejoin their bodies. For body and soul not to be reunited, the vision must come as a result of death, and as gangsters in movies are wont to proclaim, dead men tell no tales. (All humor aside, visions occasionally take place when a dead person is resurrected from either heaven or hell: Gurevich 109, 113). In addition, the visionaries are usually granted their visions not as rewards for flawless conduct, but instead as admonitions to repent while mortal fire remains: their visions warn them to overcome their failings and amend their lives once they return to corporeal existence so that they can attain heaven everlastingly. At the end of the vision, the visionary accepts the moral and religious norms of Christianity and realizes the consequences of following or not following them (Dinzelbacher 125). Pollachar escapes with a relatively light punishment, since his failure to ascend everlastingly does not condemn him to death but rather gives him another chance at life on earth—and, through it, another chance at life in heaven.

And if "To Erluin" is a parody in which Walahfrid repudiates or questions visions, it flies—or falls—in the face of all else that is known about him as a writer and person. In "Wetti's Vision" (prose dedication, ed. Dümmler, 302; trans. Traill 37) Walahfrid revealed his stake as a writer in the distinction between meaningful and meaningless dreams because he knew that not all his audience would share his opinion on the validity of Wetti's vision. (The skeptics were most likely Erlebald and Tatto: Beyerle 1925b, 90.) Later developments prove that this statement is not just the sort of rhetorical ploy typical in a preface: in one of the acrostichs within "Wetti's Vision," Walahfrid offers a vivid description of the racking punishment allotted to a bishop who took a dream of exceedingly urgent content to be no more than "the empty lies of an ordinary dream!" (400–409, ed. Dümmler 317; trans. Traill 53–54). To generalize from this example, being able to discriminate among different types of dreams was a matter of life and death.

The concern with the significance or idleness of dreams did not engage Walahfrid simply as a writer, but even more pressingly as a man—as a monk. Most revealing in this regard are two of the *Tituli Augienses*, one a poem inscribed on the window above his bed and the other a poem inscribed directly above his bed (*Carmen* 67, ed. Dümmler 409). These two poems seem to indicate at least three assumptions on Walahfrid's part: that sleeping and dreaming open conduits between the physical and spiritual worlds, that the soul takes leave while the body rests, and that the soul runs the danger of slumbering and falling prey to demons during this interval. Thus the souls of sleepers face the same perils encountered by the souls of the dead, which are often depicted in visions as being the objects of struggles between angels and demons (e.g., Bede, *Ecclesiastical History*, book 3, chap. 19; Rüegg 202–3).

Although Walahfrid does not enumerate the types of thoughts or behavior that render a person susceptible to demons, he gives one hint of what he has in mind: the fact that he brackets the closing couplet between an invocation of the Virgin and an invocation of virgin saints lends weight to the theory that he is thinking of forces that might threaten the virginity of a dreamer, forces such as succubi or incubi (Kiessling, esp. 9–28). The possible allusion to the first verse of Aldhelm's *De virginitate* (ed. Ehwald 352) adds further weight to this theory. An altogether innocent alternative is that he is paying tribute to Mary, in whose honor the monastery of Reichenau had been founded (Manser and Beyerle 331–35).

Whether the Virgin or virginity was more on Walahfrid's mind, the *tituli* lend credence to the supposition that the poet had an overactive imagination and perhaps that he was peculiarly subject to dreams (Bergmann 717). The picture of a lively, even overactive, imagination that the *tituli* offer is supported by the contents of Walahfrid's literary scrapbook. The entries in this vade mecum attest to their compiler's inclination to history, but above all else, to history as a record of unusual events and portents (Bischoff 1967, 2: 47–48).

Granted that Walahfrid was a exceptionally impressionable youth, granted that he spent his formative years in an atmosphere of intense communal fascination with visions . . . we still do not have adequate information to resolve once and for all what he meant in his poem about a man "deceived by wrongful visions." How much is the dreamer to blame and how much the dream itself? Here it bears mentioning that Walahfrid calls the dream, not Pollachar himself, wrongful. If there was a real person named Pollachar who experienced the sort of dream Walahfrid described, then we could reach many different conclusions. We could decide that the eagle is the main perpetrator of the *visa iniqua*, since it initiates both the rise (*Perge!*) and the fall (*Expurga! Redi!*). We could decide that the vision was wrongful because it misled Pollachar but that the retelling of it was worthwhile as an admonition, either against having dreams that lead to incontinence, or against requesting the wrong form of purgation in dreams or reality, or against lending credence to such dreams as they take place. The emission in Walahfrid's poem was doubly improper, since it violated the sanctity not only of the monastery but even of heaven itself. The eagle takes the dreamer to task unequivocally for "spatter[ing] lofty places with corruption" (24). Then again we could reason that the vision was wrongful not for misleading Pollachar but for resulting in bed-soiling and that the poem was designed to poke fun at Pollachar for the physical debility that caused the dream or resulted from it, to chide him for having such a dream, or to castigate him for putting stock in it.

The last-mentioned interpretation would leave open the possibilities that Walahfrid had taken offense at a pseudovision that cast doubts upon the meaning of the entire visionary genre, upon which he had expended so many pains, or that he had seized upon the vision of Pollachar to parody pseudovisions in defense of true visions. Many of these same conclusions would be plausible even if we opted not to believe that there was a real person named Pollachar—and perhaps it taxes the imagination that a person who had suffered a dream of the kind Walahfrid describes would have "gone public" with it anywhere outside the confessional, although no doubt such experiences were sometimes confessed publicly in chapter meetings. Whether or not we ever feel entitled to reach a firm conclusion about these problems, we have a duty to consider how the poem accords with medieval and modern notions of dreaming and interpretations of dreams like it. Then we must explore how the cardinal event in the poem, namely, the loss of heaven through a misconception of purgation, would have been construed in the socioreligious context of medieval monasticism.

The art of dream interpretation is as ancient as it is controversial. Sigmund Freud and Carl Jung were hardly the first to wonder whether, and in what fashion, dreams can be the vehicles of important meaning: such questions were already old hat by the time Aristotle's "On Dreams" and "On Divination in Sleep" were committed to writing. Nor were Freud and Jung the first to recognize that dreams challenge their interpreters, who must determine whether they are the nighttime fulfillment of daytime thoughts and desires, meaningful premonitions of future events, or merely the results of indigestion or physical discomfort. Such determinations would seem particularly urgent in the case of a dream like Pollachar's, in which the actions that take place within the unconscious or subconscious dream leave a physical record in conscious reality. Awakening, the dreamer must wonder what reality or truth the dream had, since the shameful mess of the dream spills into real life.

To assist in achieving such distinctions, the fourth-century scholar Macrobius, in his commentary on Cicero's *Dream of Scipio* (1.3.2, ed. Willis 8; trans. Stahl 88), offers a fivefold classification that is meant to apply to all dreams: the enigmatic dream (*somnium*), prophetic vision (*visio*), oracular dream (*oraculum*), nightmare (*insomnium*), and apparition (*visum*). In dismissing nightmares because they lack prophetic significance, Macrobius explains that they are often prompted by sexual or gastric distress: "Nightmares may be caused by mental or physical distress. . . . As examples of the mental variety, we might mention the lover who dreams of possessing his sweetheart. . . . The physical variety might be illustrated by one who has overindulged in eating or drinking and dreams that he is either choking with food or unburdening himself" (1.3.4, ed. Willis 9; trans. Stahl 88). Somewhat later, Gregory the Great, when he articulates a classification on the basis of the ways in which dreams touch the soul, begins by emphasizing physical stimuli: through fullness or emptiness of the stomach, illusion, thought and illusion, revelation, or thought and revelation (*Dialogues* 4.50, ed. Vogüé 3: 172).

Although in Macrobius's terminology "To Erluin" would constitute an *insomnium* and would be unfit for productive oneirocriticism, let us suppose for the sake of argument that it can correctly be labeled a *somnium*. In this case, we might consider analyzing the events of the poem on the basis of the "Dreambook of Daniel" (*Somniale Danielis*) and its descendants, alphabetical manuals of dreams and their interpretations that circulated widely throughout western Europe from the ninth century.

The results of such consultation are more entertaining than enlightening. The manuals offer a wealth of information about individual narrative motifs in "To Erluin," but the sum is decidedly less than the total of the parts. Indeed, the most eloquent and insightful of these desultory observations may be the Middle English: "To pisse in þe bed, be-tokeneþ infirmyte" (S. Fischer 32).

Some of the insights offered by the "Dreambook of Daniel" and its descendants could be applied to "To Erluin." For the dreamer to see the eagle may indeed signify honor; to gaze upon the heavens, great joy; to fall from them, the loss of honor; and to urinate in bed, anxiety. But when assembled seriatim, such interpretations do not by themselves facilitate a coherent reading of the entire poem.

A fuller understanding of the poem may come through comparison of the dream as a whole with analogous dreams. For these we must leave the Middle Ages, since the closest comparanda to the events related in the poem are found not in learned Latin documents but in dreams recorded in late nineteenth- and early twentieth-century folklore. Like "To Erluin," many of these dreams in folklore contain elements that are considered indecent. Furthermore, they are often related as comic anecdotes (Freud and Oppenheim 25). Because of their visionary nature, these comic dreams belong among the traditional material to which Aron Gurevich referred in his statement "that Latin writings of scholars and teachers contain substantial elements of the non-literate folklore tradition almost against their authors' will" (Gurevich xvii; cf. 127).

Freud, who collaborated with a classicist nearly eighty years ago to produce an essay on such dreams in folklore, contended that their symbolism is much more overt than in actual dreams. In his view, the very comedy of dreams in folklore permits them to communicate thoughts that would have to be concealed in real dreams. Dreams in folklore "are intended as communications, meant to give pleasure to the person who tells them as well as to the listener, and therefore the interpretation is added quite unashamedly to the symbol. These stories delight in stripping off the veiling symbols" (Freud and Oppenheim 27). In direct opposition to medieval interpreters of dreams, Freud is interested in dreams "not as premonitions about a still unrevealed future, but as the fulfillment of wishes, the satisfaction of needs which arise during the state of sleep" (Freud and Oppenheim 25).

Of the dreams in folklore that Freud scrutinizes, particularly relevant to Walahfrid Strabo's poem is one collected in Prussian Silesia in which a peasant dreams of an unsuccessful ascent to heaven (Freud and Oppenheim 44–45, 89). After he has been struck by lightning, his soul flies up to heaven. At the gates of heaven he begs to be allowed to return to earth to take leave of his family. Although initially denied, eventually he is permitted to do so, but only after being transformed into a spider. He has difficulty squeezing out enough web to accomplish the descent and in the course of trying fouls his bed. As in the case of Pollachar, the peasant experiences "something very human" precisely at the instant of greatest fear (Freud and Oppenheim 44–45).

Although the needs that arise during the sleep of this dreamer are painfully obvious, Freud has much to say about the nature of the desires that they veil. In a preamble to the text of this dream, he declares that "the connection between the urge to defecate and the fear of death is extremely plain" (Freud and Oppenheim 43). Yet the nexus between defecation and death only camouflages a deeper connection between sex and death. In analyzing other related dreams in folklore the psychoanalyst comes to the conclusion, "All at once a sexual need comes to view in these dreams behind the excremental one" (Freud and Oppenheim 49). In particular, he interprets the spider's thread and the things analogous to it in other dreams as symbolizing semen. Thus, in his view, the peasant in these dreams "is striving to produce an erection and only when this is unsuccessful does he resort to defecation" (Freud and Oppenheim 49).

In the dreams that Freud analyzes, the sleeper befouls not only his bed, but also his bedmate, who is sometimes a woman and sometimes a man. Freud avers that whatever the sex of the other person in the bed, the dreamer "is overcome by a strong erotic need" for his bedmate (Freud and Oppenheim 50). In the case of the female bedmate, the dream begins by expressing the inability of a husband to produce an erection for a wife who does not attract him. This inability causes the husband to long for a woman who is more attractive, which provokes a fear of death. To escape from this dilemma, "the disappointed sexual libido finds release along the path of regression in the excremental wishful impulse, which abuses and soils the unserviceable sexual object" (Freud and Oppenheimer 50). Similarly, in the case of the male bedmate, "the rejection of the male sexual object finds an outlet in defiling him" (Freud and Oppenheim 51).

The linkage between excretion and sex that Freud points out in the folkloric dream could be relevant to "To Erluin." The dreamer in Walahfrid's poem most definitely fills his bed with the contents of his bowels rather than of his scrotal sack, as words and phrases such as *egestio ventris* (*Oxford Latin Dictionary egestio* 1), *expurga foetida quaeque* (*Oxford Latin Dictionary expurgo* 2), and *evacuare* (*Oxford Latin Dictionary euacuo* 2) bespeak; but words such as *ilia*, which refer to the private parts as well as to inner organs (*Oxford Latin Dictionary ilia* c versus e), *lues* (*Oxford Latin Dictionary lues* 4), and *sordes* (*Oxford Latin Dictionary sordes* 1b), which encompass many sorts of bodily secretions, could pertain to sexual emission as well as to a bowel movement.

Pollachar's fear, a leitmotif of the ascent, indicates that the dreamer is spiritually or psychologically unprepared for the heavenly sights ahead of him, and his unreadiness is reflected in the physical impurity of his unvoided "inner organs," the exact nature of which is left studiously vague. There would be little reason to raise the specter of a sexual undercurrent to the poem, were it not for the furtive but insistent eroticism in the possible allusions to the rape of Ganymede in Vergil's *Aeneid* 5.255–57, to the arrival of Amor in Ovid's *Ex Ponto* 3.3, to Ovid's request to Cupid in *Amores* 2.9.40, and to Canace's pregnancy in *Heroides* 11. Even the final words could contribute to this climate of eroticism, since one significant parallel to the use of the adjective *iniquus, -a, -um* in the phrase *iniquis visis* is the Book of Wisdom 4.6, "Ex iniquis enim omnes filii qui nascuntur testes sunt nequitiae adversus parentes in interrogatione sua" ("For the children that are born of unlawful beds, are witnesses of wickedness against their parents in their trial"). This latent eroticism precludes any certainty that the incontinence in the poem is limited to the bowels and that the poem is an excremental vision worthy of Jonathan Swift; for the poem could refer not just overtly to bed-fouling but also covertly to a wet dream. The poem could exploit the superficial jocularity of a classicizing style to reduce the discomfort of a Christian audience at the topic of nocturnal emission.

If this line of analysis is pursued, a Freudian reading of Walahfrid's dream-poem could explain the story broadly as depicting sexual tension that rises, pulls the protagonist higher, leads to a sudden climactic release, and concludes by falling and relaxing. Such a reading could apply equally well to the dreams of Pollachar and the Silesian peasant. A Freudian reading more closely fitted to the circumstances of Walahfrid's poem could maintain that the repressed sexuality of the dreamer (who is presumably a monk and therefore sleeps alone) manifests itself not simply in the act of flying and in "the fear of flying," but also in the element of the eagle's tail, which the dreamer takes in his mouth. Why does the eagle command Pollachar to hold its tail in his mouth? The reason could be simply to put the greatest distance between itself and the base act of which it has foreknowledge. Then again, the imperative could imply that the dreamer will need to use his hands to perform the emission, whether it be fecal or seminal. Alternatively, since the tail (*Oxford Latin Dictionary cauda* 2; Adams 36–37) can stand for the penis in Latin sexual vocabulary as in many other languages (e.g., German *Schwanz*), the poem could be read as describing the repressed homosexual desire of the dreamer—like Ganymede in more ways than one—for fellatio. The moral of such readings would be the concluding exclamation "Pro pudor atque nefas": the *pudor* is what the dreamer did by purging, on a literal level his bowels but on a symbolic level his semen; the *nefas* that he asked outright to do so; and the deception that he did so in a vision.

Whether or not such a travesty of a *unio mystica* is plausible in either medieval or modern terms, it distracts our attention from the climactic—if such an adjective is admissible here—element in the poem, which is not the taking of the tail in the mouth but rather the befouling of the bed—the emission. With the befouling or emission we have reached the monastery, in the cells of which the dreamer, Erluin, and Walahfrid all had their beds.

Many medieval visions arose in cloisters or were at least transmitted by monastic tradition. As such, they are potentially a valuable source of cultural-historical information for the daily life and concerns of the monks who produced them (Dünninger 41). Conversely, a knowledge of cloister life is necessary for understanding many of the monastic visions, of which "To Erluin" is most definitely one. Whereas "Wetti's Vision" (although deeply concerned with the Benedictine Rule; see Knittel) offers a clear and broadly aimed criticism of the secular clergy, and whereas the dream-poem dedicated to Empress Judith, wife of Charlemagne's son Louis, has pronounced political dimensions (Traill 5; Dünninger), this poem responds almost exclusively to the concerns of a monkish audience.

The existence of no fewer than three monks named Erluin at Reichenau in the early Middle Ages can be documented in the abbey's confraternity book (Beyerle 1925a, 1167, no. 289; 1168, no. 313; 1173, no. 518). For want of information, the identity of the dreamer himself is more difficult to pinpoint. If the name Pollachar is Germanic, then its second element brings to mind names that are attested in the Reichenau confraternity book, such as Cundachar/Cundheri, Paldger, and Ruadachar/Ruadker (Beyerle 1925a, 1161, no. 139f; 1163, no. 186; 1166, no. 271; 1174, no. 545; 1176, no. 614; 1172, no. 451; 1169, no. 353; 1173, no. 520).

Regardless of whether a real person called Pollachar ever existed, and regardless of whether he was a monk or a layman, it is likely that the Erluin to whom the poem was addressed was a monk; and it is certain that the Walahfrid who composed it was one. To them, as to any monks of the early ninth century, the issue of soiling beds was no trifle; for unlike the folktales about the incontinence of dogs or peasants in heaven, a "nocturnal illusion" ("illusio nocturna") that led to a bodily emission was no laughing matter to medieval theologians and monks. A bodily secretion of any sort was an impurity, perhaps indicative of incontinence and sin.

Beliefs about the dangers of impurity are central to many religions, among which medieval Christianity is definitely to be included. Such beliefs serve two main functions. First, they maintain moral values (Douglas 2–3). When enacted ritually, they reflect "upon the body politic through the symbolic medium of the physical body" (Douglas 128). Especially in the case of monasteries, the opposite is equally true, since what the physical body of the individual does reflects on the whole of the community—the body politic. The second function of beliefs about impurity is that, beyond maintaining moral values, they provoke spiritual meditation: "reflection on dirt involves reflection on the relation of order to disorder, being to non-being, form to formlessness, life to death. Wherever ideas of dirt are highly structured their analysis discloses a play upon such profound themes" (Douglas 5–6).

The events in Walahfrid's poem take place along a clearly delineated axis of impurity and purity. At the pole of impurity is the earth. On earth people suffer misery beneath "oppressive mists" (7). On earth people live in darkness and are weighed down (15, 18) by the double burden of physical weight and sin (Matthew 11.28–30). At the pole of purity are the stars that frame the poem. In heaven all is light, both weightless (18) and bright.

In the beginning the dreamer sets his sights on the sky, especially the distant stars (2). Midway through his dreamtime misadventure he questions whether or not he deserves to enter "the gleaming hall of the star-studded firmament" (16). After his abortive flight the stars are every bit as distant, when the eagle in its parting words admonishes the dreamer not "to aim at the stars again with filth" (26). The bird's words seem to imply that there can be no shortcuts in what the dreamer calls "the long quest" (10), the long quest of rendering a body and soul free from sin. For the ascent to succeed, the dreamer must be a realist who sheds his sins while still in this world.

Monasteries were holy spaces devoted to the maintenance of celibacy. The sanctity of an individual monastery depended upon the devoutness, by both day and night, of each monk within it; and the sanctity extended even to the smallest spaces and the furthest removed cells within its precincts. Thus instances of nocturnal emission were of urgency to monks as well as to the theologians who rationalized the framework in which they operated (Payer 49). Such emissions posed a serious challenge to monasticism, a system strongly devoted to governing the entrances and exits to the bodies of its adherents so as to keep them intact (Douglas 122–23, 126, 140).

The medieval Christian emphasis on intactness charged men with the challenging task of overcoming an essential aspect of their natures. Chaste men such as monks were required to leave their sexual drives unsatisfied, since those drives were considered sinful. Even though sexuality is a characteristic that cannot be eradicated from human nature, men who wished to be pure and worthy of heaven were supposed to destroy and transcend it as a base and sinful quality. It would not be surprising if the irreconcilable tension between male sexual drives and religious imperatives produced a complex that manifested itself in dreams—and even in nocturnal emissions.

But such psychologizing should not blind us to the medieval theological views on nocturnal emissions. Expanding the view enunciated in the Hebrew Bible (Leviticus 15.16–17, Deuteronomy 23.10–11) that a man who undergoes nocturnal pollution is cultically impure, Christian theologians tended to indicate "that such an occurrence is of itself *spiritually* polluting—that is, it places the man in a state of ritualistic impurity which must be cleansed by some sort of spiritual activity" (Payer 49–50). But the dogmatists established many gradations between the two possible extremes of unremitting condemnation and complete exoneration. According to them, the level of spiritual activity required to remove the impurity depended upon the culpability of the man who had emitted semen in his sleep; for such pollution of the self and the community could result from a number of causes, ranging from superfluity or infirmity of nature through drunkenness and depraved thought to the illusion of demons (Jacquart and Thomasset 148, 150–51).

Because the causes of pollution were so various and subtly gradated, theologians had to formulate a casuistry governing the complex of guilt and impurity. In this hierarchy of sin, an act of impurity committed unwillingly is not as wrong as the same act committed willingly. By this measure Pollachar is "deceived by wrongful visions," but he is not a sinner: unwittingly exposed to the devil while he sleeps, his body does not act in concert with his volition.

According to Gregory the Great, a sleeper incurs guilt only for the waking activities and proclivities, such as gluttony, that induce the wrongful dream. From the limited information about Pollachar's state of mind and digestion that Walahfrid places at our disposal, the dreamer's only failing appears to be his excessive delight in the luxury of sleep. Whereas the poems inscribed in Walahfrid's bedroom memorialize the eternal vigilance of God and the aspiring watchfulness of Walahfrid himself, "To Erluin" opens with a vignette of Pollachar reveling in the carefree oblivion of sleep (3–4).

Each cause of pollution requires its own remedy, in the determination of which monks were gradually equipped with a vast array of penitentials (Müller 1934, 442). The most comprehensive early treatment is in the "Response of Gregory to Bishop Augustine" (*Responsum beati Gregorii ad Augustinum episcopum*), which purports to be Gregory the Great's response to one of the questions posed to him by Archbishop Augustine of England (on the question of authenticity, see Müller 1932, Brechter 1941, Deanesly and Grosjean, Meyvaert 1959, Brechter 1967, Meyvaert 1971). If the question and response are authentic, their existence confirms that the issue was sufficiently momentous to cause Augustine to consult the Pope about it while in the midst of his campaign to convert the English. Even if they are inauthentic, their inclusion in Bede's *Ecclesiastic History of the English People* (book 1, chap. 27, *quaestio* 9, ed. and trans. Colgrave and Mynors 98–103; cf. Gregory, *Epistola*, 11, 56a, ed. Ewald and Hartmann 2: 332) offers eloquent testimony to the importance of nocturnal emission as a theological concern in early medieval Europe. The response of Gregory or pseudo-Gregory indicates plainly that under many circumstances a dream accompanied by nocturnal emission was not dismissed as a manifestation of the subconscious beyond the dreamer's control but rather as an activity inextricably connected to the dreamer's conscious life. When the eagle denies Pollachar the privilege of entering heaven after he has purged himself, it is applying a principle manifest in the Bible passage upon which Gregory or pseudo-Gregory comments (Leviticus 15; Deuteronomy 23.10–11).

Later treatments abound in the penitentials, of which the penitential attributed to Theodore of Canterbury is but one of many examples (Payer 219: "seminal emission"). Under the eighth heading *De diverso lapsu servorum dei* come such niceties of sexual protocol as that "the monk who has often ejaculated because of wayward thoughts should do penance twenty days. The monk who has ejaculated while sleeping in church should do penance three days" (ed. Finsterwalder 301). Theodore's penitential has especial relevance here, since it is known to have enjoyed great prestige at Reichenau (Manser and Beyerle 319).

Besides the penitentials, the library at Reichenau had a copy of the lengthy entry on nocturnal emission contained in the relatively scarce medical works of Caelius Aurelianus, a writer of the A.D. fifth century (Reynolds and Rouse 33; Lehmann 1925, 653). The chapter of Caelius's *Chronic Diseases* (5.7.80–86, ed. and trans. Drabkin 958) entitled *De somnio venerio* opens with a sentence about nocturnal emission. As Caelius proceeds to determine, nocturnal emission is not a disease but a consequence of what a man, especially one who has been subject to constant desire or prolonged continence, sees while sleeping.

In view of the penitential and medical literature, it is plain that a medieval monastic audience would not have found the topic of bodily discharge any more out of place in a vision than the issue of other possibly wrongful sexual activities. For instance, what could guardedly be called the sin of canker of *Sodom* is a preoccupation of "Wetti's Vision" in both Heito's prose and Walahfrid's verse versions. According to Walahfrid, an angel admonished Wetti strenuously about sodomy ("Wetti's Vision" 780–84, ed. Dümmler 328; trans. Traill 67). Indeed, Walahfrid's training as a liturgist, theologian, and naturalist would have rendered him particularly qualified to discuss and reconcile the theological distrust of the body and its functions (especially sexual) with the natural occurrence of wet dreams.

Long before the conception of purgatory had been standardized (Le

Goff; contrast Gurevich 148–49), long before Dante wrote the *Purgatorio*, the related topics of bodily and spiritual purgation had become important elements in visions. Already in the late fourth-century "Apocalypse of Paul" (16, trans. James 533; ed. Gardiner 23) the soul of a sinner is rejected from heaven at the request of angels who complain of its stench. In other words, the stench of a wicked soul was as real to medieval visionaries as its opposite, the odor of sanctity.

One poignant, and even pungent, paradox of Walahfrid's poem is that the hapless Pollachar deprives himself of heaven's sweet fragrance through his own perverse literalism about purgation. He loses the honor of entering heaven not so much because of the filth he carries in his body as because of the means he employs to rid himself of it. Whereas entrance to heaven should result through the purification of the soul from its sins, which is effected through the practice of spiritual remorse, Pollachar acts as if purgatory were a form of bodily cleansing—of corporeal *purging*. Whereas he should undertake a spiritual catharsis to cleanse his soul, he instead performs a medicinal catharsis to drain his body. Though not spiritually intent on sinning (on the contrary!), he sins nevertheless in his misguided effort to free his soul from the captivity of the flesh—in voiding not only mortal evils but everything else mortal as well. And he sins in his poor choice of place. His challenge is to free himself from his earthliness, his blunder to meet the challenge by defiling the most unearthly of places, heaven. For such literal-mindedness he endures a threefold chastisement: first the scolding of the eagle (23–26), then the fall and ignominy of his bed (27–28), and finally the chiding of the narrator (29).

But where does this survey of monastic doctrine on nocturnal emission leave us? Because "To Erluin" lacks any of the telltale verbs, such as the passives of *polluere*, *coinquinare*, *inquinare*, or *maculare*, or the expression *semen fu(n)dere* (Payer 49), there are no incontrovertible grounds for construing the poem as a disquisition on wet dreams. The furthest we can go is to speculate that, although on first inspection the poem seems to belong to a class of stories in which the emission of bodily filth causes ejection from heaven, it combines that tradition with the theology on the emission of semen in wet dreams. Whether Walahfrid's poem touched even indirectly upon the issue of nocturnal emission, it seems likely that a monk as well versed in medieval theology and natural science as Walahfrid would have been disposed to view any type of major physical discharge, especially in bed, from the perspective of nocturnal emission.

Whether seminal, urinary, or fecal, the emission in "To Erluin" offers a twofold spiritual and physical significance. When the eagle directs Pol-lachar to "pay heed to the filth of [his] bedding," it means him—and through him the reader—to clean up his life, rid himself of sins, and purify his soul before again trying to enter heaven.

Perhaps Walahfrid's poem *is* amusing in the incongruity between its thickly classical language and latrine atmosphere. Perhaps the situation it describes recurs so often in dreams and reality that it had, already in the ninth century, earned a lasting niche in folklore of the sort Freud analyzes. But even if this is so, the poem is no mere trifle. Rather, it probes such essential topics as the relationship between the worlds of consciousness and unconsciousness, the dichotomy between mind and body, and the conflict between Christian abstinence and physical insistence. Thus while the poem is entertaining on literal and literary levels, it is deadly earnest on a theological level. Its contrast of a heavenly epiphany with nocturnal impurities is not a degradation of the dream-vision genre but a warning that our thoughts can be perverted by demonic visions.

In "To Erluin" Walahfrid dares to grant his eagle a voice with which to provoke and express religious concerns. He records a dream that be-came a reality, both of which remind the dreamer of his inadequacy as a monk and the reader of the pitfalls in dreams that are not based solidly on physical and spiritual continence. Like his bird, Walahfrid admonishes dreamers to control the urgencies of their bodies so that they can attend more to their ailing souls (the "aegra . . . anima" mentioned in 9–10). In particular, he advises dreamers to strive for purity, not to overreach their limits, and to resist the guiles of evil demons. In the end his poem has qualities of *both* a parodic vision *and* a serious *illusio*, since it presents the tragicomic struggle of a dreamer—a man—to find equilibrium between his body and spirit.

The concerns of the poem are so anthropocentric, even so androcen-tric, that "To Erluin" fails to meet the test of being a beast poem. Its failure results not from the anthropomorphic—or theomorphic—character of the eagle but from the secondary role that the eagle plays in the poem. The eagle is not significant for what it does but for what it says. In other words, it is not the principal actor but a moral voice that preaches to the principal actor, who is a human being—it is a talking animal (or rather, a talking bird), but it is not the protagonist. Because Pollachar's inappropri-ate conduct is the main theme of the poem, the eagle (for all its impor-tance) is only a supporting character, and thus Walahfrid's "To Erluin" is not strictly a beast poem on the order of Alcuin's "The Cock and Wolf,"

"The Sick Lion," or Sedulius's "The Ram." This conclusion leaves open a major question, as unanswerable as it is tantalizing: would Walahfrid have risked such a walk on the borderline between scatology and eschatology if he had not been writing about the never-never land of talking birds, where much more seemed permissible than in the real world of black wool and cold monastic cells?

Mystical Poems with Talking Birds

The anonymous "Swan Sequence" (see Appendix 28) has a better claim than Walahfrid's poem to be called a beast poem. Although not nearly so well known as "The Swan Lament" (see Appendix 27) in the *Carmina burana* (and in Carl Orff!), this poem is much admired today—as it seems to have been in the Middle Ages. It is preserved in eight or more manuscripts (Stäblein 1962, *Tabelle* between 492–93). The earliest of these is Paris, Bibliothèque Nationale, MS. lat. 1240, which is the oldest collection of sequences from Saint-Martial in Limoges (Chailley 79, 316). Here the poem is found between two Easter sequences (Liver 1982, 146, n. 1). In another manuscript it is identified as a hymn for Pentecost (Chailley 316). In various manuscripts the poem is accompanied by musical notation (Stäblein 1975, 114–15; 1962, 494–98).

The poem is entitled variously *Planctus cigni, De cigno, Candidi planctus cigni,* and *Cinnica* (Stäblein 1962, *Tabelle* between 492–93; Spanke 1977, 110–11), all of which refer to the swan who is the sole speaker and focus of attention in the poem. The first 2 1/2 strophes of "The Swan Sequence," sung by the narrator, set the scene: a swan has left behind the flowery land and is flying over open waters. Then the sequence sweeps into a plangent lament, 3 1/2 strophes delivered by the swan itself. The swan's adversary is the sea, over which it is flapping its wings in exhaustion and which threatens to engulf it. The tormented bird discerns food beneath the surface but prefers going hungry to risking death by landing on the troubled waves. The next 3 1/2 strophes relate the swan's renewal of strength at dawn and its subsequent salvation.

Why did the poet write about a swan? The situation "The Swan Sequence" evokes is one he could have observed in nature. In the *Life of Columba* (48b: ed. and trans. Anderson and Anderson 312–13) Adomnan presents a similarly touching picture of a crane that collapses exhausted on the ground after being tossed by the winds through the air:

> On the third day from this that dawns, you must watch in the western part
> of this island, sitting above the sea-shore; for after the ninth hour of the day
> a guest will arrive from the northern region of Ireland, very tired and weary,
> a crane that has been tossed by winds through long circuits of the air. And
> with its strength almost exhausted it will fall near you and lie upon the shore.

But whether or not "The Swan Sequence" poet drew inspiration from observation of nature, his poem is not meant to be a realistic portrayal of a natural occurrence.

The poet extends the significance of the swan's vicissitudes to make them meaningful to a Christian audience. He begins by introducing himself, as an individual poet (or solo singer), through the first-person verb *clangam*. He proceeds to draw in his human listeners by addressing them as "my sons" or "people" (*filii*: Blaise 1966, 53). Lest his hearers mistake the swan for a flesh-and-blood bird, he changes the grammatical gender of the swan abruptly from masculine (*cygnus*, 2a) to feminine (*avicula*, 3b and following). Finally, he concludes the poem on a metaphysical note by calling together the birds—who could be either real birds convoked by a real swan or the sons of the Church who sing bird-like songs such as the sequence. He invites them to join with him in pronouncing a brief thanksgiving to a higher being: "Regi magno sit gloria" ("Glory be to the great king").

If despite its brevity the concluding line is a doxology, it is the only explicit reference to religion in "The Swan Sequence." Yet in one manuscript the poem is labeled an "allegoria ac de cigno ad lapsum hominis" ("an allegory on the fall of Man, as if about a swan": *Analecta Hymnica* 7: 253). Interpreters have been sharply divided over the relationship between the rubric in the manuscript and the poem itself. At one extreme are readers who view the rubric either as a scribal mistake (Spanke 1977, 156) or as an attempt to christianize a song of Germanic origin that lamented the death of a hero or prince (Stäblein 1962; Dronke 1965, 54–55). At the other end of the spectrum are those who accept the rubric as describing the original function of the poem (Steinen 1946, 129; Godman 69–71).

There are no firm grounds for connecting the bird imagery of "The Swan Sequence" with Germanic heroic verse or folksong (Godman 69). Indeed, the presentation of the swan in this poem differs markedly from Germanic or Greco-Roman folklore (Wilmore 203–16; Arnott). According to the Greeks and Romans, the bird sang beautifully only as it died (pseudo-Aristotle, *History of Animals* Book 10.615^b, 2–5), whereas "The Swan Sequence" swan sings even though it is saved before dying. A further difference is that the Greeks and Romans believed the swan to enjoy death, since death brought it closer to God (Plato, *Phaedo* 84e–85a; Cicero, *Tusculanae Disputationes* 1.30.73). In contrast, the swan in the sequence desires to reach "the flower-covered dry land" (*terra florida*, 3a) rather than to die.

Last but not least, there is no resemblance between "The Swan Sequence" and the later "Swan Lament" (see Appendix 27), which is widely known through the *Carmina burana* (no. 130, ed. Hilka and Schumann, 1/2: 215). "The Swan Lament" jocularly presents the pensive musings of a swan as it contrasts its state while being grilled and served as a dinner dish to its appearance and habits when free; "The Swan Sequence" contains not a wisp of such levity.

"The Swan Sequence" has two formal resemblances to liturgical sequences which support the supposition that the rubric belongs with the poem: its strophes alliterate on *a*, and it ends with a doxology (Spanke 1977, 110; Godman 69). But whether or not "The Swan Sequence" was ever employed liturgically, there is little room to dispute that the combination of images, symbols, and metaphors with which the poem abounds is more typical of early Christian literature than of non-Christian literature (Liver 1982, 148–54).

Although the image of the bird as the soul is prominent in many religions (Courcelle 1974; Weicker), the general progression from darkness to light, from low to high, and from peril to safety is reminiscent of symbolic patterns in patristic exegesis (Godman 70). Most important, the metaphor of the present life as a dangerous voyage upon the sea runs through Old English elegies such as "The Wanderer" and "The Seafarer" (Dronke 1965, 58, n. 36; Godman 69–70; Liver 1982, 150–51). In view of these metaphors, it is not difficult to understand why the swan sequence was interpreted by one scribe as "an allegory on the fall of Man, as if about a swan" ("allegoria ac de cigno ad lapsum hominis"): the state of humanity after the Fall is an exile at sea, whereas the return to God is a spiritual landfall.

Although the swan sequence is in many regards unique (Liver 1982, 147), it is not the earliest extant medieval Latin poem in which a bird serves the purposes of Christian allegory. "The Hawk and Peacock" is an abecedarius written in twenty strophes of rhythmic verse, probably composed and copied at the beginning of the eighth century (see Appendix 21). This *rhythmus*, or poem in rhythmical verse, qualifies as a beast poem even less than Walahfrid's poem, since its two birds never speak. Yet "The Hawk and Peacock" is helpful in establishing the background of later beast poems, since they are believed to have been used either liturgically or paraliturgically as an Easter hymn (Schaller 1970a, 98).

The poem opens with praise of the creator in the voice of the peacock (strophes 1–2). After this exordium, the poem describes the beauty of the peacock's plumage and song (3–4), presumably with the implication that the peacock represents the wondrousness of creation. In later strophes the poem reveals further characteristics of the bird: that it will mount to heaven at the end of the world (5), that it cannot be conquered by the hawk (6), that it rejoices in its feathers and song (7), and that it resembles an angel in its marvelous appearance (8). Together with other birds, the peacock sings at Easter in praise of God the Father (9–10) and in commemoration of bodily resurrection (11–12). Presenting the theology of the resurrection in concrete terms, the following strophes describe the indestructibility of the peacock in its battle with another bird, probably a hawk (13–14). After extolling the taste of the peacock (the eucharist?), the poem closes with praise of the Trinity and Christ resurrected (18–20).

As the final strophe indicates, "The Hawk and Peacock" explores and celebrates the mystery of Easter:

> Xristus est natus,
> Xristus est passus,
> Xristus in cruce,
> Xristus decessit,
> Xristus sepulchro
> Xristus surrexit.
>
> Christ was born,
> Christ suffered the Passion,
> Christ was on the cross,
> Christ died,
> Christ was in the tomb,
> Christ was resurrected.

The peacock harmonizes well with the theme of Easter, since through the *Physiologus* the bird had passed from being a pagan symbol of immortality to being a Christian one of everlasting life, particularly of the resurrected flesh (Lother).

From around the millennium is a poem in many respects comparable to "The Hawk and Peacock." "The Peacock and Owl" was composed by Cuono of St. Nabor (Conrad of St. Avold). A lament in thirty-three hexameters (see Appendix 3), it first relates how an albino peacock is slain by an owl, then calls for curses to be uttered against the owl, and finally presents an epitaph. At the end the poet reveals that his name is Cuono and that he wrote the poem at the request of boys, probably schoolboys. The poem is followed by a prose interpretation that includes a malediction of the owl and concludes with a doxology. Like Theodulf's "The Fox and Hen," "The Peacock and Owl" claims to be based upon an actual occurrence; indeed, the villainous fox in Theodulf's poem is reported to have made off with the monks' peacock before it committed the fatal theft of the hen.

Whereas "The Hawk and Peacock" and Walahfrid's "To Erluin" survive in only one manuscript apiece, "The Swan Sequence" was copied repeatedly (Stäblein 1962, *Tabelle* between 492–93). Still, "The Swan Sequence" was not so well known that any of the later beast poets can be presumed to have read or heard it. Thus none of the bird poems is useful to the history of medieval Latin beast poetry—if the history must be one that traces direct influences. Yet, when taken together with the other two bird poems, "The Swan Sequence" gives proof of the symbolic and allegorical importance that medieval Latin poets attached to birds. The bird poems are evidence of the ease with which poems about birds or animals could be attached to ritual moments. For these reasons, we should not be surprised to see that later beast poems include birds in visions (in Eugenius Vulgarius and Nigel) and as seers (in the *Ecbasis captivi*)—and that a few later beast poems were designed to be read aloud on religious holidays.

4. Toward Narrative Complexity

> Zwischen den Zeugnissen frühmittelalterlicher Tierdichtung und dem ausgebildeten Tierepos des 12. Jahrhunderts lässt sich weder stoffgeschichtlich, noch gattungsgeschichtlich eine fortschreitende Entwicklung aufweisen. (Jauss 70)
>
> Between the evidence of early medieval beast poetry and the extended beast epic of the twelfth century, a progressive development cannot be demonstrated in the history of either the content or the genre.

The harvest of narrative beast poetry that survives after the ninth century but before the *Ecbasis captivi* in the mid-eleventh century is so meager—only two poems—that it does not deserve to be called a harvest. Furthermore, the two poems have little in common with each other. One was written in the south of Italy at the beginning of the tenth century, the other in Lombardy a century later. The one seems to have been substantially an animalization of people and circumstances in the poet's own life, whereas the events of the other—although also connected with the poet's political situation—appear to have been drawn from both beast fable and folktale. Yet the two poems share an experimentalism that marks them apart from the other compositions of their authors and that carries them beyond the earlier beast poems.

Eugenius Vulgarius's "Comic Visions"

There is good reason to infer that staffing a poem with animals afforded Eugenius Vulgarius a means of recording political events and editorializing upon them without risking his neck. More than any of the earlier poets—more even than Theodulf of Orléans—Eugenius had ample cause to fear the consequences of openly expressing his opinions.

Much of Eugenius Vulgarius's life (Wattenbach and Levison 4: 445–47) was wrapped up in papal politics of the early tenth century, in particular in the so-called Formosan controversy (Pop; Fuiano 99–115; Bacchiega). To repudiate Pope Formosus (A.D. 891–96), Pope Sergius III (A.D. 904–11) invalidated all the appointments Formosus had made. One person who lost office was Eugenius, a priest who lived and taught in Naples. (The cognomen Vulgarius more probably indicates that he was of foreign background than that he was foreign born; see Meyvaert 1966, 356–57, n. 3.) In 907, Eugenius retaliated by writing a treatise (*De causa Formosiana*) in which he defended Formosus and the validity of offices assigned during his papacy. Sergius, ever adept at annihilating his rivals and opponents, responded by attempting to bring Eugenius to trial in Rome. Sergius was greatly to be feared: to give an impression of his vindictiveness, one need only recall his ghastly posthumous trial of Pope Formosus, in which he had the dead Pope exhumed, tried, and decapitated (Ullmann 112–13). In a panic, Eugenius tried to regain his security and good name through the same means as had lost them, his writings. He bombarded Sergius, the Pope's relatives, and various secular authorities with ingratiating poems. His toadying served its purpose: Eugenius, although probably confined against his will in a monastery, was never tried in court.

The servile poems that Eugenius wrote tend to be recherché in style and construction. Many rely on etymological wordplay or on riddles; some are sculpted into visual patterns (crosses and a pyramid: *Carmina* 14–16, 36); and others vaunt their unusual meters (*Carmina* 3, 5, 17, 18). At times they are even accompanied by discursive glosses to clarify their obscure vocabulary (*Carmina* 16, 25–27, 37). Eugenius's other compositions are equally abstruse, yet for different reasons.

Three of Eugenius's poems deal with animals or birds, but two are only very short and incomplete:

> Cattus dum ructus refluit de sorice grandi,
> Relliquias mense musca deroserat audax;
> Precipitem hinc cattus mensam libamine plenam
> Calce ferit madidus probroque sepultus . . . X
> Hoc quoniam gallum milvum rapuisse dolebat
>
> (*Carmen* 11)

> As the cat poured forth belches from (eating) a great shrew, the bold fly gnawed at the leftovers of the meal. After this the cat, drunken and immersed in wickedness,

strikes the libation-filled table with its heel. Seeing
that he lamented that the kite had seized the cock

His dictis gallum milvum rapuisse ferebant
    Cornice sub quercu gesticulante diu.
Cattus enim ructus refluens de sorice pingui
    Relliquias musca roserat ardalia.
Precipitem at cattus mensam libamine plenam
    Calce ferit tumida, sternit ad hima sacra.

(Carmen 30)

They reported that when this had been said the kite
seized the cock, as the crow gesticulated for a long time
under the oak. For the cat, which was pouring forth
belches from a plump shrew, and the gluttonous fly gnawed
the leftovers. [5] But the cat strikes with its swollen
heel the teetering table filled with the libation, and
knocks the sacred items to the ground.

Are these two poems nothing more than awkward redactions of an otherwise unattested fable? Perhaps. Then again, they could be animalizations
of political events upon which Eugenius intended to pass judgment—but
not openly. Little that is certain can be said about the two poems, except
that the one reworks in elegiac verse the subject matter of the other in
hexameter lines (ed. Winterfeld 409–10) and that both pieces join elements of three fables or proverbs: cat and shrew-mouse; cat and fly; and
kite and cock. It is worth adding that the Latinity of these poems, the
authorship of which has never been called into question, is not as care-
ful as that of many of Eugenius's other poems (Dümmler 1866, 44–45;
Manitius 1: 434).

The third poem is a bonafide beast poem (see Appendix 5). Although
complete, it is no less problematic than the two fragments. Entitled
"Comic Visions" (*Species comice*), it comprises two sections that are distinct
in both meter and content: the first part comes to seventy-six lines in iambic dimeter acatalectic (Raby 1957, 1: 287–88; Norberg), the second to
seventy-five in Adonics (Lapidge 253–71).

Eugenius's authorship of "Comic Visions" has been contested (ed.
Winterfeld 430–32, and notes to *Carmen* 31A; Raby 1957, 1: 287; Szövérffy
1970, 702). As in the case of "The Sick Lion," the language, syntax, and

prosody of the beast poem are alleged to depart from the author's normal practice. Yet the case of "Comic Visions" is not as hopeless as that of "The Sick Lion": Eugenius's authorship can be established by studying the relationship of "Comic Visions" to his other poems, almost all of which are preserved with "Comic Visions" in a single manuscript written before the year 911 (Meyvaert 1966, 349–50). The second section of "Comic Visions" can be proven authentic on the basis of stylistic comparison with another poem by Eugenius. Since the first and second sections of "Comic Visions" are themselves closely linked, it stands that the whole of "Comic Visions" is the work of Eugenius. The unusual stylistic features of "Comic Visions" are not hard to explain: like the other two animal poems, "Comic Visions" may not have been polished as painstakingly as the poetic homages Eugenius dedicated to aristocrats and ecclesiastics who were potential supporters.

"Comic Visions" has the structure of a diptych—a structure found in such diverse medieval poems as *Beowulf*, Hrotsvitha of Gandersheim's *Gallicanus* I and II, and the Middle English *Awntyrs of Arthur*. It is divided into two halves, discrete but interconnected. The first segment begins with a thinly veiled boast about the Anacreontic meter, after which the poet sets the stage: in the countryside on a sunny spring day (compare *Carmen* 18.4). As the turtledove, heron, blackbird, and swan break into song, the nightingale orders them to harmonize their voices. Animals of all species rush for seating so that they may hear the concert, but instead they see a scuffle. Led by the ravens and kites (could these kites be related to the one in *Carmina* 11 and 30?), all the birds vie to overcome the nightingale in singing. When they lose in the extemporaneous contest, they flee to escape the ignominy.

When the second half of the poem begins, the meter is no longer Anacreontic but instead Adonic. There has been a shift in content as well as in form: a total of five or six years have elapsed. The animals retrace their steps to celebrate an unspecified festival in the place where the singing competition took place. The gods utter boisterous sounds, different beasts contribute their characteristic cries to the convivial scene, and the resultant medley approaches being a *voces animantium* (*Carmen* 31B: 32–38):

Sibilat ydra,
Ulula plangit.
Arguta vulpes

Improbe gannit,
Rudit asellus,
Garrit agrinus
Bosque remugit.

The Hydra hisses, the screech-owl laments. The sly fox yelps wantonly, ass brays, wild ass chatters, and ox lows.

Besides the animals that are making noise, the assembly offers two sights typical of a peaceable kingdom (Schwarzbaum): a wolf cradling a lamb in its arms and a bear dealing out its honey (*Carmen* 31B.45–48). A capon and an eagle, together with Falernus (a Falernian?) and Silvius (Silvanus?), bring gifts (49–56).

To complete the confusion, "exalted Charles" enters with a retinue that includes Seneca, Apollo, Cato, and Cicero (57–75):

Karolus altus
Ut leo frendens,
Grandia colla
Sub pede calcans,
Franco superbus,
Ense coruscus
Aestuat armis,
Spicula limans,
Proelia clamans.
His quoque gestis
Seneca signat,
Cantat Apollo,
Saltat *Ioannes* [MS, iena],
Cato fabellas
Mente serena
Dictat et ornat,
Cicero magnus
Organa quassans
Haec rhetorizat.

Exalted Charles, raging like a lion, trampling the necks of great men underfoot, the proud Frank, flashing with his sword, rages with weapons, sharpening darts, crying for battles.

When these events as well have taken place, Seneca writes,
Apollo sings, John [MS, the hyena] leaps, with a peaceful mind Cato
composes and adorns fables, great Cicero, shattering the elements of
reason, declaims them.

These historical and mythical names at the end of "Comic Visions" probably stand for actual friends and acquaintances in Eugenius's circle.

The language describing "exalted Charles" matches the words of a
poem honoring Emperor Leo—the two poems even share a line (compare
Carmina 19.13–18 with 31B.57–62, 19.8 with 31B.74)! Seeing that the two
poems are so intimately related, the "lion" (*leo*) in "Comic Visions" should
perhaps be understood not as the common noun but as the name Leo.
The name would introduce a flattering comparison between Emperor Leo
and Charlemagne, who had the valor of a lion. Likewise, the manuscript
reading "the hyena leaps" (*saltat iena, Carmen* 31B.69) should probably be
emended to "John leaps" (*saltat Iohannes*). This emendation (proposed by
Peter Dronke) would improve the flow of the poem, since otherwise the
hyena is the only animal mentioned in the last twenty lines. This John
could be Eugenius's contemporary, the Roman deacon who reworked
"Cyprian's Supper": John, who was also involved in the Formosan affair
(Bartholomaeis 169–86), referred to himself as "leaping John" (*saltantem
Iohannem*, ed. Strecker 870). Eugenius's poem to "Iohannes levita" (*Carmen* 25) would have been sent to the same person.

Eugenius's other surviving works explain neither why he wrote a
poem such as "Comic Vision" nor what he intended to convey in it. In his
prose treatise he wrote only of the sheep and wolf conventional in Christian symbolism (ed. Dümmler 122, 127, 132, 133, 135); and his two fables are
too disconnected to allow any conclusions.

The obscurity of "Comic Visions" may have been Eugenius's ploy to
protect himself. As we saw in Theodulf's verse letter, beast fable was a safe
form of self-expression for people whose luck had run out and who feared
offending the elite. Eugenius himself, in a letter begging for aid against
Pope Sergius, said that he was not at liberty to speak openly (*Sylloga* 7,
line 9, ed. Winterfeld 418). He was terrified that he would be dragged
to court or, as he described his fear, that the *spectacula* would require
his attendance (*Sylloga* 7, lines 14–15, ed. Winterfeld 418). When he calls
the competition among the birds in "Comic Visions" *spectacula* (*Carmen*
31A.11), he perhaps refers to Pope Sergius's trials.

If in writing "Comic Visions" Eugenius had in mind his narrow escape from trial and death, the chronological gap between the two halves of the poem would correspond to the time that had slipped away since he evaded Sergius's manhunt. The festivities in the second half would be the exuberance that he had felt once he was out of mortal danger in the first half. The other merrymakers would be the friends who had rallied to his support (e.g., Leo) or who had outlived Sergius's purges (e.g., John the Deacon). If the poem was written in celebration, it should be associated with John the Deacon's version of "Cyprian's Supper." In "Cyprian's Supper" members of John's intimate circle are presented under joking code-names. Like "Cyprian's Supper," "Comic Visions" would have been well suited for delivery as a mime-play (Vinay 1952, 240–41).

"Comic Visions," although evidently written for a coterie of intimates and not accessible to later beast poets, shows the same accretive use of sources as in Sedulius Scottus's "The Ram." Like the poet of "The Sick Lion," Eugenius portrays an assembly of animals. Like Theodulf, he describes groups of birds as military formations. Like later nightingale poets, he records how the nightingale sings beautifully and triumphantly (on nightingale poems, see Baird and Kane; Gellinek-Schellekens; Maximilianus; Raby 1951; Shippey). "Comic Visions" also includes a mysterious *voces animantium* (cf. the ninth-century *De carminis impeditione causa thematis tropologice*). In short, "Comic Visions" and Eugenius's other two poems about animals and birds demonstrate that in the tenth century as in earlier centuries, poets were ready to experiment by modifying and combining conventional forms of short animal fiction that they knew from their schooling.

Leo of Vercelli's "Meter"

Of the narrative beast poems that were composed before the middle of the eleventh century, two share a number of features with the *Ecbasis captivi* and the *Ysengrimus*. The earlier of the two is "The Sick Lion," which relates the story of "The Sick Lion, Fox, and Flayed Courtier" that reappeared in the *Ecbasis captivi* and the *Ysengrimus*. the later is the poem in rhythmic Adonics ascribed to Leo of Vercelli, which brings together two distinct stories: the story of an ass that disguises itself in a lion's skin and the story of a wolf that pays with its life for eating the ass instead of keeping it safe for the judgment of the lion-king.

Despite its importance, Leo of Vercelli's "Meter" has been dismissed as hopelessly fragmentary and obscure since it was first printed a hundred years ago: of the few who even mention it, Ross (276–77) and Jauss (83) are typical in giving it a mere page in their studies of medieval beast poetry. The obscurity is partly the result of the poor condition of the MS, but it could also reflect a deliberate obscurantism. By referring to the "Meter" as "a nut left for the schools" (7.56), Leo simultaneously disparages and exalts the poem. Since the expression *linquere nuces* could mean "to abandon childhood concerns" (*Fecunda ratis* ed. Voigt 129, n. to lines 701–2), on one level Leo acknowledges the unimportance of the "Meter" in comparison with the Psalms. On another level he has the same serious goal as two later fabulists who employed the nut image, which was widespread in medieval literature of all sorts (Robertson). In the so-called *Anonymus Neveleti* the anonymous author concludes his prologue with such an image (lines 11–12, ed. Hervieux 2: 316): "Verborum leuitas morum fert pondus honestum, / Vt nucleum celat arida testa bonum" ("The levity of the words conveys an honorable moral gravity, just as a dry shell conceals a good kernel"). In the fifteenth century the Middle Scots poet Robert Henryson expands upon the same image (Prologue lines 15–18, stanza 3):

> The nuttes schell, thocht it be hard and teuch,
> Haldis the kirnill, and is delectabill.
> Sa lyis thair ane doctrine wyse aneuch,
> And full of fruit, under ane fenyeit Fabill.

> The shell of a nut, though it be hard and tough, affords delight because it holds the kernel; in the same way there lies a doctrine of substantial wisdom, full of fruit within a fictitious fable. (Trans. Gopen 40)

Like the two fabulists, Leo employs the image to indicate that his poem needs to be cracked—that the true message of the "Meter" will be revealed only when the shell has been removed.

In the following pages I will attempt to crack the "Meter" in three different ways: first, through looking at the historical circumstances in which it was written; then, through examining its structure; and finally, through describing its style. Only after using such means to analyze the poorly preserved remains of this poem will it be possible to appreciate the extent of its originality and relate it to other medieval Latin beast poems.

Leo of Vercelli lived around the millennium, during the cultural flowering known as the Ottonian Renaissance. Like Eugenius Vulgarius in the preceding century, Leo experienced firsthand the vicissitudes of ecclesiastic power in Italy, but there the resemblance ends. Where the Neapolitan priest failed, Leo succeeded as a major player in the politics of northern Italy.

A confidant of Otto III (reigned 983–1002, crowned Holy Roman Emperor 996), Leo was named Bishop of Vercelli in 998 after a quick ascent. When Otto died in 1002, Leo's position was temporarily precarious. He looked for aid to Henry II (reigned 1002–24), who eventually became the new Holy Roman Emperor (crowned 1014), but instead suffered many reverses in the two decades of Henry's reign. While Henry busied himself with the German dominions, a local king, Arduin, wrested control of the Italian realm from Leo and the other bishops who had been installed by Otto III. Not until Henry's expedition of 1013–14 was Arduin crushed and the Bishop reinstated in his former glory. But Leo had barely regained power when Henry II died (13 July 1024). Casting his lot a third time with the Germans, Leo secured the Italian throne for Conrad II (1024–39). Once again, death spoiled his triumph: Leo himself died in 1026.

As a close adviser to Otto III, Leo of Vercelli was entrusted with the composition of letters to the pope. Some of these letters survive in part, as do rough drafts of letters that Leo wrote to Henry II in 1016–17 to warn the Emperor of impending trouble in Lombardy. In addition, four poems have been ascribed to Leo (Bloch 1897, 122–33; Bloch 1902, 752–54). Two of them (*Carmina* 2–3), rhymed *rhythmi* in strophes of three lines, round off our picture of Leo as a politician eager to curry favor, above all with kings and popes. A third, probably the earliest chronologically, is a lament in elegiac distichs for Peter of Ivrea, who preceded Leo as bishop of Vercelli by only a year and whose term ended abruptly when he was slain by Arduin of Ivrea. A line in this poem describes Arduin, who owned a castle named Sparono (or Sparone) near Turin (*Sparono castellum*: Bloch 1897, 126; Bloch 1902, 753): "Bestia Sparonis vomuit portenta doloris" ("The beast of Sparono belched forth portents of grief," *Carmen* 1.3).

Leo's inclination to conceive of enemies as animals also shows up in his prose. In his third letter to Henry II (dated 1016–17), Leo recounted how he had foiled an attempt on his life by a certain Ubertus Rufus and his gang. Leo summed up gleefully (ed. Bloch 1897, 21): "Ea die effugata est vulpes rufa cum omnibus vulpeculis suis" ("On that day the red fox was put to flight, together with all her cubs"). The fox would have been an obvious nickname for a wily opponent, but Leo had two additional grounds for calling Ubertus "the red fox." The "fox" (*vulpes*) alluded to a stretch of property, "Foxland" (*Vulparia*), that belonged to Ubertus (Bloch 1897, 31, n. 5). The "red" (*rufa*) referred to Ubertus's second name, Rufus, which probably indicated the color of his hair (Bloch 1897, 34–35, 107).

In a later formal writ of excommunication, Leo discarded this mocking nickname of "the red fox." After calling Ubertus a fool, Leo had to avoid the inconsistency of comparing him with the sly fox. Instead, he linked Ubertus metaphorically with an animal emblematic of foolishness: he wished that Ubertus and his henchmen would "receive a burial befitting an ass" ("sepultura asini sepeliantur," ed. Bloch 1897, 107).

Associations of man and beast no doubt came freely to a person named Leo ("Lion"). They could have served two different purposes in Leo's fourth poem, the so-called "Meter." One would have been to enable Leo to criticize his enemies safely even at times when he was in danger. Another would have been to insult his enemies: although many animals have good associations, none of the animals in Leo's "Meter" is presented favorably.

Whatever motivated Leo, associations of man and beast play a role in the "Meter." The poem as it stands and our grasp of early eleventh-century Lombard history are too incomplete to permit identification of animals in the poem with historical figures, but the general thrust of the presumed historical allegory—to lampoon disloyal Italians—is easily recognized (Manitius 2: 517). The three juxtapositions of the names Leo and Sparono hint that the poem deals with the squabble between Leo and Arduin (2.4–19):

De . . *d* . . ere
Iura Leonis,
Fana Sparonis,
Nec repetita
Multa Leoni‹s›
Longa cohercet
F‹u›rta Sparonis.
Hoc modo grande,
Maius inante.
Nocte sol‹u›ta

Curta Sparonis
Ferrea rupit
Mula capistra,
Cuius ut olim
Si Leo lumbos
Sepe dolaret . . .

[They forgot] the laws of Leo, the temples of Sparono; and Leo's long punishment does not restrain the thefts of Sparono. This is great now, but will be greater henceforth. As night came to an end, the bob-tailed she-mule of Sparono burst her iron halter, as if at that time Leo cudgeled her loins often . . .

Who or what the she-mule of Sparono would have been is impossible to specify. Sparono may be metonymy for Arduin, since *Sparono castellum* was one of his possessions (Bloch 1897, 126; Bloch 1902, 753; ed. Strecker 5: 477 n.). But whether the mule would have been Arduin himself or one of his men is uncertain.

The possible historical allegory is not limited to the mentions of Sparono. Ubertus Rufus and his supporters may figure in the allegory as well, since the narrator likens his oppressors to a "timid fox" (*inaudax vulpes*, 1.48–49) and calls the despoilers of the realm foxes (1.12). Quite uncertain is the identity of the *Ugo* addressed much later in the poem. This person cannot be the margrave Hugo (*pace* Bloch; ed. Strecker 5.483), since the "Meter" would have to be dated before Hugo's death in 1001— whereas the poem must have been written after the death of Otto III. The mentions of Leo and Arduin enable only a very rough dating in the first two decades of the eleventh century: at most times between the death of Otto (January 1002) and that of Arduin (15 December 1015) Leo, like the narrator of the "Meter," could have complained that he had been made a fugitive (1.5 and 1.29), that he had been turned into an object of ridicule, and that he had lost all that he had acquired under Otto (1.31–35).

One final historical reference that may lurk in the poem is a mule mentioned in Leo's correspondence. In late 1025, Leo wrote the following letter to Duke William V of Aquitaine:

Do not be disheartened, my dear friend, if the Lombards have deceived you. For my part, I shall counsel you as best I can if you will trust me. Be strong and play the man. As regards the past, put it out of your mind; and as for the future, be on your guard ["et de preteritis ne cures, de futuris caveas"]. Send one of your most trustworthy servants to let me know what you wish, and I shall counsel you as best I can. Send me the wonderful mule ["mulam mirabilem"], the precious bridle, and the marvellous hangings for which I asked you six years ago. Amen I say to you, you will not lose your reward, and whatever you should want of me, I shall give you. Farewell. (Ed. and trans. Behrends 198–201)

In return Leo received from the Duke a reply, of which the following are excerpts:

So write and let me know how you want me to trust you and what benefits you will advise C[onrad] to give me if I abandon my efforts to obtain the kingdom of Italy, which has been promised to me and which I might be able to secure, God willing, if I really wanted to. As to your request for a mule, I cannot send it to you at present because I do not have one that I would want you to use, and there is none to be found in our land that has horns, or three tails, or five feet, or any other feature that would warrant your calling it wonderful. But I shall send you as soon as I can the very best one that I can find in our land along with a precious bridle. As for the hangings, I could send them to you if I had not forgotten the length and width of those you asked for earlier. So I beg you to refresh my memory as to the length and width you want, and I shall send them to you if I can find them. Otherwise I shall have them made for you if there is anyone here who can make them. . . . In the preceding part of our letter, we have been jesting with you, my dear friend Bishop L[eo]; now we shall speak in all earnest. (Ed. and trans. Behrends 200–203)

What are we to make of the wonderful mules to which these letters refer? Possibly Leo was genuinely fascinated by freaks of nature and wished to acquire one for his own menagerie. In this context it bears noting that rulers did regard mules of certain types as suitable gifts; for instance, the entry for the year 798 in the *Royal Frankish Annals* relates that:

During the winter King Alfonso of Galicia and Asturias, after plundering Lisbon, the remotest city of Spain, as tokens of his victory, sent coats of mail, mules, and captive Moors to the Lord King. (Trans. Scholz, 77; I thank Adam Kosto for pointing out this passage.)

Alternatively, it is tempting, on the basis of Leo's propensity to use animal designations for people in his life, to conjecture that the very odd she-mule in these letters functions as the codename of a particular man or woman. And could the mule in this letter, whether real or cryptic, be connected with the mule-ass who stars in the first part of Leo's "Meter?"

Despite the strong indications that the "Meter" contains references to the history and politics of Leo's times, the poem is not just a roman à clef but a work of fiction. To appreciate it as such, we must first consider the state of the poem in the unique manuscript and then try to piece together the story. The poem is written in an eleventh-century hand in eight columns on the verso of the penultimate leaf of Vercelli, Chapter Library, MS. 82 (Bloch 1897, 122; ed. Strecker 5: 483). Through damage that affected all eight columns, approximately one hundred lines have been lost from a poem that was initially roughly five hundred lines in length.

The poem is frustratingly incomplete. Indeed, the first ten or more lines are wholly illegible. Of the next ten only an occasional letter or cluster of letters can be deciphered. The first unblemished line ("Effuga regno") commences a long elegiac on the misfortunes of the narrator. In one of Leo's letters he complains bitterly:

> Omnes inimici mei risum et derisum de me fecerunt, quia preceptum de quibusdam liberis, qui in Sancta Agatha contra me erant, firmare noluistis, cum enim non vultis, quod lex vult et iubet. (Ed. Bloch 1897, 21)

> All of my enemies laughed and mocked me, because you had no desire to confirm an order concerning certain free men, who were in Saint Agatha against my express command; for you do not wish that which the law itself wishes and orders.

Likewise, the narrator of the "Meter" expresses his disgruntlement at the shabby treatment he receives from his countrymen.

The narrator heightens the gloom of his plight by repeating, with variation and at irregular intervals, the refrain: "Hoc modo grande, / Maius inante ("This is great now, but will be greater henceforth" or "This is great now, but was greater before"). The refrain is as cryptic as the one in the Old English *Deor*: "Þaes ofereode; þisses swa maeg" ("That has passed; so may this"). Nonetheless, the Latin can be elucidated somewhat by a sentence in a letter Leo wrote to the Emperor in 1016 to complain about possessions taken away by Arduin's men:

> Peius enim modo quam ante, neque quicquam ita indecens tibi ab Ardoino vivente quam modo eo sepulto. (Ed. Bloch 1897, 17)

> For it is worse now than it was before, and not anything so unseemly was done to you [i.e., the Emperor] by Arduin when he was alive as is being done now that he has been buried.

As in the later *Ecbasis captivi* (7, 66, 71–72) and *Speculum stultorum* (58–80), the storyteller makes a transition from a personal statement to the beast poem proper by comparing people in his own life with animals. First he mentions people who assaulted his kingdom "like foxes" (1.12). This simile is reminiscent of a verse in another of Leo's poems, in which he said that if Henry had not replaced the deceased Otto "Vorassent lupi populum, / finis esset omnium" ("Wolves would have devoured the people, it would have been the end of everyone," *Carmen* 3.7) Then the narrator of the "Meter" laments that he has been reduced himself to being the talk of town, "a fable" (1.41). Finally, he introduces as a character the perplexing "she-mule of Sparono" (2.14–16).

Although the topical allusions early in the second column somehow coordinate the events of the poem with those of Leo's career, they later recede into the background. In spinning the story of the she-mule, Leo takes greater pains with its mulish, rather than with its human, features, and he soon passes from the mule to the wolf and other animals.

From elements of two very different stories Leo creates his own framework. The "Meter" is not itself a fable, since it offers no explicit moral. Yet, like the latter *Speculum stultorum*, it incorporates the story part of the famous fable about the ass in the lion's skin. Although known best in the Middle Ages through Avian's version (Fable 5), this fable was already beloved in antiquity (Aarne and Thompson, no. 214; Perry 1965, Appendix nos. 188, 358; Thompson 1955–58, nos. J512, J951.1): for instance, it was recorded on the third-century wax tablets known as the *Tabulae ceratae Assendelftianae* (Crusius 228–53). Without any explanation or transition, the she-mule that is discussed in the first column is metamorphosed in gender and genus into an ass. The ass, predestined by its model in Avian, gives away its true nature by showing its ears and by shedding the poorly secured lion's hide. As soon as they see how they have been misled, the other animals give the impostor a sound thrashing. The punishment links the second column with the third. After beating the ass, the animals vote to submit it to the judgment of the lion, but they must find someone who will guarantee to keep the ass safe until the lion summons it. The fox, the only beast to have a speaking role in the "Meter," nominates the wolf as bailiff, and unfortunately for the ass, the other animals second this choice. The inevitable happens and the wolf devours the ass, blood and all.

The first three columns prove that Leo was not trammeled by the conventions of any one genre. He grafted the story part of the well-known fable about the ass in the lion's skin onto a tale of the wolf whose trial is engineered by his rival, the fox. In addition, he played upon the proverbial image of the sheep foolishly entrusted to the guardianship of a wolf (Otto 198–99, no. 984).

The stories of the ass in the lion's skin and the trial of the wolf are held together by a shared theme. The "Meter" presents in order of increasing gravity three instances of deplorable treachery: the ass's in pretending and swearing to be a lion, the fox's in deliberately proposing an untrustworthy animal as custodian of the ass, and the wolf's in perjuring himself by eating the ass.

But the poem is far from over after the wolf has devoured the ass. In the third column the throng of animals has discovered the wolf's perfidy. In the fourth the beasts determine that the wolf deserves to be executed (4.9). Their scribe during the proceedings is the camel, possibly because in the New Testament the scribes and Pharisees are once accused of swallowing camels (Matthew 23.24); whether or not the same play upon the Bible led the author of *Branche* 5a in the *Roman de Renart* to make a camel the grandiloquent, would-be Latinist of a papal legate is an interesting speculation (Knapp 1983, 272). When the animals reconvene in the fifth column, they call upon the wolf to explain why he so disgraced the king, court, and law of the kingdom. The wolf is uncharacteristically shy and tongue-tied, but in the sixth column he confesses despite himself: he first breaks wind and then, in a cloacal crescendo, excretes the corpse of the ass. This vivid scene inverts a motif common in early hagiography: thieves who denied having stolen sheep were sometimes shown to be liars when the sheep would bleat or poke their ears from the mouths of the thieves (Donatus 68).

The burlesque tone holds strong as the wolf is shown cowering within a monk's cowl. This detail may be a scornful nod to Arduin, who took the tonsure near the end of his life (A.D. 1015). More important, it marks the debut of the wolf as monk in beast poetry. Many cultures have satiric literature in which animals are presented as religious figures: Japanese literature treats the fox and badger in this manner (Nozaki); Chinese, the monkey (Waley). In Western Europe of the Middle Ages the favorite was first the wolf (Kaczynski and Westra 1988), later the fox (Varty 51–59).

The seventh subdivision of the text commemorates the festivities following the restoration of order. It also provides further evidence of Leo's willingness to reach out for different means of representing animals in poetry. At a banquet the animals distribute the limbs of the dead wolf. This motif is reminiscent of the Late Latin "The Testament of the Piglet" (see Appendix 30), but since the wolf has been executed for eating an ass, the poet perhaps took the idea for the distribution of body parts from an early version of the later medieval Latin "The Testament of the Ass" (see Appendix 29). In the latter work, a dying ass recites a long list of people in specific professions to whom he wishes to bequeath appropriate body parts. In the "Meter" the lion-king receives the blood of the wolf (presumably to right the earlier wrong of the wolf in licking the blood of the ass); the avid kite takes the loins; and the he-goat dons the tail as a beard.

Now that justice has been done, the poet has nothing to add except a paraphrase of a verse from a Psalm (7.50–52): "Your judgment, kind Christ, is a great abyss" ("Grandis abyssus / Est tua, Christe, / Causa, benigne"). Then Leo breaks from Adonics for the first time in the poem and declares his wholehearted agreement in a different measure (7.53–54): "Hoc falsum nusquam; nihil est quo verius usquam. / Non iustum numquam; nihil est quo iustius umquam" ("This is nowhere false; nothing is anywhere truer than this. It is never unjust; nothing is ever more just than this"). This world is treacherous, he states unambiguously at the end of this column (7.61–66). Still, Psalm 35.7 assures us that both man and beast have hope, provided that they trust in God's providence: "Thy justice is as the mountains of God, thy judgments are a great deep. Men and beast thou wilt preserve, O Lord" ("iustitia tua quasi montes, Domine; iudicium tuum abyssus; multa homines et iumenta salvos facies, Domine"). The paraphrase of the Psalm conveys a clear message; evil men and beasts will be punished, whereas good will be rewarded. By implication, evil men will suffer the fate of the ass and the wolf in the "Meter."

The poem ends in mystery and incompleteness, just as it began. Of the eighth column only five lines survive (8.1–6):

> . . . *ere sci*ret,
> Verba prophete
> Stringere Christi
> Si meruisset
> Regula Flacci.
> Sed nec erit semper, mihi, mi Leo, crede December.

> . . . would know, if the rule of Flaccus was entitled to constrain the words of the prophet of Christ. But not always will it be December for me, believe me, my Leo.

Leo seems to wonder aloud whether or not it was proper to translate the words of the prophet of Christ (the Psalmist) into a Horatian meter, but does Leo mean that he is in the December of his life, near death? Or does he imply that a festive season is about to begin or has nearly past? The meaning of these lines is elusive.

The "Meter" is complex not only in narrative structure but also in style. In the penultimate line ("Regula Flacci"), Leo calls attention to his dependence on Horace, a dependence that goes beyond chance assimilation of phraseology. This reliance is not surprising, in view of the vogue that Horace enjoyed in the tenth and eleventh centuries and in view of the fact that Horace uses several beast fables in his own poetry. Yet although Leo reveres "Flaccus" as a master, at the same time he plays allusive games with Horace's poetry.

Leo's permutations of Horace may be subsumed under four headings. One class is awareness of authority, the response of the well-read reader to seeing Horatian phrases of exordium, transition, or peroration in Leo's verses. An example is Leo's refusal or inability to name all the gifts that Otto III gave to him: "Quae modo versu / Dicere non est" (1.36–37 [MS *quem*] "it is not possible to name now in verse"). These lines echo Horace, *Satire* 1.5.87: "mansuri oppidulo, quod versu dicere non est" ("to stay in a little town it is not possible to name in verse"). Another instance, which hangs on a single word but would nonetheless have struck Leo's listeners, comes as the bishop draws together the final threads of his poem: "Quid modo dicam? / Quid modo scribam? / Nil magis addam" (7.44–46 "What shall I say now? What shall I write now? I will add nothing more"). These words should be compared with the closing words to the last line of Horace's first satire: "verbum non amplius addam" ("not a word more will I add," *Satire* 1.1.121). In both cases, the language of Horace's *Satires* renders the movement of the medieval poem respectable as Leo's own words could never have done by themselves.

Another type of quotation provides a simple pleasure of recognition, not a special cachet of Horatian authority. Of this sort are the expressions *fuste saligno* ("with a willow-rod": cf. 2.57 with *Satire* 1.5.22, "ac mulae nautaeque caput lumbosque saligno / fuste dolat") and *fabula factus* ("the talk of the town": cf. 1.41 with *Epistle* 1.13.9 "cognomen vertas in risum et fabula fias"). A third sort of quotation aims at a comic incongruity between the original Horatian and the new Leonine contexts. For example, Horace coined the phrase "speechless shame" (*Satire* 1.6.57: "infans namque pudor prohibebat plura profari") to describe his trepidation upon encountering Maecenas for the first time. In a burlesque needing no explanation, Leo dropped these words into the sixth column of the "Meter":

the wolf, who has just defecated the ass, fears to move forward or backward because he knows that he will not receive clemency, not even for his "speechless shame" (6.54). Similar humor may be at work in the description of the young buck (7.37), which evokes ever so slightly Dido's vision of a little Aeneas playing in her halls (*Aeneid* 4.328–29).

Different from the three preceding methods of quotation are those quotations which, to achieve an ironic effect, demand intimate knowledge of their original Horatian contexts. In the first fragment Leo complains that, as a result of his undeserved disgrace, he receives no response to his greetings and benefactions. He considers this to be "treatment that would make slow-witted Apella shudder" ("Nam, quod et hebes / Horret Apella," 1.21–22). The relevance of the name is incomprehensible without reference to Horace, one of whose *Satires* mentions a credulous, superstitious Jew named Apella: "Apella, the Jew, may believe it, but I do not" ("credat Iudaeus Apella, / non ego," 1.5.100–01). By this allusion, Leo implies that his dishonor is frightful only to the stupid person who is not a true Christian; and toward the end of the poem he declares that the only sensible reaction to the duplicity of men and to undeserved disrepute is a forbearing trust in providence (7.50–54, 8.6).

At the height of the treachery in his poem, Leo turns again to Horace's *Satires* to enrich the significance of his language. Leo's description of the wolf licking the juicy blood of the ass (3.52–54) is built on Horace's expression "tepidumque ligurrierit ius" ("and has greedily licked up its only somewhat warm sauce," *Satire* 1.3.81). The Horatian phrase occurs in a passage on unjust retribution: the person who crucifies a slave merely for licking the sauce off a dirty plate is insane. Their original context plants a seed of doubt about whether the wolf was as much to blame for the death of the ass as was the fox; for if the wolf plays the role of the slave in Horace's *Satire*, then the fox resembles the master whose punishment of the slave exceeds reason. Also undercutting is the description of Orcus, who is warden at the wolf's trial: "ianitor aulae" ("the keeper of the hall," 4.41). In both of its occurrences in classical poetry, the expression is applied to guards of Hades who were tricked into failing in their duties (Cerberus in Horace, *Ode* 3.11.16, and Orcus's watchdog in Vergil, *Aeneid* 8.296).

The "Meter," even in its tattered condition, is longer than any extant medieval Latin beast poem composed before it. It achieves this length partly through an unprecedented conjoining of beast tales. Sedulius seemed adventurous when he set the Old Testament event of Abraham

and Isaac in apposition with the story of the stolen ram, Eugenius Vulgarius, when he loosely hooked together two poems about animals and birds
to produce a longer whole; but Leo went further by hinging three stories
as a triptych on treachery. In connecting three animal stories with the same
basic message Leo, intentionally or not, carried out an exercise that had
been stock in ancient rhetorical training: to link similar fables that were
suited to confirm the same moral (Hausrath 1898, 313: Theon 177W).

Leo's ingenious method of fastening together stories is only one element of what makes the "Meter" longer than the other poems. The other
part would have to be Leo's thorough acquisition of language and motifs.
Like the earlier beast poets, the Bishop of Vercelli achieved special effects
with the Latin language by quoting the Bible and classical poetry. Like
Theodulf and the poet of "The Sick Lion," he took a hint from riddlers
and directed the reader to solve his poem, to crack it like a nut. While
fusing these already existent techniques for presenting animals, Leo also
added several not seen in previous medieval Latin beast poetry. He based
his plot on the ass in the lion's skin and introduced both the fox-wolf
enmity and the wolf-monk figure, which are otherwise not documented
before the mid–eleventh century *Ecbasis captivi*. He even seems to refer
obliquely to the tale of the wolf as doctor, in which the wolf ended up
being flayed so that his hide could be used to cure the lion of a fever:
"Frigora tutus / Solis et iram / Transiget omnem, / Qui sibi credit" ("He
who trusts in the wolf will pass safely through chills and every hot spell,"
3.36–39). He took burlesque to a new extreme and, for good measure,
included the distribution-of-body-parts motif, otherwise unattested between the fourth and twelfth centuries.

Conclusion

There is no one feature of form or content that unifies the narrative beast
poems composed between the late eighth and the early eleventh century.
The poems are written in a half dozen meters, both quantitative and rhythmic: they encompass dactylic hexameters (Alcuin's "The Cock and Wolf"),
elegiac couplets ("The Sick Lion," Sedulius's "The Ram"), iambic dimeter
acatelectic (Eugenius's "Comic Visions" A), Adonics (Eugenius's "Comic
Visions" B, Leo's "Meter"), a sequence ("The Swan Sequence"), and an
abecedarian *rhythmus* ("The Hawk and Peacock").

No two of the early poems are organized identically. Alcuin's "The
Cock and Wolf," "The Sick Lion," and Leo's "Meter" are the three early

poems that use fabular material or methods the most prominently, and yet each of these poems is carefully distinguished from fable by departing from the customary story-and-moral structure: Alcuin's poem has two morals rather than one, "The Sick Lion" ends with a riddle-like challenge to be solved, and Leo's "Meter" relates three fables that share one unstated moral. The other poems are equally varied structurally.

The early narrative beast poems also differ in terms of their audiences, when any guesses can be hazarded on this topic. The coteries for which they were composed or performed include the retinues of emperors (Alcuin's "The Cock and Wolf"), the entourages of bishops (Sedulius's "The Ram," Leo's "Meter"), and monks ("The Swan Sequence").

Because in the early Middle Ages there was no fixed genre of beast literature apart from fable and the *Physiologus,* the heterogeneity of the early beast poems is unremarkable. The poets were free to reach in many directions for stories and motifs. Thus they turned to oral literature for beast folktales, to classical and early medieval literature for *voces animantium,* epitaphs, and riddles.

Perhaps to compensate for the seeming levity of their subject matter, many of the early beast poets demonstrate their earnestness through frequent use of quotations from classical poetry and the Bible. Such use of quotations is manifest already in Alcuin's "The Cock and Wolf," but it reaches new heights in Sedulius's "The Ram" and Leo's "Meter."

The "Meter" is the longest and most complicated of the early beast poems. The next beast poem is even longer and more complicated. Like Leo, the anonymous author of the *Ecbasis captivi* imbues the animals in his stories with both autobiographical and religious significance. Also like Leo, he focuses on the fox-wolf rivalry and the wolf-monk, and closes his poem with a Psalm. The most telling similarity between the two poets is stylistic: they both quote Horace profusely, even citing four of the same lines (cf. "Meter" 1.36–37 and *Ecbasis captivi* 793 with *Satire* 1.5.87; "Meter" 3.52–54 and *Ecbasis* 628 with *Satire* 1.3.81; "Meter" 6.54 and *Ecbasis* 118 with *Satire* 1.6.57; "Meter" 7.46 and *Ecbasis* 1229 with *Satire* 1.1.121).

The similarities in motifs and lines quoted do not prove that the author of the *Ecbasis captivi* knew the "Meter." Despite Leo's international connections with such notabilities as Duke William V of Aquitaine, Heribert of Cologne, and Gerbert of Aurillac, the later Pope Sylvester II (Fleckenstein 90–111), it is improbable that a copy of Leo's poem, now extant in a single Italian manuscript, ever reached the hands of the author of the *Ecbasis captivi* at St. Evre.

What the similarities between the poems do substantiate is that the two poets were exposed to many of the same sources of inspiration and that their reactions to them often coincided. Both authors created new narrative structures out of two or more stories; both laid claim to a place in Latin poetic tradition by quotations, the original contexts of which expand the meaning of the new ones; and both attempted to endow beast fables and folktales with Christian values. But whereas Leo combined a strictly fabular moral (the theme of the deceiver deceived, or *fraus frau-data*) with a Christian moral (faith in providence), the *Ecbasis captivi* arrived at a different solution.

Narrative poems are only half of the picture that can be painted from medieval Latin beast poetry. The other half is nonnarrative poetry about talking animals—beast dramas and dialogues that are extant in tantalizing tatters from the early Middle Ages. The circumstantial evidence is very strong that the *Ecbasis captivi* was meant to be read aloud, with different readers for most of the different parts (Gompf). Its author could have been familiar with beast dramas and dialogues similar to the ones that happen to have survived or to have been mentioned in medieval literature.

5. Dramatic and Dialogic Beast Poems

Besides sometimes being the protagonists in medieval Latin narrative poems, talking animals at other times appear in medieval Latin dramatic and dialogic poems. Among the nonnarrative poems, there are none of the playful exchanges with animals that were a staple of ancient philosophical dialogue, particularly of Cynic dialogues influenced by the philosopher Menippus of Gadara (first half of third century B.C.). The ancient philosophical dialogues were of two sorts, both of which were developed toward the end of comedy. One was between men and animal-like monsters; for example, Lucian's "Menippus and Cerberus" describes a humorous conversation between Menippus and the mythical dog that guarded the entrance to the underworld. The other was between men and men-turned-animal; for example, Lucian's "The Dream, or the Cock" (early second century A.D.) takes the form of a dialogue between a cobbler and his cock, who is Pythagoras reincarnated, and Plutarch's "Gryllus" (ca. A.D. 100) records the futile attempt of Odysseus to persuade one of his men, who has been turned into a pig by Circe, that it is better to be a human being than a pig.

Medieval Christianity did not admit such drollery in discussion of the afterlife, the uniqueness of human reason, and other philosophical issues. It had no room for the debates over reincarnation and animal intelligence that had provided the inspiration and momentum for the philosophical dialogues. But although many philosophical issues were beyond the pale in the Middle Ages, there are poetic exchanges of insults and threats between animals that provide a special perspective on medieval beast poetry. In addition to having intrinsic merits as poetry, the beast flytings and debates raise intriguing questions about the influence of popular theater on medieval monks and pupils—and on beast poets.

Before investigating the nature and ramifications of medieval Latin beast flytings and debates, we should clarify what is meant by *flyting*; for the term has been applied loosely to very different sorts of literature. The noun *flyting* had a relatively unambiguous meaning in Scots English.

According to the *Oxford English Dictionary* (4: 332 *fliting, flyting* 1b), it denoted "poetical invective; chiefly, a kind of contest practised by Scottish poets of the 16th century, in which two persons assailed each other alternately with abusive verse." Craigie's *Dictionary of the Older Scottish Tongue* (2: 504 *flyting* 1b) states concisely that a flyting is "a contest of poets in mutual abuse." Both definitions are useful, although they should be expanded to encompass the threats, boasts, and challenges which frequently accompany the abuse (on the relationship between flyting and contest, see Parks).

It is also important to keep the meaning of *flyting* separate from other technical terms. As a self-contained poem, the flyting is not the same as a stichomythic scene in a Greek drama (Hammond and Scullard 1013; Myres; Schwinge). Likewise, *flyting* is not always an apt designation for invectives in Norse sagas (called *senna* or *mannjafnaðr*), which are not necessarily self-contained or in verse. Above all, the flyting, in which the interlocutors make their own personalities the focus of strife, differs from the medieval debate poem (often known by the modern German term *Streitgedicht*), in which the disputants argue over an abstract or impersonal issue (Walther 1920; Steinschneider). (The topics of these compositions include the comparison of different nationalities, the relative worth of wine and beer, and the advantages of hetero- as opposed to homosexuality.) For this reason, the term *flyting* should usually be kept distinct from such forms as the Latin *conflictus* and *altercatio*, Old French *débat* and *jeu-parti*, Provençal *tenson* and *partimen*, and Italian *tenzone*.

Although the existence of beast debate poems has long been recognized, the beast flytings have been overlooked. Because the flytings have gone unnoticed and uninterpreted, their relationship with other disputations involving birds and animals has not been appreciated. For want of countervailing evidence, people have felt that a verbal conflict between two animals cannot be a flyting, since just by having nonhuman participants such a conflict belongs to the contrived, learned world rather than to the simple, native traditions from which the habit of flyting is supposed to have arisen. Attitudes toward both Middle English and Scots bird debates betray the prejudice: "The Thrush and the Nightingale," "The Cuckoo and the Nightingale," Richard Holland's "Book of the Owl," and William Dunbar's "The Merle and the Nightingale" are held to be altogether bookish debates (Dickins and Wilson 71; Hume 37–38; Wittig 75–76, 123) after the fashion of such Old French and Anglo-Norman bird parliaments as Jean de Condé's "La messe des oiseaux" (Oulmont 122–222).

No doubt most of the Middle English and Scots bird poems are purely learned. For instance, a highly intellectual debate on the issue of whether or not women should be esteemed such as "The Clerk and Nightingale" is far removed from the earthiness of flytings. Still, at least two medieval debates come close to flytings, for in them the topic of the quarrel is the animal antagonists themselves and in them the language abounds in the coarseness typical of flytings.

The earlier of the two poems is the eleventh-century "Debate of the Sheep and Flax Plant" (*Conflictus ovis et lini*). Although the incorrect attribution of the poem to Hermannus Contractus dies hard, "The Sheep and Flax Plant" has been properly credited to Winrich of Trier (Werner 1907, 602–4; Vyver and Verlinden). Like beer-and-wine or body-and-soul debates, "The Sheep and Flax Plant" revolves around the stock question of usefulness: which serves mankind better, wool or linen? Thus at first glance "The Sheep and Flax Plant" differs little from such later learned disputes as the anonymous thirteenth-century Old French *Dit du denier et de la brebis* or John Lydgate's fifteenth-century *Debate of the Horse, Goose, and Sheep*, in both of which animals argue over their respective power and importance in the world. Nonetheless, "The Sheep and Flax Plant" contains personal slurs and scatology more characteristic of flyting than debate. As the poem opens, the flax plant accuses the sheep of being filthy and stinking (line 17). Both the flax plant and the sheep continue to trade gibes about bodily appearance and odor (29, 37, 85–86, 89). The seamiest moment comes when the sheep states that if the flax plant had a proper awareness of their respective qualities, she would give up and ask the sheep to destroy her "either with her foot or with her droppings" ("vel pede vel potius subruta stercoribus," 32). The other flyting-like poem is the famous Middle English bird quarrel, *The Owl and the Nightingale*. The poem is regarded as a learned debate, even though it is introduced as anything but a coolly logical disputation: "An aiþer aȝen oþer sval / & let þat vvole mod ut al; / & eiþer seide of oþeres custe / þat alre worste þat hi wuste" ("And each one swelled up [with rage] against the other and let out its foul mood completely; and each said of the other's character the very worst that it knew," 7–10). The birds themselves know that they are squabbling rather than debating, for later in the poem the nightingale proposes that they leave off their "wrangle" (*cheste*: 177, 183) and instead argue their points in an orderly manner. As to be expected in such a brawl, *The Owl and the Nightingale* begins in angry defamation of character and passes to insults and threats (e.g., 49–50, 51–54, 56–58, 71–82, 91–138, 147–48). Even when the poem becomes more a debate and less an altercation, the owl feels impelled to punish the nightingale tit for tat for her earlier aspersions on the physical appearance and personal hygiene of the owl (577–96). Throughout the first section of the poem, the owl behaves much more as the enraged butt of the shameful words and mockery which fly freely in a flyting than merely as the losing partner in a rational exchange of views. The owl gets her revenge later when she outdoes the nightingale at the game of flyting. Coining a contemptuous phrase which is now commonplace in spoken American English but which had never before been used, she calls the nightingale "a little dirt ball" ("a lutel soti clowe," 578).

Although the tenor and language of "The Sheep and Flax Plant" and *The Owl and the Nightingale* are often unlearned, the poems have both been considered learned for two reasons which have more to do with the present state of medieval scholarship than with the nature of the poems themselves. One reason is that genuine flytings are not nearly so well known as are learned debate poems and are frequently confused with them. The second reason is that there has been little effort to seek connections between folk rites, especially those involving beast disguise, and invective poetry. Such connections have been posited only in the case of the Edda poems (Phillpotts 115–17; Ellis Davidson 25–46). Happily, a stronger case can be made for the existence of links between invective poetry and animal disguise in the Middle Ages, since folklore collectors have now gathered rich materials on the presence of animal disguise rituals throughout Europe in both antiquity and the modern period (Alford; Cawte; Meuli 1955; Meuli 1932–33, col. 1771–72, 1777–82; Strömbäck 1948, 1955).

In the face of the new folkloric data and the growing body of medieval Latin pieces available, we should consider afresh whether or not animal debates in vernacular languages are as undilutedly academic in origin as has been supposed. The debates may be akin to beast flytings—to flytings in which the contestants are animals. Even if animal debates and flytings should prove to be wholly unrelated, the beast flytings still deserve appraisal on account of the difficulties that they raise regarding the presence of folk customs in monasteries and the association between ritual animal disguise and invective in early European culture. The flytings offer a glimpse into a world of talking animals that looks very different from the one of fable, *Physiologus*, and Latin literature.

Beast Flytings

The shortest beast poem that can be called a flyting survives in a ninth- or tenth-century German manuscript, originally from Regensburg but now in Munich, Bayerische Staatsbibliothek, Clm 14101. It is only four hexameter lines long but seems to constitute a complete little poem:

> "Cur me torquetis morsu lacerante penali?
> Si non dimiseritis, adest mors vestra parata!"
> "Vos audite, canes, quid dicit perfidus ursus!
> Fugite, sin alias, iamiam discerpimur omnes."

> [The first speaker:] "Why are you wrenching me with a punishing, lacerating bite? If you do not yield, then prepare to meet your maker!"
> [The second speaker:] "Do you hear, dogs, what the treacherous bear is saying? Flee, or otherwise we will all be torn to shreds."

The four verses appear to be a conversation between a bear and the leader of a pack of dogs. They are not a reworking of any identifiable bestiary account, Aesopic fable, or animal riddle. Furthermore, the lyric is too long and polished to have been simply a pen test (*probatio pennae*), one of the maxims with which pupils practiced the alphabet or scribes readied their writing tools (Bischoff 1966). Finally, the lines in their present form are not part of a narrative beast poem, inasmuch as the dialogue in them stands by itself and not in a fable or in a narrative about a character such as Renard the Fox.

Another ninth-century manuscript, perhaps originally from the monastery of Saint-Aubin in Angers but now in Berlin, Deutsche Staatsbibliothek, MS. Philipps 1825, contains two poems (Rose 374–80). Like the four Regensburg lines, these two poems are narrative-less exchanges between two animals. The first piece has the incipit, "Quid mihi caprigero cornuque minaris" (the manuscript has the nonsensical reading *caprigeno*). Although acephalous, these nineteen hexameters survive in adequately sound condition for one resemblance to the Regensburg lines to be manifest: the "Quid mihi caprigero" is composed of a death-threat from one animal (a lion or wolf?) and a response from another (a goat?).

"Quid mihi caprigero cornuque minaris abunco,
Frangi qui facile nostra virtute valebit,
Si fuga non poterit nostros vitare triumphos?
Quod si tanta tuum lusit dementia pectus,
5   Ut non terga petas armata fronte supervus,
Te velud avulsum lactantis ab ubere caprum
Dentibus adtritum partes per mille resolvam."

RESPONSIO
"Grandia iactanter bumbosa fauce cacinnas,
Pauca sed in rebus quibis monstrare cruentis.
10   Nam si tam preceps chaus non discerneret ambos,
Ilia per media acuto te findere cornu
Instanter poteram pedibus seu sternere nostris.
Partibus in multis merito te frustra secabo,
Quamvis magna tuas orrescat bestia voces;
15   Cumque tuum fuerit tabum foetumque cadaber
Dirruptum volucresque tuo de sanguine pastae
Carnibus atque tuis satiatae denique gripes,
Ridebit pecual, gaudet tunc bestia saltus,
Tristia quae dudum carpebant pascua campi."

"Why are you menacing me with your hooked goat's horn, you who can easily be shattered by my force, if you cannot avoid my triumph by taking flight? But if so great a madness has deluded your heart [5] that you—proud of your armed forehead—don't retreat, I'll undo you, torn by my teeth into a thousand bits, like a kid rent from the teat of its mother."

RESPONSE
"You laugh out great words so boastfully with a booming mouth, but you're able to perform only a few tricks when it comes to bloody deeds. [10] For if a precipitous gap did not keep us apart, I would be able at once either to split you with my sharp horn, right in the middle of your groin, or to trample you with my hooves. I'll cut you, as you deserve, into many bits, piecemeal, even though great beasts shudder at your call; [15] and when

your corpse has rotted foully and it has been ripped apart, and when the birds have fed on your blood and when the griffins are at last sated with your flesh, then the cattle will laugh, then the beast of the grove will rejoice, which for so long grazed sadly in the field."

Like the Regensburg lines, the "Quid mihi caprigero" stands apart from the *Physiologus* and from classical fables. Its setting points in a very different direction: the "precipitous gap" that keeps the two beasts apart serves the same function as "the sundering flood," the body of water that separates the disputants in one of the two standard settings of the Old Norse *senna* (Clover 447; Phillpotts 158).

If the short poem and the "Quid mihi caprigero" were debates on specific issues, they could properly be called *Streitgedichte*, but because they limit themselves to a threat and a response, they would better be termed *beast flytings*, which may be defined as exchanges of insults, threats, boasts, and challenges between two animals. Yet to pin a generic name on the poems does not dispel the problems pertaining to their audience and delivery. Fortunately, the poem which follows the "Quid mihi caprigero" in the manuscript leaves clues that assist in unraveling the mystery of all three poems.

The poem, which could be entitled "Learn, Lion", is a monologue of fifteen dactylic hexameters.

> "Disce, leo supplex, apices sine murmure nostros:
> 'Proderit ecce tibi, quod cantat littera libri.'
> 'Scito, miser, ferulis si non vapulaveris multis.'
> His ego sub teneris obstrictus legibus annis
> 5   Alfabetum studui multo certamine scire.
> Sic quoque perdoctus nulla feritate resistens
> Sarcinulas porto stimulo confossus acuto;
> Non me dispicias tumida cervice supervus,
> Nam dominus celi dorsum conscendit aselli,
> 10   Qui propria sevum calce calcavit leonem.
> Discipulum nostrum non te sub fronte pudebit,
> Multi nam nostris inbuti forte salibis
> Sciunt orticas et parcum carpere tursum,
> Quidam cardones obtonso mandere dente,
> 15   Quamvis spinoso subpungant vulnere labrum."

"Learn, lion, as a suppliant my letters without a murmur: 'Look here, what the writing in the book sings out will do you good.' 'Study, if you don't want to be a wretch flogged with many a rod.' Bound by those two rules at a tender age, [5] I strove with great pains to master the alphabet. Thus, thoroughly learned, not resisting with wildness, I, who have been pierced through by a sharp goad, carry bundles; don't look down on me, you who are proud with your puffed-out neck, for the Lord of Heaven mounted upon the back of an ass, [10] He who trod down the savage lion with His own heel. It won't shame you to be my student, for many indeed inspired by my enthusiasm learn how to pluck nettles and scanty thorns, while some learn how to chew thistles with blunted tooth, [15] although the thistles prick the lip somewhat with a prickly wound."

Although the manuscript does not indicate who the speakers are, the contents make evident that the speech is addressed by an ass to a lion. The speech also establishes beyond a doubt that the poem came from a scholastic milieu.

The humor of the poem lies in the incongruity of making an ass, a beast that symbolized stupidity, into a teacher. The ass tries, through his hard-earned erudition, to persuade the lion to become his pupil. To demonstrate his professional competence, the ass recites the "rules" (*leges*, 4) by which he acquired a command of the "alphabet" (*apices*, 1) in his youth. The two rules, which are like "pen tests" (*probationes pennae*), accentuate reward as well as punishment: first that literacy is valuable and then that willfully ignorant schoolchildren will be chastised (Bischoff 1966, 82–87). Probably coincidentally, the first of these two rules resembles a graffito on the Palatine that is addressed to a stupid novice, who is called an *asellus*: "Labora, aselle, quomodo ego laboravi, et proderit tibi" (Väänänen 1: 223, no. 289). The second merits comparison with Cicero, *In L. Calpurnium Pisonem* 30.73 (p. 38.11–12): "Quid nunc te, asine, litteras doceam? non opus est verbis, sed fustibus" ("Why now should I teach the alphabet to you, ass? You have need not of words but of cudgel-blows").

To judge by his words, the ass's learning is not limited to two rules. Indeed, the beast twice alludes to the Bible—to the ass Jesus rode (Matthew 21.5) and to the lion he trod down (Psalm 90.13 and 1 Peter 5.8). As the poem concludes, the ass refers to his predilection for thistles and perhaps to a proverb about basic education that recurs in fuller form in

Walter Map's *De nugis curialium* (Dist. 1, chap. 31: ed. and trans. James, Brooke, and Mynors 126–27): "Primo igitur proposui leuissima, que nemini licet ignorare, sciens quod asino cardones edente indignam habent labia lattuca" ("First, therefore, I put to them very simple questions which ought to be unknown to no one, for I was aware that when an ass eats thistles, his lips count lettuce unworthy of them").

Insect Debates

"Learn, Lion" is not the only Latin verse speech by a living creature to bear the stamp of the schools. The twelfth-century "The Altercation of the Spider and the Fly" (*Altercacio aranee et musce*), which has been attributed to an imitator of Matthew of Vendôme, records the ridicule that a spider and fly inflict upon each other (see Appendix 16). This "altercation" of 74 lines in elegiac distichs (two lines are missing) has been edited from Oxford, Bodleian, MS. Misc. Lat. D 15. In its basic conception the debate resembles "The Quarrel of the Flea and Fly" (*Pulicis et musce iurgia*) by another twelfth-century poet, William of Blois (see Appendix 15). This poem of 180 lines in elegiac distichs has been printed from London, British Library, MS. Additional 34.749. How widely "The Quarrel of the Flea and Fly" circulated cannot be gauged; although Peter of Blois claimed in a letter that the poem had won William enduring fame (Walther 1920, 14, n. 1), his assertion may owe more to brotherly loyalty than to the reality of the poem's popularity.

Both poems could owe something to the familiarity of their authors with two riddles of Symphosius (*Aenigmata* 22–23), one on the ant and one on the fly, and with fables by fabulists such as Phaedrus (4.25: Perry 1965, 340–43) and Odo of Cheriton (Hervieux 4: 293, 326), where the spider and the fly engage in sharp disputes (Boutemy 1947, 138–39; Scolari 387). The twelfth-century poems could also be indebted in spirit to "The Gnat" (*Culex*), a pseudo-Vergilian mock epic about an insect (Boutemy 1947, 139). They could be related to pseudo-Ovidian eulogies for insects such as "The Flea" (see Appendix 19), an imitation of Ovid's *Amores* 2.15 which is dated in the twelfth century (ed. Lenz 1962, 300), and "The Louse" (see Appendix 23), which was written at the latest in the last quarter of the twelfth century (ed. Lenz 1955, 64).

Even when not paired with another insect the fly's natural persistence had earned it a reputation as a verbal pest in beast literature. For example,

Phaedrus included among his fables one (5.3, ed. and trans. Perry 1965, 354–57) in which a fly and a bald man have a sharp exchange of words:

The Bald Man and the Fly

A fly bit the bared head of a bald man, and in trying to crush it he gave himself a hard slap. Thereupon the fly mocked him, saying: "You wanted to avenge with death the sting of a little insect; what will you do to yourself, now that you have added insult to injury?" The man replied: "I can easily get back into my own good graces, since I know that it was not my intention to injure myself; but as for you, miserable creature of a despised species, who delight in drinking human blood, I should be glad to be rid of you at the cost even of greater discomfort."

The theme of Phaedrus's poem was reworked in hexameters by a medieval poet, perhaps early in the tenth century (ed. Winterfeld, 4: 261, n. 1):

De calvo a culice obviato

Stridula musca volans calvum conspexit euntem.
"Calve viator," ait "quo tendis? cede parumper,
Perque tuos iuro qui restant retro capillos
Me gratam liceat rostro decerpere sedem."
Sic ait et trepidum circumvolat inproba calvum.
At contra ille timens solito caput armat amictu.
Quid valet en calvus muscae lassatus ab ictu?

(Lines 1–7)

About a Bald Man Met by a Midge

A buzzing fly as it was flying saw a bald man passing. "Bald traveler," it says, "Where are you going? Give up your journey for a while, and—I swear by the hairs remaining on the back of your head—[5] it might be possible for me with my beak to pluck out a nice seat." Thus it speaks and flies shamelessly around the anxious bald man. But in response the fearful man arms his head with its usual covering. For what can a bald man weary of insect bites do?

Of course, neither the characters nor even the situation in the twelfth-century spider-and-fly poem ("The Altercation of the Spider and the Fly") need to have had a specific written source; to oppose natural antagonists in a debate is an obvious idea. For instance, the American humorist Don Marquis (1878–1937) wrote an entirely unrelated piece entitled "a spider and a fly" (1927, p. 27) which begins: "i heard a spider / and a fly arguing / wait said the fly / do not eat me / i serve a great purpose / in the world / you will have to / show me said the spider."

Not only is the idea of opposing natural antagonists in a debate a natural one, but in addition, the practice of praising seemingly insignificant insects must have been a common epideictic exercise in the rhetorical training of late antiquity: most notably, the rhetorician and philosopher Lucian (born ca. A.D. 120) produced "The Fly," a substantial mock-encomium of the insect.

The flavor of the medieval Latin spider-and-fly poem is remarkably scholastic. The poem closes with a verdict by a third party, who is not a judge weighing the merit of the arguments advanced by the two insects, but rather a teacher evaluating the proficiency in Latin of the pupils who drafted the two sections of the poem:

IUDICIUM

65   <L>itera uix reptans de uena paupere dotes
     pectoris examen iudiciale timet.
mendicat metri series ieiuna coloris,
     expers artis, egens schemate, nuda tropis.
pigmee modulus nature uocis in usum
70   prouecte puerum luxuriare uetat.
mens preit etatem, tenero preponderat euo
     sensus et amplificat quod minus esse potest.
cortice de tenero mens spirat adulta, patronum
     in puero reddet, in leuitate statum.

VERDICT

[65] The work of literature, just barely crawling from a paltry talent, fears the gift of mind, judicial enquiry. The progression of the meter stands in need: it is devoid of oratorical color, destitute of craftsmanship, barren of rhetorical figures, bare of figurative language. The limitations of a boy's pygmoid nature forbid him to run riot in the use of an adult voice. [70] The mind gives guidance to age; sense outweighs tender age and enlarges that which could be less. An adult mind breathes from within a tender bark; it will produce a guardian over the boy, it will render fixity in place of levity.

As a teacher would do, the judge chides his charges for their feeble command of metrics and rhetoric, and he counsels them to wait patiently until adulthood hones their skills.

Flytings in the Schools

To know that the beast flytings were written in schools answers the question of where they came into being, but it leaves two further puzzles. First, what prompted a teacher or pupil to write a flyting rather than another sort of poem? Second, what led a poet to stage a flyting between beasts rather than human beings?

The pieces of the first puzzle can be fitted together in two ways. One response is that the flyting came naturally to minds accustomed to memorizing schoolroom dialogues for recitation and, conceivably, for play-acting (Garmonsway; Winterbottom). Like flytings, the dialogues would have been associated with the insults and humiliations to which pedagogues sometimes subject classes. A flyting that burlesqued a school dialogue would have been the ideal mode for a schoolboy who wished to turn the tables and voice complaints. Whereas in the colloquies that were employed widely in basic medieval education instructors and their wards chat about routine matters as normal human beings would, in the beast flytings the usual school characters are distorted into animals and solemn discussions become unrestrained raillery. Such literary transmogrification would have been similar to scenes in medieval art that rendered the human participants in schools into beasts (Wackernagel 1848).

The progression from dialogue to flyting is difficult to trace because medieval dialogue literature remains sketchily charted. There are fascinating scraps of evidence, such as the description of twelfth-century school debates in William Fitz Stephen:

> On holy days the masters of the schools assemble their scholars at the churches whose feast-day it is. The scholars dispute, some in demonstrative rhetoric, others in dialectic. Some "hurtle enthymemes," others with greater skill employ perfect syllogisms. Some are exercised in disputation for the purpose of display, which is but a wrestling bout of wit, but others that they may establish the truth for the sake of perfection. . . . Boys of different schools strive one against another in verse or contend concerning the principles of the art of grammar or the rules governing the use of past and future. There are others who employ the old art of the cross-roads in epigrams, rhymes,

and metre; with "Fescennine License," they lacerate their comrades outspokenly, though mentioning no names; they hurl "abuse and gibes," they touch the foibles of their comrades, perchance even of their elders with Socratic wit, not to say "bite more keenly even than Theon's tooth," in their "bold dithyrambs." Their hearers "ready to laugh their fill," "with wrinkling nose repeat the loud guffaw." (Trans. Butler 52–53)

This description conjures up a vivid picture of verbal conflict and display, in which even the young were expected to display their grasp of Latin and their wit in taunting abuse of each other. But little information about "the old art of the cross-roads" earlier in the Middle Ages has been gathered. As a result, we are still uncertain about how the dialogues were delivered; we do not know whether they were recited or acted out and whether or not they were affected by the techniques and subject matter of popular theater and mime.

Whatever the relationship between the flytings and scholastic dialogues, the connection between the flytings and schools themselves is tight. After all, the medieval Latin flytings, as may be inferred from the very fact that they were Latin, emanated from learned institutions such as monasteries. For this reason, Latin flytings such as the seventh-century Irish *Hisperica famina* and the tenth-century English "The Dispute of a Master and Student" (*Altercatio magistri et discipuli*) understandably tended to center upon difficulties such as the frictions between rival colleagues and between teachers and pupils.

Latin flytings sometimes managed to reconcile an academic theme with a truly theatrical presentation. The ninth-century flyting known as "Terence and His Mocker" has in its margins Latin stage directions, such as indications of asides and descriptions of movements. In this flyting an adolescent denigrates the writings of Terence, only to find the Roman comedian suddenly before him. The two fall into an astringent argument, in which Terence accuses the young man of juvenile fatuity while the mocker retorts that Terence is far past his prime. Although on one level the two combatants wage the war between the ancients and moderns (*antiqui et moderni*) that raged intermittently throughout the Middle Ages (Zimmermann and Vuillemin-Diez), on another they act out a timeless academic confrontation between callow youth and pedantic old age.

Other flytings, although lacking vividly theatrical qualities, also help in interpreting the beast flytings. Sedulius Scottus, writing in the mid–ninth century, is an exceptionally valuable witness for the medieval Latin flyting. In a *collectaneum* (a collection or compilation of texts) he wrote down a contention in prose which may be entitled *Senex contra adolescentem*. In it an "old man" (*senex*) and a "youth" (*adolescens*) bicker over the matter of which one is wiser (3.1–16, ed. Simpson 12–13). Much as in "Learn, Lion" the old man offers to teach his interlocutor: "Si uis fieri meus discipulus, ego instruam te quod nescis" ("If you wish to become my pupil, I will instruct you in your areas of ignorance"). When the youth declines the invitation, the old man threatens violence: "Scio quod proteruia tua fustibus et calcibus debet dominari" ("I know that your impudence ought to be mastered with blows and kicks").

In a poem Sedulius presents wise old men as beasts with horns longer than those of immature boys (*Carmen* 80, ed. Dümmler 229–30):

> Nostri simplicitas fratrem superare trilinguem
> Exultat victrix: palmam date, laeta iuventus.
> Qui fodit foveam, grandi ceciditne ruina?
> Victus et occubuit, voluit qui victor ut esset?
> Et cornuta quidem devicit bestia calvam,
> Rinoceron mutilam protrivit acumine frontem?
> Adversus doctos noli certare, sophista:
> Si pugnare libet, cur desint cornua fronti?
>
> (Lines 1–8)

Our victorious honesty exults in conquering our three-tongued, lying brother: give us the palm of victory, happy youth. Hasn't the man who dug the ditch for another fallen in great ruin himself? And hasn't he who wished to be a victor himself collapsed, vanquished? [5] And, indeed, hasn't the horned beast conquered the bald one, hasn't the rhinoceros crushed with its cleverness the hornless brow [of its foe]? Don't vie with the learned, sophist: if it pleases you to fight, then why have you no horns on your brow?

Froumund of Tegernsee, a monk of Bavarian origin who lived and taught in the second half of the tenth century, composed a poem (*Carmen* 19, ed. Strecker 53–55) similar to the one by Sedulius, in that it demeans a boy (equating him to such despicable animals as an ass and a cuckoo). In a final flyting-like touch, Froumund ends the poem with a challenge to the boy to retort in verse. The poems of Sedulius and Froumond both show

how easily a poet could shift from insulting a person by calling him an animal, which is a universal form of denigration (Cohn; Faust; E. Leach), to converting him into an animal.

Monks could have written flytings out of a wish to turn topsy-turvy the conventionally staid learned dialogue. Alternatively, they could have hoped to construct a suitably learned medium for the flytings they knew from their native cultures. All monks lived in non-Latin cultures and languages before entering the monastery, and few would have lost touch entirely with those cultures and languages after completing their novitiate. As a result, they were bound to bring native lore into Latin literature. Like many other monasteries, the monastery of Angers, where the "Quid mihi caprigero" and "Learn, Lion" seem to have originated, may have witnessed such exchanges between native and learned cultures. From ninth- and tenth-century Angers come two very lively *Caritas-Lieder* (Bischoff 1967, 2: 69, 72). From the ninth century or earlier comes a boisterous poem about the abbot of Angers (incipit "Andecavis abbas esse dicitur"). When the poet invokes the "townsfolk" (*cives*) in the final verse, he suggests that participation in the more exuberant activities of the religious community was not restricted to the "monks" (*fratres*).

Even if many monks would have felt free to shift vernacular flytings into Latin, are there grounds for believing that such vernacular flytings existed? The circumstantial evidence is strong that they did. According to the theories of historical anthropologists, primitive Indo-European societies operated on a bipolarity of praise and blame (Dumézil 1943, 65–78). This schema has been confirmed by the praise poems and blame poems (which encompasses invective poems) that survive from several early Indo-European cultures (Elliott 3–48). Proof of invective exchanges abounds in early Germanic sources; for although records in Germanic languages are wanting before the Old English and Old Norse periods, in Latin Gregory of Tours, Paul the Deacon, and other historians knowledgeable about Germanic cultures peppered their writings with reciprocal insults and threats like flytings (Martínez Pizarro 15–130). Even the early terms for poets and poetry are evidence that invective was an integral part of poetry and everyday life (D. Ward). In fact, the very words for poet in Old English and Old Icelandic are cognate with verbs implying invective: *scop* is related to the Modern English "scoff," *skald* to "scold" (see Steblin-Kamenskij; Werlich).

Animals in Place of People

If flytings were commonplace in medieval societies and if latinized flytings would have been ideal parodies of grammar school dialogues, then we can see why persons affiliated with monastic schools would have written flytings. Yet we still face the conundrum of why they selected animals, of all possible choices, as rivals in flytings. Once again we may offer several explanations, none of which precludes any of the others.

The animals could be construed as camouflage in a roman à clef, in which a given animal signifies a given individual. As discussed previously (Chapter 2), scholars in Charlemagne's entourage gave one another animal nicknames, and yet the Carolingian evidence proves nothing about the beast flytings, the products of a very different culture. In fact, as the very word *roman* in the expression *roman à clef* notifies us, literature of assumed names is usually narrative. A dialogue such as a flyting would make a wretched roman à clef.

Before denying all human significance to the beasts in the flytings, we should explore the possibility that the animals stand not for individuals, but rather for whole classes of people. Specifically, we should recognize that medieval teachers often referred to pupils collectively as animals. Alcuin and Froumund (see Appendix 6) both identified disorderly young acquaintances with the cuckoo. More pertinent to the flytings, a gloss on Egbert of Liège's late tenth- or early eleventh-century textbook, the *Fecunda ratis* ("The Richly Laden Ship"), informs us that talented boys are to be called calves and incompetent ones asses (*Prora* 327, ed. Voigt 72); although the glossator was not Egbert himself (*Fecunda ratis*, ed. Voigt vii–viii), his comment nonetheless provides insight into the jargon used in schools of the period.

The use of *asellus* ("ass," or "donkey") to mean a stupid boy, which is documented amply in ancient Roman literature (Cicero, *In Pisonem* 73; Persius 1.59; Quintilian 6.3.57–58), was also widespread in the Middle Ages (Froumund, *Carmina* 2.12–15, 2.35.12; Warner of Rouen, *Satire* 2.59–60, 96, 99, 123). For instance, the author of the eleventh-century *Ecbasis captivi* confesses with shame that as a ne'er-do-well teenager he was called an *asellus* (line 7). In the "Learn, Lion" flyting, the word serves a new function. It interlaces the reality of the hoofed animal with the metaphor of the lazy schoolboy to create something more than a contemptuous epithet; it becomes the name of a beast who goes to school. The new convention gained strength in medieval Latin beast poetry: the comic hero of

Nigel's *Speculum Stultorum* is an ass who spends seven fruitless years as a student at the University of Paris, and an ass in the *Ysengrimus* (3.687–704) brags to the wolf-monk of being a *magister* and urges that the wolf submit to him to learn the nuances of Latin grammar.

The scene involving the ass and the wolf-monk evidently had a strong appeal in the twelfth century. Besides appearing in the *Ysengrimus* in the Low Countries, it was carved in a capital in the cathedral of Parma (Quin-tavalle 330, pl. 506). (The capital has been dated variously 1106, 1130, and the second half of the twelfth century.) In this sculpture the wolf, dressed in a monk's habit, holds a tablet on which are visible a hexameter line of eight words: "Est monachus factus lupus hic sub dogmate tractus" ("The wolf, having become a monk, is here placed under instruction"). To the right of the wolf an ass brandishes a bundle of reeds, as if ready to disci-pline the wolf. In a thematically related scene on a tympanum in a convent in Bourges, an ass with a switch raised in its hoof is seated with two ani-mals seated before it (Deschamps 14, fig. 8). The theme of the wolf in school is so widespread as to be almost universal (Adrados 1984, 263): it appears in the Assyrian *Ahikar* (8.36), medieval Latin fables (Hervieux 2: 642; Perry 1965, Appendix no. 688), and Marie de France (*Fable* 81). Not so the vignette of the wolf being taught by the ass! This vignette could be explicated very easily as a lapidary analogue to the "Learn, Lion" flyting, with the simple substitution of the wolf-monk for the lion of the flyting.

Animals in Popular Theater and Ritual

The thought of employing animals in a dramatic exchange could have de-rived from a tacit assumption that animals have to stand for particular persons (as in the Carolingian poems) or for particular classes of people (as in the Parma capital, the *Ysengrimus*, and Nigel's *Speculum Stultorum*). But alternatively, the idea could have stemmed from the familiarity of the flyting poets with the animals present in popular theater and ritual. The importance of medieval mime plays, some of which involved live animals and animal masks, can be surmised from the recurrent Church condem-nations of them, yet few particularized descriptions of mime plays are available (Axton 17–32). A thirteenth-century penitential describes mimes masked as animals who imitated the movements and sounds of beasts, but so far as I know, no document records an instance in which a mime player masked as an animal actually speaks, nor are surviving illuminations of mime players in animal disguise helpful (Chambers 1: 59, 63, n. 1, 71–72; 2: frontispiece, 262). The contents of the plays are recorded only unintentionally, almost always by ecclesiastics who were *ex officio* foes of them. Mime plays in which men impersonated asses are attested in both ancient archaeological evidence and Shakespeare's "A Midsummer Night's Dream," which was written probably about 1595–96 (Reich), but we cannot be sure that such plays were also familiar in the Middle Ages.

One monk who by chance touches on mimetic performance is Froumund of Tegernsee, whose affinity with the flyting poets has already been pointed out. In one poem he rues the effort that he has expended upon pupils who care nothing for the erudition he offers them. If only he behaved like a mime player, he laments, then he would win their rapt attention. He says (*Carmen* 32.33–42, ed. Strecker 80–82):

> Si facerem mihi pendentes per cingula caudas
>   Gesticulans manibus, lubrice stans pedibus,
> 35 Si lupus aut ursus, vel vellem fingere vulpem,
>   Si larvas facerem furciferis manibus,
> Dulcifer aut fabulas nossem componere, menda,
>   Orpheus ut cantans Euridicen revocat,
> Si canerem multos dulci modulamine leudos
> 40 Undique currentes cum trepidis pedibus,
> Gauderet, mihi qui propior visurus adesset,
>   Ridiculus cunctos concuteret pueros.

> If I made for myself tails hanging on belts, if I gesticulated with my hands and stood unsteadily on my feet, [35] if I wished to imitate a fox, or if I were a wolf or bear, if I made masks with my rascally hands, or if I knew how in a sweet voice to compose stories, lying poems, like the ones Orpheus sang to regain Eurydice, if I sang many vernacular lays to a sweet melody, [40] *Lieder* running everywhere on metrically restless feet, then the person who came close to me to take a look would rejoice, and the jester would fell all the boys.

Later in the same poem Froumund makes the transition from mime play to a competition which may be flyting: he challenges the boys to match wits with him in verse: "Eia, confratres, certemus carmine metri; / Hoc vincens aliquis sit melior reliquis" (*Carmen* 32.63–64: "Come on, fellow monks! Let us vie in metrical song; let someone, by winning in this, be better than the rest"). In another poem (see Appendix 6), Froumund attacks a boy for his uncouthness and goads him to compete in verse. After mocking the boy a few times, Froumund slips into another imagined scene that seems to refer to mimetic performances that mimic animals:

> Nunc varios sum facturus cum carmine ludos,
> Quod genus omne hominum simul aggreget et pecus omne,
> Qui certant ut cenosum te perdere saxo.
> Hic habitu vario sit primus in ordine Gitto,
> Calceus ut ruptus circum sibi pendeat omnis,
> Quem sequitur gaudens nanorum exercitus odis.
> Ut faciant risum, suspendite cingula, caudas;
> Pannosas vestes trepidimine porgite, nani . . .
>
> (*Carmen* 19.14–21; punctuation in 19–20 altered)

Now I am going to play various games with song, to bring together the whole race of men and the whole herd of beasts who compete to destroy you, filthy scamp, with a stone. Let Gitto, in variegated garments, be the first in the line, and let every worn-out shoe dangle around him, whom an army of dwarfs follows, rejoicing in songs. So that they may arouse laughter, hang belts and tails; spread threadbare clothes, dwarfs . . .

The motif of the old shoes slung around the neck hints that mime plays influenced beast poetry in general, since the same detail occurs suggestively in "The Sick Lion." After learning that the lion-king has been offended by her absence, the fox puts "many pairs of torn-apart shoes" ("Indumenta pedum multa et conscissa," 37) upon her shoulders and makes her way to the court. The lion-king reacts by laughing "with a placated heart" and awaits her next move eagerly ("placato pectore risit / Expectatque diu, quid malefida velit," 39–40)—the sort of reaction that he would be expected to produce upon seeing a mime player or clown. Now although the appetite of foxes for old shoes was legendary in the Middle Ages (*Vita sancti Ciarani* 6, ed. Plummer 219), there is nothing inherently funny about wearing old shoes. The king is not reacting to a fox-like trait but instead to seeing the trappings of a mime player or clown.

In both of Froumund's poems invective and animal mime are associated with each other, but not even his poems prove that mime played a role in the beast flytings. Equally tantalizing, but difficult to corroborate is the hypothesis that the flytings emerged from holdovers of pre-Christian rites. True, this theory would seem to receive support from the incessant Church denunciations of boisterous New Year's masquerades in which men donned masks representing stags and calves. The penitential of pseudo-Theodore is typical of these condemnations:

> Si quis in Kalendas ianuarii in cervolo aut vetula vadit, id est, in ferarum habitus se communicant et vestiuntur pellibus pecudum, et assumunt capita bestiarum: qui vero taliter in ferinas species se transformant, iii annos poeniteant, quia hoc daemoniacum est. (Chambers 2: 290–306; Arbesmann)

> If anyone on the Kalends of January goes about as a stag or heifer, that is, they change into animal garb and clothe themselves in the hides of beasts, and don animal heads: those who thus transform themselves into the form of wild animals should do penance for three years, because this is diabolic.

Although such festivals may have been a survival of Celtic rites to honor a stag-headed god (Ahl 411 on Cernunnos or Grannos), similar rites existed in non-Celtic parts of Europe (Alford 20 and pl. 2; Dumézil 1929). None of these early medieval ceremonies of beast disguise has been tied to invective, although similar ancient Roman ones have (Meuli 1955, 217). Still, one later rite seems to have coupled beast disguise with invective: the Feast of the Ass, which was in vogue from the twelfth century to the waning of the Middle Ages (Chambers 1: 275, 287, 320–21, 327, 330–33; 2: 279–81), entailed both the leading of flesh-and-blood asses into cathedrals and the recitation of Latin satiric poems directed against the inequities of the ecclesiastic hierarchy (Spanke 1931, 204–20; Schmidt; Schüppert 35–41, 54–57). In both the ancient and medieval rites, animal masks would have had the obvious advantage of protecting the identity of the insulters. Masks continue to serve this function in modern mummeries (Schwed).

If the beast flytings themselves resulted from a popular perception of animal mimes or masks and invective as being interconnected—a perception that is easier to imagine than substantiate—then they could embody a late phase of a venerable Indo-European custom.

Ancient Greek literature contains many hints of a relationship between animal disguise and invective. A good place to start is among the iambic poets, since their meter was the standard one for invective. The earliest great iambic poet, Archilochos, includes animal fables in his verse (fragment nos. 28–34, 78, 168–74, 177, 188–99, 209–16, 224–34, ed. Lasserre and Bonnard). His fables could possibly have been suitable for miming, either by the person delivering the poems or by a group surrounding him (Nagy 1976, 196). Perhaps relevant is that the target of Archilochos's scorn seems to bear a *nom parlant* in which an animal name (*lýkos*, "wolf") and the word for invective (*íambos*, "iamb") are joined: Lykambes (West 25–28).

Even among iambic poets in the generation after Archilochos, the alliance between theriomorphic disguise and invective might have remained in effect. For instance, Semonides unleashes a pack of mordant comparisons with animals in his iambic satire against women (for analysis, Marg 6–42; ed. Lloyd-Jones). Once again, invective and a suitability for animal mime seem to complement each other.

Another point of departure in Greek literature is Old Comedy, in which animal choruses figured prominently. Their nature may be guessed from the titles of plays, which were generally taken from the creatures that the chorus imitated. In all, eighteen plays are known to have had the names of animals as their titles: *Frogs, Birds, Gall-flies, Beasts, Goats, Wasps, Storks, Griffins, Ants, Fishes, Nightingales, Bees,* and *Horse-riders* (Sifakis 76–77). In addition to the titles, illustrations on vases show how these theriomorphically disguised choruses operated. Some vases picture men arrayed as horses, roosters, and other birds (Sifakis 73–75, pl. 1–8). Finally, Aristophanes' comedies include animal choruses that deliver invective (Sifakis 26, 39, 41) in various meters, of which iambs are one (Sifakis 33–36). To compound the verbal violence, each of these choruses becomes embroiled in a battle scene (Sifakis 102).

Conclusion

For all the evidence in Greek literature, the proposal that the medieval Latin beast flytings preserve traces of an Indo-European context must remain very tentative. More secure is the notion that the flytings were composed by boys in monastic schools. If so, the medieval Latin beast flytings may owe something after all to popular poetry and practices. Perhaps the flytings should be admired as remnants of what once was, but has perished: mime plays in which monks donned animal masks.

The beast flytings and debates add a new perspective on the beast literature that preceded the *Ecbasis captivi*. If the theory that the beast dialogues were staged could be verified, they would be especially illuminating for the eleventh-century poem; for the *Ecbasis captivi* appears to have been designed for declamation, with one reader for each animal or for each pair of animals (one in the outer story and one in the inner). The beast flytings and debate poems might have provided impetus for the fierce dialogues in the *Ecbasis captivi* and *Ysengrimus*, and even for the trial scenes in the Renard cycle (Graf).

Even if the beast dialogues are not the precious remains of medieval Latin theater that they seem to be, they increase our understanding of the contexts in which later medieval Latin beast poems were written. Whereas most of the early narrative beast poems are linked with the courts of rulers or bishops, the dialogues are connected with monasteries and schools. The *Ecbasis captivi*, *Ysengrimus*, and *Speculum stultorum*—the three longest of the later medieval Latin beast poems—share both these links and connections.

6. The Calf-Monk and Wolf-Monk in Performance

Introduction to the *Ecbasis captivi*

The *Ecbasis captivi* has been scrutinized intensely since its discovery in 1834 (Knapp 1979a, 1–39). The reasons for this attention are not hard to see. Besides being the longest, it is also the most challenging of the beast poems written through the eleventh century. The four most salient features of the *Ecbasis captivi* are its artful style of quotation, envelope structure, Easter spirit, and dramatic arrangement. Although this combination is unique, the individual features were anticipated in earlier medieval Latin beast poetry.

The *Ecbasis captivi* is a Latin poem of 1229 mostly leonine hexameters. Although dates of composition throughout the tenth and eleventh centuries have been proposed (for the tenth, Ross 274, Vinay 1949, 234–52; Scalia 241; for the late eleventh, Knapp 1979a, 5–7), the poem was most likely composed between 1043 and 1046 (Erdmann; Trillitzsch 15–18). The name of the author is unknown (contrast Michel, rebutted by Brunhölzl 1961, Langosch, Lehmann 1958, Reindel, Steinen 1957–58). If we make the risky assumption that the fiction of the poem corresponds exactly to the poet's life story, then he was born in the Vosges and underwent at least part of his novitiate at the monastery of Saint-Evre in Toul (Trillitzsch 10–14; cp. Knapp 1979a), the library of which is known to have contained most of the authors that the poet cited (Glauche 93–95). But the poet seems also to have been at home in Trier.

The poem survives only in Brussels, Bibliothèque Royale, MS. 10615–729, folios 187^r–191^v, and MS. 9799–809, folios 130^r–134^v. The first manuscript was probably written around the middle of the twelfth century in the monastery of St. Eucharius-Matthias in Trier (K. Manitius 1955); the second was copied from the first later in the twelfth century (Strecker 1935, 491–98; Trillitzsch 26; contrast Comerci 1979, 7–30). In both manuscripts the poem is grouped with school texts (Voigt 1875, 68) such as Aldhelm's riddles and the reworkings of Avian's fables by the Poeta Astensis.

The style of the poem is what first meets the eye in reading. The *Ecbasis captivi* is replete with lines and phrases from the classics of pagan and Christian Latin poetry (ed. Strecker 1935, pp. 46–51): over 250 lines and phrases quoted or adapted from Horace; about a hundred from Prudentius and fifty from Vergil; over twenty lines apiece from Juvencus, Sedulius, and Venantius Fortunatus; and eight lines each from Ovid and Arator. This itemization leaves out quotations from a dozen poems, from which only a few lines were taken, and from prose works, such as the Benedictine Rule and the Bible (Schumann 1936). The many quotations give the poem an extraordinary texture. Although the style has struck many readers as crabbed and has been criticized harshly (Knapp 1979a, 20), the poet deserves admiration for his ability to create leonine hexameters by rearranging lines written in unrhymed classical meters.

The allusiveness of the *Ecbasis captivi* calls to mind the earlier medieval Latin beast poems, which profited from reminiscences as a means of simultaneously demonstrating seriousness, attaining authority (borrowed feathers!), testing knowledge, achieving audience solidarity, and last but not least, earning laughter. Like many of the early medieval Latin beast poems, the *Ecbasis captivi* borrows freely from all sorts of literature in which animals are important. Thus it incorporates animal epitaphs, beast lore from the *Physiologus* and from Christian symbolism, and animals from the Bible, as well as verses and phrases from Horatian beast fables, animal riddles, and bird poems.

Also like many earlier medieval Latin beast poems, the *Ecbasis captivi* compounds elaboration in its style with intricacy in its narrative structure: it encloses an inner story (392–1009, 1016–97) within an outer one (69–391, 1010–15, 1098–223), which it boxes in turn between a prologue (1–68) and an epilogue (1224–29). In brief, the outer story tells of a calf who escapes one Holy Saturday from his stall only to fall into the clutches of a wolf, who leads him to his den and prepares to eat him. The calf requests and receives a stay of this sentence until the following day. Soon after daybreak on Easter Sunday, the herd to which the calf belongs arrives outside the cave of the wolf. The wolf assures his henchmen (or henchbeasts!), the otter and the hedgehog, that he will win the battle, provided that the fox has no part in it. At the request of his two allies, the wolf explains that his fear of the fox goes back to a dispute that once took place between his grandfather and the fox. His account of this dispute, which makes up the inner story, is a version of "The Sick Lion, Fox, and Flayed

Courtier" tale that appears in "The Sick Lion" and *Ysengrimus*. Once the outer story resumes, the wolf suffers a rapid series of misfortunes that culminates in his death through the fox's craftiness.

Although the extensive quotation and eccentric narrative outline have been treated as side-issues in interpretation of the poem, they are in fact vital to the meaning of the *Ecbasis captivi*. The style, structure, and content of the poem constitute one unified fabric. My reading entails a minute examination of the light that the original contexts of quoted lines shed on their function in the eleventh-century poem. I use this information to explain how the inner and outer stories complement each other thematically.

In reconciling the two parts of the *Ecbasis captivi*, I also pay attention to the ways in which Easter, the occasion on which the poem was intended to be read aloud, inspirited the theme of the poem. The paschal tone of the *Ecbasis captivi* is as decisive a feature of the poem as are its style and structure (Surdel 1989). Less important to my case is the manner in which the poem would have been delivered: a very strong argument has been advanced that it was designed for recitation by a small group of readers, in the manner of a dramatic performance or play reading (Gompf). This argument can be buttressed by pointing out the many instances of recitation and chanting within the poem.

Unlike the other early beast poems, the *Ecbasis captivi* begins with a long prologue in which the poet gives several indications of the nature of the poem. He expresses discontent at the hardships of verse composition, the cavils of his foes, and his inadequacies as a poet. These considerations have discouraged him from trying his hand at theological or historical poetry, he declares. Instead, he writes what he calls a lying composition (40, "mendosam cartam": Ross 267, n. 6) and a fable (*fabella*: according to Fechter 6, n. 11, "a beast fable").

At the end of the prologue, he leaves further tantalizing and bewildering clues to the nature of the poem. He writes that he will tell the story of his youth in the form of a story of a calf. Finally, he will "weave" the story "not with a simple thread" ("non simplo stamine", 68). This textile metaphor could be merely a commonplace taken from past poetry (cf. Venantius Fortunatus, *Carmen* 2.9.53; Tatwine, introduction, ed. de Marco 1: 167; Eugenius Vulgarius, "Comic Visions" 31A.2; Hrotsvitha, *praefatio* to the legends, ed. Homeyer 37; Egbert of Liège, *Fecunda ratis Prora* 1507–8, ed. Voigt 192). More likely, the phrase refers to any one or more of three interweavings: of the narrative structures of the outer and inner stories, of fiction and the poet's autobiography, or of newly composed verses and lines gathered from past poetry. In the last case, "not with a simple thread" would allude to the etymology of the cento, a "patchwork" sewn together from the verse of other poets. The *Ecbasis captivi* has this patchwork quality.

The quotations have elicited three reactions in *Ecbasis captivi* scholarship. At first, in an anachronistic application of modern beliefs about individual authorship, they were regarded as ill-concealed evidence of rank plagiarism: the author "plundered" lines to simplify the task of composition (Voigt 1875, 26–27; Wilmotte 1918, 2; Mozley 1965, 136). This judgment is unfair, since it rests on a misuse of the term *plagiarism*. A quotation constitutes a plagiarism when one person lifts the words of another consciously, but stealthily and without acknowledgment. This definition does not describe the activity of the *Ecbasis captivi* poet, who quoted ostentatiously and who, because he had to rearrange the quoted lines to produce leonine hexameters and to fit the syntax of new contexts, made his work harder rather than easier by quoting.

More recently, the quotations have been regarded as tasteful ornaments to the style of the *Ecbasis captivi* but as irrelevant to the meaning of the poem (Billerbeck). This view can be refuted by examining quotations whose original contexts are crucial to a full understanding of the action in the *Ecbasis captivi*. The most convincing is a line taken from Symphosius's ham riddle (discussed above, Chapter 1). Another example occurs at the start of the inner story (392): to grasp the sequence of events, the reader is apparently expected to know that spring is the time of year indicated in the biblical passage (2 Samuel 11.1) to which the line alludes. These two instances signal that the eleventh-century poet pulled lines from past poetry for more than their beautiful language. He trusted that his audience would recall how certain quoted lines were first used and that it would bring this information to bear on the *Ecbasis captivi*.

From an early date the borrowings have been seen as parodic (Peiper 99). As customarily defined in English, *parody* implies mockery or criticism: a parodist cites past poetry primarily to ridicule its style and content. If parody is so understood, none of the borrowings in the *Ecbasis captivi* is "parodic." But rather than abandoning the term, *parody* should be broadened to describe citation or imitation of past literature which is not critical. Such noncritical parody achieves humor for the sake of entertainment rather than at the expense of the style of the original work (LeLièvre).

Noncritical parody is a better description of the *Ecbasis captivi* poet's technique. Unlike a critical parodist, he does not imitate earlier poets to mock them. Rather, he deepens his poem with undertones of their language and thought. Through quotations and allusions he invites comparisons between the contexts in the quoted poems and those in his own. If the contexts prove to be the same in atmosphere and tone, then such borrowings perform the positive function of supporting the new contexts. If the contexts betray a disjunction, then the borrowings undercut the new context, with either grave, humorous, or seriocomic implications. For example, the grave words of Vergil's Turnus (*Aeneid* 12.677), when uttered by the hedgehog in the *Ecbasis captivi* (698), in no way diminish the majesty of Vergil's epic, but rather highlight the pompousness of the beast who speaks them as he is dismissed to the kitchen. In other instances, the lines transferred to the eleventh-century poem have contexts with a serious, rather than comic, relevance to their new circumstances. Many of the quotations from Juvencus, Sedulius, and Prudentius provide a Christian backdrop to the actions of the calf and wolf. These quotations follow the pattern we have seen in Alcuin and Sedulius Scottus, among others.

The quotations in the *Ecbasis captivi* have been studied, not one after another as they arise in the text, but instead in groups determined by the author quoted. They have been of more assistance in finding the stance of the eleventh-century poet toward a given classical poet (usually Horace) than with illuminating events within the *Ecbasis captivi* (Ermini, Wilmotte 1937, Sorrento 145–46, Fechter 21–23, Billerbeck). As shown below, the quotations will be interpreted according to a different principle. They will be analyzed in the order of their appearance in the *Ecbasis captivi*. The circumstances in which they first come up will be used to illuminate their new functions, as if they were a commentary that the poet incorporated directly into his verse, a kind of gloss that the poet used in lieu of marginal or interlinear notes (Ziolkowski 1985b). Ultimately, they will help to determine how the two sections of the poem fit together, a problem that has not been resolved satisfactorily.

The full title of the poem is *Ecbasis cuiusdam captivi per tropologiam*. These five words continue to spark intense interest (Gülich; Comerci 1979, 1980), even though there is no proof that they originated with the author of poem. They occur only in the older manuscript of the poem, where they are misspelled: EC.BASIS CUIUSDAM CAPTIVI PER TOPOLOGIAM (ed. Strecker, note *ad loc.*). Because of the problems raised by *ecbasis* and the emendation *tropologia*, the ambiguity of the title has become a topos of *Ecbasis captivi* scholarship (K. Hauck 137; Michel 4; Strecker 1933, 485; Wattenbach and Holtzmann 1/2: 186–87). *Ecbasis* has been understood both in the sense of "exit or flight" (of the calf from the stall or from the wolf's den) and in the sense of "literary excursus or digression" (Kindermann 319–20). Although the manuscript reading *per topologiam* could be defended on the grounds that the poem achieves its effect "through the quotation of commonplaces" (Kindermann 320), the conjectural *per tropologiam* is generally preferred. The expression *per tropologiam*, found already in Augustine and Jerome (Blaise 1954, 831), would signal that the poem is allegorical or, put differently, that its literal significance is subordinate to a figurative one. Following this lead, critics have uncovered one allegory after another in the *Ecbasis captivi*.

In the main these readers adhere to two approaches. On the one hand are those who assume that the *Ecbasis captivi* is a historical allegory—that it satirizes specific individuals and events. Readers of this sort match animals with people either known from history or else hypothesized to have existed. On the other hand are those who, taking the poem to be a religious allegory, view the animals as monks and devils or as virtues and vices.

The readings of the poem as a historical allegory have seldom explained the basic movement of the poem, the linkage of inner and outer stories. On the contrary, they concentrate on a single animal at a time. They see the hedgehog as caricaturing a real person whose name happens to be unknown to us (Peiper 90; Seiler 1878, 298; Ross 271; Fechter 29), identify the fox with a real historical personage such as Poppo of Trier (Hoffmann), and propose that the wolf was a Lotharingian nobleman who held the poet hostage (Zarncke 123–25, Hoffmann). Readings based on such assumptions have been received quite unenthusiastically (Scalia).

The interpretations of the poem as a religious allegory follow an opposite procedure, since they aim to explain the overall meaning of the poem rather than the details of each scene. Most religious allegorical readings build from the premise that the wolf in the *Ecbasis captivi* represents the devil (Rathay 677; Seiler 1877, 366; Ebert 3: 283; Manitius 1: 617; Ehrismann 1: 371; Michel 36; Brinkmann 119). With this key, they open the door, although every such reading leads through a different portal. To one, the wolf is the devil, while the herd is the monks who save their wayward comrade from perdition (Seiler 1877, 366). To another, the calf is a monk; the wolf, desire for the world; and the herd, the other monks. In this schema, the world stands for the destruction of the soul and the cloister for the road to heaven (Ehrismann 1: 371). To a third, the steer that mauls the wolf embodies the abbot who leads the calf-monk back to the cloister (de Boor and Newald 2: 398–99).

The religious allegorical approaches suffer major defects of their own. Rather than examining the whole text closely, they generalize about the outer story alone (the exception is Brinkmann 2: 119). Even these broad inferences are flawed, because the religious allegories proceed from the misapprehension that the outer story is a variant of a biblical parable: specifically, a parable about a lamb captured by a wolf and then saved by the good shepherd (Voigt 1875, 56; Seiler 1877, 368–69; Ehrismann 1: 371; Misch 2/1: 467). Yet although the New Testament conception of the wolf in sheep's clothing (Matthew 7.15) and that of the lost sheep and shepherd (Matthew 18.12, Luke 15.4) may underlie the calf and wolf in the *Ecbasis captivi*, a single biblical parable featuring both the lamb and wolf does not exist (Strecker 1935, 498, n. 6).

A graver failing of the religious allegories is that they vacillate between historical and religious interpretation. One animal stands for an actual person or type of person (Seiler 1878, 298), while another represents a concept or an institution (Brinkmann 2: 119). To justify these swerves, the allegorical readings condemn the *Ecbasis captivi* as a poem that is impossible to read logically (Raby 1: 276; Fechter 13).

Whether religious or historical, the allegorical expositions fail to address the three most challenging features of the *Ecbasis captivi*. No reading has unraveled the nature of the relationship between the inner and the outer stories (Knapp 1979a, 12, 14). Whereas the historical readings minimize the discrepancies between the two parts (e.g., the hedgehog of the outer story is the same as that of the inner story), the religious ones ignore the inner story altogether. None of them scrutinizes the poet's extensive incorporation of verses from pagan and Christian poets and of allusions to the Bible and to *Benedict's Rule*. Lastly, none has broached the question of how the meaning of the poem is designed for a particular occasion, Easter.

There are many reasons to believe that the *Ecbasis captivi* was written to suit the spirit of Eastertide, perhaps even to be read on Easter Sunday. In the outer story, the action takes place during Easter Eve Vigil and on Easter. The outer-story wolf calls the calf his "festive paschal meal" (272), a statement that the horrified calf later repeats to his mother (1217). In the inner story, events culminate in an Easter banquet. The nightingale reads a long homily on the Passion (859–905); the celebration of Christ's resurrection is mentioned twice (935, 973), the birds are detected to intone "paschal praises" (946), and the assembled animals chant "Salve festa dies," a line that was well known from Easter hymns (977: Venantius Fortunatus, *Carmen* 3.9; *Cambridge Songs* no. 22, ed. Strecker 62–63).

Because Easter marks the end of the long Lenten abstinence, the *Ecbasis captivi* returns again and again to the dichotomy between feasting and fasting. Even the quotations bring up this opposition, since most of the verses from Horace come from the satire on gourmets and gourmands (*Satires* 2.4). In its structure the *Ecbasis captivi* is framed within mentions of the poet's hunger: in the prologue he complains that the rigors of poetic composition deprive him of food and drink (12), while in the epilogue he describes himself as "fierce with hungry teeth" (1228). He fills the intervening beast tale with incessant reminders of abstinence and indulgence. The outer story, put baldly, is about a wolf's thwarted plan to break a meat fast. Incidentally it touches upon dozens of delicacies in the wolf's vegetarian diet (165–73, 176–79). The inner story also dwells upon menus in loving detail (542–47, 1024–27).

Since the special concerns and customs of Lent and Easter permeate the surface of the stories told in the *Ecbasis captivi*, it is logical to wonder whether they lie behind the overall narrative structure of the poem. Could the lurch from the outer to the inner story mirror the passage from the era before the Crucifixion to the era afterward—from the Old to the New Law? Could the physical movements of the animals correspond to moments in the liturgy of Easter? Could the calf's imprisonment and the wolf's death state in animal terms the events of the Harrowing, with the release of captive souls from hell and the punishment of their wrongful captors? Through a close reading of the poem and its quotational gloss I hope to answer such speculations, while helping to redeem the lack of appreciation that the *Ecbasis captivi* has received as a work of art (Knapp 1979a, 9).

The Prologue

The prologue of the *Ecbasis captivi*, while by no means woven entirely of lines and phrases from earlier poetry, nonetheless contains many swatches in which quotations dominate the texture. The allusions strike a Horatian tone that pervades the entire poem. The second line contains a possible echo of Horace's *Ars poetica* 308, the fourth verse a definite quotation of *Satires* 1.9.2. Another eight lines bristle with still more recollections of Horace's poetry (compare *Ecbasis* 11 with *Satires* 1.10.57–58; 13–14 with *Satires*

1.10.71−72; 16 with *Satire* 1.10.6; 22 with *Satires* 1.10.1; 25 with *Satires* 1.4.134−35; 28 with *Epistle* 2.1.110; 31 with *Epistle* 2.1.111; 44 with *Satires* 2.4.48). At the same time, the author twice likens himself to animals, now to a dull-witted ass (7) and now to a restive calf (66−67). As in Leo's "Meter" (1−2) and Nigel's *Speculum stultorum* (58−80), animal analogies smooth the transition to the actual beast poem.

At the beginning of the prologue the author claims that he is writing to redeem his squandered youth, a time when he was enmeshed in frivolity and was "thinking nothing sound" (3). Later, knowing that people will be curious about his motives for putting together a fanciful beast story, he proposes to supply his own critical introduction, what a medieval scholar might have called an *accessus ad auctorem* (47−49). Subsequently, he gives a vivid picture of the manner in which he wasted his youth.

One day the poet was seated, as usual, watching others toiling "to gather wheaten fruit into great barns" (52). Because wheat was seldom cultivated in the eleventh century (Zarncke 115−19, Trillitzsch 110), this agricultural observation has aroused a literal-minded curiosity, but the poet hardly has in mind a real harvest. The last four words of the line come from the parable of the wheat and the tares (Matthew 13.30), as paraphrased in Sedulius's *Carmen paschale*. To underscore the biblical reference, the *Ecbasis captivi* poet adds the word for wheat (*triticeum*), which is not present in Sedulius's verse.

The parable of the wheat and tares describes the fates that await the faithful and the unfaithful. As the poet stared out his window, he received another message about faith. According to his memory, the people gathering wheat into barns afterward tended the grapevines. By the mention of vines he draws attention to the parable of the vineyard (Matthew 20.1−16), which was often discussed with that of the wheat and the tares. For instance, the Lenten season was expounded allegorically as the time for laying aside sluggishness by "tending the vine and sowing the seed"—that is, by caring for one's soul (Amalar 1.2.5, ed. Hanssens 2: 38).

The people who labor so diligently in the fields are not necessarily monks; they could be any persons who toil on behalf of monks, pilgrims, beggars, and orphans, and who carry out the errands assigned to them (57). They realize their faith actively, through good deeds. In contrast to such fruitfully engaged workers, the poet idled his life away in a monastery that he regarded as a prison.

Troubled by memories of a happier past, the poet wept aloud (60). The verse describing his lament is also found in Sedulius's *Carmen paschale*

(4.34), where it refers to the behavior of two blind men: Christ tells them that they will see, if only they have faith (Matthew 9.27–31). The verse quoted from Sedulius's poem is followed by a mention of a cautering iron, which apparently refers to a treatment of wayward monks stipulated in *Benedict's Rule* Chapter 28 (Trillitzsch 111). Finally, the poet compares himself with a withered tree: "Like a barren tree trunk, I was becoming equivalent to burnt wood" (65; cf. "Terence and His Mocker" 30–33). This is the third verse in the prologue garnered from Sedulius's Easter poem. Significantly, all three retell moments in the gospel of Matthew in which Christ espouses his views on faith and disbelief: "Every person who nurtures nothing fertile for God will become, like a barren tree trunk, equivalent to burnt wood" (4.52–53). Thus the original contexts of the three lines add a spiritual dimension to the poet's avowal that he wasted his youth.

From which insufficiency of the heart was the poet ailing? The answer lies in the concept of *acedia*, "spiritual torpor, sloth caused by despair" (Truc; Lot-Borodine). The poet's unhealthy state of mind (3) corresponds to accidie, which manifests itself in (Wenzel 10, 19): a feeling that one's soul is accomplishing no good works, a desire to go out to perform an act of charity (51–57), a disgust for the monastic cell (58), and ultimately, either a retreat to sleep or an escape from the monastery (as in the calf-monk's flight). All three images evoked in the prologue are found in the iconography of *acedia*: the cursed fig tree and parable of the vineyard emblemize the dangers of indolence, while the parable of the tares demonstrates how people fall prey to accidie (Wenzel 102, 111, 119). These images and allusions underline the poet's declaration that his disobedience and vagrancy as a young monk were stupid. The images, since they are followed immediately by the introduction of the calf, hint that the outer story will also tell of a rebellion and a conversion. After all, the poet affirmed earlier in the prologue (47–49) that the poem reflects his personal experiences.

After the barrage of references to Sedulius and to parables in Matthew, the author likens himself to a calf bound to a post: "And [I resembled] a wretched calf quite often bound to stakes: like it, I was restrained by the reins of the fathers" (66–67). What were the author's reasons for drawing this comparison? The simile suits his policy of quoting whenever possible, since it quotes a pen test (*probatio pennae*). Equally important, the comparison could bring to mind two special monastic uses of the word *calf*. According to one use, young monks clever at reading and singing were designated calves, whereas their less skillful peers were asses

(Egbert of Liège, *Fecunda ratis Prora* 327, ed. Voigt 72). For the poet to term himself a calf in this sense would clash with his earlier assertion that he was known as an ass (7). He is likelier to have intended the word in its other sense, which equated disobedient monks with calves: "untamed calves, ever kicking up their heels against the goad of monastic discipline, cannot easily be joined to the Lord's plow under the yoke of monastic rule" (Simon of Saint-Bertin, *Gesta Abbatum Sancti Bertini Sithiensium*, p. 655). The notion of monastic discipline lies behind the phrase "restrained by the reins of the fathers" (67; cf. 133, 748), if "the fathers" refers to "monastic fathers," that is, abbots. Promising to relate the story of the calf and implying that it will parallel his own autobiography, the author brings the prologue to a finish.

The Outer Story (Part 1)

In the older manuscript of the *Ecbasis captivi* the outer story begins with a large initial letter (69; cf. 1, 353). The narrator first dates the events (Easter Sunday of the year 812) and then describes the predicament of the calf (74–80). Although his choice of Easter Sunday is demonstrably relevant to the events of both the outer and inner stories, no satisfactory explanation has been offered for the mention of 812 (contrast ed. Zeydel 9). Perhaps such a remote date could have had the same effect as "once upon a time"—the effect of fixing events in a long ago past when the impossible could happen. Chaucer chose to set the *Nun's Priest's Tale* in just such a vague but distant past when animals could speak: "For thilke tyme, as I have understonde, / Beestes and briddes koude speke and synge" (VII, 2880–81).

Just as earlier the poet opposed his own wretched fruitlessness to the exertions of people harvesting outside, here he compares a miserable calf with vigilant herdsman. In drawing this contrast he fuses typical expressions from Vergil with equally representative ones from Christian poets to create a distinctive idiom of his own. For instance, the phrases *pastores ovium* (shepherds) and *tardi subulci* (slow swineherds, 74) derive from the *Eclogues* (1.21, 10.19). In contrast, *cura pervigili* (with ever-vigilant concern, 77) has an unmistakably Christian origin and cast, particularly in conjunction with the words for herdsmen and shepherds (Prudentius, *Contra orationem Symmachi* 2.1022; Venantius Fortunatus, *Carmen* 5.3.21). As a line opening in medieval Latin poetry, *pervigili cura* became an attribute of sincere ecclesiastics (*Epistolae Tegernseenses Carmen* 42.5, ed. Strecker, p. 122).

With moans and tears, the calf entreats Jesus for two boons: that the keeper of the stable take off his bonds and that he be allowed to taste milk once more from his mother's udder. Just as the calf's desire to escape from his bonds resembles a novice's impulse to throw off monastic restraints, so the calf's thirst for milk brings to mind a monk's hunger for the milk products forbidden during Lent (Thurston 43–45). Rather than wait for his prayers to be answered, he bites and licks the thongs that hold him, until eventually he breaks loose. Now he is free to roam the meadows, to strike out where he wishes (92–94): "Greater freedom is now allowed the beast, whether he prefers to set out on the path to the left or to the right, to take a rest or continue his work." In Prudentius's *Contra orationem Symmachi* (1.335–39), these three lines form part of an affirmation that people are free to decide their destiny, by complying with God's will or by rebelling. In later Christian symbolism, the right was regarded as the direction chosen by godly people and the left by evil ones (*Cambridge Songs* no. 12.3b–4b, ed. Strecker 37–38; Hrabanus Maurus, *De Universo* 6.1, ed. PL III.158C–59B; Notker Balbulus, *Gesta Karoli Magni Imperatoris* 3, ed. Haefele 4; Chrétien de Troyes, *Perceval* 37–46, ed. Roach 2). Thanks to the Prudentian undertone and the Christian iconography, this passage demonstrates that the calf has brought himself to a decisive crossroads (contrast Comerci 1979, 65).

Will the calf turn to the right or to the left? Although the poet is too subtle to make the outcome explicit, subsequent events suggest that the calf selects the wrong direction. He sets off for the wood, where he soon meets a forester, the wolf. The wolf hails him and intones a hymn of greeting, as a proper monk should, but his song of praise (presumably a howl, like the howl of the wolf to which Alcuin also alludes lightheartedly in "The Cock and Wolf") perverts Christian usage (97–103). After a moment of seeming piety, the wolf proposes to make his guest into an animal blood-sacrifice on the grounds that every sin, such as the calf's, merits punishment. The wolf's way of behaving and thinking is emphatically un-Christian. He conceives of sacrifice as blood-sacrifice, even though blood-sacrifice was replaced when Christ instituted the eucharist. Likewise, his notion of sin is that which existed prior to the first Easter, when Christ inaugurated the New Law of mercy (Amalar, *Liber Officialis* 1.12.51).

Once he has escorted the calf to his lair, the wolf enlarges his greeting and threat. He announces that the calf should feel privileged to slake his bloodthirstiness, since he is in his third month of abstinence from meat.

The span of time alludes to the common monastic custom of commencing fasting with the third Sunday before Lent (Septuagesima), with the effect that by Easter many monks would have been in their third month of fasting.

The breathtaking blasphemy of the wolf's plans is underscored through the tissue of quotations that holds together his speech:

> Dicito, quid venias, qua nos ratione revisas.
> Tu mihi nunc, sodes, optatus diceris hospes.
> Laudes dic superis, silve novus incola surgis,
> Tu recreare venis tenuatum corpus ab escis.
> Tercius est mensis, quod frustror nectare carnis,
> Nec biberam cratum pecudis de sanguine tinctum.
> Cum prorepserunt primis animalia terris,
> Mutum et pingue pecus nobis fabricaverat usus.
> Ordinis est virtus, placetur sanguine divus.
>
> (Lines 108–16)

Tell why you come, for what reason you visit us? If you wish, you will now be called a welcome guest by me. Praise the gods: you are becoming a new denizen of the forest. You come to restore by food a weakened body. It is the third month in which I have gone without the nectar of flesh, and I have not drunk a goblet tinged with the blood of a beast. When animals crept forth upon the primeval earth, necessity fashioned for us dumb and fat cattle. It is an excellence of the order that god should be appeased with blood.

The first line of the wolf's salutation echoes words with which the devils addressed Christ in Prudentius's *Apotheosis* 419, "Quid sis, quid venias; qua nos virtute repellas" ("What you are, why you come; with what power you drive us away"), whereas the end incorporates Horace's contention (*Satires* 1.3.99–106) that laws came into being after an epoch when men were brutish:

> *Cum prorepserunt primis animalia terris,*
> *mutum et turpe pecus*, glandem atque cubilia propter
> unguibus et pugnis, dein fustibus, atque ita porro
> pugnabant armis quae post *fabricaverat usus*,
> donec verba quibus voces sensusque notarent

nominaque invenere; dehinc absistere bello,
oppida coeperunt munire, et ponere leges,
ne quis fur esset, neu latro, neu quis adulter.

                    (Lines 99–106, emphasis added)

When animals crept forth upon the primeval earth, dumb and filthy
cattle, they fought for their fodder and shelter with nails and fists,
then with clubs, and so on until they fought with the weapons
which necessity fashioned later, until they discovered words and
names with which to make known their sounds and sentiments;
from this point they began to desist from war, to build towns,
and to lay down laws that no one should be a thief, a robber, or an
adulterer.

But in the maw of the wolf the lines are reconstructed to mean that cattle
were designed to be food for wolves, as they have been from the beginning
of time. Twisting two phrases from Horace (*Ars poetica* 42, *Satires* 2.3.206),
he asserts in the last line of his greeting that the sacrifice of the calf will
maintain the proper order of the world and please God. The latter phrase
was, in Horace's *Satires* (2.3.205–7), part of Agamemnon's insane boast of
having offered his own daughter to the gods: "'Verum ego ut haerentis
adverso litore navis / eriperem prudens *placavit sanguine divos*,' / nempe tuo,
furiose. 'meo, sed non furiosus'" ("'But I, in order to wrest away the ships
clinging to the hostile shore, wisely appeased the gods with blood.' To be
sure—with your own, you madman. 'With my own, but not a madman'").
In sum, this speech is as ominous on a covert, quotational level as the wolf's
shameless desire to drink a chalice of calf's blood is on an explicit level.

Adding to the congeries of clever quotations, the *Ecbasis captivi* poet
presents the physical and verbal reactions of the calf to the danger: "Incipit
hec vitulus, singultim pauca loquutus, / Infans namque pudor prohibebat
plura profari" (117–18, "The calf begins these words, speaking few in sobs,
for speechless shame prevented him from saying any more"). The comedy
is a sort familiar from Leo of Vercelli's "Meter": the poet describes the
sobbing little bovine in words taken from Horace's vignette of his own
behavior when he met Maecenas for the first time (*Satires* 1.6.56–57). The
tragedy is that the calf still suffers from the muddleheadedness that led
him into his desperate plight. He prays, not to Christ who liberated him
from his last captivity, but to Jupiter (119). Of all the expressions of worship in the poem, this is the only one to invoke a pagan deity ("Hercle"

in 444 is simply an exclamation), and its heathen qualities include the calf's oath to sacrifice a goat if he is freed. At this instant the calf appears no less amenable than the wolf to the practice of animal expiation.

Another element of humor in the calf's prayer is that it presents an animal not only praying to the gods, but even offering another animal as a victim: "Jupiter, ingentes qui das adimisque labores, / Peccatis noctem, quin fraudibus obice nubem. / Si redeam gratis, grates exolvero divis, / His et pro meritis dabitur caper omnibus aris" ("O Jupiter, you who give and take away vast toils, spread night over my sins and a cloud over my offenses. If I should return unharmed, I will give thanks to the gods, and in recognition of these merits a goat will be sacrificed on every altar," 119–20). Yet the original contexts of the three lines quoted in this passage are anything but jolly. The first verse, in Horace *Satires* 2.3.288 (*"iuppiter, ingentis qui das adimisque* dolores"; emphasis added), mocks a mother who vows to have her child stand naked in the Tiber, if only the gods cure him of the quartan chills. Horace concludes that the woman's approach is deranged, since for the child to recover would only put him once more in peril of ill health:

> "O Jupiter, you who give and take away vast sorrows," says the mother of a child who has been lying abed for five months, "if the quartan fever leaves my child, then on the morning of the day on which you appoint a fast, he will stand nude in the Tiber." If good luck or the doctor raises the sick child from critical illness, his crazy mother will kill him by setting him on the frozen bank and will bring back his fever. With which illness has her mind been stricken? With fear of the gods. (2.3.288–95)

The first borrowing is followed directly by another from Horace (*Epistle* 1.16.62, "Noctem peccatis et fraudibus obice nubem"), in which a sanctimonious thief, pretending to invoke Apollo, instead calls upon Laverna, the patroness of thieves:

> This supposedly good man, whom the entire forum and tribunal watches, whenever he placates the gods with a pig or ox, says aloud loudly "Father Janus! Apollo!" But fearing to be heard he mouths the words: "Beautiful Laverna, grant me the power to deceive, grant me to pass as a just and holy man, spread night over my sins and a cloud over my offenses." (1.16.57–62)

To complete the undercutting of the calf's prayer, the last line is plucked from the *Contra orationem Symmachi* (1.129, "His nunc pro meritis Baccho caper omnibus aris"), where Prudentius disparaged the god Bacchus as being no more than a man with an overblown reputation (1.122–30, trans. Thomson):

> A young man of Thebes becomes a god because he has conquered India and comes wantoning in triumph for his victory, bringing home the gold of the vanquished nation, and in the pride of his spoils abandoning himself to indulgence in company with his emasculate following, in his lust for wine soaking himself with many a draught and with the Falernian juice that foams from his jewelled cup besprinkling the dripping backs of the wild beasts that draw his chariot. In recognition of these merits a goat is now sacrificed to Bacchus on every altar.

The original contexts of all three quoted lines discredit the very act of petition in which the calf is engaged, and suggest that the calf itself is either mad or hypocritical.

After the aside, the calf responds openly (the passage is labeled "Responsio eiusdem publica" ["Public response of the same (character)"] in the margin of the manuscripts) to the wolf's proposal to devour him. In this speech he confesses to having committed a youthful sin, admits his guilt (125–26), and seems keenly aware that he erred in disobeying his master (126). The master was on one level the herdsman of the calf's stable, who was responsible for the bonds on his neck (84 and 127), and on another the abbot of the monastery, where the "calf" was a disaffected novice (124: *Benedict's Rule*, chap. 2; Gompf 35). In his recalcitrance, the calf yielded to a special feeling (127), perhaps a physical lust (this circumstance would explain the repeated quotations from Prudentius's passage against abuses of touch: Ross 272–73), and worked his way loose. His gravest error was to go to the wolf's den (128). By forsaking the protection of the master, the calf-monk put himself in jeopardy. Knowing this, he accepts blame for his death, which he sees on the horizon (128–29). Nonetheless, he refuses to perish without a struggle. He wheedles the wolf for a truce (133) and for the forgiveness stipulated in *Benedict's Rule* (chap. 24 and 28).

Despite many nefarious habits and desires, the wolf remains enough of a monk (98, 185, passim) to honor the calf's request, because God is so disposed (136); but in return he demands a kiss. The calf takes exception to this request: "Why do you pretend to be an ally and why do you greet me with supposedly friendly deceit?" (139). As a defenseless calf he is naturally uneasy at the thought of being so close to a wolf's deadly jaws. But there is more to this scene than the natural fear of a calf for a wolf. As a monk, however misdirected he may be, the calf feels uncomfortable about receiving the kiss of peace (*pax*) on a day and during a time of year when it was often omitted from the liturgy. Out of abhorrence for the kiss of betrayal that Judas gave to Christ, the kiss was left out at mass on Maundy Thursday and during the Easter Vigil (Amalar, *Liber Officialis* 1.13.18; Eisenhofer and Lechner 194, 212; Perella 27–29). Judas was the person who, to follow one exegete, "by a bestial joining of lips expresses a sentence of death rather than a covenant of love" (Ambrose, *Exameron* 6.9.68, ed. Schenkl 256.13–14). The *Ecbasis captivi* poet does not leave the resemblance between the wolf's kiss and Judas's to the reader's imagination. Instead, he brings it home through the quotational gloss: the calf's question repeats verbatim Sedulius's *Carmen paschale* 5.66, a verse that censures Judas for his betrayal of Jesus through a kiss. Thus the *Ecbasis captivi* expresses through a quotation the sentiment that one of the *Roman de Renart* poets stated less periphrastically: "And surely it was a grievous sin / To attack the titmouse, his close kin, / Trying to lure her with a kiss— / Judas betrayed God just like this!" (5a.759–62, trans. Terry 78).

To mollify the calf (and to amuse the hungry monkish audience of the *Ecbasis captivi*!), the wolf guides their discourse to the subject of food. He promises the calf that his two assistants, the hedgehog and otter, will bring humble but healthy fare for dinner. Then he directs the calf to take cheer and live well while he can, for the calf's fate has been decided: the calf is "buried by the law of hell, a victim of Pluto who shows no mercy" (153–54: cf. Horace, *Ode* 2.3.24). Even at his most benign, the wolf is hell incarnate, holding the calf captive by infernal privilege.

The calf, still too confused to act sensibly, samples eagerly the assorted foods that the wolf brings to him. To explain the emotions motivating the calf, the poet inserts two verses from the *Hamartigenia* (325–26), in which Prudentius admonishes the reader not to overeat late into the night and, above all, not to abuse the sense of touch. With sly humor, the poet also packs the passage with lines from Horace's *Satires* 2.6 about the country mouse's ill-fated visit to the city mouse (Wilmotte 1937, 263–64; Trillitzsch 114–15). Like the country mouse, the calf enters the wolf's cave with naïve expectations of pleasure but instead narrowly escapes death.

As the night wears on, the wolf's errand boys, the otter and hedgehog, return with an impressive farrago of fish, spices, and fruits (164–79). Once the animals have sat down to feast, the wolf reminds his servants that he has lived as a monk for seven years. By monastic life he means adherence to the letter of the dietary code. His elaborate Lenten menu illustrates how literally he construes the laws. Although he touches no meat, he gluts himself with every imaginable sort of fish and fruit. Such perversion of the spirit of Lenten fasting was censured and satirized from the early years of the Church (Thurston 35).

To thank his servants for upholding him in his regimen, the wolf bequeathes his property to them. The hedgehog and otter, although properly delighted, are still perplexed that a calf is in the den. The wolf explains that the young animal, having spurned his stable and come to the cave, is now "surrendered into my control" ("nostris addictus habenis," 194). The phrase, recalling the first appearance of the calf and author ("patrum frenatus habenis" ["restrained by the reins of the fathers"], 67), implies that the calf has gone from a protective subjugation to a potentially lethal one.

The wolf admits readily that he is in the wrong (195–96). His one self-justification is that he acts out of love, but his love is no more than a craving to slake his wolfish thirst for blood (197–99). His vow that he will drink "from a chalice of blood" (198) crudely literalizes the canon of the mass and the biblical passage from which the canon of the mass derived (Luke 22.20). Both the Bible text of Christ's words and the words of the mass were prominent during the Easter Vigil services, where they were contrasted with the chalice and blood of the Old Law which they replaced: "The chalice of the Old Testament overflowed with the blood of dumb animals" (Amalar, *Liber officialis* 3, *Epist.* 4). To heighten the disparity between the Old and New Laws, the section of Exodus dealing with the dispensation of the Old Law was read aloud during the Vigil (Righetti 2: 251, 265). In Exodus 24.5 the Old-Law sacrifices were described as "pacific victims of calves to the Lord." The wolf has in mind just such an Old-Law sacrifice of a calf; in other words, he plans to celebrate the eucharist with real blood (Vinay 1949, 245–46).

The wolf's selfishness taints even his generosity to his two servants, for he soon makes apparent that in return for the gifts he expects the otter and hedgehog to keep watch over the captive and murder him if he attempts flight. Fortunately for the calf, the otter instead intends to be a "foresighted guardian" (204) as concerned for the calf's well-being as the "guards" (76) from whom the calf made his misguided escape. Like the earlier guards, the otter offers the calf protection rather than the oppression that was proverbially the lot of domestic animals which fell into the clutches of wolves (Köhler 187–88).

After posting the otter and hedgehog as sentinels, the wolf whiles away the evening in a travesty of a proper Easter Vigil. Rather than think of Christ's Resurrection, he listens to the hedgehog strum a zither and sing of pagan Rome. The hedgehog's selection of material contrasts with typical Easter Vigil readings, which were chosen carefully to highlight the fundamentals of Christianity; indeed, the readings for acolytes were not allowed to include even Old Testament selections, for fear of distracting them from newly learned truths (Amalar, *Liber Officialis* 1.21.3–4). With the help of the hedgehog's music, the wolf falls fast asleep—even though the Easter Vigil was supposed to last the entire night or, at the very least, until midnight (Righetti 2: 252).

As the wolf snores (215), the otter offers the calf entertainment better suited to the occasion. Over food and wine, they read the *Restoration of a Fallen Man* (*Reparatio lapsi*), the Latin version of John Chrysostom's homily on a young man who succumbed to vice but later was saved (Looshorn). In a poem in which the original contexts of quotations often amplify the significance of their new contexts, it is not surprising to find that the mention of a title is meant to recall the contents of the entire work. After this edifying recitation, the calf prays to God, who brings "consolation to those in bondage" (223), to deliver him from the hellish pit (224) so that he may praise God and see his parents once more. The prayer reminds one ironically of the calf's earlier entreaty to be released from the "bonds" of his stable, since his present bondage makes his former one look appealing.

No sooner have the calf and otter finished worship than the wolf awakes in shock from a nightmare. Eager to have the dream interpreted, he relates it to his monastic brothers (229). A wasp, gnats, dog-flies, locusts, and two hornets were swarming around him, trying to bite him. The calf and fox were both present, singing "as if a skilled hand were directing the measures of the song" (237). Having heard the dream, the otter proves his oneiromantic skills. He assures the wolf that he need not fret, if only he lets the calf go, but if he withholds the young beast, he will damn himself (241). The "herd" of flies signifies the animals in the calf's herd who will rend the wolf limb from limb; the stings of the wasp represent the forces of death, the two hornets the calf's two parents. The fox's jubilation is the antithesis of the sorrow that the wolf will feel, because the calf "bound by an unpleasant fetter" (248) will escape once the battle is under way.

At the end of his interpretation, the otter distills the message of the dream into a single phrase: "What good will you bestow? —That is the meaning of the dream" (250). But the wolf, though fearful, refuses to part with the calf, even if King Henry should give him fifty pigs and "the same number of fatted calves" (255). This statement, besides being an amusing hyperbole, recalls the "fatted calf" thrice mentioned in the parable of the prodigal son (Luke 15.23–30), the fatted calf butchered to mark the home-coming of the wayward son. The wolf has no intention of treating the errant monk in his cave like the wayward son in the parable, and he has a ready excuse for his conduct. He feels that the calf, by taking nourishment in the realm of his captor, surrendered all claim to personal liberty. Like Hades in the myth of Persephone, he adheres to the primitive belief that a soul could not return from the dead once its possessor had consumed food in the kingdom of the dead (MacCulloch 7).

To compensate for the food that the animal has eaten, the wolf in-tends to go better than an eye for an eye: he insists upon fourfold resti-tution (261). The word *fourfold* is a reminiscence of 2 Samuel 12.1–14 (cf. Exodus 22.1): in a similitude that a prophet addresses to King David, a rich man takes a lamb from a poor man. Moved by the story, David orders the rich man to be executed and the poor man to be awarded four lambs. David was not aware at first that the story was meant to rebuke him for his own behavior in having had a man murdered so that he could commit adultery with the wife (Augustine, *De doctrina* 3.21 [31], trans. Robertson 97–98). The scene in 2 Kings is echoed in the New Testament in the heart-felt conversion of Zacchaeus, who promised to Christ: "If I have de-frauded anyone of anything, I restore it fourfold" (Luke 19.8). The wolf is far from the penitence of either King David or Zacchaeus. If need be, he himself will officiate as priest and sing the Psalms (262) to speed the ser-vice. To which service is he referring? Presumably to the blessing of the paschal lamb. The medieval Church encouraged lay people to bring their eggs and meats, especially lambs, to parish priests on Easter morning; for then the first meat enjoyed after Lent would be hallowed (Thurston 477–79). For the wolf, the benediction is only a final technical nicety be-fore he may once again eat flesh and blood.

The narrator reveals at this point that, in the wolf's den, the usual priest was the hedgehog (263–66). The hedgehog-priest is a dwarf (al-though men with this deformity were forbidden to be priests: Leviticus 21.18–20) and, no less, a dwarf dressed in feathery clothes (267: Pruden-tius, *Hamartigenia* 295). To this dubious character the wolf issues exhaus-tive instructions for the preparation of the calf, whose "nectary flesh" is to be his "festive paschal meal" (272). But whereas an essential element of Easter was the sharing of the sacrifice (Luke 22), the wolf insists that his offering not be divided in any way (270).

This wolf has wearied of his vegetarian life: in a remark that many monks would have appreciated (especially toward the end of Lent!), he urges that beans be left to barbarians (Trillitzsch 120; Ross 270). He wants to resume his old habits (285–86): "One attains no honor in that way: I prefer the old custom, I will follow this custom, I will now revert to my former habits." The line and a half in which he states his intention are taken from Prudentius's portrait of a stubborn adherent of the Old Law (*Contra Symmachum* 2.274, 293), the law of physical rather than spiritual offering. The quotation from Prudentius's *Contra Symmachum* is soon followed by others from his *Apotheosis* and *Cathemerinon*, all of them uprooted from their original contexts and made to express a wholly different meaning (289–92): "From it I will draw juice and health from its rich fluid, ruddiness appears in my face, paleness withers away from my face, an appealing taste, a fragrant scent, a fitting delight; I will try everything to dispel the impurity from my breast." In Prudentius the first verse in this section describes the Holy Ghost, from which the earth draws sap and salvation (*Apotheosis* 696), but the wolf has in mind sucking juice from the calf's flesh. In the second line the wolf, claiming that his face will turn ruddy again once he has eaten the calf, uses terms with which the fourth-century poet extolled the virtue of fasting (*Cathemerinon* 8.26–28). In the next line, praising the effects of meat-eating, the wolf takes three phrases that Prudentius applied to Christ in *Apotheosis* 395–96. From the same poem (*Apotheosis* 231) is quoted part of the wolf's last sentence, about his aspirations toward purity: in its initial context the first two words referred to Christ, who endures all stages of human life so that he may resurrect all people who have died.

Without exception, the Prudentian settings of the verses cited make us suspect that the wolf's scheme runs counter to Christian custom, and the Easter liturgy confirms this intuition. Throughout the Middle Ages the liturgy prescribed set Bible readings for Easter (Baumstark 46–54). One of these was the twelfth book of Exodus, which documents the inception of the Passover feast. Exodus specified that the Passover lamb be neither raw nor boiled, but rather roasted; and yet the wolf demands with vehemence that the calf not be cooked in any way (271). According to medieval exegetes, the eating of raw lamb signified a heedless rebuffing of Christ (Hrabanus Maurus, *De Universo* 22.1, ed. PL 111.592AB). The wolf's rejection of salvation comes into still sharper focus when, after insisting that his Easter victim be prepared improperly, he balks at sharing it with anyone (270). His greed is simultaneously a laughable act of wolfishness and a damning refusal to be unselfish with the eucharist.

The otter, who has already admonished the wolf not to threaten the calf, calls his machinations "illegal" and "perverse" (293). After lauding the wolf's seven years of temperance, the otter scolds him for now "spurning holy monkhood" (302). The wolf, on the verge of committing a crime and subverting the holiest principles (305–7), is a monk in name only. A man of God ought to be vigilant and "bound with a very large fetter" (308). The phrase is a reminder of the calf's first servitude from which he so rashly fled and also, by contrast, of the calf's new shackles; for sixty lines earlier the otter described the calf as "bound by an unpleasant fetter" (248). Now the otter explains that the monastic fetters are the behavior set forth in *Benedict's Rule* (309–11): all belongings are communal, and a brother should not do unto another what he would not have done unto him. The wolf, who does not live by these tenets, will perish "according to the law of the plunderer" (312) and will die "a death of brigands" (313). These expressions, in conjunction with the words "by canon law" ("judicio canonum," 313), pertain not to secular codes for the treatment of common thieves but to canon law for un-Christian behavior. They point to a spiritual shortcoming of the wolf, perhaps like the hard-heartedness of the unrepentant robber crucified alongside Christ.

The wolf as much as admits the inadequacy of his soul when he says that he has deaf ears (315; cf. 1033). In contrast to blindness, deafness was regarded in Christian symbolism as an intentional disobedience against God's bidding (Hrabanus Maurus, *De Universo*, ed. PL III.75C); as the New Testament indicated (Matthew 11.5, Luke 7.22), deafness was an ailment easily cured by faith. To make clear that he has no plan to repent, the wolf then makes what might be an obscene allusion to the calf (316–17): "for the loins of an ass will be joined to the tail of the calf; thus Mother Nature has bidden us to pass our days." Although the second line quotes Lucan 10.238, its original context provides no clues to the meaning of the exceptionally enigmatic passage. The first could refer somehow to Deuteronomy 22.10 "Thou shalt not plough with an ox and an ass together." At any rate, the otter finds the lines somehow vulgar and upbraids the wolf but is only rebuked in return for his trouble. As a result, he decides not to waste any further breath in trying to regenerate such an obstinate beast (318–21). The wolf has had, and has declined, his chance to reform. What happens to him from this juncture is his fault, and his fault alone.

At this instant the setting shifts from the wolf's den to the calf's stable. A very pleasant day is breaking, one that promises to fulfill the otter's earlier assurance to the calf that "an hour of grace that is not hoped for will arrive unexpectedly" (219). The herdsman (if the word *corniger* means "a man who carries a hunting horn" rather than a "horn-bearing steer": Trillitzsch 122) scours the stalls to see if any of his wards is missing. Just after the animals discover their loss, a dog comes and relates that he knows where the calf is to be found. He guides a troop of cattle toward the cavern.

The story of the dog's appearance and of the wolf's reaction to the army massed outside his cave forms a marvelous comic interlude. In an example of the poet's Bible wit, the dog purports to be the hunting dog of Esau (332–37). But the scene revolves around mock-epic rather than biblical humor. The cows who follow the dog are called infantry and cavalry. The noise that they create is expressed in a grandly Vergilian expression (cf. 352 with *Aeneid* 9.752): "There is a crash on earth, as if the whole world were tumbling down." Most amusingly, but also most ominously, the wolf is depicted as being "buried in sleep and wine" (353), just as the city of Troy on the eve of its destruction was described in *Aeneid* 2.265. This allusion is highlighted in the older manuscript by being written with a large initial.

Although fearful at the prospect of a battle, the wolf puts on a show of courage for his two allies and urges them to take heart, since their citadel is impregnable. Unless the wily fox tricks them, all will turn out well, because they are mightier than their opponents. Rather than allaying the fears of the hedgehog and otter, however, this philosophy of "might is right" exacerbates them. The two beasts do not want to incur guilt by spilling the blood of their relatives. They wish to repay God with thanks, not with crass offenses, for the laws that He established. They berate the wolf: "Those things which you could not bestow, you held by a hostile law" (385). Their charge echoes the final words of the otter's dream interpretation: "What good will you bestow? —That is the meaning of the dream" (250).

As the first part of the outer story draws to a close, the *Ecbasis captivi* poet has established both on the surface and on the quotational level a sharp opposition between the wolf and the other animals, all of whom are monks. At stake is a calf, identified with the monk-poet in his early years, who yielded to despair and went astray. Unlike all the other animals, the wolf feels that the calf's one mistake is irrevocable and that it must be expiated through blood-sacrifice. Although the phrases "Old Law" and "New Law" are not used explicitly, such an antinomy describes the contrasting views of the wolf and the other animals. For the crisis to be resolved, the poet must prove that the New Law has primacy over the Old. In the inner story he endeavors to demonstrate in animal terms why the wolf's law is no longer valid and why the calf must be set free. As in the outer story, he strikes a balance between the earnestness of the legal-theological theme and the playfulness of the quotational style and animal characters.

The Inner Story

Immediately after speaking of God's laws, the otter and hedgehog ask to be told what caused the vendetta between the fox and wolf. The abruptness of the transition implies that they see an underlying connection between the two topics, divine law (384) and the old quarrel. In response, the wolf tells the inner story, the long tale of the conflict between his ancestor and the fox. Interestingly, the opening passage (392–96) contains, in lieu of allusions to classical and Christian poets, one possible reminiscence of the Old Testament and one of the New. The first line may allude to 2 Samuel 11.1, where the words indicate that the action takes place in the spring. If so, the line hints that the inner story, like the outer one, occurs during Eastertide. A bare four lines after the possible Old Testament allusion, the wolf makes a pointed New Testament allusion to set the stage for the story of the ailing lion-king (396–97): "A decree went out [*Exiit edictum*] that the beasts of the forest should run to the cave and bring anything healthful [or salvational] for the limbs of the sick lion-king." In the New Testament the first two words announce Caesar's order that a census be taken, the census that led to Christ's being born in Bethlehem (Luke 2.1): "And it came to pass, that in those days there went out a decree from Caesar Augustus, that the whole world should be enrolled." Apart from a reference to the Psalms and one Old Testament expression in the prologue, the *Ecbasis captivi* up to this point has drawn attention only to those parts of the Bible which record episodes in Christ's life: the miracle of the fig tree, the parable of the prodigal son, the tale of Zacchaeus, the parable of the wheat and tares, and the miracle of the blind man. Now, after almost four hundred lines, the poem suddenly and emphatically retreats to the time before Christ was born—in other words, to the time before the New Law.

The worlds of the inner and outer stories differ in spirit as well as in date. The lion-king is sick and the animal must bring remedies. In accordance with a newly instituted rule, the wolf is elected chamberlain and takes charge of the roll call (400–401: on the manuscript *decanie* and the emendation *decatie*, Trillitzsch 125; Zeydel 105). In his sedulous hunt for absentees he recalls the herder who searched for the calf (325–26), but the resemblance is only superficial. The one animal missing from the assembly is the wolf's archenemy, the fox. The wolf has no intention of saving his foe; on the contrary, he intends to murder her. By slandering the fox to the king, he arranges for her to be declared a most wanted criminal, to be killed on sight. If the fox is caught alive, the wolf plans to subject her to "marvels of torture" (407) before she dies. For this purpose he constructs a lofty gallows (although *crux* also means "cross" 408).

Only one beast at the court, the pard, cares enough for the fox to find her and warn her of the impending danger. The fox responds with a mixture of vulpine slyness and monastic devoutness: she prays with outstretched arms to the alpha and omega for salvation (414–15), but smilingly pretends not to believe in the pard's report. The phrase that describes the pard's placement of her arms is appropriated from Vergil's *Aeneid* 6.685 ("palmas utrasque tetendit"), where it records Anchises' response upon seeing Aeneas in the underworld. Long before the *Ecbasis captivi* poet, the expression caught the attention of centoists (Ricci 181–83), who used it to describe the cruciform position of prayer employed in both the liturgy and ascetic practice (Gougaud).

Nearly every time when the fox enters the scene of action in the *Ecbasis captivi*, she is both crafty and genuinely pious, on the one hand the age-old victor over the wolf and on the other the champion of righteousness; the ambivalence of the later *Roman de Renart* tradition, in which the fox is admired for being shrewd but deplored for being immoral, is already evident (Best). In this first look at the fox, her sanctity and monastic obedience are the keynote. She worships after eating and then, in accordance with *Benedict's Rule* (chap. 42, 48), falls silent. Once en route to the lion's court, the fox and pard recite Psalms, and finally they complete the entire Psalter. Although the normal monastic custom was to chant the entire Psalter in a week, it is not necessary to interpret the psalm-singing of the fox and pard as satirical exaggeration (Fechter 11; Gompf 38). Especially on Easter monks often recited the entire Psalter in a day, sometimes several times and sometimes in torturous postures (Le Déaut 156–66; Eisenhofer and Lechner 88; Righetti 2: 219).

The fox does more than recite Psalms; she also pours forth prayers (425), just as the virtuous otter prayed for the calf after their meal (216).

She asks Christ to be her helmet, calling to mind the "helm of salvation" in both the Old Testament (Isaiah 59.17) and the New (Ephesians 6.17, 1 Thessalonians 5.8), and to cast down the false witness (cf. 429 with Proverbs 6.19).

The richest of the Old Testament allusions occurs not in the fox's speech but in the narrator's account of her preparation to enter the lion's cave: "She looses the bindings around her feet and heads toward the lion's cave" (430). A similar verse in Prudentius's *Dittochaeon* (8.4) depicts Moses as he readies himself to approach the burning bush: "He looses the bindings around his feet; he hastens to Pharaoh's citadel." Prudentius's line paraphrases the very words God is reported to have spoken to Moses in the Bible (Exodus 3.5; cf. Joshua 5.16): "Come not nigh hither, put off the shoes from thy feet: for the place whereon thou standest is holy ground." This passage from Exodus was remembered on Maundy Thursday, the day of ritual footwashing, and on other days during Eastertide (Pascher 141–42). According to Amalar (*Liber Officialis* 1.12.37–38; 1.29.8), shoes, which are fashioned from dead animals, represent Adam, from whom we derive death. People should remove their spiritual shoes (that is, refrain from all impropriety) when they enter a church, just as Moses took off his shoes before nearing the bush (Hrabanus Maurus, *Carmen* 52, ed. Dümmler 217). Not to take off footwear in a place of prayer symbolizes a preoccupation with earthly matters.

After undoing her shoes, the fox fortifies herself to face the lion. Her gift of gold to the pard and her trepidation at the threshold of the lion's den are both cast, with comic effect, in epic language from the *Aeneid* (cf. 434 with *Aeneid* 11.845, 437 with *Aeneid* 6.427, 11.423). Upon entering the cave, the fox asks the sovereign to bless her, but the lion's benediction at once turns into an accusatory question: "O beast of many heads, you are paying a visit to me on my deathbed?" (440). The expression "beast of many heads" originated in Horace's version of the fable of the sick lion and the fox (*Epistle* 1.1.76). In the fable, the fox stays away from the cave of the ailing lion-king when she notices many footprints leading into the cave but none emerging. With a playfulness characteristic of the *Ecbasis captivi*, the phrase that Horace's fox addressed to the lion is spoken here by the lion to the fox, but the result in both stories is the same, since the fox outfoxes imminent death!

The fox answers the lion's questions with a long self-vindication. According to her, she has come to visit because she has found, at long last, a cure for the king's ailment. The tale of how she came upon this remedy and in what the remedy consists begins at the lake of Gennesaret (446). Gennesaret is named only once in the Bible, as the place where throngs gathered to hear the word of God and where Christ's miracle convinced the apostles to be fishers of men (Luke 5.1). At the same lake of Gennesaret the fox conferred with a coot who told her of the great lamentation over the lion's dire illness. The coot's words imply that salvation for the lion lies in the very outpouring of grief, in the spirit of the place where Christ once preached: "Great lamentation is being made in these seaside regions. Run, hasten: life is hidden in this medicine" (450–51). She gives the fox a kiss of peace, and the fox leaves the Holy Land with the unnamed remedy, which perhaps should be interpreted as true belief (Brinkmann 119).

The fox's account of her itinerary mingles satire, local allusions, and travel lore. The blend evidently placates the monarch, who ceases to demand an explanation for the fox's tardiness and instead pursues the charge that she leads a wicked life. In reply, the fox refers her case to a higher authority, a *circator* (468–70). According to many monastic customaries (see *Mittellateinisches Wörterbuch*), a *circator* was an official who inspected monastic establishments to make sure that they were in order. Such an official fits well within the inner story, which is both monastic and courtly (K. Hauck): the fox is a monk as well as a queen, the lion is an abbot (748) as well as a king (848, 936). The animals are *fratres* (400, 442) and *confratres* (409, 780, 1172), are described collectively as *clerus* (587) and *conventus* (494, 610, 635: Seiler 1877, 368), but are also soldiers (848). Here the *circator*—a minor bureaucrat—is wittily transmogrified into an arbiter of life-and-death cases. Seen in a more serious light, the *circator* stands unobtrusively for God, the only judge capable of pondering every crime. For this reason, the fox's invocation of the *circator* sobers the group at once (471).

In the next passage, the fox enumerates the changes which the march of time and her indefatigable quest for a remedy have wrought in her. Her ten-line speech is pieced together entirely from verses and phrases of Horace, Boethius, Nemesian, and the anonymous poet of the "Poem on Old Age" (*Carmen de senectute*). In the wolf-narrator's opinion, the oration is a feat of epic deviousness: he lavishes upon it the same praise with which Horace extolled a successful epic (*Ars poetica* 151–52): "And ⟨s⟩he invents in such a way, ⟨s⟩he mixes falsehoods with truths, so that the middle is not discordant with the beginning, ready to follow a twisted path rather than the truth" (482–84). Whatever the wolf thinks, the fox's words move the animals of the court: "All cry out together: 'Let the Olympic fox be revered!'" (486). The Latin *conclamant omnes* comes from Juvencus, who uses it on two occasions to describe the reactions of crowds to Christ (3.639, 4.565). As the beasts of the *Ecbasis captivi* prostrate themselves, commiseration with the fox's sufferings during her arduous travels replaces the anger which they had felt. Intoning a solemn song, they conduct the fox to her liege lord.

As a gesture of peace, the fox touches the king's scepter. As at the outset of the inner story, the poet takes pains here to show that the customs are old and that the action takes place in the distant past (491–92). He alludes once again to the Old Testament, in this case to Esther (4.11, 5.2, 8.4). His motives are manifest: like the fox, Esther was a queen who went before a king (Ahasuerus) to have an unjust sentence repealed and who succeeded in having an unethical traducer (Haman) himself punished upon the *crux* that he had erected. Even the fox's gesture recalls how Esther laid her hand upon the king's scepter to secure his clemency for herself and peace for her people.

At the lion's urging, the fox gives particulars of the medical treatment that she recommends. Reluctantly, she says that her godfather should be dragged out of the court and flayed, and that the king's back should be anointed with a fish's brain and enveloped in the wolf's hide. After these steps have been taken, the fox first takes the drink to which she is entitled by *Benedict's Rule* (chap. 38) and then lectures the troop of animals. Her first two lines set the tone for the whole passage of nearly two dozen lines: "Alas, you unfaithful throng, in concert in a badly joined pact, / how rashly you impose an unjust law upon yourselves!" (514–15). With them begins the fox's meticulous assessment of the court's legal system: in the coming disquisition the term *lex* occurs five times, *fedus* twice, and *iniquus, decretum, iudicium, placitum,* and *precepta* once each. The fox takes the assembly to task for "inverting all virtues" (521). In her opinion the beasts have passed judgment upon themselves, not upon her.

Above all other legal failings of the court the fox censures the policy that "a person may be condemned although he be absent" ("absens damnetur," 524). Her reasoning alludes to Festus's defense of Paul against the Jews in the Acts of the Apostles 25.16: "It is not the custom of the Romans to condemn any man, before that he who is accused have his accusers present, and have liberty to make his answer, to clear himself of the things laid to his charge." Taken narrowly, the allusion suggests that the fox's opponents are similar to the persecutors of Christ and the apostles. In a broader sense the fox rejects one clause of the law that prevailed until

Christ's Resurrection. The Old Law provides that the fate of a person who breaks one of the Ten Commandments is determined irrevocably at the moment of transgression; the verdict is reached long before the person, by dying, comes into the presence of God.

The next five lines of the fox's speech (525–29) support the interpretation of *absens damnetur* as a clause of the Old Law. The fox predicts that the person who follows her new law will be glorified. In contrast, the person who denies the call three times and has no excuse will be hanged or crucified on the *crux* and receive no dispensation. The fox's new system differs from the court's old one in allowing a person three chances for redemption. In fact, the fox's rule grants a person the same number of opportunities to embrace salvation as Christ gave to Peter; and the verse defining the rule comes from Sedulius's depiction of Peter's three denials (526, cf. *Carmen paschale* 5.107). In the next line the fox puts aside the minutiae of jurisprudence and considers how a judge should comport himself: "But the pious right hand of the king will commit no crime" (530: cf. Psalm 117.16). Like the earlier word *circator*, this verse pertains equally to the lion-king and God.

Once the animals have duly praised the fox's legislation, she dictates a menu for the convalescent king. Like the evening repast of the outer-story wolf, the foods comply with the letter of monastic practice by including no meat (541), but the heaps of fruits and fishes once again make a mockery of monastic spirit. In another touch of Bible wit, the lion-abbot of the animals is to eat even the whale that swallowed Jonah (546–47). The lion is pleased at the prospect of such dainties and, in gratitude, deputizes the fox to handle affairs of state while he recovers. The crowd reacts fearfully to this news (561–64): "A greater fear runs through their hearts more than was usual, and no voice can speak, no show of pride shines. Then the frightened band ["Tunc tremefacta cohors"] carries out what their lord bade; all rise and bend their necks to their commander." Here again, the poet selects lines from different poets but with related contexts in order to comment on the circumstances in the *Ecbasis captivi*. As well as being the instinctive (and funny) response of wary animals to the guileful fox (cf. the situation in *Reinaerts Historie*: Best 129), their fright is the awe that human beings feel in Bede's description of Doomsday (Bede, *De die judicii* 84–86, 93, ed. Hurst 438–44). It is the terror that, according to Prudentius's *Apotheosis* ("dum tremefacta cohors," 501), surreptitious Christians experience when Christ disrupts a pagan sacrifice that they are attending.

After the animals swear fealty to the fox, they are assigned tasks to help restore the cave and its environs to a sound state. With a verse drawn from Venantius Fortunatus's Easter hymn (*Carmen* 3.9.7), the fox calls for the cave to be decked with flowers (579). She emphasizes most that she wants the animals to listen attentively as the unicorn recites the *Life of St. Malchus* (*Vita Malchi*). As was the case with the *Restoration of a Fallen Man* (*Reparatio lapsi*) in the outer tale, the mention of Jerome's *Life of St. Malchus* is meant to recall the contents of the work. The *Life* relates the unhappy consequences of a monk's flight from his community. Against the advice of his abbot, Malchus succumbs to filial feeling and leaves his monastery. Shortly he is carried off as a slave by bedouins, who set him to work as a herdsman. Although for a time Malchus delights in his pastoral life, eventually he is reminded of his earlier days as a monk. To avoid being forced to marry, he takes flight to the desert. After narrowly escaping being devoured by a lion and being recaptured, he makes his way back to his community.

The fox is keen for the lion, in particular, to heed the lovely and educational melodies that the unicorn intones (588: cf. Horace, *Ars poetica* 344). The description of the unicorn as maidenly and high-voiced need not be a mocking reference to a high-voiced monk in the poet's community (*pace* Gompf 36, 40); it could be simply a humorous twist of the lore that only a virgin could capture the unicorn.

After the fox has helped the feeble king away from the cave, the leopard brings out a pressing message: the pack of beasts inside deserves a meal after three days of fasting (608–11): "I mourn for the throng: they have been holding out in the cave for three days now, they have gone without food or drink, they are exhausted in their fasting hearts; all the assembled mourn for the illness of the king, they pretend nothing false, but greet with friendly peace." This passage hints strongly that the animals have been altered spiritually as well as physically. The leopard's statement that the crowd is growing weak with "a fasting heart" (609) adverts to the conception of Lenten abstinence and, more especially, of the fasting on the three days preceding Easter as a token of sorrow for Christ (Amalar, *Liber Officialis* 1.1.14). The first line of the speech (608) paraphrases the New Testament description of the pity that Christ took upon the throngs which had fasted with him three days beside the sea of Galilee (Matthew 15.32): "And Jesus called together his disciples, and said: I have compassion on the multitudes, because they continue with me now three days, and have not what to eat, and I will not send them away fasting, lest they faint in the way." By a self-quotation in the fourth verse (cf. 611, 139, both indebted to Sedulius, *Carmen paschale* 5.66), the leopard contrasts the spiritual abstinence and good faith of the crowd with the planned blood sacrifice and Judas-like treachery of the outer-story wolf.

Moved by the leopard's counsel, the fox permits the animals to refresh themselves with food and drink. The leopard rushes off with the glad tidings and allots further tasks to the animals. In the manner of "Cyprian's Supper" the assignments play on associations that the animals have in the Bible: the camel, which according to the parable in Matthew 19.24 has difficulty in passing through the eye of a needle, superintends the fabrics, and the stag, which thirsted after a fountain in Psalm 41.2, serves as the cupbearer (Ross 270).

In contrast to the gentle and casual humor of the biblical references the comedy in the leopard's colloquy with the hedgehog is sharp-edged. When the leopard tries to send off the hedgehog to collect apples, the proud little beast objects that he is too good for such menial service. The blustering about his ancestry which follows is as packed with witty allusions as any passage in the *Ecbasis captivi*. Like the pedantic cook in comedy of the third century B.C. who used Homeric jargon (Holtz 6), the hedgehog speaks in a stream of pretentious quotations, allusions, and references. He belongs to the class of vulgar pedants known in French as *cuistres*—a word that derives from a Vulgar Latin term for a scullion or cook's boy. The hedgehog calls himself "a standard-bearer of the city Rome" and "a marquis of the Rutulians" (675), who were the implacable foes of the Trojan settlers in Vergil's *Aeneid*. In the same breath he brags that his covering of prickles offers such insuperable protection that "ten thousand attackers are driven back by one sling of it" (678). The hyperbole recalls the song sung of David after his sling felled Goliath (1 Samuel 18.7): "Saul slew his thousands, and David his ten thousands."

His allusions and quotations notwithstanding, the grandiloquent beast is consigned to the kitchen. Such banishments to the kitchen appear to have been stock elements in beast stories since the Egyptian epic of the cats and mice, in which a cat was sometimes reduced to being a scullery-slave (Brunner-Traut 13–29). In the *Ecbasis captivi* even the words in which the hedgehog is dismissed are humorous, recalling the instructions that Horace addressed to one of his *Satires*, personified as a slave-boy, and likewise those that Propertius spoke at the end of an elegy: "I puer atque mee citus hunc impone coquine" ("Go, boy, and quickly put him in my kitchen," 695); "*I, puer, atque meo citus haec subscribe libello*" (*Satires*

1.10.92, "Go, boy, and quickly add these words to my little book," emphasis added); "*I puer*, et *citus haec* aliqua pro*pone colum*na" (*Elegy* 3.23.23, emphasis added). As the farce ends, the hedgehog accepts his lot with all the dignity and stoicism that he can muster—and with a phrase that Turnus spoke to his sister before he faced his last, fatal battle with Aeneas (698; cf. *Aeneid* 12.677)!

Once the hedgehog has been put in his place and the court finally brought to rights, the fox concentrates her thoughts again on the well-being of the lion's soul. The king wishes to have a companion who sings the Psalms and divine hymns; the fox believes that the pard would discharge these offices handsomely; and the leopard expresses agreement, in a line echoing both the Lord's Prayer and Horace. Compare "Fiat velle tuum, simplex dumtaxat et unum" ("Thy will be done, but let it be simple and uniform," 719) with "Fiat voluntas tua" ("Thy will be done") and "denique sit quodvis, simplex dumtaxat et unum" (*Ars poetica* 23, "In short, let the work be what you wish, but let it be simple and uniform"). After the leopard has sworn an oath that he and the fox will never fall into discord, the two allies kiss on the lips (725). The fox responds to this kiss of peace with words that in Prudentius praise Christ for the boundless love he showed in assuming human form. Compare "Quantus amor celi, tanta est dilectio nostri" ("As great as is the love of the heavens, so great is our affection" 726) with "tantus amor terrae, tanta est dilectio nostri, / dignatur praepinguis humi conprendere mollem / divinis glaebam digitis, nec sordida censet / haerentis massae contagia" (*Apotheosis* 1027–30, "Such is his love of earth, such his affection for us, He deigns to grasp with the divine fingers a soft clod of soil very fertile, and thinks it not mean to touch the clinging lump"). Through this quotation, the poet insinuates that this kiss is the opposite of the one offered by the wolf to the calf—that it is a spiritual exchange of good will rather than a physical act.

Still preoccupied with the lion's heart, the fox turns to him and makes an oracular pronouncement: "It is the hour of rising: your realm is like the realm of Croesus" ("Hora est surgendi: tua sunt quasi regia Croesi," 729). Like other verses in the *Ecbasis captivi*, this one conflates the Bible with the poetry of Horace. The first half line recalls Paul's summons to the Romans to awake from sleep to their salvation (Romans 13.11)—a verse of Scripture quoted very early in *Benedict's Rule*: "It is now the hour for us to rise from sleep. For now our salvation is nearer than when we believed." "The realm of Croesus" (Horace, *Epistle* 1.11.2) reminds the lion that his kingdom has been enmired, as was Croesus's, in the riches of this world. In fact, the ruler of the animals still hesitates to relinquish his earthly perquisites. For the time being, he wants to quaff strong imported wine, but the fox persuades him to drink the local vintage instead (730–39). At the end of a jesting digression on the charms of Trier's wine, she makes the lion remember the aim of her mission: "I have brought gifts of salvation / health" (739). The lion, after puzzling over these words, realizes that he may trust the fox (740–45). The two agree that the wolf met a fitting end.

As the lion recalls the wolf's fate, he grows nervous about his own future and wonders aloud where the pious pard, his spiritual counselor, has been. The fox goes to the tree where the pard has been huddling, and they chat together before rejoining the king. With a quotation from a Psalm the fox assures the pard that the wolf's attempt to entrap her failed: "He has fallen into that very snare which he laid in his deceit" (767: cf. Psalm 34.8). Apparently reminded of the Psalter by this verse, the pard informs the fox of how many Psalms he has recited on that day. The pard mentions that he worshipped "with unbent knee" (772). This was the liturgically correct posture during Eastertide, a symbolic avoidance of the mocking genuflections that the Jews reputedly performed before Christ (Amalar, *Liber Officialis* 1.13.17, 4.37.7). In unison the fox and pard chant more Psalms, but they finish with a panegyric on the three boys whom Nebuchadnezzar ordered to be thrown into a furnace. The subject would seem to be a curious match for the Psalms, were it not that the incident of the three youths was one of the fixed readings on Easter (Thurston 425; Righetti 2: 265).

When the pard meets the king and the others, great rejoicing takes place. After the pard has been blessed and anointed as king, the entire party moves to the dining table. When the fox first arrived and defended herself against the wolf's treachery, the animals were tongue-tied with fear (471), but now they are silent because she has restored tranquility to the court (788–89). The fox rises, brings forth cups, and commemorates the calm with a mass, although the poet jokingly declines to name it as such (793). The animals sing two prayers, the one to God the creator and savior (*pace* Gompf 41–42), the other for the king's health and prosperity. The second prayer concludes with the request: "May your life be wealthy and rich with the gift of Christ!" (805). The lion, though proprietor of a realm like Croesus's, lacked Christian wealth until the fox "woke" him (729).

At the ensuing banquet the lion interrogates the pard about his long absence. The pard replies that, although he was distant from the court, he nonetheless suffered acutely during the king's illness and that now he brings gifts surpassing those which the queen of Sheba bestowed upon Solomon (814, cf. 3 Kings 10.2). Soon he shifts the conversation to a glory that Solomon lacked, but not the lion-king: songbirds. To back this claim, the pard orders the king's birds to come at once. The first to arrive is the nightingale, who takes a propitious seat to the right of the pard and promises to sing of the Annunciation (825–27). A pious bird, she turns down the drink offered her and seeks instead the sublime nourishment that comes from Christ. Accompanied by the blackbird, she warbles the story of Christ's Conception and Passion.

The nightingale's dolefulness exasperates the pard, who insists that she temper her wailing. Their conversation runs seventy-five lines, of which roughly fifty are usually considered an interpolation or two interpolations by one or two authors (852–80, 881–907: Voigt 1875, 63–67, Kindermann 315, 317–18). The two main reasons for considering the lines spurious are first that if they are removed the line count provided at the end of the poem is accurate; and second that they are more explicitly religious than other parts of the poem.

Even if the passage was added later, as the response of an eleventh- or twelfth-century reader to the poem it can still shed light in several ways. The first is its emphasis on life in this world as an incarceration (873, 878). Another illuminating feature is the notion that Christ's arrest, although prefatory to the sadness of the Passion, cleared the path to joy (884). These two views of imprisonment may be compared with the calf's two confinements, initially in the monastery and subsequently in the wolf's den (224). A third feature of the interpolation is that it likens Christ to a calf (898–99), an identification that is suggested in Christian glosses on the sacrificial calves of the Old Testament and in early medieval Latin poetry (*Glossa ordinaria* on Leviticus 16.3, ed. PL 113.341B; "De ratione duodecim signorum," stanzas 6–7, ed. Strecker 693–94; "Cyprian's Supper," ed. Strecker 892).

At the end of the conjectured interpolation, the pard sends the nightingale to cool her zeal in the river. As the nightingale and blackbird preen themselves after bathing, they are met by the swan and parrot. When the newcomers inquire about the king's health, the nightingale answers that they should sing together to celebrate the "paschal feast of the one who is undergoing resurrection" (935). The phrase refers both simply to the lion, who is recovering from his illness, and subtly to Christ, whose death and resurrection were identified with the stillbirth and subsequent rebirth of lions as described in the *Physiologus*; thus Easter was viewed as the "feast of the lion who undergoes resurrection" (Walahfrid Strabo, "Wetti's Vision" 16, ed. Dümmler 303).

For a moment the birds are on the verge of having the sort of competition that nightingales often inspire. The parrot vows to outstrip the Sirens in the beauty of his voice (941). The swan promises to outdo all human brass instruments, for he has David's own ten-string harp and, what is more, was instructed by the psalmist Asaph (944–45). The last vaunt alludes, with wit characteristic of the *Ecbasis captivi*, to a verse from the first Psalm by Asaph (49.11): "I know all the fowls of the air." With its humor it settles the conflict among the birds and nudges them toward their true goal, to praise Easter in hymns (946).

The birds fly without delay to the lion's den, where the pard welcomes them with a fond kiss. After telling of their journey and encounter with the nightingale, they ask the pard to lead them in both song and conduct. At the pard's command, they sing a variation upon a famous Latin Easter hymn (977: Venantius Fortunatus, *Carmen* 3.9.39). Then all the beasts and birds chant the liturgical prayer composed of the Greek words *kyrie eleison* ("Lord, have mercy") so energetically that the cave thunders with their sacred song (980). To complete their performance in the three holy languages (McNally), they break into Hebrew: "Lingua Iudaica ructant Grecaque Latina" (983). This finale cleverly marks a major transition in the inner story: the official commencement of Easter; for what is the Hebrew that the birds and beasts intone but "Alleluia," considered the Hebrew word par excellence (Thurston 472–75; Amalar, *Liber Officialis* 1.1.16, 1.31.7, 1.32.3, 3.13–14)? The alleluia and the lovely melodies to which it was set were a cherished feature of the liturgy in medieval churches, but the alleluia was laid aside as inappropriately joyful during Lent and was restored to the ritual, with great pomp, only on Easter (Thurston 26–34; Amalar, *Epistula Amalarii ad Hilduinum* 19, ed. Hanssens 1: 344).

Beginning with the parrot, the members of the lion's court drink in celebration. In his cups, the lion extols the canny fox for having nursed his body with the "fire of health / salvation" (996). The next verse develops the underlying theme that the lion was restored to health by Christian spirit, not by earthly medicine, since it begins with a phrase from Sedulius's description of a cripple whom Christ healed (3.184). The lion expresses his gratitude readily by declaring that what belongs to him belongs to the pard, and what belongs to the pard belongs to the fox (1000). In spite of this auspicious pledge, the fox feigns sadness and, when the lion demands an explanation, asks to be given the wolf's cavern. The lion accords this boon before witnesses.

The wolf, too agitated to continue his narration, now interrupts the inner story to tell the otter that the cave conceded to the fox is the very one in which they are seated. Of course, the wolf regards the fox's acquisition of the cave as an unconscionable swindle. The otter replies sagely: "A descendant has succeeded him, a perverted heir has succeeded him: the fathers sin, their offspring pay for their sins" (1013–14: contrast Zeydel and Strecker on the division of speeches). The otter's statement, with its strong Old Testament undertones (Exodus 20.5, 34.7; Deuteronomy 5.9; Ezechiel 18.2), applies to the wolf and not to the fox; for only the wolf has progenitors mentioned in the poem. To all purposes the fox is the same creature in both the inner and the outer stories, whereas the outer-story wolf is a descendant, perhaps the grandson, of the inner-story chamberlain (395). Interpreted in this light, the otter's interjection means that the sins of the inner-story wolf will be visited upon his outer-story progeny. It represents a further, by now redundant, confirmation that the wicked wolf of the outer story is near catastrophe.

Before the tone of the poem becomes too grave, the otter breaks off his analysis of the wolf's error and asks which foods the animals ate after they drank. The wolf resumes the narration of the inner story on a bright note, with the pard's description of banquet foods and etiquette. Then the lion addresses the entire assembly one last time (1033–36): "Hear, then, all of you and hearken with the ears of your hearts. Thanks be to you, that you took pity upon me; let no one lord over you as an enemy when you go forth in all regions, where the broad world extends." Of his four verses, fully three have significant resonances in past poetry. The first comes verbatim from Christ's speech to the Pharisees, as versified by Juvencus (3.147, 2.812): Christ asked the sectaries to open the ears of their hearts to understand the spirit of his words. The lion expects the animals to reach a similar soulful understanding of the king's peace which he promulgates. The last line of the regal oration is transferred from a passage in Sedulius (5.420), in which Christ bids his apostles to compass the world and to baptize everyone in it. Finally, the second verse is a self-quotation which juxtaposes the spiritual gift of serenity that the lion-king grants his court and the physical gift of property that the outer-story wolf presented to his two servants, in an effort to suborn them to keep the calf his captive: "Thanks be to you, that you have thus supported me" (187).

Now that the company has been enlightened by the fox and by their reinvigorated king, the poet uses the quotational gloss to compare the animals with the hordes fed by Christ through the miracle of the loaves and fishes: "Seque per immensas diffundunt agmina silvas. / Mox magni

parvique lupum lusere gavisi, / Accessit lete turbe glomeratio tante"
(1041–43, "And the bands pour forth through the immense forests. Soon
large and small in delight mocked the wolf, and the assemblage of so great
and happy a throng drew near"). The gloss comes through Prudentius's
Apotheosis 714 "*seque per in*numeras in*fundunt agmina* mensas" ("and the
crowds spread themselves about at countless tables," emphasis added) and
Matthew 15.30 "et *accesserunt* ad eum *turbae multae*," ("and great multitudes came to him," emphasis added). By two such pointed invocations of
the miracle, the poet equates the recent experiences of the animals to a
communion with Christ, a spiritual feeding diametrically opposed to the
physical bloodshed that the outer-story wolf plots and that the inner-story
wolf failed to achieve.

As the animals file away from the cave, they pause beneath the wolf
to deride the force that they have overcome. They inform the wolf that
God judges men by their intentions and, we are to infer, not just by their
deeds (1049). As they thus tax the wolf with spiritual insufficiency, they
address him with the words in which the good sower apostrophized the
malefactor, the devil, in Juvencus's version of the wheat and the tares parable (1051: cf. Juvencus 2.807). While the animals berate the wolf, the parrot advises the lion about how he should manage his life (1053–60). To
instill meaning into his existence and to banish his dread of death, he must
relinquish his lusts (1055). The world deceives its friends, who end up only
as worm food; for worldly glory is as ephemeral as a flower's bloom.

In reaction to the parrot's lecture, the lion goes to sleep for three days.
This period of time was drawn from *Physiologus* lore, according to which
the whelps of the lion are born dead and remain lifeless for three days until
the lion breathes upon them and brings them to life (see Appendix 8).
After awakening, the lion in the *Ecbasis captivi* leaves the cave for the Black
Forest and Germany. The swan takes the region held by the Northmen,
the parrot India, and the pard the West (1073–76). Like the gospels, the
message of the lion's court is spread to the four points of the compass: the
lion travels east (Germany is east of where the poet lived), the swan north
(Trillitzsch 152), the parrot south (according to medieval geography, India
lay south of Europe: Isidore, *Etymologiae* 14.3.5), and the pard west.

Once the animals have dispersed, the fox goes to the cross or gallows
(*crux*) and composes a didactic epitaph for the wolf. From the style in
which the inscription commences, it bids to be a repository of practical
wisdom for the courtier, especially regarding what he should and should
not say, but it brings home two serious points. In the middle it teaches

the wolf, and anyone who happens to read it: "Avoid speaking falsehoods; keep your ears open" (1083). Whereas the first clause recalls the Ninth Commandment (Exodus 20.16), the second half of the sentence alludes again to the Christian concept of the "ears of the heart" (Curtius 136, n. 17), and both parts of the line call to mind the baptismal ceremony that customarily took place during the Easter Vigil (Amalar, *Epistula de baptismo*, ed. Hanssens 1: 244; Righetti 2: 253). At the end the epitaph spells out the punishment that the wolf has received for violating the injunction against falseness (1091–93): "You were duplicitous, you prepared torments for your nephew, and punishment is to be suffered no less for what is wished than for what is done: you will lie as attractive food for worms and wasps." These verses, particularly the second one, explain infractions against the Ninth Commandment in a Christian sense: that sinful intentions and not only sinful acts are blameworthy. Not surprisingly, the second line comes word for word from Christ's speech in Juvencus (1.522) about adultery of the heart. In the closing line, the epitaph provides a graphic picture of the punishment that the wolf will suffer for his error. That the body would serve as food for worms was a platitude of Latin and vernacular medieval literature, but the wasps are unique to the *Ecbasis captivi*. Whether or not the insects came to the poet through oral tradition (Hélin 1967, 793–94), the poet employs them here to achieve a learned effect. The insects should be interpreted here as they were sometimes by medieval Bible commentators: as demons sent to plague the wicked (*Glossa ordinaria* on Joshua 24.12, ed. PL 113.520CD). They tie the fate of the inner-story wolf to the nightmare in which the outer-story villain was beset by insects— and the insects included wasps.

Although the setting of the inner story is a fusion of a court and a monastery, its message corroborates the message of the more purely monastic outer story. Furthermore, both stories are set during Eastertide and both are equipped with quotational glosses that at once lighten and deepen the style of the poem. More important, both contrast two methods of dealing with apparent sin, on the one hand ineluctable punishment and on the other three opportunities to achieve forgiveness. The inner story serves not to glorify the fox, but instead to show how and why the law by which the wolf operates in both the inner and outer stories has been superseded. The inner story is linked to the story of the calf (and through the calf to the biography of the monk-poet) by the mention of the *Life of St. Malchus*.

The Outer Story (Part 2)

As the inner story finishes, the outer story reaches its climax. From the crest of the wolf's hill the otter sees the fox coming to the cave with the deed and with the witnesses demanded by law. The accompanying herd of the calf's friends and relatives cries out against the wolf (1107–19), whom they consider a devil striving to subvert justice (1112). Although the wolf feigns to bring salvation, he offers nothing but death (1114). In medieval iconography Christ was the bait put on the cross to take Leviathan and thereby to win release of imprisoned souls (Zellinger; MacCulloch 204). The wolf, because he represents the opposite of Christ, inverts the symbolism: "he is the hook of death, covered with poisonous bait" (1113). As an acknowledged lawbreaker, the wolf is doomed to die an outlaw's death (1116). The New Testament passage (Romans 2.12–13) which inspirited this line indicates that the wolf's lawbreaking arose from hearing the word of God without hearkening to it: "For whosoever have sinned without the law, shall perish without the law; and whosoever have sinned in the law, shall be judged by the law. For not the hearers of the law are just before God, but the doers of the law shall be justified." All the legal talk and the threat that the wolf's servants will be enslaved terrify the otter, who returns to his master and exhorts him once more to release the calf, but his persuasion has no effect.

In recording the subsequent mêlée, the poet returns to the playful tone that alternates with the didactic so amusingly throughout the *Ecbasis captivi*. His account of the otter's flight (1134) perhaps echoes the denigration of Judas in Sedulius's *Carmen paschale* (5.135–36). The other quotations are also slight, though potentially roguish: the dog which heads the vanguard of the invading force recalls a dog in Vergil's *Eclogues* that barked when a goat was stolen (1139; cf. *Eclogue* 3.18), while the report of the invasion begins with the same word that Vergil used for the capture of Troy (*invadunt* is the first word in both 1140 and *Aeneid* 2.265).

Even without mischievous quotations, the fox's rhetoric is comic. The crafty beast cajoles her "uncle" to emerge and to let the herd admire him (1142; on kinship terms, see Lynch 48). For fifteen lines (1141–55), nearly all of them borrowed from Horace, the fox flatters the wolf on his natural graces and on his grand achievements.

The ploy succeeds. As the wolf ascends, the calf draws the bolt and runs free. While the calf sucks happily at his mother's teats, the scoundrel is impaled upon a tree by a bull (1163). The line ending alludes, unobtrusively but significantly, to the death that his ancestor had planned for the fox, since the tree often stood for the cross or the gibbet (Ricci 181–82; Thornton 130–31): cf. "Arbore de celsa vulpi crux *figitur alta*" (408) and "At lupus a tauro trunco con*figitur alto*" (1163, emphasis added). His enemy drafts another sepulchral inscription, which the narrator labels "an apt description for a wicked plunderer" (1165). Through the word "plunderer, spoiler" (*predo*), he reminds us of the otter's warning to the wolf, before the calf's rescuers had even arrived, that if he kept the calf he would break the monastic code and perish "according to the law of the plunderer" (312). The epitaph expresses the same principle still more baldly: "Ve qui predaris, quoniam predaberis ipse! / Mercatur mortem, qui fraudis diligit artem" ("Woe to thee that spoilest, for thou shalt thyself be spoiled. He who loves the art of deceit deals in death," 1167–68). The first line is based nearly verbatim on Isaiah 33.1 "*vae qui praedaris* nonne et *ipse praedaberis*" ("Woe to thee that spoilest, shalt not thou thyself also be spoiled?" emphasis added). The *Glossa ordinaria* on this verse explains (PL 113.1276B): "Against Sennacherib; these words can also be applied to anyone who seizes or to the devil himself."

As in the inner story, the fox crowns her victory over the wolf with a homily to her beloved fellow monks (1172). She stresses that there is no greater pestilence than "an enemy in one's own home" (1178) and that such an enemy should be eradicated on the spot. The home in question must be a monastery, since both the calf and wolf are monks (Comerci 1979, 38–39). The phrase *domesticus hostis* trims Boethius's conception (3.5) of a *familiaris inimicus* to fit monastic usage (cf. Knapp 1979a, 91–92; see Comerci 1979, 44): it describes a monk who abuses another one of the brethren. The wolf is the *domesticus hostis* because he is a monk who misbehaves and yields to the devil.

The rest of the fox's speech defines the wolf's misdeed. Custom dictates that a prisoner be freed if bail is posted or if entreaty is made (1182–84). Any fool who entices a captive to his chamber, feeds him, and induces him to unspeakable acts is destined to die as the wolf dies (1185–90). Like the wolf, such a senseless idiot is effortlessly and bloodlessly vanquished by a sensible person (1190–94). The fox attributes her own sense to the grace of Christ (1195–97). The last line of her admonishment insists that a monk's behavior should be the opposite of the wolf's treatment of the calf (1197: cf. 311).

The calf's mother asks her child to report what his savage host did to him, but the young animal demurs for fear of making himself and his listeners squeamish. Instead, he tells of the pleasant night that he spent in the company of the otter. When he does mention the wolf, he avoids using the word *wolf*—as if it were taboo—and instead calls him Herod (1216–17). The calf has three reasons to call the wolf Herod. First, because the calf, his intended victim, is still a suckling infant; for Herod Antipas was known to the Middle Ages as an infanticide (Matthew 2.16). Second, because the wolf has been characterized as a devil, and Herod was a well-known type of the devil in exegetic writings (e.g., Isidore, *Allegoriae* 137.143, ed. PL 83.118A; Adam Scot, *Sermo* 43.8 (193), ed. PL 198.398CD). Lastly, because Herod was described as a beast by Christ himself: "And he said to them: Go and tell that fox, Behold, I cast out devils, and do cures to day and to morrow, and the third day I am consummated" (Luke 13.32). Under the influence of this verse in Luke his bestial violence became proverbial in the Middle Ages (*Hymnus de natale innocentum* 3–4, ed. Dümmler 246; Egbert of Liège, *Fecunda ratis Prora* 887–88, ed. Voigt 150).

The inner story concludes with the calf's thanksgiving to Christ, a happy antithesis to his prayer to Jupiter when he first fell into the clutches of the wolf. The toil-worn poet, in an epilogue, vows to leave the frivolous realm of poetry for the more serious profession of singing the Psalms. The poet evidences his characteristic humor in his closing self-description (1228–29): "Angry at the same time, fierce with teeth that have gone hungry, / I will conclude my speech, I will not add a word more"). How fitting, to cap the *Ecbasis captivi* with the last line of Horace's first *Satire*! How appropriate, too, for the author of the *Ecbasis captivi* to style himself "fierce with teeth that have gone hungry," a phrase that in Horace referred to a wolf (*Epistle* 2.2.29)! With a respectful nod to the authority of Horace and with a final joke to charm his learned, but hungry audience, the poet brings to a close the quotational gloss which he began in the prologue.

Conclusion

A reading of the quotational gloss in the *Ecbasis captivi* reveals that Lent and Easter are more than simply the season in which the events take place. Alongside the open bantering about the Lenten diet and its circumvention are numerous references to the liturgy of the Easter Vigil: to the kiss of peace, positions of prayer, set readings, paschal lamb, and eucharist. Furthermore, Lent and Easter imbue the poem not just with their outward observances but also with their spirit. As the day on which the New Law replaced the Old, Easter is the key to the otherwise puzzling relationship between the inner and outer stories in the *Ecbasis captivi*. The outer story presents a calf-monk who has sinned through both despair and a desire to infringe the Lenten dietary strictures by drinking milk. The wolf, who follows the letter of the Old Law, believes that the calf should be chastised for the crime. The inner story is interposed to validate the institution and meaning of the New Law: that people should have the chance to reform and that they are to be judged by their intentions and not by their actions. The outer story resumes to show the penitent calf freed, under the terms of the New Law.

The capture and liberation of the calf are described in terms that recall the Harrowing of Hell, which is supposed to have taken place between the crucifixion and the resurrection. Even in early accounts of the Harrowing there are numerous references to the two dominant motifs of the *Ecbasis captivi* outer story, chains and captivity (Venantius Fortunatus, *Carmen* 3.9.6; John Scot Eriugena, *Carmen* 2.6.11, 21; *Analecta Hymnica* 7: 59, no. 45, stanzas 7a, 11b; 7: 73, no. 60, stanzas 3b, 4a). The shackles of infernal law shattered when the lamb (Christ) descended to the cavern and freed the sheep from the wolf (Venantius Fortunatus, *Carmen* 3.9.84). Satan was cast as a monster forced to disgorge his prey (Venantius Fortunatus, *Carmen* 3.9.83; John Scot Eriugena, *Carmen* 2.6.14). In popular belief, the Harrowing recurred annually on Easter: souls in hell were released from confinement (MacCulloch 35–36, 41). In view of these resemblances, it is enticing to see parts of the *Ecbasis captivi* as reenacting the Harrowing legend within an animal fiction.

Yet even if from one perspective the *Ecbasis captivi* is a theriomorphic account of the shift to the New Law and of the Harrowing, from another it retains a humor all its own. Easter was a time of solemnity, but it was also a time of ecstasy. These two qualities are mirrored in the *Ecbasis captivi*, a poem that is entertaining as well as instructive (Ross 269–70; Gülich 89–90). The systematic chicaneries of the wolf with monastic rules are both laughable and profoundly impious. In mixing comedy and didactic, the *Ecbasis captivi* anticipates the evolution of vernacular Easter plays, in which Herod and Judas are funny (even in dying), but evil (Weimann 111–21).

The *Ecbasis captivi* has very special features. Though not all of its quotations require the reader to test the original context against the new one, the poem is in many places furnished with a quotational gloss. Besides having the stylistic sophistication of a quotational gloss, the poem has a structure that boxes one story within another. Both stories are arranged to be recited or performed economically by a few readers or actors. This recitation or performance was meant to take place on a particular occasion: its themes of fasting versus feasting, proper sacrifice versus improper sacrifice, and captivity versus freedom are especially suited to Eastertide.

Although the combination is unique, not all of these features were wholly unprecedented. Rather, they develop trends suggested in earlier beast poems. The beast flytings and Froumund of Tegernsee's remarks about miming offer evidence that school skits about animals were recited or performed in the century before the *Ecbasis captivi* was written. In addition, there were earlier poems associated with particular holidays; for instance, "The Swan Sequence" was sung on the day of Pentecost, "The Hawk and Peacock" on Easter. Finally, quotations with original contexts which enrich the new ones occur in the beast poems of Alcuin, Sedulius Scottus, and Leo of Vercelli. Leo even anticipated the *Ecbasis captivi* in his fondness for allusions to Horace.

Although it cannot be shown that the poet of the *Ecbasis captivi* read any of the early medieval Latin beast poems which are today extant, his familiarity with fable and medieval school traditions about animals is indisputable. In addition, he exhibits the readiness to explore all potential sources of beast lore that typifies the early medieval Latin beast poets. He quotes knowledgeably from the beast fables of Horace and from the animal riddles of Symphosius and shows further versatility in writing a nightingale lament and animal epitaphs. He studs his composition with jests about the animals in the Bible and refers to the *Physiologus* when describing the lion's recuperation.

The *Ecbasis captivi* poet declared explicitly that he yearned for the poem to be both useful and entertaining, in the manner of a *fabella*. In voicing this desire, the poet placed himself among the number of beast poets from Alcuin through Leo of Vercelli who regarded their poems as an outgrowth from beast fable. But like the earlier poets, the *Ecbasis captivi* poet took pains to differentiate his poem from beast fable. He underpinned it with an autobiographical and religious significance, a narrative complexity, and a style uncharacteristic of classical fable. Like many of his predecessors, the *Ecbasis captivi* poet combined religious meaning (what has been termed allegorical meaning) with deft humor (*pace* Knapp 1979a, 34).

How did the achievement of the *Ecbasis captivi* affect the future course of medieval Latin beast poetry? The *Ecbasis captivi* was written in Toul or Trier, roughly the same area as the next long beast poem (the *Ysengrimus* was written in Ghent or thereabouts). It is more likely that the *Ysengrimus* poet knew of the *Ecbasis captivi* than that the *Ecbasis captivi* poet had read Leo's "Meter" or any other foregoing beast poem that is still extant.

Yet the two works, the *Ecbasis captivi* and *Ysengrimus*, share only those traits that could have been commonplace in the eleventh and twelfth centuries, most notably a rigorously literal-minded, insatiable wolf. Indeed, when the *Ysengrimus* uses a tale of a wolf-monk and a version of "The Sick Lion, the Fox, and the Flayed Courtier," it reverses the order in which they appear in the *Ecbasis captivi*. Whereas in the eleventh-century poem the wolf-monk of the outer story narrates the tale of "The Sick Lion" to explain the basis of the wolf-fox antagonism, in the *Ysengrimus* the story of the wolf-monk is told to entertain "The Sick Lion" as he convalesces. Was this a deliberate reversal, or is it a sign that the *Ysengrimus* poet was not familiar with the *Ecbasis captivi*?

In overall emphasis and tone, the *Ysengrimus* differs from the *Ecbasis captivi* and other earlier beast poems. In the twelfth-century poem the animals are humanized but not to represent individuals important in the poet's personal life; in this regard, the *Ysengrimus* is unlike Leo's "Meter," with the ass of Sparono, or the *Ecbasis captivi*, with the calf-monk whose fate describes that of the poet. Furthermore, although the *Ysengrimus* concludes apocalyptically, it is not marked by the sustained attention to theology of Sedulius Scottus's "The Ram," "The Swan Sequence," or the *Ecbasis captivi*. Nor is it tied to a specific occasion. Unlike Leo's "Meter" and the *Ecbasis captivi*, the *Ysengrimus* is written in a polished style but relies less for effect and meaning upon allusions to canonical classical texts; it lacks a quotational gloss.

Since both the wolf-villain and calf-hero of the *Ecbasis captivi* are monks, the actions of the animals have an immediate relevance to the human world: whatever any of the characters does can be construed as a comment upon the attitudes or actions of monks. Yet the *Ecbasis captivi* poet set his sights not on the conduct of a specific class—namely, monks—but rather on the meaning of an important holiday to his own salvation and to the salvation of the reader. The tropology of the poem consists in the poet's realization that Christian salvation is open to anyone who repents.

The wolf-monk is at once the greatest similarity and the greatest difference between the *Ecbasis captivi* and the *Ysengrimus*. In both poems the wolf tightens the pertinence of the events to monastic life, but there the resemblances end. In the *Ecbasis captivi* the poet introduces the wolf as the villain who victimizes the calf, his main concern. The poet brings in the antagonism between the fox and wolf only as background to the relationship between the calf and wolf. In the *Ysengrimus* the poet makes the wolf his central concern. Around the wolf-monk he builds a towering structure of stories taken from both beast fables and animal folktales. By making the wolf the antihero of the poem he enables the use of trickster stories that pit wolf against fox, among others. By making the wolf a monk he guarantees that the rapacity of the wolf will comment satirically upon the behavior of monks.

7. Ysengrim, the Wolf-Monk with a Name

Die meisten Tierschwänke sind zweifelsohne umgeformte Tierfabeln. Ebenso sicher haben jedoch auch andere Gattungen wie Märchen, Mythen und "Naturgeschichten" Motive beigesteuert. Gelehrte Tradition und Folklore haben Anteil an der Stoffvermittlung. Der Schritt vom Tierschwank zum Tierepos ist zuallererst ein formaler: Statt einiger weniger Episoden werden eine ganze Reihe aneinandergefügt und mehr oder minder geschickt verknüpft. Eine gewisse Länge ist unabdingbare Voraussetzung. Diese ist selbstverständlich sowohl im Fall des *Ysengrimus* wie des "Van den Vos Reynaerde" und dessen Bearbeitungen erfüllt.
(Knapp 1979a, 113)

Most comic tales about animals are doubtless recast beast fables. However, other genres as well, such as fairy tales, myth, and "natural histories," just as surely contributed motifs. Learned tradition and folklore had a share in the transmission of material. The step from comic tales about animals to beast epic is first and foremost a formal one: instead of a few episodes, a whole series is joined together and more or less skillfully assembled. A certain length is an indispensable precondition. This is obviously fulfilled in the case of *Ysengrimus* as well as in the case of *Van den Vos Reinaerde* and its reworkings.

"The Cock and Fox" and "The Wolf"

Apart from the *Ecbasis captivi*, two shorter beast poems survive from the eleventh century (Schaller 1970a, 97; Voigt 1878, 19–21). Like all other Latin beast poems of the eleventh and twelfth centuries, both "The Cock and Fox" and "The Wolf" use stories about animals to express thoughts about Christian values in general and ecclesiastics in particular, and yet they differ starkly in their means of attaining such religious relevance. Whereas "The Cock and Fox" follows an essentially fabular approach seen in the early narrative beast poems, "The Wolf" moves in a different direction— one that culminates in the *Ysengrimus*. For this reason, describing the differences between "The Cock and Fox" and "The Wolf" will help to illuminate the transition from the short, early medieval Latin beast poems to the longer twelfth-century ones.

As seen in Chapter 2, the first medieval Latin beast poem, Alcuin's "The Cock and Wolf," is the earliest version of a fable about a cock whose one moment of overweening pride caused it to be caught by a wolf, but whose ingenuity enabled it to escape (Voigt 1884, lxxxi; Baldo, ed. Hilka 18, 52–53; Graf 25–47). Alcuin's poem departed from the most common form of a beast fable by adding a Christian moral to a conventional fabular one.

Coincidentally, the anonymous eleventh-century "The Cock and Fox" reworks the same fable of cock-and-predator and follows an identical procedure of recounting the fable and of appending a Christian moral (Appendix 18; compare Yates 1983). Yet whereas Alcuin's poem told the fable in a compressed thirty-one dactylic hexameters, "The Cock and Fox" swells to seventy-four rhythmic Ambrosian strophes. The later poem reaches this length partly through modifications to the narrative. It substitutes the fox for the wolf and makes the new antagonist a speaking character. It turns the capture of the cock into a feat of vulpine cunning, so that the fable narrates two instances of trickery (a capture and an escape) rather than the one seen in Alcuin's "The Cock and Wolf" (an escape). In not the least of the alterations, it brings human beings into the fable by adding a scene in which villagers chase the fox with the cock in its mouth.

But even with the various sorts of amplification, the narrative section of "The Cock and Fox" extends only thirty-four strophes; the remaining forty strophes are devoted to a Christian moralization, which the poet hopes will redress the triviality of a literary form he disparages—the beast fable (strophes 35, 56, 63, 71, 72). Unlike Alcuin, the poet is nowhere concerned with the moral of *fraus fraudata* ("The person who deceives another will himself be deceived") that is implicit in the story part of this fable (Servaes 24). Ignoring the conventional moral completely, he begins the moralization by likening the crowing and fluttering cock to preachers who shout and gesticulate to prevent their listeners from becoming sluggish. To maintain this identification throughout the fable requires inventiveness. At one point, to explain the lamentations of the cock after it has been seized, the poet compares the bird with priests who repent and are absolved of their youthful peccadilloes (strophes 52–55). At another stage he connects the cock no longer with priests, but with the congregation; and he implies that in this instance the priests are represented by the crowd which obliges the fox to drop his booty (64–68). Conscious of the surprise that this sudden reversal in his exposition might occasion, the poet produces an unexpectedly neat justification: it is right that the cock represent the people at some times and the swarm of scholars at other times, since together these two groups constitute the whole body of the Church (69–70). In his contentment with teasing two seemingly conflicting meanings from the fable "The Cock and Fox" poet is once again reminiscent of his Carolingian predecessor.

Both Alcuin and "The Cock and Fox" poet buttress the morals of their fables by uniting their fabular cocks with cocks familiar in Christian symbolism. In two gospel accounts (Matthew 26.75; Mark 14.68–72), Peter is depicted weeping as, at the crow of a cock, he realizes to his distress that he has fulfilled Christ's prediction of the three denials. In the theology and hymns of the early Christian period this cock stood for Christ himself, alert to retrieve souls from the sleep of spiritual death (Ambrose, "Aeterne rerum conditor"; Augustine, *Enarrationes in Psalmos* 118.147, "Sermo" 29.3–4, ed. Dekkers and Fraipont 1765; Prudentius, "Hymnus ad galli cantum"). In the eyes of biblical exegetes, the bird symbolized the Christian vigilance that awakens the heart to its sins and leads it to the daylight of repentance (Ambrose, *Exameron* 5.24.84–92, ed. Schenkl 199–203).

Even before the time of Alcuin, the cock sometimes embodied the anointed representatives of Christ on earth, the priests, whose wakefulness keeps the souls in their custody alive to the Christian spirit (Hesbert 455–56; Pintus). This cock was made a visible and tangible symbol: its likeness roosted on the highest weathervane of most churches (Honorius Augustodunensis, *Gemma Animae* 1.144, ed. PL 172.589B; "Multi sunt presbyteri qui ignorant, quare"; Pangritz 141). Like the connection of the fox with Satan and of Peter with Leviathan, the equation of the cock to preachers could have been found in such a standard of patristic exegesis as Gregory the Great's *Moralia in Iob* (19.2, ed. Adriaen, 143A: 956, lines 9–18; 33.17–34, ed. Adriaen, 143B: 1702–4; 30.9–13, ed. Adriaen, 143B: p. 1510, line 12 to p. 1524, line 66: see Hesbert 455–56). "The Cock and Fox" poet took advantage of the conventional cock symbolism to redeem what he regarded as a trivial fable (35–36): the moral tells the reader to understand that the cock represents preachers (47). Whether by design or not, the poet's use of a fable to identify the cock with preachers is an amusing twist on the widespread use of fables by preachers (Grubmüller 1978; Whitesell).

Both Alcuin's poem and "The Cock and Fox" are fables in which the morals are given a strong Christian flavor. Although the story part of the cock-and-fox fable influenced later beast poets, the moral was discarded when the story was related outside the context of fable collections. When the story of the cock and fox was next told (*Ysengrimus* 4.811–5.316), it was not moralized. This lack of interest in retaining a separate and explicit moral could help to explain why "The Cock and Fox" is extant in only one manuscript (Brussels, Bibliothèque Royale, MS. 10708, folio 172^{r-v}).

A poet writing a longer beast poem cannot follow the conventional story-and-moral format of fable without modification. Once a poet decides to elongate the story part of a fable or to incorporate it as an episode in a longer poem, a blunt decision about the moral is required. The moral interpretation can be made an integral component of the poem by moralizing each incident in the narrative as it occurs, but in this case the narrative flow will have to be interrupted repeatedly. The opposite approach would be to save the moral for the end; here, the disadvantage is that the poem will lack the intimate connection between story and moral point that is characteristic of fable: the reader will enjoy the long narrative and be edified by the long moral but will not experience the virtually simultaneous enjoyment and edification that is characteristic of true fables.

Because of these structural problems, the moral raised a barrier in the face of poets who wished to join together the story parts of several fables into a unified longer narrative. One ingenious alternative to stopping the narrative at the end of every story part and providing its moral was to assemble several fables with one and the same moral—the procedure that Leo of Vercelli followed in his "Meter." Of course, such a restrictive alternative would not have been useful to most poets, even if it had occurred to them. Fortunately, although the story-and-moral structure of Latin fable was familiar to anyone trained in medieval Latin, it was only one of many literary forms to which medieval Latin beast poets were exposed—and only one of many more to which their fecund imaginations were capable of leading them.

With the exception of stories about animals that purport to be realistic (such as those by Ernest Seton and Jack London), most fiction about animals achieves its relevance through establishing identifications between animals and human beings. For instance, in a mock-epic such as *The Battle of the Frogs and Mice* animals are identified with human characters in a revered form of literature, all for comic or parodic effect. To take another example, in classical fable animals are identified with ethical types: the wise, foolish, greedy, rash, and so forth.

In the eleventh and twelfth centuries a shift occurred in beast literature. Whereas in earlier Greco-Latin fable collections the pertinence of animals to the human world tended to come through their ethical associations, in medieval collections animals were identified instead with particular social classes and especially with particular types of ecclesiastics (Henderson 1973, 1978, 1981, 1982). Rather than being restricted to fable collections, this shift from ethical to social morals can also be seen in individual art fables, such as "The Cock and Fox," and in nonfabular beast literature, such as the "The Wolf."

Unlike "The Cock and Fox," the eleventh-century "The Wolf" (see Appendix 31) is not a retelling of a fable found among the poems of Alcuin or in any earlier poetry. Its one link with preceding medieval Latin beast poetry is that it deals with a wolf who is a monk, but "The Wolf" develops the wolf-monk from Leo of Vercelli's casual mention into a full-blooded figure, the cynosure of fifty-four elegiac couplets.

Because the animal who plays the title role in "The Wolf" is so thoroughly a monk, each event in the story related there is automatically a comment on monks and monastic practice. The story is as follows. A wolf is caught in a trap. The shepherd who laid the snare finds the beast and tries to stone him to death, but to no avail. Ultimately, he undertakes to cudgel out the beast's brains. The wolf cries for mercy, pledges fourfold restitution for the sheep upon which he has preyed, and eventually secures his liberty by leaving his whelp as a pledge of good faith. Directly after his release, the wolf locates a monk and feigns conversion so as to obtain a tonsure and a monk's habit. Flaunting these, he returns on the assigned day to the shepherd and asks to take the place of his whelp, for his spiritual rebirth has prevented him from carrying out the earlier vowed reparation. The shepherd, moved by the wolf's new-found piety, lets loose both wolf and whelp. Of course, the gullible man is shocked when the wolf recommences his sheep-eating ways, but the animal enlightens him with the scornful words: "Sometimes I am a monk, sometimes I am a canon [secular cleric]" ("Et modo sum monachus, canonicus modo sum").

The wolf who becomes a monk when it suited his convenience was not restricted to "The Wolf" or even to its two later redactions, "The Wolf by Ovid" and "The Wolf Goes to Hell." Rather, he occurs in a broad range of literary and artistic evidence from the eleventh and later centuries. Among the early parallels, one of many vignettes in Egbert of Liège's *Fecunda ratis* depicts a wolf who alternates between being a monk and a layman, depending on the availability and the quality of monastic food (*Prora* 1554–67, ed. Voigt 195–96):

ABOUT THE WOLF SOMETIMES A MONK, SOMETIMES A SECULAR

A wolf was running about on a journey, hastening to plunder, and he got hold of fish, which he bestowed upon his gluttonous stomach. The easily procured food he collected rendered him so arrogant that he vaunted he was to be considered a monk. Then, as he was going away, he found some hams and ate them as well. To those who enquired why he suddenly rushed away and gave up his intention, he said, "Spare me in this matter, I beg of you. Sometimes I am a monk, sometimes a secular when it comes to the food I procure. I don't need attendants to call so that I will be agreeable and ready to eat; I don't need a baker and a cook as elegant noblemen do. Unaccustomed to such things, my parents raised me so that I would never be a fussy eater with aversions for food. I do not feed on cooked food—delay is odious to my thefts—instead, this throat of mine demands raw offerings."

The punch line ("Nunc monachus, nunc sum parto popularis in esu," "Sometimes I am a monk, sometimes a secular when it comes to the food I procure") was sometimes retained by later authors, even those who substituted a cat and mouse for the wolf and sheep of the earlier version (Odo of Cheriton, no. 23, trans. Jacobs 85: Perry 1965, appendix no. 592). In other cases the conceit of the wolf-monk was given a different shape but retained the same spirit of satire and condemnation against those who become monks for material comfort rather than for spiritual reasons (Hervieux 4: 270) or those who repent falsely (Hervieux 3: 334–35, 4: 406).

The *Ecbasis captivi* presents the most comprehensive picture of the wolf-monk, complete with minute parody of monastic duties during the Easter Vigil and on Easter Sunday. Either the *Ecbasis captivi* or one of its sources was known to the author of "The Wolf," which shares the motif of fourfold restitution (compare *Ecbasis captivi* 261 and Zacchaeus in Luke 19.8). At any rate, "The Wolf" is also thorough in monasticizing its wolf. He takes the tonsure, wears a Benedictine cowl, and greets people with the pious blessing "Benedicite." He even grumbles to his whelp about the insipid food that monks eat.

Revealingly, the monastic humor was expanded in a later reworking of "The Wolf" that was fathered upon Ovid, "The Wolf by Ovid" (*Ouidius de lupo*; see Lehmann 1927, 2–8). In this version of the story the wolf actually enters a monastery, where he becomes a trusted key-keeper. (How a poem that centers upon a monastery and monastic practice could ever have been fathered upon Ovid is an interesting question!) The trouble starts one day when he is sent with a fellow-monk to catch fish at the river. He catches sight of an ass browsing at the riverside, claims that it is a crab,

and devours it. (The same story later appears as a fable, with a bellwether
or lamb in place of the ass and a salmon instead of a crab: see Perry 1965,
Appendix nos. 655, 655a; Marie de France no. 50.) After this taste of blood,
the wolf goes on a rampage, eating the food and poultry of the monastery.
In the end he is beaten fiercely but allowed to leave. The dealings of Ysengrim with monks end similarly (5.1041–1128).

Where did the wolf-monk originate? His lineage cannot be traced
smoothly to a single source (Graf 12, 83–88; E. Erb 1/2: 1020 n. to 801;
Kaczynski and Westra 1988; Papademetriou). One body of literature that
can be ruled out is beast fable: although outside the corpus of Greco-
Roman fables there are animals that play the role of an ascetic or clergy-
man (Adrados 1984, 253; Curletto 119, n. 20; Gupta: *Pañcatantra* 3.4, p. 315;
Jatakas nos. 127–28), within the corpus no animal serves a comparable
function.

One part of the wolf-monk's family tree leads to the Bible, the same
place where the cock-as-priest in "The Cock and Fox" originated. Already
in the Old Testament there is a metaphor likening a predatory man to a
wolf: "Benjamin a ravenous wolf, in the morning shall eat the prey, and in
the evening shall divide the spoil" (Genesis 49.27). But as has been recognized for a century, the metaphoric use of wolf and sheep in "The Wolf"
and related texts is most likely to have been inspired by a few New Testament parables (Willems 132). One metaphor depicts Christ as a shepherd,
his charges as sheep, and the wicked as a wolf (John 10.11–16). Another
warns of false prophets as wolves in sheep's clothing: "Beware of false
prophets, who come to you in the clothing of sheep, but inwardly they are
ravening wolves" (Matthew 7.15). There are two parables of the lost sheep
(Matthew 18.12, Luke 15.4), and two similes equating the apostles with
sheep sent into the midst of wolves: "Behold I send you as sheep in the
midst of wolves" (Matthew 10.16) and "Go: Behold I send you as lambs
among wolves" (Luke 10.3). Christ's metaphors were not lost upon the
Apostles: when Paul warned the Ephesians against heretics, he said, "I
know that, after my departure, ravening wolves will enter in among you,
not sparing the flock" (Acts 20.29).

Christian thought fused these metaphors, parables, and similes into
one overarching metaphor of good Christian leaders (the *pastors*) as shepherds tending the flock of the faithful (the con*greg*ation) against the wicked
as wolves. The spiritual relationships implicit in the metaphor were given
physical form in the crozier that popes, bishops, and abbots bore; and they

were also memorialized in language (Walther 1963–68, nos. 30541–42; 6: 10, 110) and literature (Cooper 24; Schüppert 153–59).

The fiction of a wolf who disguised himself as a sheep that arose in the Middle Ages (Perry 1965, Appendix no. 451; Thompson 1955–58, no. K828.1) surely owed something to the Christian metaphor of shepherd, flock, and wolves. Voigt hypothesized (1884, lxxxi–lxxxii):

> Des Wolfs Debüt als Schafhirt V 548 ff. und dessen Rechtfertigung V 573–580 ist offenbar nach Evang. Ioh. X 1–5 gearbeitet: er ist diesmal nicht, wie sonst, als 'fur et latro, aliunde' sondern 'per ostium in ouile ouium' eingetreten, um nun, getreu der biblischen Vorschrift, als 'pastor bonus ouium' mit dem heimischen und anheimelnden Rufe 'kum!' seine Lämmer zutraulich zu be-grüssen, ins Freie zu locken und aud der Weide, wohin er immer will, nach sich zu ziehen.

> The wolf's debut as shepherd (5.548 ff.) and his justification (5.573–580) are obviously embroidered on the model of the Gospel of John 10.1–5: on this occasion he entered not, as elsewhere, as a "thief and brigand, from some-where else" but rather "by the front gate into the sheepfolds" so as now, faithful to the biblical prescription, to greet his lambs without reserve as a "good shepherd" with the homey vernacular call "Come!," to entice them into the open, and to draw them behind him to the pasture, where he always wishes to go.

His idea has won warm support (Knapp 1983, 279–80). But the wolf as shepherd and the wolf in sheep's clothing would also have been encour-aged by the imagery of many non- or parabiblical proverbs, in which a juxtaposition of wolf and sheep epitomizes the uncomfortable relationship between the strong and weak or oppressors and the oppressed: "to leave wolves to guard sheep, to entrust the sheepfold to a wolf" (Otto 198–99, no. 984; Köhler 187).

The source of inspiration is less important than the effect. If a writer felt that an ecclesiastic leader was failing to execute his responsibilities toward the congregation, he could compare the ecclesiastic—whether or not a monk—with a wolf in sheep's clothing or with a pastor turned wolf. Just among the beast poets, the metaphor occurs in the writings of Eugen-ius Vulgarius, Sedulius Scottus, and Nigel. The metaphor was applied both to classes of ecclesiastics (English clergymen, in the case of Nigel: *Tractatus* 185, 195; *Speculum Stultorum* 2665–706) and to individual church-men (e.g., Pope Sergius, in Eugenius Vulgarius, *De causa formosiana*, ed. Dümmler 122–23, 127, 132–33, 135).

Of special interest to the reader of medieval Latin beast literature is the connection that developed between wolf and monk (Mann 1987, 130–31): the wolf passed from being a metaphor for a monk to being a real monk. The notion of making an animal a monk is not peculiar to medieval Western literature; for instance, in Japanese legend the badger is often depicted as a fat-bellied Buddhist monk. But at least one special circumstance would have encouraged people to accept the notion of the wolf-monk in particular. Because a wolf in sheep's clothing is a wolf dressed in wool, the image led almost irresistibly to the image of the wolf-monk. If a wicked person is a wolf who assaults the flock of the faithful, then a bad monk is a wolf dressed in wool garments who has gained entrance into the sheepfold. Thus the anonymous poet who attacked Heribert of Losinga for simony wrote (ca. 1095):

> Filius est presul, pater abbas, Symon uterque.
> Est Petrus exclusus: modo Symon in arce locatur,
> Sub specie sancta vestitus veste cuculla.
> Cerne lupum monachum! bene gyrat abante retrorsum;
> Est bene subtonsus, botis tunicisque politus;
> Iurat: "crede mihi!" cui Christus credere nescit.
> Stat lupus ad caulas; premit agnum dira leena.
> Hic tremit, illa premit; canis abstat, opilio dormit.

> The son is a bishop, the father an abbot, and both are Simon. Peter has been shut out; now in the citadel Simon is set, clad beneath a holy outward appearance in a cowl. See the wolf-monk! Well does he turn topsy-turvy [literally, frontwards backwards]; he is well trimmed, refined in his boots and tunics; "Trust me!" he swears, whom Christ cannot trust. The wolf stands at the folds; a fierce lioness attacks the lamb. The lamb trembles, the lioness attacks. The dog keeps its distance, the shepherd sleeps. (*De symoniaca heresi* 17–24; for commentary, see Lehmann 4: 317; Mann 1987, 130–31; Manitius 3: 54–55; Yunck 69–70.)

With this transformation the resemblance between the Christian symbolism of the wolf and that of the cock ceases. Whereas the cock stayed "like a priest," the wolf became a monk.

In art the wolf-monk is depicted in accordance with the story of "The Wolf in School." This story is found as early as the *Ahikar* (Adrados 1:

364–65). In medieval literature it is attested in fables and nonfabular animal stories in Latin, German, French, and English (Du Méril 156–57, n. 4 and 1; Hammann 7–12; Lämke 82–91; Marie de France, no. 81; Perry 1965, Appendix no. 688; Tubach no. 5338; Warnke 237–39; Voigt 1884, lxxxi; Kaczynski and Westra 1988, 122–24) and which either became proverbial or else derived from a proverb (Wackernagel 1848; Seemann 196–97). The heart of these stories and proverbs is that no matter how earnestly a priest or monk tries to instruct a wolf in the alphabet, paternoster, or creed, the beast cannot restrain himself from thinking of sheep. In the blunt words of one proverb, "As the wolf learns Psalms, he longs for lambs" ("Cum lupus addiscit psalmos desiderat agnos," Walther 1963–68, no. 4220; cf. nos. 4987, 6587, 11731, 23422a, 34157). According to another, "Nature always constrains a person to her laws: the wolf-monk becomes a roving plunderer as he was before" ("Semper natura quemvis trahit ad sua iura: / Fit lupus hic monachus raptor ut ante vagus": Walther 1963–68, no. 27977). Pope Urban II elaborated upon such proverbs in a bull of 14 April 1096 for the monastery of Montierneuf of Poitiers, in which he took to task the secular clergy of Poitiers for their demands against the monks:

> Indeed, as I realized that they were not pleading for spiritual but for fleshly privileges, I spoke in seriousness a certain proverb that ought to have shamed them, if they wanted to heed it, about the wolf set to learn the alphabet: when the teacher said A, he would say "lamb," and when the teacher said B, he would say "pig." They did the same, because when we promised psalms and prayers, they in response demanded things which are not beneficial to the profit of souls. (Bull of 14 April 1096; Voigt 1878, 21)

Urban II's use of the wolf-monk specifically to chide the secular clergy to the advantage of monks offers tentative support to the idea that the wolf in school was a piece of *Mönchspädagogik*, similar to the figurative explication of beast fables (Martin 277).

The usual form of the artistic representations is of a tonsured monk or cleric holding a bundle of rods and pointing to a book while a cowled wolf (sometimes a wolf-pupil or wolf-novice as much as a wolf-monk: Meissner 271) looks eagerly away toward a sheep. This scene and closely related ones are found in various artistic media throughout Western Europe (for references, see Panzer 1906; Wackernagel 1873, 310–11): on a frieze in the cathedral of Freiburg im Breisgau (Cahier and Martin pl. XXIV, 124–26; Panzer 1906, 16; Stammler 9), on church decorations at Marienhafe and elsewhere (McCulloch 12–13; Budde 83–84, 86, 90, figs. 61–63), in German manuscripts (Panzer 1906, 19–20, pl. 30–31; Panzer 1931), on bricks and tiles from western Switzerland (Hammann fig. 2; Panzer 1906, 18, pl. 29; Voigt 1878, p. 21; Reinle, xlii), on a spandrel in San Paolo fuori le mura (Seroux d'Agincourt 4: pl. 33), on a capital in the monastery church of St. Ursanne in Doubs (Panzer 1906, 18, pl. 28), and on a capital in the cathedral of Parma (Decker 328, pl. 229; Quintavalle 330, fig. 506).

The emergence of the wolf-monk held unrivaled importance not just for beast fable (Wooller), but for beast literature as a whole. As a critic commented long ago, "The favorite character of Latin poetry was, if not from the very beginning, at least quite early, and in any case already some time before the *Ysengrimus*, the wolf-monk" (Voretzsch 420). The popularity of the wolf-monk can be explained partly in terms of the advantages that he brought to poets who sought to write long stories about animals without accepting the limitations of the fable form. In both "The Cock and Fox" and "The Wolf," the human world is pushing against the animal one: in both, people and animals converse and interact with one another. The increased contact coincides with the desire of beast poets to make their stories about animals relevant to Christian readers. "The Cock and Fox," like fables before and after it, achieved Christian relevance through a moral added to the story. In contradistinction, "The Wolf" comments on Christian life implicitly: whatever the wolf-monk does reflects on human monks, without the need for appending a moral or for making the animal represent an actual human being.

Once the need for a separate moral disappeared, a second difficulty was solved: how to make long narratives out of beast stories. For the early poets, lengthening poems appears to have been a painful process of incorporating stock scenes that prolonged one simple narrative rather than joined together several tales. With the introduction of the wolf-monk, the tendency of Leo's "Meter" and of the anonymous *Ecbasis captivi* to join fable-like episodes, but to forgo the morals, was confirmed. Poets could now relate several stories without having to pause between them to announce their ethical meanings or social commentary.

To judge by the number of manuscripts, "The Wolf" won great favor with its readers (Voigt 1878, 1–15). Copied repeatedly, it was refashioned with additions that are proof of how easily new scenes can be grafted onto a narrative about the wolf-monk. Yet "The Wolf" marked only a midpoint in the evolution of the wolf-monk. Later in the eleventh- or twelfth-century, the wolf-monk was further individualized with a nickname.

So well-known was the wolf-monk that before long the nickname was applied metaphorically to a real man. In the *locus classicus*, Guibert of No-gent chronicles how the ringleader of a rebellious mob trapped and taunted his enemy, the bishop Gaudri, in the barrel where the terrified prelate had concealed himself:

> Et retuso obice sciscitabatur ingeminando quis esset. Cumque vix eo fusti-gante gelida jam ora movisset, infert: "Captivus" inquit. Solebat autem epis-copus eum Isengrinum irridendo vocare, propter lupinam scilicet speciem; sic enim aliqui solent appellare lupos. Ait ergo scelestus ad praesulem: "Hic-cine est dominus Isengrinus repositus?" (Ed. Bourgin 167: cf. 237)

> [As they sought for him in every vessel, Thiégaud halted in front of the cask where the man was hiding,] and after breaking in the head he asked again and again who was there. Hardly able to move his frozen lips under the blows, the bishop said, "A prisoner." Now, as a joke, the bishop used to call this man Isengrin, because he had the look of a wolf and that is what some people commonly call wolves. So the scoundrel said to the bishop, "Is this my Lord Isengrin stored away here?" (Trans. Benton 176)

Unfortunately, it is impossible to determine whether Bishop Gaudri and the rebel Thiégaud knew the wolf's name from Latin tales current among clerics (Foulet 75–89), or whether the Bishop was likelier to draw from popular humor than from cloister wit (Torrance 94–95, 302, n. 33). It is also beyond our means to grasp the full significance of the etymology: the proper name is composed of the elements *isen-* ("iron") and *-grijm* (battlemask), with the full meaning "the iron-masked or iron-helmed one" or "wolf-mask" (Menke 130–31). The etymology of the name could suggest either a cult-animal worshipped by a tribe of warriors or an animal used in masked performance. In regard to the latter possibility, it is worth noting that the name (in Guibert of Nogent) is first attested in an ironic exchange and in a moment of role reversal—in a world upside-down. Fi-nally, there is the folklore of the Swiss *isengrind*, a ghastly spirit that goes around on Christmas Eve and New Year's Eve to steal children. In some localities the spirit is represented by a person wearing a dog-mask (Meuli 1932–33, 1771–72). It is possible that the author of the *Ysengrimus* was aware of the etymology, since he refers to a wolf-mask on two occasions (3.736, 6.435), but he gives no real details.

Whether the tale of Ysengrim was learned or lewd, we can tell from the episode in Guibert of Nogent that by 1112, when the altercation be-tween Gaudri and Thiégaud took place, the name *Ysengrim* was in com-mon usage as a designation for wolves and was associated with satire on clerics. By the time when the *Ysengrimus* was composed, it was no longer necessary to point out either that Ysengrim was a wolf or that he was a monk. Under any name, the wolf-monk remains the passe-partout to the meaning of the *Ysengrimus*. The twelfth-century beast poem pays subtle but unmistakable homage to the wolf-monk when it records that the convalescing lion asked to hear, before any other story, the one of Ysengrim's mishaps in the monastery (3.1185). No one, not even the king of the beasts, could resist the entertaining and edifying allures of the wolf-monk.

The *Ysengrimus* and Its Author

The author of the *Ysengrimus*, despite 1-1/2 centuries of efforts to puzzle out the chief points of his biography, remains almost a cipher (for a review of scholarship, see Knapp 1979a, 41–47). On the basis of one manuscript ascription he was known for a time as "Nivard of Ghent," but the documentation for this name and place of birth or residence has not stood the test of time, since other manuscripts attribute the poem to "Balduinus" (Knapp 1979a, 41–42); the poem has also been ascribed by a modern scholar to Simon of Ghent (Geertsom), although this attribution has received only two votes of confidence (for, Barnouw 163 n., Yates 1979; against, Mann 1987). Because the one indication of his rank in society (*magister*) came with the now-uncertain name Nivardus, we cannot even be sure what his occupation was. On the basis of internal evidence we can posit with confidence only two facts: that the poet was a Dutch-speaking inhabitant of the Low Countries and that he finished the *Ysengrimus* in 1148 or 1149 (Mann 1987, 160–61).

The *Ysengrimus* itself, at 6574 lines of elegiac distichs, is the longest of the medieval Latin beast poems. It is widely recognized as a work of genius, even unprecedented genius (Jackson 332–40, 359; Knapp 1975b, 407, n. 157; Mann 1987, ix). At the same time it is, by all accounts, a troublesome poem to understand. Unlike the three next longest poems (Nigel's *Speculum*, the *Ecbasis captivi*, and Leo's "Meter"), it has neither an author's prologue nor an epilogue. It throws readers *in medias res*, and there it leaves them to fend for themselves.

One major problem is to divide the poem into narrative units (Knapp 1979a, 48–52): one of the least satisfactory divisions is the seven-book system of the standard editions (Mann 1987; Voigt 1884), since it cuts across the twelve main stories within the narrative (Willems 153–56; reproduced by Mann 1987, xi–xiv).

Most of the dozen stories in the seven books are concerned with the feud between the wolf (Ysengrim) and the fox (Reinard), but in several episodes the crafty fox is not involved. He is nowhere in sight when the wolf encounters the stallion Corvigar (5.1129–322). Nor is he mentioned as Ysengrim meets his fate through the agency of the sow, Salaura, and her pig-accomplices (7.1–442).

In addition to the difficulty of its unity, the *Ysengrimus* presents complexities in the style and content of the individual scenes. It sometimes quotes past authors as deliberately and meaningfully as the *Ecbasis captivi* does—and sometimes as wittily (compare *Ysengrimus* 5.449 with *Aeneid* 6.126–29; 3.82 with *Amores* 1.2.33; 6.318 with *Metamorphoses* 11.377); there are half lines or turns of phrase from Lucan, Juvenal, Boethius, Sedulius, Cato (author of the *Distichs*), Vergil, Horace, and Ovid (Manitius 3: 769; Voigt 1884, lxix–lxx; Yates 1979, 155). Although these quotations merit further exploration, on the whole the classical turns of phrase in the *Ysengrimus* are a matter of embellishment (Schneider 523), and in no sense do they constitute an internal gloss comparable to the one in the *Ecbasis captivi* or even to the one in Leo's "Meter."

Counterbalancing quotations from Latin literature are numerous proverbs (Mierlo 1943b, 89), which seem often to have been translated from vernacular sayings (Singer 1: 145–78; Mann 1984–85). Thus these proverbs add a popular dimension to the style of the poem that exceeds that of any earlier medieval Latin beast poem. Furthermore, the proverbs contribute to the fabular tone of the *Ysengrimus*, making the poem sometimes seem to be composed of hundreds of little fables, each outfitted with its own moral. In a random three pages of text the reader's eye alights on such sententious or proverbial morals as "A bird in a snare is worth eight in the air," "Honesty achieves results by honest means," and "One shouldn't look a gift horse in the mouth." The frequency of such observations camouflages the absence of explicit morals.

For all the quotations and proverbs, the major complexities of the *Ysengrimus* are unlike those of Sedulius Scottus's "The Ram," Leo's "Meter," and the *Ecbasis captivi*. They arise not so much from its style as from its dark references to topical events and places (for instance, Berschin; Yates 1981), to aspects of monastic rite (Geertsom), and to the liturgy (Peeters). The actions of the anthropomorphized animals seem often to have a satiric "other meaning," but the precise meaning of the satire is elusive. It is easy to agree with a glossator who wrote in the one manuscript that "certain things seemed to me so unheard of and uncommon that for want of knowledge and insight I could not come to understand their meaning" (Latin quoted by Voigt 1884, vi–vii).

Although in my opinion it is an exaggeration to maintain that Matthew 7.15 "is the imaginative kernel around which the whole of the *Ysengrimus* is constructed" (Mann 1987, 139, on Knapp 1979a, 70, and Voigt 1884, xci), a productive way to approach the *Ysengrimus* is through the metaphor of the wolf-monk; indeed, I would propose that the *Ysengrimus* poet structured his disparate stories around this metaphor. To support this proposal, we must examine how the poet interlaced his satiric declarations on monasticism, monastic life, and specific monks with the metaphor of the wolf-monk. With this foundation we will be able to interpret how the wolf-monk enabled the poet to bring more tacit satire on monasticism into the poem. In particular, we will see how the introduction of the wolf-monk permitted extensive noncritical parody of liturgy and of monastic rite. The parody functions as the fulcrum around which the separate stories pivot.

The just-mentioned approach (first advanced in Ziolkowski 1981) differs from many past literary appraisals of the *Ysengrimus*. In the first place, it is not embroiled in tired old questions about the sources of the stories. Were they oral tales in a Germanic tradition (Grimm ccxciv; Voigt 1884, lxxxviii–lxxxix)? Had the same tales circulated in Latin before the *Ysengrimus* (P. Paris 346; Faral 1923, 29)? Was the *Roman de Renart* influenced by the *Ysengrimus* (Donovan; Foulet; Mann 1988), was the Latin poem a reworking, under clerical and monastic influence, of Old French tales which later evolved into the *Roman de Renart* (Willems 36; Sudre), or were the Latin and Old French poems wholly unrelated (Mierlo 1943b, 99–103; contrast, Flinn 29–31, Knapp 1979a, 65)?

There was no single wellspring of inspiration for the *Ysengrimus*. One dimension of the poet's genius was that he could unite stories of disparate origins in a coherent framework. He weaves together the story parts of fables with animal trickster tales; both the fables and the trickster tales were probably of both Latin and vernacular origin.

The *Ysengrimus* retains much of the tone intrinsic in fables and trickster tales. For instance, the cartoon-like violence and brutality in the *Ysengrimus* (Mann 1977) has its match in trickster tales such as the Brer Rabbit stories, in which Brer Fox's head is served in a stew to his wife and children, Brer Wolf is scalded to death in a chest, and Brer Bear is stung to death by bees. Both the *Ysengrimus* and Joel Chandler Harris's Uncle Remus stories evidence the same sort of rich double or multiple meaning, in which the very practical lessons that the stories conveyed to earlier audiences are supplemented with very different significances as the stories are integrated into literary frameworks for a new reading public. Thus the *Ysengrimus* poet conserves themes intrinsic to animal folktales. For instance, hunger is constant: one of the few personifications is "magistra fames" (5.64), and attempts to secure food, real or imagined, are almost omnipresent in the activities of Ysengrim (Charbonnier 1984a, 405). And the fight for survival is unending.

In the *Ysengrimus* the violence and brutality of the trickster tales are transcended to express criticism of the ecclesiastic hierarchy. Furthermore, the narrative of the *Ysengrimus*, for all its flaws, is not a string of related but separate folktales, whether by a single author (as in Joel Chandler Harris's Uncle Remus stories) or by a number (*Roman de Renart*); rather, it joins the stories as episodes within a coherent plot. Whether or not the *ordo artificialis* of the plot was in any way modeled upon the *Aeneid* and the Latin epic tradition (Knapp 1983, 287), the messages that the *Ysengrimus* conveys owe next to nothing to the heroic adventures of Aeneas and his epic brethren. The characters who hold center stage in the *Ysengrimus* come from a very different world.

Instead of concentrating upon the source of the materials in the *Ysengrimus*, I offer ideas about the shape that the poet gave to them. But whereas most past studies of literary technique in the *Ysengrimus* have looked at consolidating themes and motifs (Jauss 93–113; Knapp 1975a; T. Erb; Mann 1977), this one focuses exclusively upon the character of the wolf-monk and the satire that became possible through his presence in the poem.

Monkish and Wolfish Rules

The *Ysengrimus* poet made ambitious use of the monastic rule (Knapp 1983, 296–97). Since the wolf-hero of his poem was a monk, the author had a pretext for commenting upon monks and monastic life. It is as if changing the plain and simple wolf into the personalized Ysengrim enabled a poet for the first time to particularize his satire against monks. The individuation can be seen as reflecting two twelfth-century tendencies: the increasing emphasis on individuality (Hanning; Morris) and the treatment of beasts as accountable, like humans, for their actions; for priests pronounced maledictions not only against entire species of animals, but even against specific individual animals which had somehow erred in the eyes of the Church (Franz 2: 144; Plöchl 2: 331; Tubach nos. 4556, 4645).

In the *Ysengrimus* explicit satiric remarks about monks fall into two categories. One comprehends those criticisms of monks, abbots, bishops, and popes which do not identify by name the person being attacked. The narrator and characters of the *Ysengrimus* take monks to task for many failings. Among these is the predilection for roving outside the monastery: the brothers return very reluctantly to their communities after they have vagabonded in the free world (4.549–58). Thus Reinard pretends that the demonic peasants (2.229) who beat Ysengrim at the fishpond were monks trying to force him back to the cloister.

Above all other vices, the poem castigates the monks for greed and gluttony (on such satire, Schüppert 93–95). Monks rush like lightning bolts to gain riches (1.639–40). They are especially grasping when food is at stake. For example, they never sing so happily as when a sumptuous feast is approaching (1.1045–46). In their voracity they outstrip wolves: Ysengrim finds his monkish cravings fiercer than his wolfish hunger (1.642–44). As the superintendents of monks, abbots must be preeminently acquisitive and gluttonous (Schüppert 101–6). Reinard reminds his "uncle," Ysengrim, that no self-respecting abbot refuses to follow the rule of grabbing (1.201–2). Later he persuades Ysengrim that his truncated tail is a badge of success, since any competent abbot overindulges to the point where his abscesses require the surgeon's knife and cause a physical disfigurement (2.243–48). According to Ysengrim, abbots excel in the religion of the stomach (5.949–54): although the typical monk drinks wine in great quantities, his abbot swills three times as much (5.940).

In the opinion of the personalities whom the poet created, monkish coveting has passed beyond the cloister and has vitiated other ecclesiastics (Schüppert 58–90). Bishops are selected from the monks, because regular clerics are not as talented thieves as monks "whose rule is to leave behind nothing" (5.1010, 5.997–1004). Bishops win their posts through pilfering and gourmandizing and prove their capacity to guard sheep by stealing all that they can wrest with their hands. Once rooted in the episcopacy, the cloister vices of greed and gluttony sprout to the very top of the ecclesiastic hierarchy, the papacy. The sovereign pontiffs, too, are monks recruited on account of their extraordinary greed (7.465, 7.685–87).

Besides assailing monks in the cloister and the upper reaches of ecclesiastic power, the *Ysengrimus* singles out real-life monks who, to the poet's way of thinking, abused their offices. Like the diatribes against the monks as a class, satire against individual monks (especially against those promoted to being abbots, bishops, and popes) strikes hardest at the vice of greed.

The longest section devoted to individual monks purports to compliment Abbots Walter of Egmond and Balduin of Liesborn on their outstanding management of their respective monasteries (5.455–540: Willems 108–11; Mierlo 1943b, 32–34, 46–48). Scholars have been sharply divided over the significance of this long passage, with one group believing that the panegyric is sincere (Grimm, lxxxiii; Voigt 1884, cvi–cxii; Knapp 1979a, 77–80; Mann 1987, 145–54) and another that it is only an ironic surface to a bitter indictment of Walter for avarice and Balduin for hypocrisy (Willems 108–14, esp. 113; Mierlo 1943b, 32–34). If positive, the passage is unique in the poem. Small wonder that it has been misinterpreted, since the reader is ill-prepared to encounter straightforward praise in a poem that has no heroes, and since the passage begins with a highly ambiguous couplet, which advertises Walter as the "Lucifer of abbots" (5.456). Whereas in the rest of the passage Walter is ostensibly the "morning star of abbots," through ironic implication this phrase could signal that he is the "Satan of abbots" (5.442: interpretation advanced in Ziolkowski 1981, 1: 125; discussed by Mann 1987, 152).

Although the interpretation that the passage is honestly laudatory has many strengths, I am not persuaded that even this one passage, even if strategically placed, proves the *Ysengrimus* "to have been motivated by a desire to win patronage" (Mann 1987, 146, n. 441) or that it should be "the starting-point for all inquiry into the author's particular situation in life" (Mann 1987, 174). For an artist to include praise of a person, even of a prospective patron, within a work of art or literature does not mean necessarily that the work was motivated entirely or even mainly by a desire for patronage. And if a poet had written the *Ysengrimus* in the hope of winning support from a patron, why would he have been shy of advertising his own name and that of his patron—as Sedulius Scottus did in the ram poem and as Nigel did in the *Speculum stultorum* and the prose letter? Finally, the passage makes an unusual keystone in the architecture of the poem, since omitting it would not cause the average reader to notice that anything had been omitted from the *Ysengrimus* (Sypher 1980, 229–30; cp. Mann 1987, 152, n. 460).

If positive, the description of Walter of Egmond and Balduin of Liesborn stands alone in its favorable tone. In another passage, Reinard, while cursing his teeth for having allowed the cock to escape, expresses the wish that they could have the tenacious bite of Anselm, the first Bishop of the diocese of Tournai (5.109–30: Voigt 1884, ciii–cv; Willems 106–8; Mierlo 1943b, 45–46). The poet here makes use of the convention in both medieval literature ("The Cock and Fox" stanzas 33–34) and medieval biology (pseudo-Hugh of St. Victor, *De bestiis et aliis rebus*, book 2, chap. 20, ed. PL 177.67C) that animals curse parts of their bodies. More important, the poet once again attacks what he pretends to glorify. As a rule, the few historical figures who are mentioned in the *Ysengrimus* are monks and are sharply criticized. And the poet hesitates no more to round on a monk-pope than on a monk-abbot or monk-bishop. In fact, the last person to be named in the *Ysengrimus* is Pope Eugenius III, who the author mistakenly claimed had undermined the Second Crusade and had squeezed the life-breath out of Christendom in order to fill the coffers of Rome (Voigt 1884, cxiii–cxvi). Thus the author savaged not only the basic principles, or lack of principles, of twelfth-century monasticism and monastic promotion, but also four flesh-and-blood beneficiaries of those policies: Abbots Walter and Balduin, Bishop Anselm, and Pope Eugenius III.

To integrate such frontal assaults on monastic life and ecclesiastics with the implied satire of presenting a greedy wolf as a monk, the poet accentuates the wolf-like features of the human ecclesiastics against whom he inveighs. Reinard's curse, which makes the Bishop of Tournai seem more bestial and rapacious than a fox, is not isolated. Besides a spurious couplet stating that Geroldus of Tournai and Ysengrim are blood-relatives (3.506ab: Voigt 1884, civ; Mann 1987, 161), there is a scene in which Ysengrim is repeatedly served the severed head of a wolf, each time with the announcement that it belongs to a different churchman. Once the animals say that it was detached from the body of a hermit of Anjou (4.272: Voigt 1884, xcvi). On other occasions they compare it with the heads of monks at Sithiu and at Vedastus, near Arras (4.285–86). Finally, when Ysengrim has entered the monastery of Blandigny the narrator refers to the abbot of that institution as "another wolf" (5.870). For the purposes of the satire the poet tightens the resemblances between man and beast or, to be more precise, between monk and wolf (4.286).

The broadsides against monks—and especially against those brothers who rose to become abbots, bishops, and popes—are interspersed through the *Ysengrimus*. At the same time, the wolf Ysengrim embodies monks of all degrees in the ecclesiastic hierarchy. At one time or another he is presented as a hermit, monk, abbot, priest, deacon, bishop, archbishop, and pope (Voigt 1884, lxxiv–lxxv, n. 1, and 437; Mann 1987, 13). The wolf, who takes his monastic status seriously, will endure any pain or indignity, so long as his forbearance earns him the reputation of being a good monk (2.685–86). What is more, Ysengrim devotes considerable attention to observing, after his fashion, *Benedict's Rule*. Since in his view (5.360) food and tonsure make the monk, he takes the tonsure and renews it in the Corvigar episode (5.1129–322). He wears a black cowl and says matins. When able, he hails the people whom he encounters with monastic salutations (*benedicite* in 1.1029, 4.141, 5.451, 5.835; *dominus vobiscum* in 5.547–48; *pax vobis* in 4.141–42, 7.13).

So closely has the wolf pored over the regulations that he feels qualified to propound a number of amendments. For a start, he insists on adherence to three tenets: "I give nothing, I spurn moderation, and I have sworn off faith" (1.576). Although these tenets are reminiscent of the wolf in the *Ecbasis captivi*, the rule of the wolf here is much more detailed. As regards the finer points of monastic etiquette, he sees no reason to forbid sleep after the midday meal, nor to impose long sessions of holy song (5.586–88). Most of Ysengrim's suggested revisions pertain to dietary laws because to his mind the monastic code should be "a religion of the stomach" (5.412) and "a law of devouring" (5.407; cf. 5.422). Of course, he believes that monks should eat meat (4.223–40). He proposes that the brothers dine upon sheep instead of rolls, with each brother receiving a per diem allotment of five (5.591–608). To finance the purchase of the sheep, the brothers would sell their useless holy vessels (5.681–86). In recompense, the new diet would enable them to substitute wool for hay in the outhouse (5.609–10). If they ate their mutton raw, they would multiply the savings, since they would keep all the shipworthy wood usually squandered in cooking meals (5.667–80).

Both Ysengrim, who is a supposedly authentic wolf, and monks, who in the satire are metaphorical wolves, aim to victimize sheep. According to the poet, Pope Eugenius III hoarded coins like a good pastor gathering errant sheep (7.685–86). The Pope, despising the admonitions in the Bible (Acts 8.18), fleeces the sheep (5.107–8). The Supreme Pontiff is more than imitated by the bishops: he is outdone in his fleecing by Bishop Anselm of Tournai, who tears off flesh along with the fleece (5.109–21). Ysengrim, privy to this knowledge, suggests that bishops should be selected on the basis of their adeptness at stealing sheep (5.997–1012). His understanding of pastoral duties runs in a similar vein. He equates the duties of a "shepherd of the sheep" with those of a cook (5.441–46, 5.544, 5.569–609), even after the monks explain that he ought to construe the noun *pastor* ("shepherd") as a figurative term rather than as an etymological derivative from the verb *pascor* (5.544, "to feed on"). The human beings and animals who are made a party to Ysengrim's philosophy of sheep react apprehensively (5.563–66) and compare the wolf unflatteringly with human monks of all ranks: monastic, abbatial, and papal (1.971–72, 4.175–88). Although Ysengrim alludes only once to the metaphor of the wolf in sheep's clothing (4.153), he makes no secret of his overriding ambition to be in the middle of a flock; and the sheep in his fantasies are not merely animals, but religious functionaries in their own right. They form choruses that recite and sing (1.999–1018), and are "brothers" (*fratres*) in a monastic order with a very pleasing rule (2.372–78).

The author of the *Ysengrimus* constantly likens real-life monks to animals and his fictional animals to real-life monks, so that at times the two worlds join seamlessly. But although he attributes to true monks and to Ysengrim the same predatory goals, he presents the wolfish monks as far more successful than the real wolf in the race to complete control, and corruption, of the world through their rapacity. Human ecclesiastics abuse the rights accorded them through the liturgy and, like wolves, despoil their flocks. In his fiction the poet refuses to allow Ysengrim the same impunity. The wolf aspires to many religious powers, all in order to eat his fill of sheep, which he considers a perquisite of ecclesiastic office. Instead of sating his appetite, however, he is gored again and again by the flock. Whenever he comes upon sheep, his lupine hopes are dashed. He is the one who, like a sacrificial lamb (3.1017–20), is fleeced and victimized. Ysengrim, who is twice flayed, turns inside-out the image of the wolf in sheep's clothing (Mann 1977, 506).

To discover how the many opponents of the wolf triumph over him, it is necessary to consider monastic rite and liturgy. In response to Ysengrim's unwelcome attentions, his enemies turn ritual upon him in a way opposite to his greedy intentions. In the *Ecbasis captivi* the liturgy of a special day acted as a touchstone for the behavior of the wolf. The more wildly he contravened the liturgy and the spirit of Easter, the more imminent his downfall became. The final debacle resulted from the wolf's abuse of liturgy but was not in itself a liturgical act. In the *Ysengrimus* the plethora of liturgical allusions and parodies serves a different purpose: all of Ysengrim's would-be debauches fail when the liturgy is wielded against him. Examining the parody of monastic rite and liturgy will, in addition to highlighting the similarities and differences between the twelfth-century poem and the earlier *Ecbasis captivi*, explain in part how the author of the *Ysengrimus* managed to consolidate twelve diverse stories in a coherent beast epic; for he shaped much of his narrative around monastic rite and liturgy.

The Liturgy Strikes Back

The *Ysengrimus* seems chock-full of anomalies. Although concerned with the disasters engineered by Reinard and inflicted upon Ysengrim, it begins with the sole victory of the wolf over the fox and ends when he is killed, not by Reinard, but by a horrendous sow and her clan of swine. These inconsistencies are typical of trickster-tale cycles, of which a preeminent folklorist has written:

> The adventures of the Trickster, even when considered by themselves, are inconsistent. Part are the result of his stupidity, and about an equal number show him overcoming his enemies through cleverness. Such a trickster as Coyote, therefore, may appear in any one of three roles: the Beneficent Culture Hero, the clever deceiver, or the numskull. As we look at these incidents, we find that this mixture of concept is continually present, so that any series of adventures is likely to be a succession of clever tricks and foolish mishaps. (Thompson 1946, 319)

Such is the fox who appears in ancient Sumerian proverbs and fables. Like Coyote, he is capable of astounding failures and successes. Like Reinard (contrast Gordon 1962, 236), he is conceited, false ("The fox's mind [and] mouth are suited for falsification" Gordon 1962, 234), and even litigious ("The fox had a stick with him [and so he could say]: 'Whom shall I hit' He carried a [legal] document with him, [and so he could say: 'What shall I challenge?'" Gordon 1962, 235). But the exceptional failures of the fox in the *Ysengrimus* are not simply ragged edges left from the slapdash reconfiguration of putative sources. Rather, they are exploited deliberately as cues to the reader that none of the animal characters in the poem is an invincible hero.

Although the first story (1.1–528) is also an exception in not showing the liturgy enacted to the detriment of Ysengrim, it contains a travesty of an ecclesiastic court. The wolf daydreams that a synod takes place in which he is defended successfully against charges of having misappropriated a ham. As Ysengrim envisages the court, a learned attorney first establishes his client's strength of character by describing his recent sojourn in a monastery. Indeed, the lawyer soon proves that the wolf, by eating the ham singlehandedly, followed two precepts of *Benedict's Rule*: firstly, that the monk who needs more is entitled, even obligated, to take more (1.432; cf. chap. 34), and secondly, that the brothers should hasten to the table as soon as the dinner-bell has been rung (1.433–34; cf. chap. 43). Ysengrim and Reinard agreed to share whatever food they found. For a short while after coming upon the ham while Reinard was out of sight, Ysengrim waited; but when he calculated that it was time for monks to dine, he sat down to his meal. He would have erred against the gospel if he had saved for the future (1.453; cf. Matthew 6.34), and against the *Rule* if he had risen unsatisfied from the table (459–62). Thanks to such sophistries, the attorney in Ysengrim's daydream demonstrates that the wolf was a good monk to eat all of the ham except for the strings.

In the first tale Ysengrim dreams of employing the letter of the monastic rule against its spirit in order to feed himself. He contorts a religious institution, monasticism, to satisfy his own base appetites. In the second story (1.529–2.158) Reinard turns this process against Ysengrim, by arranging for religious ritual to foil the wolf's hope of obtaining food. He encourages Ysengrim to persevere as a monk and to honor the monastic diet by eating fish, albeit in gross quantities. As the wolf, squatting with his tail in the chilly water, misconstrues monastic usage, the fox rushes off and interrupts the celebration of a religious rite, a mass. He steals a cock that belongs to the officiant; the priest breaks off the service so that he can give chase; and the pursuit culminates in the punishment of Ysengrim.

Within this story of a fishing expedition, parody of liturgy and satire of ecclesiastics abound (cf. Yates 1984). Upon seeing the cock stolen, the possessive priest stops singing a proper hymn, "Hail, festive day!" ("Salue, festa dies!") and proclaims instead, "Woe to you, sad day!" ("Ue tibi, mesta dies!") In his improvised hymn he blames his superiors for his woes, since he would not have been celebrating the mass and therefore unable to protect his poultry if the bishop had suspended him for his past negligence as a priest. Later he rails at the office of the mass itself for not having safeguarded the bird to repay him for the many times when he had presided over services. The greed of the priest comes out especially when he demands a pledge from the members of his congregation, who have just appeased him by promising him a cock and a hen to replace his purloined rooster. His irreligion, already apparent in his blasphemous curses, becomes wild comedy when he leads his deacon and sexton in a mad chase after Reinard, all of them hurling church vessels at the fox. There is hardly need to report that church regulations fulminated against this sort of abuse of vessels (Plöchl 2: 303). With such a priest as spiritual guide, the boorish congregation has evolved a strange worship. An old woman, Al-drada, hisses through her 11-1/2 teeth a "lower-class canon" (2.60) of saints who never existed, mainly words from the liturgy which she took to be the names of holy men. The roster includes: Saints Excelsis, Osanna, Al-leluia, Credinde, Pater Nuster, and Celebrant (Peeters).

More liturgical parody revolves around the punishment meted out to Ysengrim as he sits frozen to the pond. Reinard initiates the grotesque imitation of rites when he speaks with his "uncle" as the villagers hurtle toward the pond. After making Ysengrim anxious about his predicament, Reinard reassures him that the priest wants only to renew the wolf's ton-sure and to sprinkle holy water on his head so that he will once again be a monk in good standing. As the wolf pleads desperately for help in escap-ing, Reinard reminds him obliquely of their last meeting. He declares that he would worry, if he freed Ysengrim from the ice, that he would be hauled before a synod and held responsible for the loss of the fish which the wolf had caught with his tail. At the last possible moment Reinard leaves, telling his uncle: "I have read what I was going to read; I leave to you the last words, 'Tu autem.' The reading is finished, lord abbot; say 'Tu au . . .'" (1.927–28). "Tu autem domine miserere nobis" was a prayer pro-nounced by the lector at the end of recitations; it was spoken both by monastic lectors reading before meals and by church lectors in services. Here it has a threefold significance. In the first place, by *Tu autem* Reinard means literally that "You, too, Ysengrim, will suffer failure, just as I suf-fered when we last met." Reinard had to learn his "lesson" (*lectio*) and now Ysengrim will have his turn. Secondly, the fox equates what is to follow with a church service: Ysengrim is to be punished by the liturgy. Finally, the sounds of the two syllables *tu au* foretell with gruesome onomatopoeia the cries that Ysengrim will emit as he is drubbed.

The peasants, as if collaborating with Reinard, treat their many at-tacks on the wolf as religious rituals. They recognize Ysengrim as an abbot who came to collect sheep-fleeces and sheep-flesh to take back to his mon-astery (1.967–72). They interpret his posture on the ice as a manifestation of penance, and they believe that he should absolve his guilt publicly and not privately (1.975–76: Righetti 4: 249–79). To help him decide between the two methods of self-mortification, they insist on subjecting him to trial by ordeal (1.977–82). They will toss at him the church candelabra, crucifixes, casks, and other vessels. If he does not feel the blows, he will be proved innocent, and if he does, he will be guilty.

When Ysengrim does not respond to this palaver, the priest assures his congregation that the wolf is silently expressing a blessing before a meal (1.1027–30). The priest and his charges are quick to supply Ysengrim food so that his benediction will not have been pointless. The priest, giving Ysengrim a long "bless you," swats him on the head with a Bible (1.1041–42). This action parodies the rite of consecration of a bishop, during which the officiating bishop and two assisting bishops or deacons held the gospel book upon the head and shoulders of the bishop being consecrated (Righetti 4: 440). With vicious irony, the poet compares the slapping of the book against Ysengrim's temples with the way in which platters of food and goblets of wine contact the lips of monks on feast days (1043–46). He has the wolf, who seeks to acquire lambs through abuse of the liturgy, chastised by buffets that are called food and are imparted through a travesty of the liturgy. Just as aptly, the poet, to describe the actual punishment of a wolf who tries to eat figurative sheep (the flock of the faithful), uses very literally the words of a metaphor about distinguishing the meaningful, figurative value of a story from the doctrinally valueless, literal surface. The pummeling of Ysengrim is the winnowing of grain and chaff (1.1063–64), a metaphor commonplace from Augustine (*De doctrina* 3.7.11) onward (Spicq 14).

The peasant woman, Aldrada, bungles her move to tonsure Ysengrim everlastingly by decapitating him (2.33–34); instead, she chops off his tail. As in earlier phases of the scene, her mistake translates instantly to liturgical parody. Ysengrim, tumbling forward as he is suddenly released from the ice, is a priest who genuflects prematurely (2.121). The unfortunate embrace of the old woman with the wolf is a ritual kissing of a bishop— but on his anus (2.122–28). Even the flight of the wolf, when he disentangles himself from her and sprints away as quickly as his feet can carry him, emerges as an act of liturgical parody: Ysengrim is a bishop who, in his unseemly haste to depart, neglects to excommunicate the guilty (2.138–39), pardon the repentant (137), bless the congregation (143), and sing the closing hymn and Psalm (147) as he quits the altar (Voigt 1884, notes ad loc.).

Thanks to Aldrada's misdirected swing of the ax, Ysengrim survives for his next adventure. As the third story commences (2.159–688), Ysengrim moans and rails about the duplicity of his nephew, Reinard. The fox jumps out of the bushes and commiserates with his uncle on the poor state of his "cowl." To make Ysengrim forget that he was ever angry, Reinard tells him how to secure a new cowl from the bellwether, Joseph (2.199, 2.267). The scheme requires that Ysengrim be engaged as a surveyor by four rams squabbling over their territorial boundaries. Instead of setting property lines, however, the maladroit wolf finds himself made into a boundary-marker, which the rams jostle from spot to spot with their horns.

During most of the story, the tribulations of the wolf give occasion for mathematical witticisms (Schwab 1969), rather than for liturgical parody or monastic satire, but at the end Ysengrim becomes a monk once more, and his torments are likened to a ritual. As the poet earlier characterized a beating as a threshing of wheat (1.1063–64), Reinard now calls one a pruning of a useless tree (2.651–52: compare Matthew 21.19, *Ecbasis captivi* 65, "Terence and his Mocker" 30–33). In both cases, biblical metaphors pertaining to the separation of the good from the bad are put into gruesome practice. In both scenes, physical violence is presented to Ysengrim as a Christian rite designed to satisfy his longings. In this instance, the fox incites the four brothers to bow to the already incapacitated wolf and give him "loving-cups" (2.655–56). The "draught of love" (*Minnetrank* in German) was a custom widespread among Germanic peoples, including those dwelling in the Low Countries (Bächtold-Stäubli 6: 375–80). Often the draught was preceded by an obeisance and took place in conjunction with prayers to St. John, St. Gertrude, and other saints (Bächtold-Stäubli 4: 745–60; 3: 708–12; 6: 378). It was meant to protect the guest and to mark the Christian goodwill of host and guest alike. Its evocation in describing the goring of Ysengrim is therefore appropriate: the rams mimic the proper protocol with great exactitude when they lower their heads and offer the wolf their horn-shaped goblets, as often as any guest would wish. Their visitor, the monk who came to acquire a new cowl, is aware of the liturgical undertones to his beating and keeps still so as to uphold his reputation as a monk (2.685–86).

In the fourth story (3.1–1198), about the sick lion-king, Ysengrim's habitual desire to eat takes second place to his eagerness to retaliate against his enemies. As usual, he hopes that his respectability as a monk will help him to obtain nourishment. He assures the skeptical lion-king that he went through advanced medical training during his time in the cloister (3.111–12; cf. 1.27). When he proposes that the lion devour his recent torturer, the ram, he justifies such a harsh measure on the grounds that "more than once the expedient was found more pleasing than the right in the cloister" (3.171). Also as usual, the rash actions of Ysengrim rebound to his own injury. He presses his plan too importunately, the king turns away in revulsion, and the ram and goat juggle Ysengrim back and forth on their horns. Just as he bore in silence the beating at the fishpond, he holds his tongue about the rough treatment dealt him by his two enemies: he still wishes to pass for a monk (3.217–18).

The blows are treated as a liturgical office, with one blow for every word spoken in the ceremony (3.214). Sadly for Ysengrim, the brutality in this office, rather than ending the service, sets off a series of liturgical harassments. The ass, Carcophas, asserts that Ysengrim never sang so well in the monastery as he did at prime and maintains that he will learn still better if he is flayed. By the song at prime, Carcophas means the howling as Ysengrim was battered at the icepond. This definition of breviary "singing" adds a sinister edge to the contention of Carcophas that Ysengrim, if flayed, will produce the songs for all eight canonical hours at once. Thus in this passage "singing" assumes the ominous colors that it did in the *Ecbasis captivi* (262), when the wolf threatened to "sing" the service himself if the priest delayed.

The flaying of Ysengrim is the axis of extensive liturgical parody. To the bear, for instance, the excoriation of the wolf is a reading (3.963–67), presumably because the ripping off of the hide resembles the turning of a book's pages. Reinard calls to mind hagiography as he urges the recalcitrant wolf to relinquish his pelt as St. Martin surrendered his cloak to the beggar. Above all, the flaying of the wolf becomes the ritual unrobing of a priest, abbot, or pontiff (3.874, 3.936). The boar reprimands Ysengrim for not thanking Bruno, the bear, for having flayed him. In view of Bruno's skill at removing vestments, Ysengrim would be well advised to cultivate his friendship; if the wolf ever became a priest, he would want to have the bear as his deacon.

The flaying must have reminded medieval readers of the defrocking of church officials or monks, for the similarity between a wolf stripped of his "hide" (*pellis*) and a bishop deprived of his "robe" (*pellis*) or a monk of his tunic is too suggestive to have been missed (Geertsom 12; Mann 1977, 506). An additional irony would be present if the scene recalled the injunction in *Benedict's Rule* that good monks turn the other cheek when denuded: "when deprived of their tunic surrender also their cloak" (chap. 7.42).

In the topsy-turvy world of the *Ysengrimus* the flaying or defrocking leads to a promotion, not to a demotion. In "The Sick Lion," the excoriation of the fox's antagonist leaves strips of hide on the head and paws which resemble the gloves and miter of a bishop, as well as the gloves and cap of a worldly potentate. At the close of "The Sick Lion" (65–66), the bear is taunted with the similarity. In the *Ysengrimus*, the wolf's condition elicits many derisive comments from the rabble of the lion's court. The ram blames Bruno for having carried out his office poorly (3.987–88), since he left the miter on Ysengrim's head. Soon referring to the left-over hide as hair, the ram urges that they renew the wolf's tonsure by removing it. As blood cascades from Ysengrim, Reinard expostulates with him for having hidden the scarlet dalmatic of a bishop beneath his shabby skin: such duplicity insults the majesty of the monarch. When the bleeding wolf collapses into a prone position to supplicate the king for mercy (*Benedict's Rule*, chap. 44), Reinard accuses him of throwing down his gloves and cap to challenge the sovereign to a duel. In the face of such a grave allegation, Ysengrim is lucky to escape with his life.

The lion, wrapped in the wolf's cowl, shows a great interest in hearing about Ysengrim's mishaps in the monastery, but before an account of that adventure is given, he hears about the pilgrimage of the roe, Bertiliana, and her companions. A boar is drafted to read these stories. This boar could be a reminder of the ham division, which precedes these stories in the narrative (although it anticipates them chronologically): the boar chews the story of the wolf-monk just as Ysengrim earlier chewed the ham. In the first tale (4.1–810), Ysengrim is a hermit who wishes to join a pilgrimage. The investiture of a pilgrim was a religious ritual, as significant to some people as donning a monk's habit (Sumption 172–73). The ritual included the blessing of the pouch and mantle and the presentation of the staff, hallowed on the altar. As usual, the wolf's high hopes of abusing religious ritual are disappointed: the customs of monasticism and pilgrimage are parodied in order to castigate him physically.

As Ysengrim enters the hut of the pilgrims, he advertises his monasticism with a hearty "Peace be with you" ("Pax vobis," 4.141–42). In his words, he has come "as a hermit to caution brothers to abide by peace and justice" (4.147–48). He asks the he-goat for a votive cross to indicate his participation in the pilgrimage party (Sumption 171–73). The travelers are uneasy about Ysengrim's "introit" into the hut (4.192) because they perceive that the wolf is interested far more in provisions than in shrines. But at the urging of Reinard, they lavish dainties upon the wolf, even the meat that his idiosyncratic rule permits (4.223–40; contrast *Benedict's*

Rule, chap. 39). But the animal flesh consists of the heads of wolves—wolf-abbots and wolf-bishops. Following the repast, which Ysengrim declines to eat, the ram, he-goat, and stag present the wolf with goblets of drink to wash down the food. Like the earlier love draughts, these draughts are strokes of their horns and antlers (4.450, 456, 470).

After the drinks have been served, Ysengrim groans in pain. The horned animals decide that the wolf is not singing mass or reading the lesson but rather seeking the remission of his sins. They absolve him with a ruthless threefold amen, "bless you," and other "benign words" (4.611, 620, 627). Finally, they initiate the wolf as a full-fledged pilgrim by outfitting him with a cross, wallet, and staff, all in the form of horns and antlers butted against his hide. When at last Ysengrim escapes from their brutal attentions, he swears to get revenge: though Reinard has sung part of the matins service, Ysengrim will be back with his brethren to finish the service. The fox, who always has the last word, is unperturbed. He bids farewell to Ysengrim with an ironic echo of the wolf's first cheery "Peace be with you" ("Pax vobis," 4.714–15). Ysengrim, a hermit who came to institute a *pax* of eating pilgrims, leaves reeling and bleeding from the love-draughts, monastic song, and investiture as a pilgrim that he was accorded by the fox and the friends of the fox. The liturgy has once more defended itself successfully against his onslaughts.

Whereas liturgical parody is extensive in the stories about Ysengrim, it is extremely rare in those about other animals. For instance, liturgical parody is absent from the sixth story (4.811–5.316), about Reinard and Sprotin the cock. The absence is all the more striking when one realizes that the same story as an exemplum contained extensive plays on the kiss of peace (Tubach no. 3629). But the presence of this episode in the *Ysengrimus* in no way diminishes the wolf-monk. Rather, the tale clarifies the reasons for Ysengrim's misfortune by shedding light on his opponents. The encounter between Reinard and Sprotin shows that not even the fox is invincible. But whereas Ysengrim's career traces an unended line of failures after his initial success in the division of the ham, Reinard's is a record of initial failures (against the cock and Ysengrim) later made good.

There is no liturgical parody in the central incident of the seventh story, the meeting of Reinard with Ysengrim's wife (5.705–820), but it is rife in the two episodes of the seventh story which treat of the wolf's stay in the monastery of Blandigny (5.317–704, 5.821–1128). That the liturgical parody centers upon Ysengrim suggests that it came into the poem as an apanage of the wolf-monk. It is hardly fortuitous that, in a later shortened version of the *Ysengrimus* in which the wolf is not a monk, both parody and satire disappear from the story (*Ysengrimus abbreviatus*).

Ysengrim enters the monastery after Reinard gives him a sample of monastic cuisine. In other words, the wolf becomes a monk only because he likes the fare. As far as he is concerned, religion and monasticism are very much matters of the stomach (5.407, 412). His obsession with eating impels him to suggest many changes to the monastic rule and makes him incapable of executing his responsibilities. How can he sing properly, when he considers good singing the ability to open one's mouth wide (5.429–34)? How can he thrive as a monk or officiate as a priest, when he cannot learn to say "bless you" (5.451–52) and when he mispronounces the two formulas of liturgical greeting (Righetti 1: 214–16), "The Lord be with you!" (*Dominus uobiscum*) as "This way, sheep, come!" (547–50: *cominus ouis, cum!*) and *amen* as *agne* (559)? The plays on *Dominus uobiscum* and *amen* call to mind many other versions of the wolf-monk, especially the wolf-monk in the school (Kaczynski and Westra 1988, 121–24).

The monks laugh away the suggestions and incompetences of the wolf, but they cannot shrug off his interference in their monastic duties. Their first inkling of trouble comes when Ysengrim takes his singing assignment, the tenth responsory of the night office, for an indication of how many sheep he will be served at the next meal (5.631–60). As soon as his turn to sing arrives, he breaks out in animated chatter about sheep (821–38). The monks hiss for him to be still, and as he protests that he has not yet been fed, they struggle to stifle their guffaws at his ineptitude. Seeing that Ysengrim disrupts every liturgical ceremony in which he involves himself, the monks have to eject him by force to bring the night office to rights. Indeed, *Benedict's Rule* (chap. 45) stipulates that monks who err in singing be humiliated and that young monks who do so be beaten. The abbot, besotted with strong wine, subjects the wolf to the usual monastic punishment for arrogant disobedience: he dismisses Ysengrim, like a scullery boy, to perform the menial task of pouring the wine (*Ecbasis captivi* 695–97, *Carmen Winrici*).

The punishment fails disastrously. As soon as Ysengrim sets foot in the wine-cellar, he begins to knock the bungs out of all the casks. Soon he is happily lapping up what spills out. When the monks come to dislodge Ysengrim from the cellar, where he is now floating on a sea of their prize vintages, the wolf tries to distract them by espousing his theory of how a bishop should be selected: the monk who proves himself greedier than all of his comrades shall win the post (5.989–1040). At this, the brothers

ranged around the cellar door exhort the wolf to emerge and to be or-
dained a bishop, for he is without doubt the most avaricious monk in their
company. Not mindful of the bad luck that church vessels brought him at
the fishpond, Ysengrim rushes out of the cellar to receive his reward.

In the satiric passages of the *Ysengrimus*, the poet censures a Church
which repaid a monk for his greed and gluttony by elevating him to abbot,
bishop, or pope. In his fiction, he makes any dealing with the liturgy or
any ecclesiastic promotion an excruciating ordeal. He parodies in this
scene the ceremony for the consecration of a bishop. As usual, the parody
is not a slavish, step-by-step transmogrification of an entire ceremony, but
rather an imaginative, eclectic recombination of certain elements from that
ceremony. A consecration day may be divided into three stages: what occurs before, during, and after the rite (Righetti 4: 439–45; Voigt 1884,
notes ad loc.). The poet suppresses all of the preliminaries, except for a
parade with banners (1047–48). Of the second phase he leaves out the
transfer of the pastoral staff, ring, and gospel book but includes the salving
with the chrism. Of the third he keeps the imposition of the miter, while
omitting the donning of gloves and ring and the procession to the episcopal throne. Finally, he adds the assumption of the pallium and the
presentation of consecration gifts.

The march of the monks to the wine cellar represents the parade with
banners (1043–48). One of the brethren anoints Ysengrim by stuffing his
ears full of fleas (1049–57); another rams the abbot's spittoon onto the
wolf's head so that he will have a miter (1058–74); and a third strings a
horsecollar around his neck as a stole (1075–76). After the abbot hits Ysengrim on the back with a millstone that he calls a "sweet biscuit" (1077–80),
yet another monk strikes the wolf into helplessness with a broken bell
(1081–90). Before Ysengrim can gather his forces, one brother drums on
him with a horse's head and another bores through him with a red-hot
iron: they pretend that these vicious attacks are gifts of a fiddle and a
bow, as if the new bishop were a new David—or an apprentice minstrel
(1091–116).

Once the seventh story has ended, the poet picks up the threads of
Ysengrim's biography where he had left them dangling—just after the
wolf was flayed to heal the lion. In the eighth story (5.1129–322), Ysengrim
confronts a stallion, Corvigar, in the belief that he can prevail upon him
to surrender his hide. As the flayed wolf approaches, the horse asks what
happened to his "cowl" (5.1179–82). After explaining, Ysengrim demands
the stallion's skin to replace the one that he lost at the lion's court. Corvi-

gar changes the subject with dexterity by observing that the wolf needs not only a new robe, but also a fresh tonsure, if he wishes to be taken for a proper monk (5.1225–26: Righetti 4: 371–74). He volunteers to shave Ysengrim's head, an offer which the wolf accepts only after inspecting the razor and the strop—the stallion's horseshoe and penis! The wolf makes no secret of his hope to earn a meal from monasticism, for he intends to gobble Corvigar as soon as the opportunity presents itself. In a peripeteia typical of the *Ysengrimus*, the wolf gets more than he bargained for: instead of a simple tonsure, he is given the mark of ecclesiastic authority. The iron horseshoe embedded in his brow carries more weight than the leaden seals of the popes, just as the leaden seals confer greater privileges than the waxen ones of bishops. With Corvigar's seal attached to his forehead, Ysengrim will easily regain admission to the cloister.

In the ninth, tenth, and eleventh stories Reinard reappears to reaffirm his commitment to destroy Ysengrim. He makes this dedication exceedingly clear in the eleventh tale (6.349–550), the only one of the three in which parody influences the course of action. In this story, Reinard convinces the wolf that he is owed a hide by the ass, Carcophas. Eventually Ysengrim need only swear an oath of truthfulness on a relic chest in order to receive the hide. The supposed reliquary turns out to be a wolf trap, however, and costs Ysengrim a paw. Both this tale and the next combine parody of relics with satirical comments on the Second Crusade. Possibly they were meant to criticize the adoration of relics (Schreiner), especially in drives to raise funds for enterprises such as the Crusades.

The outcome of the eleventh story brings Ysengrim and Reinard full circle from the first one, about the division of the ham (cf. Mann 1987, 33, n. 101). In that tale, Ysengrim agreed to give the fox an equitable fourth part of their booty, but broke his word and instead ate it all by himself. Reinard's subsequent behavior toward Ysengrim may be seen as repeated attempts to win redress for this inequity and for the humiliation of having been bilked. In the tenth tale (6.133–348), for instance, Reinard cuts a slaughtered cow into four portions, none of them for the wolf. The tenth tale foreshadows the eleventh; for while in the tenth the fox deliberately sets aside a hoof of the cow for himself, in the eleventh he contrives to deprive Ysengrim of a paw. At last Reinard has regained, symbolically, his quarter of the booty—and the spoil is the wolf.

The maiming of the wolf marks an achievement for the weak and oppressed over the strong, for the prey over the predators, but it is at best poetic justice. The satiric outburst in the middle of the eleventh episode exudes the conviction that in the world of men injustice is the inflexible rule (6.491–94). In the hierarchy of iniquity, the peasant must grovel before the tyrant, and the tyrant before the pope. In the real world the liturgy does not fight back. Liars turn unscathed from reliquaries, and grasping aspirants to episcopacies are not beaten insensible at their consecrations.

The definitive victory of the liturgy over Ysengrim occurs in the twelfth and final tale (7.1–708), in which both satire and parody reach their highest pitch—both literally and figuratively (Charbonnier 1984b, Schouwink 1984). As in the pilgrimage of Bertiliana and her companions, the wolf appears proclaiming his monastic benevolence with the liturgical greeting "Peace be with you!" (7.13–14 "Pax!"; cf. 2.99, 4.141–42, 6.56; Righetti 1: 214–16); in his naïvete he expects that a few sweet words will allay the worries of the old sow Salaura and persuade her to let him administer a kiss. In the story of the pilgrimage, the "Peace be with you!" greeting was echoed ironically by Reinard and sounded ominous, as if by antiphrasis it indicated Ysengrim's true intentions. Here in the tale about Salaura and the sixty-six swine, Ysengrim's "Peace!" is both a liturgical greeting and the kiss with which it was related (Perella; Righetti 1: 385–88, 3: 486–89). Of course, the kiss which the wolf would like to press upon the sow and upon any other available victim is the kiss of death, identical to the one the wolf wished to give the calf in the *Ecbasis captivi* (138–39).

Salaura invites Ysengrim to learn about the rule of her order, since she has a good notion of his. Not at all parodic, her rule stipulates that the kiss of peace not be exchanged between a man and a woman and that it take place at its proper time, after a mass has been celebrated (7.29–36). Since Salaura is of the opposite sex from the wolf and since it is not yet prime, she and Ysengrim are not entitled to kiss. Even if they agree to overlook the difference in gender, the problem of the requisite mass remains. Ysengrim would offer to perform a mass, but his lameness disqualifies him from officiating (Leviticus 21.20). Yet by his gastrointestinal clock the wolf knows that it is prime and consequently time for a mass to take place. What solution can be reached?

To settle the matter, Salaura takes upon herself the task of celebrating a mass and of bestowing the kiss of peace, but she needs the assistance of her monks and nuns. By biting her on the ear Ysengrim helps her hail her charges and sound the introit to the perverted mass (7.105).

Once Salaura has squealed, sixty-six younger pigs arrive to commence the ceremony. Although there is no need to look for special symbolism in the pigs (Schouwink 1984, 1985), the herd of pigs that would have come first to the mind of medieval Christians was the Gadarene swine—the herd into which a legion of unclean spirits entered after being exorcised from a man by Jesus (Mark 5.2–16; Luke 8.20–35). Whereas the man was exorcised and the swine threw themselves to their death, here the wolf is killed and the swine survive. The devilish associations of the pigs would only have been strengthened by the legend of the demon-swine, devils in the form of swine who attacked a Carthusian brother, but who were driven away through the power of the paternoster and the Virgin (Peter the Venerable, *De Miraculis* 2.29, PL 189.946C–947B; H. Ward 2: 588, no. 12). If the author of the *Ysengrimus* and his audience knew the legend of the demon-swine, then they would have seen an irony in the failure of the wolf to save himself despite all his pretensions of liturgical knowledge.

Salaura had promised Ysengrim that her sixty-six charges would have lips fuller and more pleasing to kiss than her own puckered old mouth. But once the pigs arrive, their menacing snorting and slavering fill Ysengrim with terror that they will give him the kind of kiss he wished to give them (7.149–54). They confirm his worst expectations by reading him an epistle that consists of tugging flesh from his hindquarters (7.189–92). The epistle is followed by the gradual, which the crowd of pigs "sings" as it tugs chunks of the wolf's flesh (7.193–214). Ysengrim has become the offering, the eucharistic host.

Later in the mass, the sow Bekka rips off one of his three remaining feet so that he falls flat on his face, into a position of prayer. Then Salaura eviscerates his liver, which because of its two lobes she pretends to mistake for a stolen book (7.289–91: Sypher 1973, 132; Mann 1987, 533 notes that "no book is involved in the ceremony of the kiss of peace at Mass" but a book was of course involved in the mass itself: 7.187–89). Now that the volume has been recovered and peace restored, all the pigs are allowed to press the "kiss of peace" (*pax*) upon Ysengrim, but first Ysengrim asks and is granted his last request, the chance to prophesy the future (7.301–62). Here, at the point in the mass where the homily should have been read, the reader is treated instead to a series of vulgar imprecations. The wolf, in a fitting end to a life of gluttony, invokes the spirit of flatulence rather than the Holy Ghost as he faces the animals who are to eat him.

The wolf, who regularly receives greater and more painful returns from the liturgy than he foresees, finds that the kiss of peace results in his canonization as a saint. For his preternatural holiness, Ysengrim deserves to be buried in numerous reliquaries, namely, the stomachs of the sixty-six pigs and Salaura. Salaura authorizes this unusual type of sanctification with a twisted quotation from the Bible, like the ones that Ysengrim brought forth so often in defense of his dietary habits: since the Sacred Scripture tells us to love our enemy (Matthew 5.43–44; Luke 6.27, 6.35), and since her two closest adversaries are her stomach and Ysengrim, she can make no more magnanimous gesture than to unite the two within her by eating Ysengrim (7.395–414).

After the wolf has finished his prophetic last speech and Salaura has announced how his epitaph will read, she swallows his liver and the other pigs join in dismembering him. Sonoche tears out his diaphragm and heart, which she believes to be the text and seal of a peace declaration (7.427–31). Another sow, Cono, develops the parody by calling the wolf's gullet a peace trumpet (7.432–36). She claims that, now that the pigs have the emblems of peace, *pax* reigns. What had begun as parody of a liturgical *pax* has been transformed into a political and legal *pax* (Mann 1987, 104).

The parody of a peace declaration accords poorly with the preceding travesty of religious and monastic ceremony. Indeed, the twelfth episode as a whole could be faulted for including inconsequential parody and for fitting awkwardly with the rest of the poem. After all, it breaks the continuity of the poem by having Salaura execute Ysengrim, even though Reinard was the chief antagonist throughout the earlier stories. But are these two features, the parody of a peace declaration and the change of an archenemy, truly discordant with what came before? Or do they enhance the unity of the poem in ways not immediately obvious?

Ysengrim offended against Reinard only once, in the first story. He was punished fittingly and fully for this injury in the tenth and eleventh tales, and needed to pay no further redress to the fox. In contrast, Ysengrim transgressed repeatedly against Christian liturgy and monastic custom. To mention only the first and second stories, he showed a willingness to abuse the legal process of a synod and contributed to the interruption of a mass. Subsequently, he disrupted the night offices of monks and of pilgrims. If Ysengrim owed satisfaction to anyone at the end of the poem, he owed it to the rites and institutions of Christianity, which he had so often wronged.

Because the Christian institution most often violated by the wolf was monasticism, it is proper that his executioners be an abbess and her followers. To underscore the notion that monasticism itself is retaliating, Ysengrim suggests that his encounter occurs on the vernal equinox, which is the feast-day of Benedict, the founder of Latin monasticism (Schönfelder 1929, 50; 1955, 156, notes). Because Ysengrim perverted the liturgy whenever he tried to get food, the avenging monks turn his own weapon against him. In the episode at the fishpond, a mass was cut short at prime (2.93–274, 1.735). When a priest tried to resume the service by swatting Ysengrim with a Bible, the wolf was accidentally set free by an old woman who kissed him on the rectum. In the story of Salaura, the mass which had been arrested in its course recommences and finishes at prime. The officiant, rather than clubbing Ysengrim with a copy of the Bible, tears one out of his bowels (7.289–91). In this second mass, the old woman is a sow who, instead of caressing the wolf on the anus, amputates his buttocks (7.190–92). And not only through the symmetry of imagery in the second and twelfth tales is the death of Ysengrim linked with the liturgy of the mass. Even the number of the sows, sixty-six, may point to the sixty-sixth Psalm, always read at the morning service in monasteries (*Benedict's Rule*, chap. 12–13: contrast Schwab 1969, 246, who relates sixty-six to the number of the beast in the Apocalypse 13.18).

The last two hundred lines of the *Ysengrimus* juxtapose the poet's treatment of the fictive wrongdoer to his attitudes toward real-life ecclesiastics—the monks who become abbots, bishops, and supreme pontiffs. As Salaura is grieving for the death of the wolf, Reinard emerges from a nearby hiding place and enquires of her what has happened to his "uncle." After informing him of the many masses that have been read over the wolf, the sow bursts into a long song of lament—a *planctus*—in which she questions the efficacy of baptism and the presence of the Holy Ghost on earth (7.607–14) and warns that the depravity of human conduct would lead to destruction on the Day of Judgment. Reinard cuts her short before she can make her criticism of twelfth-century Christianity more specific. In the process of pretending to defend Pope Eugenius III, he produces a long invective against him for betraying the crusaders and for hoarding coins.

In the fantasy that is the *Ysengrimus*, the poet condemns to death a wolf-monk who strives to accomplish on a literal level that which the human beings were already achieving metaphorically: the devouring of the flock. The author betrays ample confidence that the ceremonies of monasticism and liturgy can protect themselves from interlopers: he has the mass, by killing Ysengrim, restore to the world the peace that the wolf had disturbed throughout the poem. Thus the poem combines a trust in the institutions and ceremonies of religion with a disappointment in the ecclesiastics who oversee them. The bitter-sweet mixture of faith and chagrin strikes one most at the end of the *Ysengrimus*. The nefarious wolf-monk is brought to justice by a nun, but the holy woman is cast unflatteringly as a sow! How reliable a spokesman for church reform is such an abbess? And how good a nun is Salaura, who has no fewer than twenty-two children (7.141–42)?

The lesson of the *Ysengrimus* is not that a person with the cunning of the fox can get the better of everyone else. As Reinard's failures are evidence, the principle behind Uncle Remus's trickster tales holds true in the unique landscape across which the animals of the *Ysengrimus* move: "There's always someone that's stronger." None of the characters in the poem deserves the name of the hero. Rather, the *Ysengrimus* depicts an antiheroic world of unmitigated vice, in which the wolf embodies greed and gluttony, the fox slyness and false pride. In contrast to the idealism of such beast literature as Kipling's *Jungle Books*, the animals of the *Ysengrimus* are not models of virtue. They are appropriated to depict the lowest conception of humanity; they are avatars of the worst in the world of human beings. The purpose of the poem seems to anticipate Gerard Leeu's *Die Hystorie van Reynaert die Vos* (1479) and Caxton's *The History of Reynard the Fox* (1481), both of which have a prologue and an epilogue in which the reader is told to learn from the wicked animals how to avoid wickedness. One spectacular achievement of the *Ysengrimus* poet was that he could make his characters exemplars of evil while managing at the same time to personalize the animals more fully than in any previous work of beast literature.

Although all of the characters are villains, the darkness in the *Ysengrimus* is not unrelieved. The poet did not leave his reader with a fictional world of ineluctable and unceasing dialectic between predator and victim (*pace* Jauss 105–7; Mann 1987, 52), with a world in which Fortune wreaks havoc with one and all (*pace* Jauss 188–89); he also shows the reader that villainy will be punished: the corrupt ecclesiastic will be subverted by his greed, the corrupt statesman by his craft. Thus the absence of heroes does not signal the lack of anything positive, since behind the vituperation abides a faith in the system. The author of a satiric medieval beast poem need not have been opposed to the ideal behind the system he satirized, any more than George Orwell had to reject the notion of true socialism when he wrote *Animal Farm*.

Conclusion

Saepe condita luporum fiunt rapinae vulpium.
(*Querolus*, ed. Emrich, 70)

Often the caches of wolves become the plunder of foxes.

When medieval narrative literature burgeoned in the second half of the twelfth century, beast literature flowered as spectacularly as romance (Martin 287). Stories of Renard the Fox and his peers spread rampantly throughout Europe (Flinn; Best), transmitted in artistic as well as literary monuments (Varty): the main *branches* of the *Roman de Renart* were written between 1170 and 1205 (Foulet), while Heinrich der Glîchesaere composed *Reinhart Fuchs* toward the end of the century. *Van den Vos Reinaerde* followed in the first half of the thirteenth century. The *Physiologus* tradition crept out of its well-established but confined location to enter many new ones, as successive vernacular authors of bestiaries extended its applications. Largely new works of animal fiction, such as Nigel of Canterbury's *Speculum stultorum*, won enormous popularity.

Little of this florescence depended directly on earlier developments in medieval Latin beast literature, although the *Ysengrimus* was undoubtedly important in the gestation of the Renard cycle. Yet all of it vindicated the efforts that the earlier medieval Latin authors had made to produce hardy grafts, rooted in stories that were too humble to merit preservation but eventually growing into written forms that could compete for attention and admiration in the world of Latin learning.

When medieval authors wrote in Latin, they reached a decision, whether conscious or not, that had a great bearing on the prospective audiences and literary contexts of their compositions. By the middle of the twelfth century, the choice of languages was as demanding as it had ever been. Consequently, it is only fitting that language, writing, books, and texts should be a major concern in the *Ysengrimus* (Westra; Scheidegger; Mann 1987, 58–77). In some respects the choice of Latin limited the appeal of compositions; for since most people in the Middle Ages received no

training in Latin, full appreciation of Latin poetry belonged to the relatively few people—usually men and usually clerics—who were educated.
In another respect, writing in Latin guaranteed that a work of literature
could travel with relative freedom across the many linguistic borders of
medieval Western and Central Europe, since at most times and in most
places knowledge of Latin was an essential component of being literate.
Furthermore, the choice of Latin meant that authors could assume on the
part of their audiences a shared cultural background, in particular a familiarity with both Christian liturgy and a substantially classical menu of
school texts.

Medieval authors who decided not only to write in Latin but also to
make a talking animal the protagonist of a composition faced further vistas
and further impasses. Medieval Latin poets came in contact with large
bodies of written and oral beast literature not only in Latin but also in
vernacular languages, much of which has been lost. This literature encompassed such diverse material as oral and written beast fables and trickster
tales, the symbolic animals of the *Physiologus* and bestiaries, and beast riddles. Because many of these literary forms were represented in the earliest
readings in the grammar schools, the most enterprising poets were eager
to give their works a special cachet by experimenting. They had their own
messages, created their own narrative frameworks, struck their own tones,
and developed their own styles and voices.

As the surviving medieval Latin beast poems demonstrate, the range
of possible responses to beast literature and lore was unlimited. To look
only at the two longest poems written before 1150, the poet of the *Ecbasis
captivi* wrote a recitative play, the poet of the *Ysengrimus* an epic. Yet although each composition is sui generis, it would be mistaken to allow a
standardizing generic taxonomy to obscure the similarities among these
works of fiction—similarities that arise from the fact that all of these works
have talking animals as their protagonists.

Etiological animal tales and animal trickster tales are one protoplasm
of beast literature, but this protoplasm underwent substantial changes in
passing back and forth between oral and written literature. A story that a
preacher told to a congregation of peasants or that a peasant related to
family or friends could have been reshaped in Latin verses by a monk or
cleric to be read in a refectory or episcopal court—or vice versa.

Because the most established form of written literature with talking
animals as heroes was beast fable, the authors of many medieval Latin
beast poems presented their poems as outgrowths from fable and related

genres such as the exemplum. This stance brought with it a mixture of pride and defensiveness, a desire to capitalize upon the conventional strengths and popularity of fable while avoiding its childish associations.

One of the fable's strengths was that it fulfilled Horace's principle (*Ars poetica* 333) of being delightful and useful, of entertaining and edifying its readers. In the view of Conrad of Hirsau (*Dialogus super auctores* 384–89, ed. Huygens, p. 84), Aesop and the other fabulists weave together entertainment and edification:

> Et quia poetis propositum est aut prodesse aut delectare, auctor iste ex qualitate morum humanorum contexuit mendosa commenta fabularum suarum, res fingens insensibiles, vel certe irrationabiles, ludos vel seria invicem conserentes, omnia ad similitudinem humanae vitae referens.

> And because the objective of poets is either to provide benefit or to delight, this author fabricated the lying fictions of his fables on the basis of human conduct, imagining inanimate or at least irrational things engaging alternately in games or earnest activities, and relating all these events to the likeness of human life.

It is no accident that beast poets also used the medieval version of the Horatian principle (Suchomski) to justify their poetry, pointing out that, although fictitious, their stories of animals concealed useful lessons (Knapp 1979a, 38–39, 112). They take pains to emphasize both their playfulness and the difficulty of their poems. For instance, the author of the *Ecbasis captivi* acknowledges his poem to be a "one-of-a-kind fable" ("rara fabella," 39) and "a lying composition" ("mendosa carta," 40), but he goes on to say that "There are nevertheless many useful lessons to be observed in it" ("Sunt tamen utilia que multa notantur in illa," 41). Nigel lays a similar claim in the prologue of the *Speculum stultorum* (5–14).

The goals of entertaining and edifying can be met in many ways. The entertainment can stem from the humorous actions of the animals or from their presumptuous appropriation of lofty rhetoric or classical style. The edification can be expressed explicitly, as in the moral of a fable, or left implicit. Thus the edification need not be expressly didactic. Rather, it can come through a satire that depicts evils to be avoided or through an allegory that tells of heavenly joys. It can be achieved through the worldly wisdom of animal trickster tales (a wisdom never too far from the surface of the Renard cycle), the ethical home truths or social commentary of fables, the eternal religious verities of the bestiary, or a combination of these elements.

Another freedom—or necessity—embraced by the beast poets was the freedom to invent narrative structures that suited their individual purposes. The poets are consistent only in avoiding the compact "story and moral" structure of conventional fable. Instead, they opt to box one story within another, to string several stories together—in short, to experiment. But perhaps it is misleading to represent this experimentation as a freedom the poets elected. In a sense, the freedom was forced upon them, since they had no written models for substantial works of beast fiction. From oral culture (and oral culture was found among monks as well as among the common people), they could have drawn stock characters and individual stories, but there is no reason to suspect that any longer narratives existed: the *Ysengrimus* anticipates by many decades any coherent epic elaboration of the Renard cycle. Likewise, from the treasury of Latin Classics the beast poets would have known many simple forms, such as fable, epitaph, and testament, but no longer ones: even the *Golden Ass*, a novel of man-animal transformation that is loosely related to later beast literature, was practically unknown and unavailable. One sort of edification can be offered inside another: so thoroughly did the beast poets take to heart the goal of edifying that even within their poems animal characters are often told exemplary stories. In the *Ecbasis captivi* the wolf tells of the old struggle between his grandfather and the fox; in the *Ysengrimus* the lion's court hears of the wolf-monk and of the fox and cock; and in the *Speculum stultorum* not only is the main character an exemplum to the reader, but in addition he tells and is told numerous other stories as exempla to him— and to the reader.

Because the authors of the longest beast poems wrote without models, they showed considerable diversity in their means of structuring their narratives. They were willing and able to innovate because they had to toe the line of no existing genres, once they had paid lip service to fable. Whereas the *Ecbasis captivi* poet took the risk of allowing a huge inner story to interrupt the course of the outer story, the *Ysengrimus* poet tied together many episodes in an outer story with a few in an inner story. Later, Nigel contrived a frame tale within which he inserted exempla, dreams, and visions.

Such narrative structures, in which events and meanings are enclosed within events and meanings, take to an extreme a tendency implicit in all of the medieval beast poems, as in all ancient and medieval beast fables: to require readers to locate human messages within animal forms. The beast poems differ from the beast fables only in their refusal to reveal directly the messages encoded in them. From Alcuin and the Carolingian poets on, readers are challenged, almost teasingly, to determine the relationship between the beast stories and the human world. Is the cock of Alcuin's poem a hero or a villain, a good Christian or a bad, a befeathered Orpheus or a Eurydice? Is the bear in "The Sick Lion" a churchman or a nobleman? Did Sedulius the Irishman own a ram, or was his poem a complete fiction? In either case, was the poem really a plea for patronage in the form of a ram or was it an expression in animal form of political problems in Sedulius's life (Ratkowitsch)? Is the ass or mule in Leo of Vercelli's "Meter" related to his wrangles with Arduin? Do the mishaps of the calf in the *Ecbasis captivi* correspond to moments in the biography of the anonymous poet?

Most of the poems touch upon the issues of disguise, flaying, or stripping of disguises: the bear in "The Sick Lion" is flayed, the ram in Sedulius's poem is accused of being a wolf in sheep's clothing, the ass in Leo's poem is expelled from the body of the wolf, the wolves in the *Ecbasis captivi* and *Ysengrimus* have their hides torn off after seeking to do the same to the foxes, and the ass in the lion's skin is never far from the surface in Nigel's *Speculum stultorum*. While within the brutal arenas of the poems animals struggle to tear away the coverings under which would-be predators hide, within the hermeneutic circle around the poems readers engage in an analogous process of peeling the surface of the poems to find hidden meanings. But the analogy should not be pressed too far, for the stylistic and structural surfaces of the poems cannot be detached with surgical precision from the multiplicity of meanings that lies behind them.

Appendices: Translations

1. ALCUIN, "THE COCK AND WOLF"

There is a bird called by the special surname "cock." This bird announces daybreak, dispels shadows from the earth, marks the times of the day, and is girded in his loins. The flock of chickens is ruled subject to his authority. [5] God praises the cock by saying that he has understanding: to be sure, he brings the times of the day from beneath an obscure cloak.

Oh what a sorrow! A barrier of roads once constrained him as he was hastening a long way off, testing for food with his beak. Therefore, as he seeks food by himself and ranges over the crossroads, [10] alas! boasting, too bold, and very proud, he is snatched by the lurking wolf.

Oppressed by this burden, the cock at once finds for himself this scheme for escaping: "Often your fame, O wolf of exceeding strength, has come to my ears and has told in a strange rumor that your great voice can produce a deep [15] sound with bright harmonies. I do not grieve so much to be devoured by a hated mouth as to be cheated of being allowed to learn from you what was possible to believe about your voice."

The beast put credence in what was said, and the wolf, swollen with love of the praise that had been offered, [20] opens his hellish throat, spreads wide his gluttonous jaws, and unlocks the innermost chamber of the vast cavern.

But swiftly the bird, harbinger of daybreak, is rescued, and in a bound flies and quickly clings to a tree branch. As soon as he has gained sudden freedom, [25] the bird sitting on high brings forth songs with these words: "Whoever grows proud without reason is deservedly deceived, and whoever is taken in by false praise will go without food, so long as he tries to spread about empty words before eating."

This fable applies to those people, whoever they are, who have obtained salvation rightly, but are then deprived of it by black deceits, in paying heed to false breezes with their empty rumors.

2. ALCUIN, LETTER 181

The first letter [of the alphabet, *A* for Alcuin] sends greetings to the first [Adalhard of Corbie], and the fifteenth [*p* for *pater*, "father"] to the sixth [*f* for *filius*, "son"], the number consecrated in the fifteen gradual Psalms [Psalms 119 to 133] to the perfect number of six in the works of God.

Why did that brother come empty-handed? On his tongue he carried a "Greetings!" for our ears, but in his hands he brought nothing for our eyes. You indeed, who sit in the intersection [Corbie: cf. Genesis 38.14], why did you hand over nothing definite to him, who dwells in Maresa [Michah 1.15]? The ravens cry out, flitting about the peaks of the roofs, and the dove nourished on the paving stones of the church is silent.

Whom should I believe, if he said anything about the eagle [Pope Leo III (795–816)]? He who recently left the peaks of the Roman citadel so that he could drink the fonts of the Saxon countryside [Paderborn] and see the lion [Charlemagne], who rules over all living creatures and wild beasts; or what our blackbird, flitting among them, handed over to the monastic cock [Adalhard], who is accustomed to wake the brothers for their morning vigils; so that through him the solitary sparrow on the roof [Alcuin] should know what was being agreed between the lion and the eagle; and if the youth of the eagle was renewed into its former joyousness according to the prophecy of the psalmist [Psalm 102.5]; and if new roofs were rising up in the swampy lairs of perfidy [the church of Paderborn]; and if the lion [Charlemagne] was considering following the ibis by crossing the Alpine hills.

The sparrow has its ears open. But, as I see, the proverbial cat [Devil] has taken the tongue of the cock [Adalhard] [literally, "the proverbial wolf in the fable has taken the voice from the cock"], lest by chance as he sings the pope's denial of his crimes should be repeated in the city of ancient power [Rome], and lest the most recent mistake should be worse than its predecessor [Matthew 27.64].

Why has charity sinned, which did not see the written "Greetings"? In the meantime I hear that partridges running through the fields have come to the dwelling-place of the cock [Corbie]. Perfect charity dismisses fear [1 John 4.18]. With the gleaming pupils of its eyes it notices everything, and with its bright gaze of piety it will always find a sure standard of rightful counsel. As it seems, the cock [Adalhard] has been turned into a cuckoo which tends to be silent as the sun ascends into the summer constellation of Cancer; whereas the nest-making sparrow [Alcuin] shrills on the sooty roofs in the same way, no matter what the sign of the zodiac.

Now in the month of September the sparrow flies to revisit its beloved nest [the monastery of St. Martin in Tours], so that it may feed its chicks [pupils], yawning with greedy beaks, with granules of piety; hoping that sometime over the banks of the fish-filled river [Loire] it will hear the voice of the cock [Adalhard] sound out "Greetings!" and that the bird which is accustomed to rouse itself to morning song with its own wings will come to exhort the sparrow in the midst of its chicks.

O how sweet is the voice of charity, which the amiable encouragements of brotherly love are accustomed to sound out in the ears of the heart. Do not close your hands full of seeds, because the person who hides grain will be cursed, and the person who multiplies it will receive a blessing [Proverbs 11.26]. What sort of verdict will he receive, who denies to a beggar that which he ought to press upon even an unwilling recipient? How does that which is not sown increase? What profit can be hoped for by the person who does not bear fruit? Or how does the fruit increase, if seeds are not spread about? Blessed are those who sow seeds upon all the waters, sending there the foot of the ox of the ecclesiastic order and the ass of the lay court [Isaiah 32.20]. And if you have not acted in the morning of your youth, you should act even now in the evening of your final dotage. It is better to be the dispenser of everlasting bread than to be the agent of transactions among peasants. Because as a man sows, so shall he reap [Galatians 6.8].

Look where charity has led me! Forgetful of myself, bringing goatskins to the sanctuary of Christ. For your heart is known to be the treasure of Christ, whence rivers of living water are wont to flow [John 7.38]. If I have exceeded proper bounds, let the charity which has no bounds and which endures all things pardon me [1 Corinthians 13.7]. Draw me behind you through your prayers, so that we may run together to the prize of being summoned on high [Philippians 3.14]. Virtue has failed if brotherly consolation does not help up the tired and raise up the person lying. What is there that charity cannot accomplish, seeing that it is in him who can accomplish everything? Do not neglect the salvation of your brother. Christ gave himself on behalf of sinners; why do you deprive of encouraging words a person to whom Christ did not deny his very blood? Is it truly possible that you ought to consider someone an outsider, when all people are fellow citizens in Christ? Charity does not hold individuals in awe; it does not have bags with holes [Aggeus 1.6]; and it does not load itself with thick clay [Habacuc 2.6], but it is modest, kindly, merciful, and clement. May he protect you in charity, he who gathered you in the sheep-fold of charity, taking you from the waves of the wild sea [Jude 13], so that you should be a ram, which no power of iniquity could resist [Proverbs 30.31]. Give aid to the person who beseeches you, so that he may triumph in him, who conquered the vanities of this world in you—and who said in a consolatory speech to his disciples: "These things I have spoken to you, that in me you may have peace. In the world you shall have distress: but have confidence, I have overcome the world" [John 16.33].

May Christ the son of God make you a victor and may he hearken to your every prayer, dearest brother.

3. CUONO OF ST. NABOR, "THE PEACOCK AND OWL"

Just when we surrendered our limbs to rest last night, then suddenly a very great disquiet and an immense grief, which we can scarcely control, awakened us. For this reason it is pleasing to sing, because singing assuages mourning.

[5] A rare bird on earth and one quite similar to white swans, alas, our peacock passed away from the present life; a natural death did not carry off the peacock, but rather a savage owl slew it. Otherwise unable, the owl killed it by deceit as it was sleeping; but nevertheless not easily, for they struggled with vigor.

[10] But when the peacock was tired and wished relief from us, it cries out with its characteristic cries redoubled. Stupefied, we arise—but the bird was already close to death. As we stand weeping, it abandoned us in our grief.

Now in tears we make this known to you, abbess; [15] we entreat urgently that you grieve compassionately and that you conduct it obsequies, as you are able; indeed, then we promise to you a love equal to our love for it.

So that the creature which restrains you [O peacock] pitilessly may grieve because of us, may the owl—[20] which brought sorrow to those who in no way hurt it—be accursed above all other birds. May curses be heaped upon the owl by the whole world; may it never be safe or outlive either its mother or father.

This epitaph should be engraved above the bones of the peacock:

"Here lies whiteness, which dark blackness has afflicted; [25] indeed, the peacock here buried will be likened aptly to a star, there is nothing whiter in either heaven or the underworld. The envious owl bit its body and struck it dead, and stained its throat with the blood undeservedly shed. From this time henceforth may the owl be accursed in all things in the world; [30] may the phrase 'May the peacock be blessed' be pronounced by every creature."

You, whoever you are who have laid your eyes diligently upon these verses, speak, so that Cuono may thrive forever in the life-giving God of heaven. Requested by the voices of boys, he composed these verses.

[*Prose Interpretation*]
"The blessing of the Lord is upon the head of the just" (Proverbs 10.6). It is therefore a consequence that the curse of the Lord should be upon the head of the unjust. Accordingly, the owl will be rightly subject to every sort of malediction.

When it laid an ambush, it stumbled upon ambushers. When it wished to capture, it perceived captors. [5] When it wanted to seize, it came upon those who seized it. When it longed to deceive, it found deceivers. When it desired to slay, it saw slayers. Nevertheless, it has not yet suffered death, because we waver about the appropriate manner of death in which it should perish.

In all things God, who delivered our enemy into our hands, is blessed.

[10] We chose to make this matter known especially to you and to the dominion of your nuns since we judged it fitting that, just as you were companions in our most grievous lamentation when the dearest peacock was slain, in the same way you might share in the great laughter when the most hated owl was captured.

Moreover, on account of the great happiness may it please everyone to shout out: "Let us serve in sanctity the Lord, who will free us from the assault of our enemies; [15] let us sing to the Lord, for he is to be extolled gloriously [Exodus 15.1], since he cast down at our feet the neck of the attacker."

4. EGBERT OF LIÈGE, "THE BEAR, WOLF, AND FOX"

About the Three Officials: The Bear, Wolf, and Fox
Once upon a time, when the bishop of a certain see died, [1175] free choice about it is granted to two counsellors. Now the wolf and fox gave

by way of response: "In our opinion the bear should not become bishop. As provost he consumed the brothers' communal food. Unable to share, he took the communal property for himself."

[1180] Then the wild bear attacked the wolf, tearing him to shreds. The fox, the vintner, now reminds the brothers; she says, "You know about our brother and deacon, the wolf? Look: you see him bloodied for the sake of the brothers' funds. The bear tore the flesh from his neck upon his fierce claw—for the outcome is plain from his bright red cap. His ruddy headdress taught me to be cautious: I hope that it will be possible to keep a distance while he rules us: a person treacherous in small matters in rarely trustworthy in a great one."

May he lose honor who takes everything for himself alone.

5. EUGENIUS VULGARIUS, "COMIC VISIONS"

A.

[1] It is a pleasure to weave a web in Anacreontic verse, to fasten metrical foot to foot, and to lead them through their poetic course. [2] The times are most excellent, the meadows most springlike, everything is beautiful and rejoicing, and our dwellings are charming. [3] Therefore, let bodies be joyful and hearts laugh, let all things celebrate as love seeks out neighboring regions.

[4] Phoebus spins through his phases, whirling the lights of the heavens; rivers murmur of sleep; and birds sing sweet things. [5] The turtledove first gives forth songs of favorable omen; later the heron utters hoarse sounds; while the blackbird mixes in the harmony, the swan completes the melody.

[6] The nightingale seated on a myrtle says, "You, dear children, listen to the words of your mother, so long as the upper air circles the constellations. [7] Singing the same notes I sing, sweet-sounding scions of our progeny, gradually rein back for God your throats, most worthy of song. [8] For you are the happiest people, only you are the psaltery of God, singing divine songs in the inmost parts of your heart. [9] Come now: so that by following your mother's pattern you may outdo feathery beaks, make haste to temper the coming notes of your voice."

[10] The nightingale said this, and soon fine cries of joy follow; a tune arises from a pleasant voice and puts to sleep the secret concerns of the mind. [11] For this reason the seating grows crowded, as every

sort of animal runs up—the lioness, lynx, and deer—as the tailed vixen stands. [12] The fishes desert the waters, and the shallows creep backward; the poetaster Codrus is present, thumping his flanks because filled with envy. [13] The eagle, the king, sits on gold—the rest around him in columns. The peacock with its jeweled back is there, and the talkative crow as well. [14] And there is more: a company of ravens and a phalanx of kites are hot with anger, they discuss the omens of war, that the nightingale may be conquered. [15] But a youthful ring-dove anticipates victory; first the cock and blackbird lament that their flanks have burst. [16] The cicada, puffing out its wretched and angry spleen, makes crackling noises in the field; the nightingale, prolonging its verses in warbling, takes the palm of victory.

[17] Then the beaked clan is distraught, and the eagle turns bloodless and cold, and strength fails in its bony midriff. [18] The owl becomes the herald of flight, urging them to retreat to hidden spots, lest their minds conscious of shame pay the penalty forever. [19] Then the feathery camp turns around and selects hideaways scattered about and blasts of the breeze that have been broken; they seek the high places of the woods.

B.

It comes to pass that, while the above events took place, a five-year orbit and [5] a circuit of the theatrical world—a year—went by. Then the rebuffed crowd makes its way to that place, following a path that is dusty and everywhere well-worn, [10] but passable.

The creatures are happy, the wind and the breeze are full of song, [15] and the skies are clear. They stand ready to serve, each one according to the due lot of its parent, each one working [20] eagerly to be of service in some way. So Mars furnishes anger, Zephyr the grasses. The south wind thunders; [25] and a shaggy Fury goads the limbs. The demon Abyssus enters, removing what is dirty, offering goblets; [30] and the ghoul Orcus, bringing the shades of the dead, smokes. The Hydra hisses, the screech-owl laments. The sly fox [35] yelps wantonly, ass brays, wild ass chatters, and ox lows. All the creatures [40] behave in the fashion proper to them.

The din goes to the stars, the hall resounds, the joys of the fête reverberate prodigiously. [45] Then the wolf, happy with this honor, carries the lamb in its arms; the bear gives out its honey, the capon favorable omens. [50] The Falernian provides wines, Silvius a wild boar, the eagle a goat, pot-herbs pounded to a pulp, ground gum resin, [55] and under the edge a golden meal.

Exalted Charles, raging like a lion, trampling the necks of great men [60] underfoot, the proud Frank, flashing with his sword, rages with weapons, sharpening darts, [65] crying for battles.

When these events as well have taken place, Seneca writes, Apollo sings, John leaps, with a peaceful mind Cato composes and adorns fables, great Cicero, shattering the elements of reason, declaims them.

Notes

A.16   Literally, "liver."
B.25–26   *erinis* as *Erinys*, with change in gender? Or *erinis* as "hedgehog"?
B.37   If not a wild ass, *agrinus* could designate a type of bird.
B.69   MS *Saltat iena*, "the hyena leaps."

6. Froumund of Tegernsee, Poem 19

Why do you tear at me so many times—you, a cuckoo without wings, who are more sluggish than any tortoise, putting yourself on a par with a human being? Look, you swell up like froth—even though you are about to rush down into the fire! Don't stop being even now the creature you were for so long in the past: [5] may you be a reeking, phlegm-filled wind-bag, rottenness incarnate!

You pretend that you fashion poetic verse with your stylus, but you produce trifling words which you learn from I know not whom. If you wish, let us vie in composing verses in poetry. Here, I say, turn your eyes, fool, and don't stare at the clouds.

[10] But look sharp! Shouldn't your hand be scrubbed, since your snivelings are hanging from it? Shouldn't your nose be washed with water, because even your chest is filthy? If you lean forward your head, which in your laziness you wiped off on your hard chest, drops of old phlegm fall.

Now I am going to play various games with song, to bring together [15] the whole race of men and the whole herd of beasts who compete to destroy you, filthy scamp, with a stone. Let Gitto, in variegated garments, be the first in the line, and let every worn-out shoe dangle around him, whom an army of dwarfs follows, rejoicing in songs. [20] So that they may arouse laughter, hang belts and tails; spread threadbare clothes, dwarfs; and put their shoes on your feet.

Let Sigihard walk here together with his friends and let the stupid servant offer rustic poetry—[25] what a competitor!—until the whole crew shows its pleasure and the brothers say, "Let this gallows-bird be stoned! In bygone days our monastery was noble with honor. Alas, from that high degree it has tumbled, spit upon and full of phlegm, leaden and muddy in feet and hands, a blockhead. [30] Look, there he stands, like a block of wood all stiffened with cold! Let us all together strike him with our heels, for he is considered a nauseating sight by all who gaze upon him. It is no hard task to destroy him, because his body is not worth a straw. Let's break him gently, like a tender nit; [35] he will have to be crushed like a little louse under the fingernail."

Let the milky-white tooth of the black Ethiop laugh at me, let a white raven croak over this untimely death. The moles also marvel at you with clapping hands, the little tongue of birds chatters at you with explosive volume.

[40] I sang this for myself and likewise for my beloved nephew, so that he might dispel his laziness and learn to play forever.

Notes

The editor of this poem commented (Froumund, ed. Strecker 53): "Man scheint in Tegernsee etwas derbe Ausdrucksweise geliebt zu haben. . . . Einzelnes bleibt dunkel" ("They seem in Tegernsee to have liked a somewhat crude form of expression. . . . Details remain obscure").

19–20   Ed. Strecker 54: "Quem sequitur gaudens nanorum exercitus odis, / Ut faciant risum. Suspendite cingula, caudas."

29   Alternatively, "maimed in feet and hands."

35   I close at the end of this line the quotation that begins in 15.

7. Leo of Vercelli, "Meter"

Column 1

5   A fugitive from the realm,
        I had been [destroyed];
        but because often
        I alone [among all]
        did this—
10   I knew them,
        I saw them,

[those who] just like foxes
[or] Pharisees
[crushed]
15   [the vital organs] of the realm—
what these scoundrels
inflicted,
I am forced to [redress].
This is great now,
20   but will be greater henceforth.
For—a situation that slow-witted
Apella, the superstitious man, fears—
I receive no response
to my greetings
25   and I do not receive recompense
[for] my earlier good deeds.
This is great now,
but will be greater henceforth.
As a peasant
30   among fugitives
I lose everything
that Otto gave,
I lose everything
that the crown of
35   the [broad] world gave,
[whom] it is not possible
to name now in verse.
This is great now,
but will be greater henceforth.
40   Broken by the burden,
made [the talk of the town],
I am pointed at [by people's fingers],
[I am beaten with the lash],
[a disgrace] to the present generation,
45   [an infamy] to the next.
This is great now,
but will be greater henceforth.
The cowardly fox
dares to mock,

50   [and] refreshed
        [by the blood] of the cock
        . . . to them,
        [but] . . . to our . . .
        [This is great now,]
55   [but will be] greater hence[forth].

        Column 2
        This is great now,
        but will be greater henceforth.
        [They forgot]
5   the laws of Leo,
        the temples of Sparono;
        and Leo's long
        punishment does not
        restrain
10   the thefts of Sparono.
        This is great now,
        but will be greater henceforth.
        As night came to an end,
        the bob-tailed she-mule of Sparono
15   burst her
        iron halter,
        as if at that time
        Leo cudgeled
        her loins often,
20   as if she wept for barley,
        as if she wept for oats,
        and as if stinking sedge
        were not
        noble bedding for her.
25   This is great now,
        but will be greater henceforth.
        The ass, covered
        in a lion's skin,
        terrified his enemies;
30   but because he neither
        moves about in a bound,

nor raises his neck fiercely
in the open air,
nor rolls about
35   raging eyes,
with his hair bristling—
just as he crept up fast,
so he sank down to the ground fast—
(this is great now,
40   but will be greater henceforth)
for because he brays
and does not scatter
sand with his hoof,
because he shakes out
45   his long ears,
because he rolls
his back in the dust
and loses the poorly
secured hide,
50   this beast is known as
what he was before,
and beaten practically
to death.
This happened now justly,
55   more justly than before.
Beaten by the he-goat
with a willow-rod
before he farted,
before he atoned for
60   the evils he had committed.

Column 3
dusty
5   .   .   .   .

swears multitudes of oaths
.   .   .   .
. . . the rods
10   [He cries] as before,
brays as before,

and the braying itself
was evidence
that he was
15   a wretched ass
who had been in hiding,
not a tooth-gnashing lion
who had raged.
How much
20   he would deserve feeding
in the assembly,
if the former name [of lion] still stood!
This happens now justly,
more justly than it happened in the past.
25   But the throng
does not have confidence in him,
unless a solemn pledge
is given by a guarantor
who would stay
30   near the ass
and who would wish
to keep the peace in every way.
"The wolf,"
says the talkative fox,
35   "is agreeable to the ass.
He who has confidence in the wolf
will pass safely through
chills and
every hot spell of the sun."
40   This happens now justly,
more justly than it happened in the past.
The wolf is trusted,
commended;
but the treacherous tongue
45   of the fox spoke falsely,
as events that become known subsequently
proved.
For the lawless wolf
takes the oath willingly
50   and in poor faith

dines upon the ass.
And that night he licks
the sweet sauce
robbed from his friends.

Column 4

This is great now,
but will be greater henceforth.
5   Thereupon the entire
bristling throng,
the shaggy throng,
suggests to the lion
that this very wolf
10   is fit for the gallows.
All the beasts
invoke the law,
invoke the king.
This happens now justly,
15   more justly than it happened in the past.
After the lion, blazing with anger,
hears these matters,
he commands
the entire kingdom to assemble
20   before the first of the month.
The scribe, a camel,
quickly notes down
these times
and instructs everyone
25   about everything
through duly sealed royal documents.
This happens now justly,
more justly than it happened in the past.
Look! At the stated time
30   the wild band
comes together.
The school of the swamps
rushes together;
and tribe by tribe

35   they seek
        the great halls
        of the lion,
        which is to say, of the king.
        Orcus, arisen from the mountains,
40   arrives,
        the doorkeeper of the hall
        by the privilege of his ancestors.
        What a fine guard
        and avenger is Orcus!
45   Indeed, if you
        put your trust in the poets,
        he does not need a doorbolt
        or sword:
        single-handedly he guards
50   the ramparts and [wards off] enemies

Column 5
        A savage bear,
        large as a high
        mountain of straw,
20   approaches
        the sheer cliff;
        he is a pillar of the world,
        with his companion the faun
        now gamboling,
25   now singing back,
        and he shouts, "Wolf,
        impious one, return
        our relative!
        Return him thundering
30   like a swan
        and emulating a priest
        with the special grace of his voice!"
        This happens now justly,
35   more justly than it happened in the past.
        After these things had been thus said
        by the entire group,

about why the senseless wolf
committed
40   an enormous dishonor
against the Pharaoh, why he committed
a lamentable crime against the realm,
why as a result of his
heinous undertakings
45   the select order
of the senate
suffers everlasting disgrace,
and why through his agency
public administration
50   and law enforcement
are impaired,
he is bidden (under the threat
of a drawn sword) to speak.
Not knowing what reply
55   to give,
he quickly becomes mute,
expert in wailing,
fluent in licking.
This happens now justly,
60   more justly than it happened in the past.

Column 6

This happens now justly,
more justly than it happened in the past.
10   . . . .

. . . just as if [a fierce
15   delirium] burned him up,
the skillful beast
feigns a feverish condition.
At this point, Leo, write;
at this point, Hugo, laugh.
20   The mouth is inclined to vomit
[all the time],

but now the rectum
is even more inclined to do so,
and the clamp when broken
25   is not to be trusted.
For he snorts badly
and rakes the ground badly,
moos and neighs,
pretends to have horns.
30   The very ear of the judge
resounds
so that you could well believe
him as he regained strength
to have rumbled
35   like the echo of a whirlwind.
The assembly stinks,
the sand stinks,
and the very sanctity
of the laws turns foul
40   on account of the excrement.
You would wish to believe
that with the deliberate
wrongfulness of wolves
he did not wish
45   to return any ass
already buried away.
But the lying beast,
unmastered by the distress
of his critics,
50   cannot go forward
and does not trust to go backward.
The cowl that he has taken to wearing
does not help him a bit;
nor does the childlike shame
55   in his supplicatory neck.
This happens now justly,
more justly than it happened in the past.
With the buck as judge
and the kite as overseer
60   (out of greed for which the wolf

never stained his lips
with any blood whatsoever) . . .

Column 7

5   This happens now justly,
more justly than it happened in the past.

.   .   .   .

10

All sing,
All leap about.

15   .   .   .   .

you would see beasts.
This happens now justly,

20   more justly than it happened in the past.
On the next night
the she-ape seeks
great meals
for the great lion

25   and cornel berries
and honey-apples for herself.
This happens now justly,
more justly than it happened in the past.
A cruet filled

30   with blood is brought to the lion, the master,
as a good omen,
while the loins go to the kite,
just as the tail goes

35   to the youthful he-goat,
for the buck
had previously played without a beard
in the hall.
The remaining pieces are distributed

40   now to those

who could be present.
This happens now justly,
than which nothing is less.
What shall I say now?
45   What shall I write now?
I will add nothing more
unless what the friend
of David plainly writes and says:
50   "Thy judgment,
O merciful Christ,
is a great deep" [Psalm 35.7].
This is nowhere false; nothing is anywhere truer than this.
It is never unjust; nothing is ever more just than this.
55   Therefore you, Leo,
leave this nut now for the schools
and instead
serve the Omnipotent
and put to flight
60   transitory laughter;
and do not ever
trust in anyone.
The one and only
faithful being is he,
65   from whose mouth
this came forth.

Column 8
. . . would know,
if the rule of Flaccus
was entitled
to constrain
5   the words of the prophet of Christ.
But not always will it be December for me, believe me, my Leo.

Notes

1.15   Alternatively, "deserved death."
1.20   Or "but was greater before"? The phrase recurs in 1.28, 1.39, 1.47, 1.55,
2.3, 2.12, 2.26, 2.40, 4.4.

2.4	Assuming the reading de*didic*ere.
2.7–10	"And the repeated / punishment of Leo / does not restrain for long / the deceits of Sparono."
2.22–24	Or "and as if she had stinking sedge and not a noble bed."
2.35	Or "with his head raised high."
4.24–25	Literally, "with the help of warm wax."

8. PHYSIOLOGUS LATINUS (VERSIO B)

Leo (The Lion)

For indeed Jacob, blessing his son Judah, said, "Judah is a lion's whelp, the son born of my seed; who shall rouse him?" (Genesis 49.9). Physiologus says that the lion has three natural properties. The first is that he walks in the mountains, and if it should happen that he is sought by hunters, the odor of the hunter comes to him; and with his tail he covers his tracks behind him, so that the hunter may not follow his tracks, find his den, and capture him.

In the same way our savior—the spiritual lion from the tribe of Judah, the root of Jesse, the son of David [Apocalypse 5.5]—having been sent by his heavenly father, covered the tracks of his divinity for those who understood, and became an angel with the angels, an archangel with archangels, a throne with thrones, a power with powers; until he descended into the womb of a virgin and by this saved the human race which had gone astray. And not knowing this, and not knowing him as he ascended to his father, those who were angels on high said to those who were ascending with the lord: "Who is this King of Glory?" To which they responded, "The Lord of hosts, he is the King of Glory" (Psalm 23.10).

The second nature of the lion is that, when he has fallen asleep, his eyes are alert, for they are open; just as the betrothed in the Song of Songs (5.2) attests, saying, "I sleep, and my heart watcheth." For indeed, when my lord fell asleep physically on the cross and in the tomb, his divine nature was vigilant: "Behold he shall neither slumber nor sleep, that keepeth Israel" (Psalm 120.4).

The third nature of the lion is that, when a lioness has borne a cub, she brings it forth dead and guards it for three days, until on the third day its father comes, breathes into its face, and brings it to life. In the same way the omnipotent father awakened our lord Jesus Christ, his son, on the third day from the dead. As Jacob said, "He will sleep as does a lion, and as the whelp of a lion; who shall rouse him?" (compare Genesis 49.9).

Nycticorax (The Owl)

Concerning the owl, David says in the same psalm: "I am like an owl in the house" (Psalm 101.7). The owl is an impure bird (Deuteronomy 14.17), and loves darkness more than light.

This bird represents the Jewish people, who repulsed our lord and savior when he came to save them; they said, "We have no king but Caesar" (John 19.15); "but as to this man, we know not who he is" (John 9.29). On this account they love darkness more than light. Then the lord turned to us gentiles and brought light to us as we were "sitting in darkness and in the region of the shadow of death" (Isaiah 9.2); and in the region of the shadow of death a light arose for us. Of this people the savior spoke through a prophet: "A people, which I knew not, hath served me" (Psalm 17.45). Elsewhere he said: "I will call that which was not my people, my people, and her that was not beloved, beloved" (Romans 9.25; Hosea 2.23). About that people of the Jews who loved darkness more than light (John 3.19), the lord says in a Psalm: "The children that are strangers have lied to me, strange children have faded away, and have halted from their paths" (Psalm 17.46).

Vulpis (The Fox)

The fox is a crafty animal, exceedingly treacherous and contentious. When it has gone hungry and has found nothing to eat, it seeks a place where there is red earth and rolls upon it, so that it should seem as if all bloody. It throws itself onto the ground and turns itself over on the ground as if it is dead. Holding in its breath, it puffs itself up so that it is not exhaling at all. The birds, seeing it so puffed up and lying as if bloody, and seeing its tongue hanging out of its open mouth, think that it is dead. But when they come down and alight upon the fox, it grabs them and eats them.

The fox therefore represents the devil. To all those who live according to the flesh the devil *pretends* that he is dead. But although he may have sinners within his gullet, to those who are spiritual and advanced in their faith he is *truly* dead and reduced to nothing. What is more, those who wish to be fattened by his flesh (that is to say, by the flesh of the devil) are people who wish to execute his works, which are adultery, fornication, idolatry, sorcery, murder, theft, false witness (Matthew 15.19), and other acts similar to these. As the apostle says, "For if you live according to the flesh, you shall die: but if by the Spirit you mortify the deeds of the flesh, you shall live" (Romans 8.13). Those then who live according to the flesh, who are occupied in the works of the devil, who are held under his domination, and who become like him will perish together with him. As David says, "They shall go into the lower parts of the earth: They shall be delivered into the hands of the sword; they shall be the portions of foxes" (Psalm 62.10–11). Finally, Herod is likened to a treacherous fox, for the lord said, "Go and tell that fox" (Luke 13.32); and elsewhere the scribe heard from the savior: "The foxes have holes" (Matthew 8.20; Luke 9.58). And in the Song of Songs (2.15) we read: "Catch us the little foxes that destroy the vines." Physiologus spoke truly of the fox.

9. SEDULIUS SCOTTUS, "THE RAM"

When high and mighty God created the animals of the world, those which the sea, land, and heavens contain, at that time he multiplied the sheep with multiple honors and made them the leaders among the bleaters. [5] The kind-spirited creator clothed them with a fleecy covering and dressed them in a well-padded robe—made of their bodies—and armed their inward-bending brows with curving horns, so that they might wage proud wars against other horn-bearers. In their twin nostrils he spread proud might; [10] he made them multiple in their multiple pantings.

But a gentle simplicity is also innate in their sacred horns, and deadly poisons do not harm these pious creatures. For this reason, I confess, my predilection for them has increased, my love of their robe and of their well-fed midriffs has increased. [15] I swear by these fingers, that in this I never lie: that I crave them, treasure them, always love them; and not even the river Lethe will wipe away this holy love. What my mouth is now announcing, my heart asserts with full awareness. My trifling verses praise them and greet them, [20] and I say nothing false, as you know, kind-spirited father. For your merciful nature has seen fit to distribute black sheep to me, since I am a black sheep, but it has also given me snow-white ones.

One of these sheep was shapelier and plumper than the rest: woe is me, by what a cruel death did he die stricken! [25] He was the guardian of the outstanding flock, nobler than all the others, peerless, matchless. His gentle-hearted strength, residing in those stiff horns, surpassed all other horn-bearing beasts and all the bright white flocks. He gleamed with his snow-white fleece and with his snow-white eyes; [30] and he was an enormous and energetic victor in fights of the forehead. Aries, the constellation of the ram, loved him with a pure love and wished to make him co-regent of his realm; Lucina, the powerful goddess of light, wished to place him on high as a bright constellation, on account of his white covering; [35] for they report that Luna, the goddess of the moon, loved the wool of fleeces, and that Pan, the god of Arcadia, deceived her with a fleece.

For him my love burned (since the cockles of my heart are not as hard as horn); for who but a fool would not love him? And then your mildness, which is rich and which denies nothing, [40] saw fit to give this ornament to me; but Fortuna, a goddess always opposed to good things, soon snatched Tityros from me, wretched, woe is me!

There was a wicked bandit, one of Goliath's tribe, dark like the Ethiops and a Cacus in his trickiness. [45] Frightful in his appearance and pitch-black in his malicious demeanor, he was crude in his actions, crude in his language. This scoundrel took you, pious sheep, and dragged you with his unspeakable hands through many thickets; alas, what an unspeakable act against you, O wretched ram! Unfortunate sheep, you were very meek and serene as you fluttered [50] through multiple fields.

The raging pack of dogs caught sight of the robber as he was going, the horned and great-spirited lamb-leader as he was being carried. Soon the spirited squadron cut capers; the sound of crashing and smashing grew grand. [55] As the pack of dogs with fast-moving mouths seeks out the thief and the stolen object, the frond-filled wood barks and every grove resounds. Why do I hold back my words? Alas, the mild-mannered sheep is caught, while the robber—faster than the wind—runs in the shadows. The sheep was left alone and fought much; [60] threatening with his horns, he inflicted multiple wounds. The hounds, vanquished by a two-horned sheep, were shocked and figured a lion was present. All were barking at him with their currish mouths, but he—not sheepish in the least—shone with his pious face.

[65] "What madness is arising in your hearts?" he said. "Recognize me as the servant of Bishop Hartgar. I'm not the wicked robber, not that sneak-thief; instead, I am a pious sheep, the illustrious leader of a flock. If you have a hankering to overcome a despotic enemy, then look: [70] the robber is nearby, fleeing. Let's grab him! But if, on the contrary, your rage and hoarse barking should incite you to gory wars against peaceful little me, then I swear by this head, by these horns, and by this proud forehead that I will give you the rewards you deserve."

[75] Having made this statement, he managed suddenly to soothe the hearts of the beasts; a peace began to dawn and the two sides leapt back.

But there was one dog which was just like the barking god Anubis, which had as grandfather the dark-spirited hellhound known as Cerberus, and which was accustomed to hunt fleet stags [80] and hideous bears in the manner of its grandfather: with a threefold throat. This creature, when it saw that the savage pack was growing quiet, snarled with its teeth and puffed out its shaggy neck. "Look at yourselves," it said, "A sheep, under the falsely assumed name of peace, is speaking sly words and tricking you, just as a fox would do. [85] This creature here is a wicked bandit and a malicious henchman of a bandit; for that reason the two of them are heading for a leafy shelter. He alone is to be held responsible for so great a wrong, I declare; for he makes peace with his words, but threats with his brow."

At this, the gigantic sheep struck with brandished horns at the mouth of the lying beast; [90] he broke two of its teeth and, in addition, he pounded with his brow its doggish brow. The ram would have been the victor, if only he had not fled the battle; for, as if a victor, he rushes away headlong, leaving his enemy behind. He runs about heedlessly and, without guile, flees. [95] Afterward he blundered into thickets and wicked thorn-bushes; alas, the pious ram became stuck in those rough places. Then next the cursed Cerberus pressed him from behind, dealt him savage wounds with its bloodied mouth. The sheep falls lifeless to the ground, a sight sad to behold, [100] and bedews the briar-bushes with his crimson blood.

The nymphs wept, all the creatures of the wood burst into sound, and the flocks of bleating beasts groaned over the crime. Quite rightly you, Luna, who are two-horned and white yourself, mourned, while you, Aries of the heavens above, wept. [105] What did he deserve, he who was just, honest, and devoid of fraud? He drank neither wine nor any other fermented drink. Drunkenness did not lead him astray from the path of propriety, nor did the banquets of kings, nor did the feasts of noblemen. To him, ceremonial food meant the grass in the fields; [110] and the clear-flowing Meuse provided him with a sweet drink. Not a greedy being, he had no desire for clothes of royal purple; rather, he was content with a tunic made of a hide. He did not range proudly on horseback through the delightful glades, but instead he traveled in the ordinary fashion—on his own feet. [115] He was not a liar and he did not speak idle words; he emitted only the mystical words *báá* or *béé*.

Just as the lamb who sits enthroned on high—the Son of God himself—tasted biting death for the sake of sinners, in the same way you, pious sheep, taking the route of death, ripped apart by the unfair dogs, [120] perish for the sake of a wicked bandit. Just as the holy ram became a sacrifice in Isaac's stead, so you remain a welcome victim in the place of a wretch. O how merciful is the piety and broad the power of the Lord, who does not wish men to pass away in a bad death! [125] The celestial right hand of God, which once promised to bring help soon to a certain man on a cross, now saves the shameful robber. Give thanks to the Lord, O worthless, wicked, and faithless robber; speak, you wretch, with the Psalmist such words: "The right hand of the Lord of Olympus then raised me on high; [130] I will live, not die, and I will sing the deeds of God. The kind-hearted power, reproving, reproved me; but it did not hand me over to death and it snatched me away from the slaughter."

The Epitaph

You, good sheep, farewell, renowned leader of the snow-white flock; alas, that my garden does not still contain you alive. [135] Perhaps, friend, a warm bath would be made for you, for no other reason than the rights of hospitality. With devout heart, I myself would administer the water to your horned head and to your heels. I must confess: I have yearned for you, I yearn at this very moment for your widow and mother, and I will always love your brothers. Farewell!

Note

12   Or "neither magic charms nor poisons harm."

10. THEODULF, "THE BATTLE OF THE BIRDS"

We can well understand certain facts from events and examples. Although I would not practice divination, I know what this event signifies; and although many marvels were seen at the same time, this one that I am ready to recount was actually seen. [135] Gairard related it to me, Paschasius to him: Gairard relates what he heard to me, Paschasius what he saw to him.

To be sure, there is a place at the outer edge of the region of Toulouse and Cahors; in this place each of the two districts borders on the other. Located there is a field, the outer edges of which are ringed by woods;

[140] people live not too far from there. Many birds filled this field in a great onslaught, and many a fowl took a seat on its plain—birds that the river, forest, and wasteland contain, birds that have the habit of building nests on rocky crags.

[145] These birds have diverse foods, songs, colors, styles of flight, plumage, talons, beaks, habits, habitat, and occupations; for the direction of the west wind brought some of them, the north wind brought others, and you would think that each of the two factions had its own battle standards. In those fields the two battle lines [150] settled on opposite sides, and a fair distance lay between them.

You would think that emissaries were shuttling between the two battle lines so that they could prepare to report the terms of war or peace. Meanwhile, a few birds from each side flew to the other side, and the birds of each side fulfill their duties.

[155] The outcome shows clearly that these peace missions accomplished nothing: after them the birds engage in great wars. And just as emissaries ran back and forth for a long time between the Carthaginians and the Romans, until they rushed into armed conflict, so it is between the birds: after quite enough flying back and forth had been done for both sides [160], they rush into wild conflict with all the force at their disposal.

On both sides the companies of birds burn to fight, and squadron encounters squadron, cohort cohort. The might of the soldiery varies, but the will is uniform: what the larger soldier wants, the small also wants.

[165] Neither the war chariot nor horse power is needed; the sword is not used, and no darts fly. In place of a helmet is a crest, in place of a spearpoint are beaks and talons; and each side sounds its songs in place of trumpets. The light wings of the birds play the part of shields, the little feathers of daggers, [170] and the fine plumage takes the place of a cuirass.

And when the sixth day of this assemblage had passed, birds from both sides rush into war in keen competition. And in turn they mangle themselves, on one side with bites, on the other with blows; on both sides the war mounts because of their unbounded courage. [175] You would think that you were seeing the Rutulians rising here, the Teucrians there, and Mars raging wildly on both sides.

Just as the acorn falls from the oak in autumn, and the leaf in its season as the frost comes, in the same way the army of birds [180] fell dead there and filled the ground with great carnage. For just as the smooth threshing floor is filled in the summer with grain, so the field was filled with birds which had been killed in this way.

A small part that came from the north returned to the north; on both sides a whole cohort lies annihilated. [185] This event is bruited about, the people come and are stupefied at what has happened; they marvel at the limbs of the various birds as they lie there. Even the bishop from the city of Toulouse, Mancio, came. The common people ask whether or not these fowl may be eaten. "Take the ones allowed, leave the ones forbidden," he said. [190] They load their carts with birds and everyone returns to his home.

A swift rumor, flying through many mouths, communicated to us that another such event also took place at this time. Those who go to and from Rome tell this—and among them a woman here is a good witness. [195] She goes from Tours and heads toward Rome to pray; upon returning from there she tells the matter to the priest Arbald, and he to me.

To come to the point, a battle of birds took place, like the one described above, in the neighborhood of the sluggish Saône and the rapid Rhone. Where amid rugged cliffs and thick swamps [200] a little countryside surrounded by level places lies open, there (as they report) come birds of every species which, Europe, your fruitful land nurtures. One group sits upon the rocks, one sits among the fields, and one very large group sits on tree branches.

[205] The young males of the soldiery are divided into two factions, and each faction thinks eagerly of conflict. Four hawks come from one side, four from the other, and four—the same number—falcons from each faction.

In the first encounter the birds of each group destroy one another mutually, [210] hawk hawk and falcon falcon. Beaks press upon beaks, talons clash against talons; inasmuch as they bear equal arms, they destroy themselves all the more. The Roman people did this in the fields of Thessaly when they waged fierce war, a father-in-law on the one side and a son-in-law on the other, [215] when brother destroyed brother and friend friend; in the course of this fighting they bore the same standards and the same weapons. In fact two great birds which did not fight are reported to have escaped; the remaining throng lies dead.

Each of the two factions triumphs, but victory soothes neither, [220] and both sides left the ground filled with carnage. As the rage of Hannibal filled Cannae with death, so the countryside becomes filled with the death of birds. Who would relate every single detail: what, whereby, why, when, or for what reason? These events shown on repeated occasions are plainly portents.

11. Theodulf, "The Fox and Hen"

There is a place that the Gauls call by the name Charroux, where the palatial door of heaven lies open to the elect, where a palace shines in the name of the savior, and where the cloisters of the monastery remain honorable. [5] This place shines forth, trusting in the blood-red guarantee of its saints, and an extraordinarily faithful throng lives there.

In short, Rothar, great count and renowned hero, founded this building together with his wife, Eufrasia. He adorns it with tawny silver, gems, and gold, [10] and it abounds in books, clothes, and sacred implements. He gave farms, meadows, houses, woods, vineyards, tenants, herds, animals, and all kinds of goods, so that by his generous hands dire need might be dispelled; and at the same time the heavenly storeroom receives these fruits, [15] so that God on high might purge him of all sin and join him devoutly to the heavenly choruses in the citadel. Christ is eager to defend this place from evil coteries; he would hallow it for his own cult.

A fox had grown accustomed to capturing in hostile plundering [20] whatever foods were being prepared for the men, and this sly creature also devours with her jaw the bird which produces a thousand colors when it spreads its feathers. At that time the worthy crowd of monks remained ignorant of which pest was inflicting such losses upon them.

[25] Immediately afterward, the deceitful fox seized a winged hen, but from this place the escape route of fraud was shown to be closed. By her own doing the uncouth predator, together with the weight of her prey, hung stupidly on part of a branch. She hung stupidly, bereft of all her sly detours, [30] and on all sides her assorted tricks were ended.

She had consumed the head of the bird in her cavernous mouth; at the same time, the other limbs remained untouched. In fact, the alderbush was smaller than a tree, but higher than the undergrowth. On this alder you, foot of the cunning beast, were caught [35] in such a way that the right paw, if the fox raised it quite high, could touch the stones, with which the wall rose steeply aloft. Here hung the fierce predator, and then the pest twisted her neck and trembling head this way and that.

Upon seeing these events the faithful throng of monks rejoices, [40] seeing marvelous portents from a well-disposed God. Every impious thief, stay far, far away from here; be gone, demonic error! Come, kindly angel! May harmony reside here and the spears of envy be suppressed, and in this place may hope and faith reign. [45] May God, granting all good things, repel adverse ones, and may our minds feed upon your nectar, Christ.

12. THEODULF, "WHAT DO THE SWANS DO?"

What do the swans do, as the ravens emit such sounds, and many songs fill my house with noise? Now the deceptive culprit, the magpie, simulates the speech of a human being; despising the other birds, it perches at the sacred meal. [5] And with its voice the parrot imitates various types of poems, defiling your Muses, bard Homer. And the seabird, a dark fisherman in the waves of the Loire, is now accustomed to inhabit the woods of Brie, and the bird which—look!—added to your praise, Lamuel [Charlemagne?], [10] thinks itself to be a peacock, handsome in its feathers. Its voice sounds equivalent, I think, but its plumage fails to measure up in color, and its does not render a varied ornamentation, golden in beauty.

Now the springtime cuckoo points out the lights of Phoebus, a stammering voice resounds in its hoarse-sounding throat. [15] Now the rascally crow, hanging on the boughs, call down the rain and boasts deceitfully that it has nine lives.

May the voice of the blackbird fall silent: the marshland goose moves the plectrum of its tongue, and with its head submerged devours all manner of dirty things. May the springtime nightingale silence its sweet songs: [20] the hostile owl reechoes nighttime sounds. Look, Balaam's ass rebukes the prophet again and produces unaccustomed sounds with its braying voice, and suddenly steers him into an opposite course of action.

May Tityros laugh at beautiful-sounding Orpheus. [25] You, Orpheus, feed the stinking nanny-goats in the woods; Tityros pursues the pleasures of the court. David [Charlemagne] remains in the citadel with a very few girls; each puffs out songs to the accompaniment of a trumpet that belongs to the Muses. First and foremost Delia makes the Muses of Horace [Alcuin] glow; [30] afterward the others together echo sacred notes. Now Delia strikes with her thumb a Thracian chord, and adorns her sacred temples with fresh flowers. A tender pipe pries into the secrets of the mellifluous Muses and—look!—sounds out fifteen tones in its throat.

[35] Old man Horace, accompanied by boys, goes off from the city; as the full daylight of summer returns, then he returns home. He is of age, let him answer for himself, he will speak for himself and for his boys. He will have bidden them either to blow the light reeds or [40] to bind festoons of flowers about the head of old man Silenus.

The psalmist David, echoing amidst the royal banquet, sees these few Muses. What is more, Vergilian Delia will interject a few womanly feet of poetry as she works amid the leashes and heddles of the loom. [45] Suddenly she saw Beselel and clumsy Wolf, on which account she fell silent, fearing their elegant words. When Wolf takes flight, sense returns to her mind and heart, and she fills the rivers, countryside, and houses with songs. And on any day when golden locks grow upon the head of [50] Thyrsis [Meginfridt or Maganfredus, the royal chamberlain], then he also will sing.

As tuneful Wolf seeks his poems in the bookchest, perhaps he will find them, as Vergil then resounds. Well-known Lucius himself represents songs in brief form, and, as it happens, the raven is unable to learn such songs.

[55] The mere little Irishman, girded with a sharp sword, is looking for you, so that he may run you through the chest, Corvinianus (member of the raven clan!). He does not fear ravens and would not spare any bird, provided only that he entertains hopes that Damoetas [Archbishop Riculf of Mainz, 787–813] is far removed. Our Irishman [Cadac-Andreas] is not a pious poet, O Damoetas; [60] in his mouth a lively frolic is turned into lamentation. But nevertheless, the Irishman, making threats with his weapons, now tries battle; he wishes to strike a Gaetulian head [Hrabanus Maurus] with his sword. This fellow will have a triple name: *Scottus Sottus Cottus*. And he shouts the name of Clan-Wolf [Theodulf] in his cavernous throat.

[65] Look, Menalcas [the royal kitchener, Audulf]: he sang this distich to us in versified song—and in his grimy mouth: "A lifeless man has pierced a living one with unjust laughter, but nevertheless these battles are helpful to boys."

Three boys who prevail over the flames through their nobility and [70] faith rejoice over the dishes of Daniel [their canticle is recited at the table]. Now Job is resplendent in a number of immeasurable honor [a canticle of Job is read], and to pious eyes the psaltery is splendid with love.

In the middle David, orchestrating the banquet in peaceable order, rules all things by his scepter. [75] And pious Aaron [the high chamberlain, Hildebold] blesses everything throughout the palace, sanctifying all the dishes with sacred words. And bald Nehemiah [Eppinus, Eberhard?], who already renewed the city of Jerusalem, in his great power over liquor will bring sweet wines.

What place is there for the black raven among these guests? [80] May he remain amid the wolves in the woods—unless Elijah should clean away the crimes of the raven and should call him again to him for sacred meals.

Harberd, the greedy protector of the Spanish drink, is armed with food in his room [85] and stirs the warm potful with his scepter in the kitchen so that he may drink in cold form what he stirs here while it is warm.

And the little Greek Potiphar, hated as it so happens by girls, armed in vain, waging no battles, whom as companions Bagao and Aegeus together accompany; [90] out of these three maimed men there will not be one true man. These fellows, I think, are not faithful of their own free will in bedchambers—the savage hand of a doctor compels them to keep their faith.

And Hiram, the son of a widow, constructs well a building for the high-throned one: may Christ speed his work.

[95] Among these people the giant Nimrod shakes his hunting spear, and prepares to strike the raven on its head with his spear. And enormous Polyphemus roils the sea which is filled with speeding sails so that the sea bird is unable to escape from the main. These two are unequal in their limbs, but threatening in their [100] disposition: the former will break the feet of the raven and the later the head.

The pygmies [Einhard and Osulf] will desire only to seek peace from you, black ravenlet, on account of the wars with the cranes. May these things suffice for you as you come, may winter, thirst, and hunger suffice. [105] Let us keep our three-footed brothers for ourselves in our hall; may you have a scant retinue. May you keep only these verses, bravest little raven, and reading them often store them in your heart, until Horace [Alcuin] comes accompanied by boys and odes; [110] then it is possible to hope for better things for you.

Now I give to you as many farewells as there are white hairs on your head; so goodbye to you, Corvinianus!

Notes

The scholar who has done the most to elucidate the meaning of this poem emphasized that some of its obscurities resist explanation: "Eine Dichtung, die wie diese auf ein ganz bestimmtes Publikum hin verfaßt ist, kann in all ihren Einzelheiten, ihren witzigen und versteckten Anspielungen auch nur innerhalb desselben voll verstanden werden: sie ist esoterish, nicht bemüht darum, der Nachwelt irgend etwas zu schildern oder zu dokumentieren. Theodulf geht hier sogar noch weiter: er versucht, selbst dieses Publikum von Eingeweihten, in welchem jeder jeden kannte, mit den einleitenden 22 Versen zu verblüffen und zu mystifizieren" (Schaller 1971, 138) ("A poem which, like this one, was composed for a very particular audience, can be fully understood in all its details and in its humorous and hidden allusions only within that audience: it is esoteric, unconcerned to describe or document anything at all for posterity. Theodulf goes even further here: with the twenty-two introductory verses he tries to stun and mystify even this audience of initiates, in which everyone knew everyone else").

97   Polyphemius.
103–6   These couplets play on the words *trispeda* and *trispedicus*.

13. Thierry of St. Trond, "Weep, Dogs"

"Weep, dogs, if you have time to weep, if you are able to weep, weep, dogs: the pup Pitulus is dead."

"Pitulus is dead? Who was Pitulus?"

"More worthy than a dog."

"Who was Pitulus?"

"The chief concern and grief of his master. [5] He was not a large dog—not an Alban dog, nor a Molossian dog—but a slight dog and a short pup. He was five years old. If he were twenty years old, still you would think him a pup when you saw how modest he was in size. He was scarcely equal to a Pannonian mouse in his whole body; [10] he was similar not so much to a mouse as to a hare. White in color, he bejeweled his face with black eyes."

"From which breed was he born?"

"His dam was a Frisian, as was his sire."

"How much strength did he have?"

"Quite little, but suited to that body; his courage was great, but his physical might was a different matter."

[5] "What was his function? Was it a useful one or not?"

"That his large master should love a small dog—that was his duty, to play before his master."

"What was the use of that?"

"There was none, if not laughter! No one failed to laugh at him as he stood or as he moved: [20] whatever he tried, there was laughter at seeing him. He was now inflexible, now flexible; savage in one instant and gentle in the next; bold and great-spirited, but then lazy and frightened. The creature who had hurt a great bear with a puny bite was terrified at the peeping of a puny mouse. [25] I believe that he, a creature born when every single Vertumnus was discontented [Horace, *Satire* 2.7.14], was equal to none and was unequal even to himself."

Such you were, beloved dog, to be laughed and grieved; you were laughter while you were alive, but look at the grief when you have died!

Whoever saw you, whoever knew you, loved you [30] and grieves now over your demise, pitiable dog.

Perhaps you deposited your limbs within the tomb of a raven's maw; to be sure, you did not deserve to be food for worms. Dear dog, all too much to be lamented, my poetry fails you as an epitaph, for you have no tomb. [35] Yet your Thierry is not guilty of this toward you: I was not present when you were on the point of dying. But what hindrance does the lack of burial pose to praise of the dead? Many great men lack the mound of a burial site. For example, Cato, a celebrated man, who brings his fame to the stars, [40] is said as an exile not to have earned a grave. And Pompey, conqueror of the world, to be feared by the whole world, was buried in a small nook. That most sacred member of the senate, slain in Thessaly, was food for a vulture: how did that harm his due rewards?

[45] Virtue is not enclosed in graves and tombs, but it fills the vaults of heaven and the ample spaces of the earth. Nevertheless I am of the opinion that there is a certain solace in the act of burial. Hence you read that tombs were made for the birds and horses. Ovid's parrot took pride in his burial mound and epitaph, [50] because the last words on his tongue as he died were "Farewell, Corinna!" And the great Macedonian arranged for his renowned horse Bucephalus a funeral procession fit for a king's burial, and in his praise founded an exceedingly famous city, called by the identical name, Bucephala.

[55] The muse of great Vergil even celebrated a gnat and appended the epitaph of the gnat to the *Aeneid*. In dying the gnat saved the life of the poet. As it happened Vergil gave the gnat no tomb, but he made an eternal song, renowned throughout the centuries, [60] and the slight gnat is famous on account of his verses. I do not wish to yield to Vergil as regards an epitaph for Pitulus: I will ennoble my dog, just as Vergil did his gnat.

Notes

5   Or "Albanian"?
7   The translation assumes a full stop rather than a comma after *fuerat*.

14. WALAHFRID STRABO, "TO ERLUIN"

It was night, and throughout the regions of the vast sky distant stars increased the splendor with their twinkling lights; Pollachar, free from all cares, was enjoying the wealth of the night, sleep infused with Lethe's gift—[5] when suddenly, as rumor reports, Jupiter's armor-bearer, breaking through the deep shadows, appeared to the man's eyes to be present.

"Come," it said, "and transcend the oppressive mists of the earth, for I will lead you to a place where great rewards await you."

Happy at these words, the man renders thanks to the [10] omniscient one, because he is willing to gratify a soul exhausted by its long quest. The bird flies heavenward, and carries the fearful man through the airs, until the clarity of the bright heavens gave him a fright.

That new Daedalus, partly persuaded by fear, partly because he dreads the precipitous path that he is treading, says, [15] "Will the gleaming hall of the star-studded firmament suffer me, weighed down as I am with this filth with which my limbs swell? No! Instead, let the waste of the distended belly run forth, let the earth keep its weight—I will go off light."

The talon-grabber, knowing what was going to take place, said, "Hold my [20] tail with your mouth and, be quick, cleanse yourself of all stenches." Then indeed, so that he might remain pure forever, he makes every effort to void his inner organs. At this the eagle said, "It is absurd to place in a divine setting a person who spatters lofty places with corruption. Therefore go back and, once you have slid back [25], pay heed to the filth of your bedding; and may you not hope to aim at the stars again with filth." Awakening, he found passing through his bed everything that he imagined pouring forth from the high vault of heaven.

O shame and wickedness, a man deceived by wrongful visions . . .

Notes

10   Alternatively: "because he [the dreamer] wishes . . . "

24   It is conceivable that *loca* could also refer to *lieux d'aisance*, or "latrines" (Blaise 1975, 543, *locus* 10).

15. WILLIAM OF BLOIS, "THE QUARREL OF THE FLEA AND FLY"

If fictions and words that prompt laughter delight anyone, let him read these words and know me to be his bard; for, since fictions delight many, and serious words few, so that I may be read by many, I choose to relate fictions.

[5] You, who read this, do not seek fruits from a thorn, or a rich work from poor material. Inarticulate poverty of words and scant resources of meter deserved poor material. I do not come to be extolled for this crime;

I desire laughter, [10] and I am not drawn by ambition for praise. Whatever reader comes to these laughable lines, let him laugh and give our Muse her just rewards.

A fly aims to be preferred to a flea; the flea, in turn, is inflamed by an equal ambition. [15] Thus pride inflames each of the two to a contest, since each one is unable to consider the other as an equal.

Disdaining the small size of the flea, the fly desires to seem great by speaking great words, and she speaks first. Therefore, she compensates for her small size with words [20] and disguises her small self by speaking great words. She is borne beyond herself by words and, having said nothing equal to herself, she transcends herself through words and speaks elevated words in thunderous tones. Saying great things about herself, she leaves great many words behind her, and she is by far less than her words. [25] The personal appearance of the speaker differs by far from the words: the words she says are great, but she herself is small.

"I marvel," she says, "I marvel that a flea contends with me. I marvel that she has not taken fright at my mastery. I take offense and I seem to be cheapened in my own eyes, that a creature of her sort [30] who has scorned me considers herself the equal of one such as me.

If the crazy flea had been worthy to have me as her mistress, she could be a companion to kings in this manner at least. For it is a known fact that kings are subject to me; thus she could be equal to kings, if she would be my servant. [35] The first seat among the guests of the king belongs to me; and I myself drink from the part of the goblet from which the king drinks. So that the king may eat nothing except what I, already satisfied, leave behind, I taste beforehand every single one of the king's dishes. Often I sit above the head of the king; from there I consider [40] proudly what my glory and honor may be. Thus the court of the king honors me in its king, and whenever he is greeted, I am greeted.

And what if my anger has flared intensely? The whirlwind of my rage disturbs and terrifies everything. [45] And as I rush about in anger, my wing, moving in a whirlwind, roars and murmurs certain threats. When angry, I neither know nor deign to fear any falls, but I go imperiously wherever I wish.

I do not fear the throat of a person eating greedily, and [50] I descend to his very stomach, intending to return nonetheless. Having become a mighty despoiler of consumed foods, I bring back from there foods that travel backwards with me. Hence, I am granted freedom to cause harm with impunity: when I harm a person, he fears to harm me. [55] Although he is injured by my tooth, his own hand arranges with deft quickness that

I not be injured by his teeth. I am saved by my enemy; he makes it so that I come out; and yet I do not fear for myself but rather he fears for me. And although he is insistent that I die, nevertheless he labors [60] that I not die; thus he suffers me whom he nonetheless hates.

The contraption that was able to overthrow the walls of Troy, that very same contraption would not be at all an obstacle to me. In addition, because I am conquerable by no human weapons, by which a human being is himself easily conquered, [65] ingenious man envies me and directs his mind to new devices, and strives to accomplish new feats. Hence the product of human zeal, the fly swatter, has a name invented from the noun of my name. *Homo sapiens* sweated in mind and body so that this device, [70] one of so many, could throw an obstacle before me.

Of so many devices one harmed, harms, and will harm: the fly swatter contraption is deadly to me. Nevertheless, great use is afforded by this disadvantage, and the deadliness itself carries the weight of usefulness. [75] Usefulness transcends the disadvantage in this particular disadvantage, and the disadvantage is less because of its usefulness. Such a device becomes damaging to me, but it becomes convenient; though injurious it proves beneficial and it harms usefully. Do you ask how it harms? Because when I am struck by its whirlwind, [80] I am driven away from the desired foods before eating my fill; and nevertheless for that very reason it helps, because thus it prevents me from becoming food to the person eating the foods among which I desire to be. Thus it prevents me from entering the throat of a person eating; for no more grievous Scylla is to be feared by me than an open throat. [85] That Charybdis is the one fear of my species, that is the only Scylla to be feared by my species.

The work of human envy is thus converted to our use, and my enemy, man, becomes advantageous to me. My enemy is more advantageous to me than any friend, [90] for the very reason for which he was more savage to me than any enemy. And man, attentive and excessively solicitous, although unwillingly, plays servant to my benefit. For shame! Therefore the flea dares to contend with me, and believes that holding me in contempt is a small matter?

[95] But what am I doing? Since I entered debate with such a creature, for this reason she could almost be called equal to me. Her who was worthless, I made so that she would not be worthless. Her who was without praise, I made so that she would not be without praise. However much honor being compared with me brings to her, [100] so much the less honor my honor has as a consequence. That she contends with me is a dishonor to me, but an honor to her; and she has carried off the prize of

the contest. Whether I win or she wins, the praise is hers for whom being conquered will be a greater glory than conquering will be for me. [105] Therefore indignation brings an end to my words, nor do I wish to speak any more words, although very many remain."

She had finished; the flea was about to speak and leaps forth into the middle from the tender bosom of a maiden. "And who," she says, "taught the slave of Beelzebub [Lord of the Flies] [110] and the bird of a degenerate guardian spirit to fashion lies? She uttered lofty words indeed, but such words spurning such a one as me do not sit properly in the mouth of such a creature as her. Her very words spurn her as she speaks and fear lest they grow vile in her mouth. [115] But because her prolonged speech kept us too long, now I will speak with controlled brevity.

There is not need for many words; on my behalf the very place whence I just came will speak, even if I myself say nothing. If now everything that she said could be ours, [120] still it is more worthwhile to be in the tender bosom of a maiden. She shares food with the king; but the daughter of the king does not shrink from sharing her bed with me. I wander through the secret places that belong to Venus in the lap of the maiden, breaking through the enclosures of her pudenda with my lusty foot. [125] Ha! How many times I have laughed at the sighs of Jove himself, [who hopes] that at some time he could enjoy the honor I do. He himself envies me and he would be more blissful than he is now if but once he could occupy the places that I occupy. Although an envious person is usually worth less than the envied, [130] all the same I do not maintain that Jove is worth less than I am.

What if she tastes beforehand every single dish brought to the king; I have tasted beforehand every single stolen pleasure of Jove. With all due respect to Jove, his Danae has felt me where she had not yet felt Jove. [135] And I have touched, and it was no small delight for me to have touched, whatever in Ganymede was a hot spot for Jove. The smooth plain and the well-turned ivory of the tender thigh, the places that Orpheus taught were appropriate for sports of love, the flesh of sensual pleasure and the charm of touching Ganymede [140] were known first to me and then to Jove. If I have touched all or if I have marked well the places touched, then all were worthy to be caressed by Jove.

Jupiter merited praise in this flesh, in my opinion; for a noble crime has the merit of praise. [145] The object of the crime made the crime to be of less weight or even did not allow it to be a crime at all. Without Ganymede as object it could be a crime, but in the case of Ganymede it could be called a sport. When the lusty hand of Jove was playing and roving

[150] through the groves of Venus, over the boyish thigh, I deceived the fingers as they were scratching and frolicking with a certain tremulousness, and instead of Ganymede I was touched by Jove. As they played together, either Ganymede bore the weight of my advances along with Jove's, or I together with Ganymede bore the weight of Jove's. [155] I was Jove's competitor or Juno's rival—I speak with due regard for Juno and Jove.

Lotis would not have sensed Priapus beforehand if she had not been touched, if that god had the possibilities I do. If what is possible for me, Faunus, had ever been possible for you, [160] the Lydian girl [Omphale] would have yielded to your desires. The places that you were seeking, Faunus, when you were deceived by the changes of clothing, I then occupied. Secret escapades of girls are known to me, and a woman will not feel the embrace of her lover without me.

[165] A nipple that stands, does not sag, is firm to the touch, and still has the sign of intact virginity, just such a breast as is usually praised and sought out by Jove represents pleasures and treasures to me. The fly cherishes discarded meats and squalid carcasses [170] in place of the greatest treasures and pleasures. She hates nothing except what she sees marred by no sore; for indeed a serious ulcer is her place of birth.

But the fact that I am spurned by her will not be unavenged, and a due punishment will strike down her pride. [175] The spider, hard-working in weaving webs, leaps about; she will be the proper avenger of the contempt shown me. When her raft gets stuck and is captured on those shoals, then, then! the fly will know well her own worth."

And because this wretched end is now upon her, [180] I do not wish to speak more words, lest I be called a boor.

Note

175   *Insultat* could be translated "jeers."

16. "The Altercation of the Spider and Fly"

I suppose that there is in the midst of good things an associated evil, which the fly strives to grab as her endowment. Oh, what a shame! See the outrage! Reason, lulled by the glowing ashes of excess, does not know the way of sobriety.

The fly—[5] a cruel stepmother to cleanliness, devoted to vices, a foul corruption—is tortured by the stings of extravagance. Unskilled, she oppresses the expert; harmful, the studious; stupid, the learned; pernicious, the righteous. Because of what worthiness does she feel entitled to reprove the worthiness of another, [10] because of what dowry to be proud, because of what virtue to puff up with pride, because of what justification to stand out above others?

Her greatest delight is dregs, her hall the scullery, her dining room the sewer; ordure is her food, a corpse is her wealth. So long as she thrives, a good taste turns out to be a false promise, charm falls flat, honor withers, worthiness grows dirty, a pleasant aroma turns tart. She, culling the first fruits for herself, exacts foul tribute from any dung and corpses you please. The burden of the dishonor outweighs the actual damage, seeing that she (decay in person!) dares to depreciate my worth.

It may be that I am ugly, yet popular acclaim speaks out about my good sense, [20] and the high repute of my skill compensates for the imperfection of my body. Indeed, the gravity of my mind gives me commendations, my sense proclaims them, my renown allots them, my odor toasts them. My sickly skin is astonished at the resources of my mind, just as the threshing floor is astonished at the harvest, the nut at the kernel, the bark at the wood, the seeds at the crop. The shadow of the nettle covers the rose, the storm of a cloud outside obscures the delight of the sun's splendor. A harmful shadow blackens ivory, and a sophist blackens what is better in appearance; a pleasant odor breathes forth from under a brittle bark. I watch, you rage; I am eager, you consume; I request, you lick up; [30] you snore, I move about; you break in pieces, I make; I weave, you flee. You roll around, I build; I have knowledge, you have none; I make ingenious devices, you make mistakes . . . . [*One line lost.*] Therefore, may the judge restrain the defendant, lest a noxious plague make bold to destroy the human race.

Response of the Fly

Envy grieves when fortune smiles, the prophet of doom feels tortured to see prosperity. Oh, what sadness! Wrath runs wild into forbidden territory, worthless corruption bears arms against worthiness. The wicked spider, [40] a noxious plague, the worst of banes, swelling with corruption, dares to act to my detriment. Tumorous dregs, grave, bad, worse, worst, horrible to see, filthy to touch, mistress of violence. A freak of nature . . . no, a ghoul. No, the anger of the gods, or the work of hellish impiety. The daughter of Tisiphone and shameful granddaughter of Megaera, she foretells ancestors who were infernal with the same plague. A vessel of impurity, a deformed trunk, in her belly . . . [*One line omitted.*] . . . belches out a deadly evil, pours it out for the benefit of death, [50] by which Claudius and Cato perish. Her harmful shape forewarns of her savage spirits; the corruption within does not know how to conceal itself outside. My highest power governs in full; I am accustomed by myself to take first fruits from the feasts of kings. Honey pours out manifold treasures to me; Bacchus, unadulterated by water, laughs in golden vessels before me. The queen gives kisses to me, her nectar its scent to me; her bed is my couch, her purple robe my seat. I taste beforehand, I sample in advance the flowery rose-gardens [60] of a maiden's lips, the lilies of her neck, the ivory of her forehead. I glory, you tremble; you hang, I fly; I rejoice, you sorrow; I rule, you groan; you lie in a torpor, I run up and down; I drink, you thirst. May your judgment, therefore, oppress this harmful one: it is fitting that those who harm by destruction be oppressed by perdition.

Verdict

[65] The work of literature, just barely crawling from a paltry talent, fears the gift of mind, judicial inquiry. The progression of the meter stands in need: it is devoid of oratorical color, destitute of craftsmanship, barren of rhetorical figures, bare of figurative language. The limitations of a boy's pygmoid nature forbid him to run riot in the use of an adult voice. [70] The mind gives guidance to age; sense outweighs tender age and enlarges that which could be less. An adult mind breathes from within a tender bark; it will produce a guardian over the boy, it will render fixity in place of levity.

Notes

13   *Quoque* in the edition: emend to *quaque?*
27   *Meliorque* in the edition: emend to *meliusque?*
65   Cf. Ovid, *Tristia* 3.14.34 "parvaque vena fuit."

17. "The Ass Brought before the Bishop"

While a certain person who was going to promote his donkey to the rank of priest was importuning the ears of the bishop with protests that it was passing the year long without performing the holy mass, the bishop said, "Are its life and morals sufficiently commendable?"

[5] Getting down to his feet, the man said that he had found the ass only with difficulty, and he asked that the ass be consecrated. The astonished prelate replied to this: "A great madness afflicts you, that anyone should dare to consecrate a dumb beast to such a high office: leave quickly!"

[10] The man, walking sadly, turns around the ass by beating it. The scorned ass, having been struck, began to bray. Under its tail a bar of ruddy gold flashed. Cheered by this gift and song, the bishop commented: "The ass sounds good and ought not to be suspended from a holy rank, [15] since the Lord bestowed upon it such great talent."

18. "The Cock and Fox"

1   Standing within an appropriate privy-chamber,
     a cock was singing
     unceasingly upon a dung heap
     out of happiness with its summit.

2   A famished fox is nearby.
     She hears the unwelcome songs
     by which the cock remained alert
     with a flapping movement.

3   Conscious of her slowness, she
     sets a snare through craft,
     and first, with ingratiating nods,
     flatters with these words:

4   "O blessed the ancestry which has given birth
     to an heir
     who imitates his father
     in such a way that he can outdo him by far in songs!

5   I see lacking only one attainment
     which I am uncertain whether you can achieve;
     for your father used to sing
     with verve while dancing.

6   For he would whirl himself with three quick
     leaps in such a way that
     in an Andalusian gyration
     he would mix a caper with a song of joy."

7   Soon the cock undertakes the effort:
     leaping and singing, he turns around
     and, coveting a little glory,
     succumbs to the words of the little fox.

8   "Why should I," he says, "be considered
     to have degenerated from my father,
     since I recreate in movement and song
     the standard set by my father?"

9   But in reply the fox says,
     "Let us bless the Lord
     because the father lives on
     somehow in his son.

10   It was not believable
     that there should be in our time
     one who could become so notable
     for marvelous deeds.

11   But that skilled father of yours
     would often close his right eye
     when, with his body in rapid motion,
     he would dance in a whirl."

12   "I can also do likewise,"
     the cock remarks at once.
     Then he turns in a circle
     and shuts his right eye.

13   But the fox, in a sly ruse,
     falls on her back suddenly,
     and, feigning amazement,
     loses her breath.

14   She shudders from sighing.
     At last with difficulty she speaks;
     with feeble delivery,
     as if tired, she begins in this way:

15   "Who will be able to believe these deeds
     if he has not seen them with his own eyes?
     If the ear alone should hear of them
     that would never suffice to make a person believe.

16   You would outdo even your father,
     if you could add only one accomplishment:
     if you could leap higher
     with both eyes shut."

17   The cock, until now the beneficiary
       of successful outcomes,
       now will exemplify
       what boasting brings about.

18   Then he recommenced the same moves
       that he had already demonstrated in leaping about,
       but as he showed his marvelous talent
       he experienced insulting treatment.

19   For closing both eyes,
       he leaps in the air.
       The fox runs up
       and catches him in her yawning maw.

20   Because of this misfortune the cock
       is carried off in a distressing form of transport;
       the alert neighbors notice
       and run after them swiftly.

21   With hue and cry they fill the clouds:
       "The little fox is carrying off the cock!
       Come help as quickly as you can!
       An outstanding bird is dying."

22   Already the fox was a long way off
       and had taken hope from her pursuers,
       when the cock out of sadness
       forms a new plan.

23   And as the crowd of common folk
       pressed on with their shouts,
       the cock turned back to the little fox
       and pronounced this opinion:

24   "Fortune has abandoned me
       and, what is more, has handed me over to you.
       If death cannot be removed,
       then surely at least let it be honorable!

25   The peasants are now attacking you.
       They charge you with the crime of theft
       and they do not know what your renowned
       foresight has accomplished.

26   They maintain that my tomb
       will be the stomach of a thief,
       that I hardly deserved
       to be buried in this pit.

27   This contention with which I am being slandered
      is becoming more irksome to me than death itself,
      seeing that this infamy damages you
      with equal dishonor.

28   Put me down for a little while, I ask,
      and address the people in this way
      and, thirdly, also say to them:
      'I am taking off what is mine, not yours.'

29   By these words whatever condemnation
      is brought against us will be washed away.
      I will find this a solace somewhat
      for my death."

30   She stopped immediately,
      placed the cockerel on the ground,
      turns back toward the crowd,
      and speaks the words of the cock.

31   But the cock rises in haste
      and flies away, beating his wings.
      The fox hurries after him,
      but feathers outdo feet.

32   Severely angered, she then
      planted her feet swiftly
      and thus with malevolent intention
      hurls imprecations:

33   "Let pustules afflict the tongue
      that falls into the possession of talkativeness
      at a time when it is dangerous to talk,
      and that is not able even so to be controlled."

34   "And let them afflict the eyes,"
      the cock replied in return,
      "that of their own accord blind themselves
      when danger is imminent."

35   From now on let us spurn vanities
      of absolutely no benefit to anyone
      and of no use to truth,
      which detests fables.

36   A severe judge threatens
      and rebukes all vanities.
      Let us exchange for better ones
      those very words that we wrote.

37   Thus we will reduce
Babylon to captivity
when the vision of peace takes away
what confusion created.

38   We know what is written
in the Gospel about the dung heap [Luke 13.6–9]—
that by using it a vineyard worker made
a fig-tree fruitful.

39   For the master of the vineyard
makes ready for him an axe
and orders the tree to be cut down to the roots,
saying: "Why does it take up space?"

40   But at once the worker obtains permission
that the fig-tree should not be destroyed
until he prepares it with a hoe
and fertilizes it with his basket.

41   For this reason penitence is signified
by the ordure of the dung heap,
by which the sterile sinner recognizes
that he stinks;

42   for when a corrupt person comes back to his senses,
he sees the wrongs he has committed,
and through lamentations he grows fertile
from the ordure of crimes.

43   Assembling a secure basis
atop the heap of them,
from this time on he subdues his former life
and raises himself higher.

44   And because lamentation has taken precedence
in his mangled heart,
from now on he claps during song,
following the procedure of Ezechiel [21.17, 25.6].

45   For this reason it was not inappropriate
for us to note at the beginning
that the cock standing in dung
beat his wings as he sang.

46   Before I append "Woc!"
in accord with the word of the prophet,
since I have described the dung heap,
I will not omit the cock.

47   In the cock you should understand
      quite appropriately the doctors of the Church
      who shout in loud voices and gesticulate
      so that listeners will not grow sluggish.

48   He first raises himself
      as he strikes his side with his wings
      so that he may first perceive
      what he announces to those below.

49   He produces extended notes
      at night, when people snore,
      for there is need of shouts
      so long as people are blinded by errors.

50   Toward daybreak he makes noise frequently,
      indicating the hour of judgment
      when the night of this world
      perishes in the everlasting morning.

51   When he thus thunders about with his voice,
      he strikes with lightning the deaf,
      warning with his exhortation
      that we should rise from sleep now [Romans 13.11].

51²   Night has gone in advance. Look:
      the day approaches in haste.
      Let us soon cast away
      the wretched activities of the darkness.

51³   Just as we noted above
      that the cock when snatched from the dung
      sang in refined laments
      and then rose,

52   it is not beyond credence
      that doctors of the Church can be
      freed of crimes
      through divine assistance.

53   Indeed, after the apostles
      idolatry, fetid with the slime
      of errors, produced
      famous preachers.

54   The savior, speaking figuratively,
      calls them salt:
      if the salt should disappear,
      there would be no seasoning [Matthew 5.13].

55 Then we can consider
    that these people can grow so foolish
    that through their vain glory
    they rush down into the mouth of Leviathan.

56 In the fable we described
    how the cock was first carried off in his whirling
    and then engulfed in the maw of the fox
    when he shut his eyes.

57 By the little fox is designated
    Satan, the ambusher
    who by dishonesty trips up
    those whom he cannot trip up by force.

58 He was the first to urge
    damnable boasting upon the cock.
    Afterward by means of impious turnings
    he obscures the cock's eyes.

59 "For the impious," said the psalmist,
    "walk round about" [Psalm 11.9]
    and "let their eyes be darkened
    that they see not" [Psalm 68.24], he added.

60 O woe! What we promised
    is now revealed in a certain sense;
    for after a joyous song
    man falls into the pit.

61 But before he is swallowed up
    entirely below,
    by the grace of God
    he leaves the mouth of Leviathan [Job 40.20].

62 The one who strangles him with a hook
    punches a hole in his jaw;
    Peter the denier is drawn
    from his savage teeth.

63 As the fable says, the little fox
    put down the cock
    and thus said to the people:
    "I am taking off what is mine, not yours."

64 The thoroughly wretched gentiles,
    formerly handed over to Satan,
    were called back to their voices
    by very great doctors of the Church.

65   Satan took a stand opposite them
        and put down his booty (so to speak)
        when he aimed his entire savagery
        at the Church.

66   He presented himself flatteringly to them,
        so that he might tear them apart in their vices;
        he roared opposite her,
        complaining that his people were being taken away.

67   Then hearing the word of God
        and shaking themselves,
        the gentiles moaned
        to have been the booty of the demon.

68   Immediately they beat their wings,
        deserted Leviathan,
        and, flying to the heavens through the power of their vows,
        claim their place of birth.

69   Small wonder if I made
        the bird figural in a twofold sense,
        in that it designates the people in some cases
        and the crowd of doctors in others;

70   for these are the members of the Church
        which rejoices in having Christ as its head,
        for the doctors together with the people
        form one body in the Lord.

71   But this same fable
        is pleasing on account of its final section,
        in which the cock and the little fox
        enjoy a truly stylish ending.

72   The fox condemns her tongue unendingly,
        the cock his sleepy pupil,
        and thus the whole fable
        is brought to a close in a definite pronouncement.

Notes

My translation can be only provisional, since Herrmann's edition is seriously flawed. My translation assumes the following corrected readings and emendations.

3.3   *mitibus* in the edition: *nutibus*.
6.3   A Morris dance?

9.4   *uiuus est* in the edition: *reuiuiscit.*
19.2   *utrumque* in the edition: *utramque.*
19.3   *subicit* in the edition: *subiit.*
22.1   *aderat* in the edition: *aberat.*
22.3   *pro* in the edition: *prae.*
25.3   *quod* in the edition: *quid.*
28.3   *quoque* in the edition: *eique.*
29.4   *repperio* in the edition: *repperiam.*
39.2   *aptans* in the edition: *optans.*
41.4   *fetore* in the edition: *fetere.*
42.1   *prorsus* in the edition: *prauus.*
45.4   *percussum* in the edition: *percussis.*
46.1   *nunc* in the edition: *"ue"* (= *vae*).
48.2   *perculit* in the edition: *percutit.*
48.4   *quod* in the edition: *quo.*
50.1   *perstrepunt* in the edition: *perstrepit.*
51³   *ipsum* in the edition: *inde.*
57.2   *insidiator* in the edition: *insidiatur.*
59.3   *et ipsi obscurent* in the edition: *et obscurentur.*
65.3   *sententiam* in the edition: *seuitiam.*
66.2   *iacerent* in the edition: *laceret.*
68.3   *uotis* in the edition: *uolis.*
68.4   *uindicat* in the edition: *uendicat.*

19. "The Flea"

O flea, little and yet a bitter plague harmful to girls, with what manner of poem shall I act against your deeds, fierce one? Hard one, you lacerate a tender body with your bite. When your skin has become full with blood from the skin, [5] you cause dark spots to come from her [white] body; and her smooth limbs, spotted with them, become rough. And when you plant your sharp proboscis in her side, the maid is forced to rise from her heavy sleep; and you wander throughout her folds, the other limbs are accessible to you, [10] you go wherever you please: nothing is hidden from you, savage. Oh, it pains me to tell: when the girl lies stretched out, you pluck at her thigh and enter her open legs. Occasionally you dare to go through her sexual organs and to disturb the pleasures born in those places.

[15] May I die, if I do not now wish to become my own enemy, so that the route to my desires can become more easily passable. If nature allowed me to be turned into you and if it granted the power to return to the form in which I was born, or if I could be changed by any incantations, [20] at my own desire I would become by incantations a flea, or by po-

tions, if potions can accomplish more, I would wish to alter the laws of my nature. What incantations conferred upon Medea or potions upon Circe is a matter that has been made sufficiently well known.

[25] Changed by these means, if I were thus capable of change, I would cling on the edge of the maid's nightgown. From there I would go swiftly and stealthily, moving over the thighs and under the clothing of my girl to the places I chose, and just as I hoped, I would lie down (not hurting her at all) [30] until I turned from a flea back into a human being. But if by chance the maid, terrified by these new portents, forced her servants to shackle me, either she would yield, excited by my entreaties, or else I would soon turn from a human back into a flea.

[35] Once changed back and pouring forth humble prayers, I would induce all the gods to fulfill my desires, until I held fast—through either entreaties or force—all the goods I had hoped for; and then she would prefer nothing to having me as her friend.

20. "GOUT AND THE FLEA"

In olden times the flea is said to have afflicted powerful men, whereas dire gout afflicted poor men. But whenever the flea by night tore at the limbs of the rich man, a light was brought at once and it was captured. [5] Whenever the other hid itself in the soles of a poor man, the poor man was unable to stand still; as a result the gout was quite tired. Thus they were worn out, driven along by bitter fates, the flea by fear of slaughter, gout by the toil of the road.

Once they come together, they report to each other their woes, [10] and they agree to change places. Meanwhile gout began to afflict the movement of the rich man, whereas the flea afflicted your bed, poor man. The rich man has leisure and lies back: you have great rest, gout. You, flea, are safe, the companion of limbs too tired to swat you.

21. "THE HAWK AND PEACOCK"

[1] This great bird heads toward the stars on high; spreading about noble words it commends the lamb, the author, for everything. [2] The good creator should be praised well. He did well when he created good

things throughout the world; carrying through to the end, he protects the good things in his kindness.

[3] It flapped its wings covered over with feathers. Its tail flashes, gleaming with color. It produces a song, it surpasses all. [4] In worthy triumphs the peacock spreads out in varying manners in two wheels, comelier than all on account of its small limbs.

[5] On its final day, when the sun has been extinguished, it mounts aloft, escapes evils; extending its wings it flies forth to the heights.

[6] The hawk is stout, the peacock stronger: trusting in itself, it scorned the fierce hawk; blessed, the strong peacock remained unconquered. [7] Rejoicing to have achieved glory for itself, wheeling in a circle, exulting in its feathers—rejoicing it sings, an ornament for the celebration. [8] In flight it has the countenance of an angel, an honorable manner, a happy countenance: its appearance is a marvel.

[9] In the season of spring flowers burst into a flame of colors, winged creatures join together, they invite to Easter, they sound in turns—and the peacock, too. [10] Then they applaud plentifully, trilling their tongues. They sing mellifluously, they make sound far and wide, and they praise the father, singing happily.

[11] The dead flesh is proven a marvel, after much time abandoning corruption, and the flies of evil hardly graze. [12] And no one ever exceeded his time, and no one is ever devoured by worms, and no one is not found.

[13] Having gone forth from the egg, having forgotten the nest, adorned with feathers—its tail is appropriate, offering war to everyone it encounters. [14] The peacock commences a beautiful battle. They go at once, brandishing their talons; each marks the chest of the other with gory wounds.

[15] How beautiful, all like a plane-tree . . . breast like an emerald. [16] In regal style the peacock shines crimson, with proper and worthy food for a king, drink for a king, eating for a king. [17] Quite rich, it satisfies greatly. Its savor and taste satisfy heart and soul, and it is the only good taste, there is none like it.

[18] Highest trinity, may you be glorified. You are the good maker, you are life to everyone, and you protect such great things under the great star. [19] Single trinity, one in triumphs. True God slain, true eternal God, flying into the heavens, living eternally. [20] Christ was born, Christ suffered the passion, Christ was on the cross, Christ died, Christ was in the tomb, Christ was resurrected.

Notes

1.6   Or "to everyone."
7.4   I translate *Gestans* as equivalent to *gestiens*.
9.2   I emend *Ignis et* to *igniscunt*.
9.2–3   Or "fires of the sun and flowers come together, birds invite Easter . . ."

22. "THE LOMBARD AND SNAIL"

A Lombard came to the grain fields: he walks around them, walks around and rejoices because he sees lush crops. As he happily admires the lush grain crop in this way, the unaccustomed sight of a snail came to him. [5] He wonders what it is; he is stunned, shudders, and loses his breath with fear; he loses consciousness and turns pale, and warmth goes out of his bones.

When at last he comes to his senses, he stands back and says: "What I see is a crime. This is my last day. This is not a wolf, bear, or viper; I don't know what it is, [10] but I do know that, whatever it is, it is readying war against me. The shield is a sign of war, the horns are a sign. Alas! Should I refuse to fight? Not I: I would rather die. If I should be able to overcome a monster of this sort, I would earn both honor and everlasting fame.

[15] What did I say? It is not proper conduct to confront a monster; other, less frightful wars are not lacking. What praise will be given, if this should be called madness, not a fight? It is not civilized to have perished in this fashion. If my wife and all my children should see this monster, [20] they would turn tail at the sight of it alone. Besides, this fight will not seem an even match to anyone, for my foe is armed but I am unarmed."

Thus he hesitates. Fear and shame fight within him: shame causes him to fight, but fear shuns such things. [25] In the end, what he judges right is established through consultation: he consults his wife, and he consults the gods. The gods respond to him that he is going to enjoy the palm of victory, although he scarcely dares to trust their divine powers.

In contrast, his timid spouse, fearful for her husband, like a loyal wife, [30] exclaims in tears: "What are you getting ready to do, madman! What sort of wars meets your approval? Leave off, I ask you, attacking monsters, put aside your animosity. Spare me, wretch that I am, spare your children, even if you do not care to spare yourself. O woe! This day will see us destroyed! [35] Daring Hector would not dare this, Achilles would not; in this the sublime courage of Hercules would fail."

"Keep your entreaties within limits, dearest wife," he said. "A daring mind is not swayed by entreaty or tears. Today the gods are going to give me a name that will last forever. [40] Now I entreat you, that you and the children fare well."

Once he took a stand in the field, he directs his course swiftly now here and now there, besets the beast, and threatens great deeds: "O beast, the likes of which nature never created, monster of monsters, deadly pestilence, [45] the horns that you are now deploying against me do not frighten me, nor does the shell under the cover of which you remain safe. By this strong right hand you shall die today, and I shall not suffer you to contaminate my grain crops any longer."

And brandishing his spear, he looks for the [50] most lethal spots and vigorously pursues the palm of victory. What fitting rewards shall be given for so great a deed? This is not a small matter: let the lawyers come to decide.

23. "The Louse"

On the sweaty skin beneath my clothes a louse took hold, broke through the skin, sucked, and swelled. After I noticed—for it forced me to notice—I guided a finger which soon caught it. [5] Having been brought into the light, fearing (I think) the blows of my thumb, the slippery louse fell from my finger and hid among the creases between the joints of my toes. But its flight brought no success: trouble followed. Having been discovered, it is snatched up; having been snatched, it is proven to be guilty; [10] and by way of punishment it is consigned to death. All the nits and black sisters bewail it, and they make a tomb and, with the tomb, an inscription: A HEAD WITH SIX FEET AND A BODY WITHOUT A HEART LIE IN THIS TOMB, FLESH BORN OF FLESH.

Notes

5   The translation assumes a comma rather than a full stop after *ictus*.
8   The translation assumes *cura secuta fuit* instead of *cura secura fuit*.

24. "The Prose of the Ass"

1   From the lands of the Orient
     came the ass,
     handsome and quite strong,
     well-suited to bearing burdens.
        Hey, Sir Ass! Because you sing,
        curling your pretty mouth,
        you will have hay enough
        and oats aplenty.

2   He was slow on his feet,
     if there was not a staff
     and if the goad
     did not pierce him in his hindquarters.
        Hey, Sir Ass! etc.

3   After being reared
     in the hills of Sichem under Reuben,
     he crossed the Jordan,
     bounded into Bethlehem.
        Hey, Sir Ass! etc.

4   Look, with large ears
     a son brought under the yoke,
     outstanding ass,
     lord of the asses.
        Hey, Sir Ass! etc.

5   With his bound he surpasses hinnies,
     does, and roebucks—
     swifter than
     dromedaries.
        Hey, Sir Ass! etc.

6   Ass power
     brought god from Arabia,
     frankincense and myrrh from Sheba
     within the Church.
        Hey, Sir Ass! etc.

7   As he draws waggons
     with many burdens,
     his jaws
     grind hard fodder.
        Hey, Sir Ass! etc.

8   He eats barley and thistle
     with ears of grain:
     he separates wheat from chaff
     on the threshing floor.
        Hey, Sir Ass! etc.
9   Say amen, ass,
     now full of grass,
     repeat amen, amen.
     Spurn old fashions.
        Hey, come on!/Hey, come on!/Hey, hey: come!/You are
        handsome as you move./Your mouth is pretty as you sing.

25. "THE SAD CALF"

A mournful calf was looking for its mother amid the meadows. A
bird with long legs encounters it. The bird says: "Hail, brother! Why are
you lowing, sad of heart? And why are you troubled as you tread down
the flowering fields?"

[5] The calf replied to her with these words: "Sister, it is now the
third day that I have not touched milk, and I am in hunger as I move."

The winged creature replies: "Lunatic, do not worry about such matters; for the third year is now ending in which I have not suckled."

The irritated calf is reported to have said to her: [10] "Just look! Your
legs show the sort of food you have eaten."

26. "THE SICK LION"

Once upon a time there was a report that the lion had lain ill and that
he had already reached almost his final days. As soon as this very sad rumor
reaches all the beasts, namely, that their king was suffering intolerable
pains, [5] they all come together weeping and calling doctors, so that they
may not lose the great support of their prince.

Here were present buffaloes, as well as aurochs with huge bodies; the
fierce bull was present, as were the oxen, the parti-colored pard together
with the broad-antlered stag, [10] together with them the steed, which
accompanied them on their route. Nor were the stags, showing their
horns, absent from this group; and the roebucks and goat family were
present also. Here are the boar with flashing teeth, and the fierce bear with
uncut claws; here are the hare and wolf. [15] Here come lynxes, here con-

verged sheep, and dogs and pups assemble together. However, only the fox was not present among these throngs, for she did not deign to visit her lord.

The bear is said to have pronounced these words then before the others, [20] and to have repeated these threats in the following manner: "O great and powerful king, unconquered chieftain of wild beasts, receive these words within your indulgent ears, and may this whole retinue hear—this whole retinue which is known to be subject to your great dominion, O just king. [25] What so dire a madness took hold of the fox, or what passion could have entered so small a beast, that only she should not wish even to approach the king, who has been visited by the entire populace which is subject to him? This impudence of the fox's attitude is indeed great, [30] and she ought to be subjected to great pains."

Once the bear has related these words, the king says to everyone: "Now let her fall, swiftly torn to pieces, to die!" Then the entire people at once raise their voices to the heavens: "Just and good is the judgment of our prince!"

[35] This matter came to the attention of the fox, and she turns her thoughts in many directions, and prepares her long-known ruses: she seeks out many pairs of torn-apart shoes and, placing them upon her shoulders, she makes her way to the royal camp.

When the king saw her, he laughed with a placated heart [40] and awaits a long time what the untrustworthy creature has as her purpose. And when she stood before the faces of the dukes, the king speaks first: "What will you bring me, as you are about to die, you who come to be torn apart?"

For a long time trembling and considering in her fearful heart, she relates topics which had been premeditated hastily: [45] "Pious king, clement king, most unconquered king of ours, receive now in your mind the precepts that I bring to you. I wore out these pairs of shoes as I searched over all the roads of the world out of my desire to find a doctor who could cure the great illness of the king [50] and take away from your people their great sadness. In the end I was able with difficulty to find an outstanding doctor, but I fear to tell you, king, what he instructed."

The king said: "If what you report is true, sweetest fox, tell me quickly what this doctor said."

[55] At this the wicked fox, not forgetful of the bear, said: "Receive quite cautiously these words of your servant: if I can envelop you in a bear-hide, without delay the illness will go away and a healthy life return."

Immediately, at the bidding of the lord, the bear is stretched out [60] and his skin is torn off by his own comrades. As they exult at covering the lion in this pelt, the tiring pain left altogether.

When afterward the fox saw the bear so bare in body, she relates these words in a happy mood: [65] "Who gave you, O father bear, this fancy head-dress to wear on your head? And who gave you these gloves for your hands?"

Look, your humble servant offers these verses to you. Seek out with vigor what this fable can mean.

27. "The Swan Lament"

1   Once I lived in lakes,
     once I was beautiful,
     when I was a swan!
         Wretched! Wretched!
         Now I am black
         and burnt to a crisp!

2   I was whiter than snow,
     fairer than any other bird;
     but now I am blacker than a raven.
         Wretched! Wretched!
         Now I am black
         and burnt to a crisp!

3   The fire burns me to a crisp,
     the servant turns and turns the spit;
     now the waiter dishes me out.
         Wretched! Wretched!
         Now I am black
         and burnt to a crisp!

4   I would rather live upon the water,
     ever beneath open air,
     than be doused in this pepper.
         Wretched! Wretched!
         Now I am black
         and burnt to a crisp!

5   Now on a dish I lie
     and I cannot fly;

I see gnashing teeth—
   Wretched! Wretched!
   Now I am black
   and burnt to a crisp!

28. "THE SWAN SEQUENCE"

1	I will cry out, sons, in a lament
2a	of the winged swan that traversed the ocean.
2b	O, how bitterly it was wailing that it
3a	had left behind the flower-covered dry land and had sought the high seas,
3b	saying: "I am an unhappy little bird. Woe is me! What am I in my wretchedness to do?
4a	Tired as I am, I will not be able to rely upon my wings here in the gleaming water.
4b	I am battered by the waves; exiled, I am dashed now here and now there by gusts.
5a	I feel anguish amid the close-packed crests of the whirling waves; moaning, I beat my wings, gazing upon all that can bring death, not able to ascend upon high.
5b	Although perceiving in abundance plants upon which fish feed, in the tumult of the whirling waves I am unable to take up these fine foods.
6a	East, west, heavenly climes: make the constellations gleam.
6b	Call upon Orion to help, dispelling the setting clouds."
7a	While in silence she was considering these matters, ruddy and helpful dawn came.
7b	Having been brought relief by the breeze, she began to recover her forces.
8a	Rejoicing, she flew now between the high seas and the familiar constellations among the clouds.
8b	Now made gay and joyful, she made her way across the streams of the sea.
9a	Singing in a sweet measure, she flew toward the dry land, lovely to see.
9b	Come together and cry out together, all you troops of birds:
10	"Glory be to the great king!"

Note

6b The risings and settings of the constellation Orion were associated with storms.

29. "The Testament of the Ass"

The peasant, when he saw his ass had died, wept for its demise: "Oh no, oh no! You are dying, ass? [5] If I had known, ass, that you were going to die of cold, I would have clothed you in muslin. Oh no!"

The peasant woman cried out [10] in a voice quite plaintive, as the neighbors came to meet her: "Oh no!"

The peasant howled and with great cries tore out his hair with his hands: "Oh no! Rise, for long enough that you can drink and draft a will. [20] Oh no!"

The ass soon arose, and immediately drafted a will orally. "Oh no!" [25] "I give my cross to papal officials, ears to cardinals, and tail to the minor orders. Oh no! My head to judges, [30] voice to singers, and tongue to preachers. Oh no! My back to porters, flesh to fasters, [35] and feet to walkers. Oh no! My hide to cobblers, hair to saddlemakers, and bones to dogs. [40] Oh no! My entrails to vultures and my phallus, together with my testicles, to widows. Oh no!"

[45] When all of his possessions had been bequeathed, the ass drifted into the sleep of death with his brothers. "Oh no!" Then the abbot and clerks [50] offer wheaten bread, since he has in mind to die. "Oh no!" The peasant and servants carry the body of the ass [55] to become wolf food. "Oh no!"

30. "The Testament of the Piglet"

Here begins the will of the pig.

Marcus Grunnius Corocotta, piglet, has made his will.

Since I could not write with my own hand, I have dictated the text.

Magirus the cook said: "Come here, destroyer of the house, [5] ground-rooter, fugitive piglet, and today I am going to take your life from you."

Corocotta the piglet said: "If I have done anything, if I have committed any sin, if I have broken to pieces any dishes with my feet, I appeal, Master Cook, I ask for my life; grant my appeal."

Magirus the cook said: "Go, boy, bring me a knife from the kitchen, so that I [10] may make this piglet bloody."

The piglet is seized by the servants, led off the sixteenth day before the Kalends of Lucerninus, when the spring shoots of cabbage abound, during the consulship of Clibanatus and Piperatus. And when he saw that he was going to die, he requested the boon of an hour and asked the cook for permission to make a will. He called [15] his relatives to him, so that he could leave to them something from his provisions.

He said: "To my father Verrinus Lardinus I give and bequeath thirty bushels of acorns, and to my mother Veturina the sow I give and bequeath forty bushels of Laconian wheat flour, and to my sister Quirina, at whose exchange of wedding vows [20] I could not be present, I give and bequeath thirty bushels of barley.

And from my bodily parts I will give and pass on my bristles to the cobblers, my . . . to the . . . , my ears to the deaf, my tongue to lawyers and speechmakers, my intestines to butchers, my thighs to the sausage-makers, my loins to women, my bladder to boys, my tail to girls, [25] my muscles to libertines, my ankle-bones to runners and hunters, my hooves to robbers.

And to the unmentionable cook I bequeath a ladle and pestle, which I brought with me: let him tie his neck with rope from Thebeste to Tergeste.

[30] And I wish for a tomb to be made for me with the following inscription in gold letters: 'Marcus Grunnius Corocotta the piglet lived for 999½ years. If he had lived another half year, he would have completed 1000 years.'

My best friends and consuls of my life, I ask you to treat [35] my body well, to spice it well with good seasoning of nuts, pepper, and honey, so that my name may be repeated forever. My lords and my relatives, have this will signed."

Lardio signed. Ofellicus signed. Cyminatus signed. [40] Lucanicus signed. Celsinianus signed. Nuptialicus signed.

Here ends the testament of the piglet, on the sixteenth day before the Kalends of Lucerninus, during the consulship of Clibanatus and Piperatus. Live happily!

31. "The Wolf"

A certain wolf often seized many of a shepherd's sheep as they wandered throughout the broad pastures. The shepherd, after he proved unable to harm the seizer by valor, strove to ensnare him by craft; [5] for he bends a stiff oak with such great effort that its top can touch the ground; and a snare is tied to the bent top, so that a movable rod holds down the snare. That rod attaches the snare to the ground in such a way [10] that anyone who moves the rod will perish in the snare; and in the middle of the snare the head of a lamb is attached in such a way that anyone who seizes the head will move the rod. Then the shepherd goes off.

The wolf goes to that device and at once seizes the lamb's head in its mouth. [15] But once the rod is moved, the snare binds its neck in an instant, and the stiff oak lofts the wolf up high.

As the shepherd sees the captured robber hanging, he hurls stones at it to speed its death. He makes a thousand wounds, so that the wolf may perish through being stoned, [20] but that evil spirit cannot be expelled. To torment it more, at length he takes it down from high and, raising his cudgel, uttered these words to the wolf: "Stones accomplish nothing; now I will dash out your brains with my cudgel and make them funeral offerings to the lambs."

[25] At once the wolf cries out, "Take pity, most pious shepherd, and, I beg, heed the few words that I relate to you. If you deign to grant my life to me, I will restore four times over everything that I seized. You may say that I have nothing here, but if you permit me to go off, [30] you will have a useful pledge that I will not be false to you: my whelp will be a suitable hostage. I shall surrender him to you, so that I will return when the day you have appointed arrives. Should I never return, negligible harm would be done to you, if the youth should perish in place of his worn-out elder. [35] The youth can do harm, whereas I will not do harm if I live, and I will provide you no benefits if I am destroyed. Take my hide: it will not be fit for making a boot for you. Take my meat: it will not be fit for food. I don't know why you should seek to destroy this wretched body [40] since neither the outside nor the inside of it will be useful to you."

To make a long story short, the gullible shepherd lets the wolf go home as soon as he has received the hostage. As the wolf goes home, preparing a stratagem by which to deceive the shepherd, he finds a monk and his servant. [45] "Hail, my father," he said, "Do not spurn the words of a suppliant and do not rebuke me because I have sinned. I repent of my error, I am tired of consuming worldly goods, and I am ashamed to have slit the throats of an innocent flock. It brings me no profit to pamper my limbs with ever-present enticements, [50] if I should have no spiritual salvation. Beat me with a switch, or strike me with any manner of whip, only render this soul to God, pious man. I ask you, clip my head of hair and shave a broad tonsure, and give me a monk's tunic, since I have converted. [55] Lest you should think that you accomplish so great a task for naught, I give you as a gift a sheep, since it was just now given to me. If the treat of mutton that I have given should not meet your fancy, then give the meat to your servant and keep the fleece for yourself."

Once the monk receives the very welcome gift, [60] he takes up shears and shears the wolf in a moment, and as he shaves the head he strives to make the tonsure so great, that a circle should run from ear to ear. In addition, he teaches what sort of monastic order the wolf should follow. Then he orders the wolf in its cowl to go.

[65] The day arrived, on which the hostage was supposed to be returned and on which the wolf had promised to return. Then it returns, but the shepherd is barely able to recognize it, for he sees that the wolf is black, whereas just now it had been gray. He says, "You have changed greatly from the sort of wolf you were, [70] who were a seizer of sheep and captured in a snare."

After the wolf, bowing its head, said "Bless you!," it uttered these words amid the tears it poured forth upon its face: "Worn down by the wounds of the stones which you had inflicted upon me, I was recently languishing, and a doctor was present. [75] Pressing my vein, he felt that my pulse was not running well, and he said, 'You will not live; rather, you will die.' In the meantime a monk comes to visit me in my illness and admonishes me to repent at last of my crimes, and he teaches me hallowed hope, in that no one whose life has been wicked would be damned, [80] so long as his death was good. In short, he persuaded me to scorn the world entirely and gave to me this monastic habit, once I had taken this tonsure. When I abandoned my old ways and former foods, I who had been languishing grew healthy in an instant.

[85] Now I seek to lay down my life lest a brother should perish, since my guarantor was supposed to lose his life. Although I have come back as I agreed that I would come back, I have nothing of my own to restore to you. I do not wish to deceive your trust. If you wish to spare me, then spare me; [90] if it pleases you that I should perish, then kill me."

The shepherd said, "This right hand of mine will never harm you. On the contrary, seeing that it harmed you in the past, please pardon me. In killing a monk I would become a murderer two times over: let the hostage go free and you go home."

[95] As they go off joyfully and loiter safely in the field, the wolf in its great hunger spoke these words to the whelp: "Believe me, brother, mutton is extremely tasty, and cheese and beans will be harsh food. I will not take up a burden that I cannot bear."

[100] So it spoke and began, as before, to seize sheep. But after a short time, as it feeds upon a seized lamb, the shepherd sees it and rebukes it as follows: "You are well and you are a monk, you ought not to dine upon meat; not so does the hallowed rule of Saint Basil instruct."

[105] Thereupon the wolf said, "The order of good men is not simple; sometimes I am a monk, sometimes I am a canon."

And as soon as the wolf went into the woods on a straight and narrow path, the shepherd realizes that he has been badly deceived.

32. "The Wrangle of the Dwarf and Hare"

Muse, outstandingly sweet to me before any of your other sisters, I ask you, in haste relate the battles which have been kept in silence so long. For while you composed, the bard once sang the battles of noble Aeneas and the notable deeds of Turnus; [5] celebrating, Homer expressed in his remarkable text the wars and the triumphant combats of keen Achilles; Statius described Adrastus, Cadmus, and tough Tydeus, and the poet described the struggles which each victor accomplished, which battlelines he overturned. [10] But none of them brought out the ill-fated battles of the dwarf, timid whelp, and fierce hare, in which the dog and dwarf were overcome and turned tail. Therefore, the bellicose hare as victor laid them low in their cowardice, bloodying their eyes and mouths with its claws fixed.

[15] The abbot (but with you outdoing him) encouraged the hare with its youthful valor to engage in savage battles with such an armed soldier and with the swift whelp, to the end that, confident in its courage, confident in its bold weapons, and forgetful of its own lightness it would not wish [20] to act forbearingly as its parents did nor yield to any enemy. On the contrary, it does not refuse to enter a struggle with many, turning its arms against each and every one in scratching.

It was devoted to a manner of warfare which none of its ancestors had employed (quite the contrary, they had been accustomed to defend their lives through flight!), [25] and the arrangement of affairs is indeed marvelously different: the coward conquers, bodies are torn to shreds which formerly had been destined by hereditary right for courage.

The unwarlike creature springs up and burns to provoke quarrels. Brandishing its weapons it moves, it pierces with sharp spears; [30] the mild one is changed into the wild one, and thus suddenly, wearing its crest, it follows struggling like an enormous bear. It becomes like a monstrous tiger, like the chimera itself; what had been a hare was now like a wolf or like a grim lion.

[35] Recalling the injuries done to its people by men and swift dogs, and the throng devastated in a lamentable slaughter by birds, it pursues enemies who were accustomed to lay low the race of hares. The most savage avenger of the slaughter assails this land and wounds with dire bite and lethal claw. Marking bloody signs with a cruel stamp, [40] it wounds those who beset it, and it detaches curved barbs.

Bibliography

PRIMARY SOURCES

"About a Bald Man Met by a Midge." *De calvo a culice obviato.* Incipit "Stridula musca volans calvum conspexit euntem." Ed. Paul von Winterfeld. *MGH Poetae* 4/1: 261, n. 1.

Accessus ad auctores; Bernard d'Utrecht, Commentum in Theodulum; Conrad d'Hirsau, Dialogus super auctores. Ed. R. B. C. Huygens. 2d ed. Leiden, 1970.

"Acts of Peter." In: *The Apocryphal New Testament.* Trans. Montague Rhodes James. Oxford, 1924. 300–36.

Adam Scot. *Sermo* 43. Ed. Migne, *PL* 198: 393–401.

Adomnan. *Life of Columba.* Ed. and trans. Alan Orr Anderson and Marjorie Ogilvie Anderson. London, 1961.

Aethelwulf. *De abbatibus.* Ed. Ernst Dümmler. *MGH Poetae* 1: 582—604.

Ahikar. Ed. and trans. William McKane. London, 1970. 156–82.

Alciphron. *Letters of Parasites.* In: Alciphron, Aelian, and Philostratus. *The Letters.* Ed. and trans. A. R. Benner and F. H. Fobes. Loeb Classical Library. Cambridge, Mass., 1949.

Alcuin. "The Cock and Wolf." *Carmen* no. 49. Incipit "Dicta vocatur avis proprio cognomine gallus." Ed. Ernst Dümmler. *MGH Poetae* 1: 262.

———. *Carmen* 57. Incipit "Plangamus cuculum, Dafnin dulcissime, nostrum." Ed. Ernst Dümmler. *MGH Poetae* 1: 269–70.

———. Letter 181 (to Adalhard of Corbie). Ed. Ernst Dümmler. *MGH Epistolae* 4: 18–481 (299–300). Berlin, 1895.

Aldhelm. *Aenigmata.* Trans. James Hall Pitman. Reprinted with new Latin text by Maria De Marco. Corpus Christianorum Series Latina 133. Turnhout, 1968. 359–539.

———. *De metris et enigmatibus ac pedum regulis.* Ed. Rudolf Ehwald. *Aldhelmi Opera. MGH Auctores Antiquissimi* 15: 59–204. Berlin, 1919.

———. *De virginitate (carmen).* Ed. Rudolf Ehwald. *Aldhelmi opera. MGH Auctores Antiquissimi* 15. Berlin, 1919.

"The Altercation of the Spider and Fly." *Altercacio aranee et musce.* Incipit "*in mediis* reor esse bonis, quod carpere dotes." Ed. J. H. Mozley. "Some unprinted fragments of Matthew of Vendôme (?). A Description of the Bodleian MS Misc. Lat. D 15." *Studi Medievali* 2d series 6 (1933): 208–38 (232–34).

Amalar of Metz. *Amalarii episcopi opera liturgica omnia.* Ed. J. M. Hanssens. Studi e Testi 138–40. 3 vols. Vatican, 1948–50.

Ambrose. "Aeterne rerum conditor." Ed. Guido Maria Dreves. *Analecta Hymnica* 50: 11, no. 4.

——. *De Abraham.* Ed. Carolus Schenkl. In: *Sancti Ambrosii Opera,* part 1. Corpus Scriptorum Ecclesiasticorum Latinorum 32/1. Vienna, 1897.

——. *Exameron.* Ed. Carolus Schenkl. In: *Sancti Ambrosii Opera,* part 1. Corpus Scriptorum Ecclesiasticorum Latinorum 32/1: 1–261. Vienna, 1897.

Analecta Hymnica. Ed. Guido Maria Dreves. 55 vols. Leipzig, 1886–1922.

Anonymus Neveleti. Ed. Wendelin Foerster. In: *Lyoner Yzopet. Altfranzösische Übersetzung des XIII. Jahrhunderts mit dem kritischen Text des lateinischen Originals (sog. Anonymus Neveleti).* Altfranzösische Bibliothek 5. Heilbronn, 1882. 96–137.

——. Ed. Hervieux. 2: 316–51.

"Apocalypse of Golias." Ed. Karl Strecker. *Die Apokalypse des Golias.* Texte zur Kulturgeschichte des Mittelalters 5. Rome, 1928.

"Apocalypse of Paul." In: *The Apocryphal New Testament.* Trans. Montague Rhodes James. Oxford, 1924. 525–55.

——. In: *Visions of Heaven and Hell before Dante.* Ed. Eileen Gardiner. New York, 1989. 13–46.

Apuleius. *The Golden Ass.* Trans. Jack Lindsay. Bloomington, 1962.

Archilochos. Ed. and trans. François Lasserre and André Bonnard. *Archiloque, Fragments.* Paris, 1958.

Aristotle. "On Dreams." Trans. J. I. Beare. In: *The Complete Works of Aristotle: The Revised Oxford Translation.* Ed. Jonathan Barnes. 2 vols. Bollingen Series 71/2. Princeton, 1984. 1: 729–35.

——. "On Divination in Sleep." Trans. J. I. Beare. In: *The Complete Works of Aristotle: The Revised Oxford Translation.* Ed. Jonathan Barnes. 1: 736–39.

"The Ass Brought before the Bishop." *De asino ad episcopum ducto.* Incipit "Ordine presbiteri dum promoturus asellum." Ed. Karl Strecker. *MGH Poetae* 4/3: 1080.

Augustine. *Ad consentium contra mendacium.* Ed. Iosephus Zycha. Corpus Scriptorum Ecclesiasticorum Latinorum 41. Vienna, 1900. 508–9.

——. *De doctrina christiana.* In: *Aurelii Augustini Opera* part 4/1. Ed. Iosephus Martin and K.-D. Daur. Corpus Christianorum Series Latina 32. Turnhout, 1961. 1–167.

——. Trans. D. W. Robertson, Jr. *On Christian Doctrine.* Indianapolis and New York, 1958.

——. *Enarrationes in Psalmos.* In: *Aurelii Augustini Opera,* part 10/1–3. Ed. D. Eligius Dekkers and Iohannes Fraipont. Corpus Christianorum Series Latina 38–40. Turnhout, 1956.

Avian. *Fabulae.* Ed. Antonio Guaglianone. Corpus Scriptorum Latinorum Paravianum. Torino, 1958.

——. Ed. and trans. J. Wight Duff and Arnold M. Duff. *Minor Latin Poets.* 2d ed. Loeb Classical Library. Cambridge, Mass., 1935. 680–749.

Babrius. Ed. and trans. Ben Edwin Perry. *Babrius and Phaedrus.* Loeb Classical Library. Cambridge, Mass., 1965.

Baldo. *Novus Aesopus.* Ed. Alfons Hilka. *Beiträge zur lateinischen Erzählungsliteratur des Mittelalters*: 1. *Der Novus Aesopus des Baldo*. 2. *Eine lateinische Übersetzung der griechischen Version des Kalila-Buchs. Abhandlungen der Gesellschaft der Wissenschaften zu Göttingen, philologisch-historische Klasse*, N.S. 21/3. Berlin, 1928.

The Battle of the Frogs and Mice. Ed. H. Ahlborn. *Pseudo-Homer*, Der Froschmäusekrieg—*Theodoros Prodromos*, Der Katzenmäusekrieg. Schriften und Quellen der alten Welt 22. Berlin, 1968.

———. Ed. and trans. Hugh G. Evelyn-White. *Hesiod, The Homeric Hymns and Homerica*. Loeb Classical Library. Cambridge, Mass., 1914. 541–63.

Bede. *De die judicii*. Ed. D. Hurst. *Bedae Opera*, part 3/4. Corpus Christianorum Series Latina 122. Turnhout, 1955. 439–44.

———. *Ecclesiastical History of the English People*. Ed. and trans. Bertram Colgrave and R. A. B. Mynors. Oxford, 1969.

Benedicti Regula. Ed. Rudolf Hanslik. Corpus Scriptorum Ecclesiasticorum Latinorum 75. Vienna, 1960.

Benedict. *Liber Politicus*. Ed. Paul Fabre. *Le Polyptyque du chanoine Benoît* (*Etude sur un manuscrit de la Bibliothèque de Cambrai*). Travaux et mémoires des Facultés de Lille 1/3. Lille, 1889.

Bernard of Clairvaux. *Apologia ad Guillelmum Sancti-Theoderici Abbatem*. Ed. Migne, *PL* 182.895–918.

———. Trans. Rudolph.

Bible. Vulgate. Latin text: *Biblia sacra iuxta vulgatam versionem*. Ed. Robert Weber. 2 vols. 2d ed. Stuttgart, 1975.

———. English translation: *The Holy Bible: Douay Rheims Version*. Baltimore, Maryland, 1899.

Boccaccio. *Genealogie deorum gentilium libri*. Ed. Vincenzo Romano. 2 vols. Scrittori d'Italia. Bari, 1951.

———. *Boccaccio on Poetry: Being the Preface and the Fourteenth and Fifteenth Books of Boccaccio's "Genealogia Deorum Gentilium."* Trans. Charles G. Osgood. Princeton, 1930. Repr. The Library of Liberal Arts. New York, 1956.

Boethius. *Anicii Manlii Severini Boethii Philosophiae consolatio*. Ed. Ludwig Bieler. Corpus Christianorum Series Latina 94. Turnhout, 1957.

———. *The Consolation of Philosophy*. Trans. Richard Green. The Library of Liberal Arts. New York, 1962.

Brinsley, John. *Ludus literarius or the Grammar Schoole*. Ed. E. T. Campagnac. Liverpool, 1917.

Caelius Aurelianus. *Chronic Diseases*. In: *"On Acute Diseases" and "On Chronic Diseases."* Ed. and trans. I. E. Drabkin. Chicago, 1950. 958–63.

Cambridge Songs. Carmina cantabrigiensia. Ed. Karl Strecker. *Die Cambridger Lieder*. MGH Scriptores rerum Germanicarum in usum scholarum separatim editi 40. 2d ed. Berlin, 1955.

Carmen Winrici. Ed. Ludwig Gompf. *"Querela magistri Treverensis* (Das sogenannte *Carmen Winrici*.)" *Mittellateinisches Jahrbuch* 4 (1967): 91–121.

Carmina burana. Ed. Alfons Hilka, Otto Schumann, and Bernhard Bischoff. Vol. 1, parts 1–3, and vol. 2. 2d printing. Heidelberg, 1961–78.

Catallus. *C. Valerii Catulli Carmina*. Ed. R. A. B. Mynors. Oxford Classical Texts. Oxford, 1958.

Chrétien de Troyes. *Le Roman de Perceval ou Le conte du Graal*. Ed. William Roach. 2d ed. Geneva, 1959.

Cicero. *In L. Calpurnium Pisonem oratio*. Ed. R. G. M. Nisbet. Oxford, 1961. 172–79.

———. *Tusculanae disputationes*. Ed. Thomas Wilson Dougan. 2 vols. Cambridge, 1905–34.

"Clerk and Nightingale." Ed. Rossell Hope Robbins. *Secular Lyrics of the Fourteenth and Fifteenth Centuries*. 2d ed. Oxford, 1955. 172–79.

"The Cock and Fox." *Gallus et vulpes*. Incipit "Stans apto consistorio." Ed. Léon Herrmann. *Scriptorium* 1 (1946): 260–66.

———. Trans. Moritz Heyne. *Altdeutsch-lateinische Spielmannsgedichte des 10. Jahrhunderts. Für Liebhaber des deutschen Altertums übertragen*. Göttingen, 1900. 64–78.

Columbanus. "Epistola" 5. Ed. *MGH Epistolae* 3. Berlin, 1892. 170–77.

Conrad of Hirsau. "Dialogus super auctores." In: *Accessus ad auctores, Bernard d'Utrecht, Conrad d'Hirsau, Dialogus super auctores*. Ed. R. B. C. Huygens. 2d ed. Leiden, 1970. 71–131.

Cuono of St. Nabor. "The Peacock and Owl." Incipit "Nocti preterite dedimus cum menbra quiete." Ed. Karl Strecker. *MGH Poetae* 5: 382–83.

"Cur me torquetis morsu lacerante penali." Ed. Karl Strecker. *MGH Poetae* 5/1–2: 521.

"Cyprian's Supper." *Cena Cypriani*. Ed. H. Hagen. *Zeitschrift für wissenschaftliche Theologie* 27 (1884): 179–87.

———. Ed. Karl Strecker. *MGH Poetae* 4/2: 870–900 (bottom of pp.).

Dante. *The Divine Comedy*. Ed. and trans. Charles S. Singleton. Bollingen Series 80. Princeton, 1970–75.

———. *On Eloquence in the Vernacular*. In: *Literary Criticism of Dante Alighieri*. Trans. Robert Haller, Lincoln, 1973.

De carminis impeditione causa thematis tropologice. Incipit "Auri stemmate nexas." Ed. Paul von Winterfeld. *MGH Poetae* 4/1: 243–44.

De ratione duodecim signorum. Pacificus. Incipit "Spera celi duodenis / signis circumvolvitur." Ed. Karl Strecker. *MGH Poetae* 4/2: 693–95.

De symoniaca heresi. Anonymous. Incipit "Crevit in aecclesia monstrum, genitore Losinga." Ed. H. Boehmer. MGH *Libelli de lite imperatorum et pontificum saeculis XI. et XII. conscripti*. Hanover, 1897. 3: 615–17.

Decretum Gelasianum. Ed. Ernst von Dobschütz. *Das Decretum Gelasianum de libris recipiendis et non recipiendis*. Leipzig, 1912.

"Dit du denier et de la brebis." Ed. Achille Jubinal. *Nouveau recueil de contes, dits, fabliaux et autres pièces inédits des XIIIᵉ, XIVᵉ, XVᵉ siècles*. Paris, 1842. 2: 264–72.

"Dreambook of Daniel." *Somniale Danielis: An Edition of a Medieval Latin Dream Interpretation Handbook*. Ed. Lawrence T. Martin. Lateinische Sprache und Literatur de Mittelalters 10. Frankfurt am Main, 1981.

Ecbasis cuiusdam captivi per tropologiam. Ed. Karl Strecker. MGH Scriptores rerum Germanicarum in usum Scholarum 69. Hanover, 1935.

———. Ed. and trans. Edwin H. Zeydel. *Ecbasis cuiusdam captivi: Escape of a cer-*

tain Captive. University of North Carolina Studies in the Germanic Languages and Literatures 46. Chapel Hill, 1964.

Egbert of Liège. *Egberts von Lüttich Fecunda Ratis*. Ed. Ernst Voigt. Halle a. S., 1889.

———. "The Bear, Wolf, and Fox." *De tribus ministris • urso • lupo • vulpe*. Incipit "Olim defuncto cuiusdam presule sedis." *Fecunda Ratis Prora* 1174–1189. Ed. Ernst Voigt. 174–75.

Epistolae Tegernseenses. In: *Die Tegernseer Briefsammlung* (*Froumund*). Ed. Karl Strecker. MGH Epistolae Selectae 3. Berlin, 1925.

Eugenius of Toledo. *Eugenii Toletani episcopi carmina*. Ed. Friedrich Vollmer. *MGH Auctores Antiquissimi* 14. Berlin, 1905.

Eugenius Vulgarius. "Comic Visions." *Species comice*. Incipits "Anacreunti carmine" and "Accidit, ut, dum." *Sylloga* 31A–B. Ed. Paul von Winterfeld. *MGH Poetae* 4: 430–32.

———. *De causa Formosiana*. Ed. Ernst Dümmler. *Auxilius und Vulgarius: Quellen und Forschungen zur Geschichte des Papstthums im Anfange des zehnten Jahrhunderts*. Leipzig, 1866.

———. *Sylloga*. Ed. Paul von Winterfeld. *MGH Poetae* 4: 406–44.

Eusebius. *Aenigmata Eusebii*. Ed. Maria de Marco. *Tatuini Opera Omnia*. Corpus Christianorum Series Latina 133. Turnhout, 1968. 209–71.

The Exeter Book. Ed. George Philip Krapp and Elliott Van Kirk Dobbie. The Anglo-Saxon Poetic Records 3. New York, 1936.

"The Flea." *De pulice*. Incipit "Parue pulex, sed amara lues inimica puellis." Ed. Friedrich Walter Lenz. "De Pulice Libellus." *Maia: Rivista di letterature classiche*, N.S. 14 (1962): 299–333 (here: 313).

Fredegar. *Chronica*. In: *Fredegarii et aliorum Chronica. Vitae Sanctorum*. Ed. Bruno Krusch. MGH Scriptores Rerum Merovingicarum 2. Hanover, 1888.

———. *Chronicorum Liber Quartus cum Continuationibus*. Ed. and trans. J. M. Wallace-Hadrill. London, 1960.

Froumund of Tegernsee. "Poems." *Die Tegernseer Briefsammlung* (*Froumund*). Ed. Karl Strecker. MGH Epistolae Selectae 3. Berlin, 1925.

Gilgamesh. Trans. N. K. Sandars. *The Epic of Gilgamesh*. 2d ed. London: Penguin Books, 1988.

Glossa ordinaria. Ed. PL 113–14.

"The Gnat." *Culex*. Ed. and trans. H. Rushton Fairclough. *Virgil*. 2d ed. Loeb Classical Library. Cambridge, Mass., 1934. 2: 370–403.

"Gout and the Flea." Incipit "Temporibus priscis pulix lacerasse potentes." Ed. Neff, 1908. 198.

Gregory the Great. *Dialogues*. Ed. Adalbert de Vogüé. 3 vols. Sources Chrétiennes 251, 260, 265. Paris, 1978–80.

———. *Moralia In Iob*. Ed. M. Adriaen. Corpus Christianorum Series Latina 143–143A–143B. Turnhout, 1979–85.

———. *Registrum epistolarum*. Ed. Paul Ewald and Ludwig M. Hartmann. 2 vols. MGH Epistolae 1–2. Berlin, 1891–99.

Guibert of Nogent. *Guibert de Nogent: Histoire de sa vie (1053–1124)*. Ed. Georges Bourgin. Collection de textes 40. Paris, 1907.

————. Ed. and trans. John F. Benton. *The Memoirs of Abbot Guibert of Nogent*: *Self and Society in Medieval France*. Medieval Academy Reprints for Teaching 15. Toronto, 1984.

"The Hawk and Peacock." *Versus de accipitre et pavone*. Incipit "Avis hec magna." Ed. Karl Strecker. *MGH Poetae* 4/2: 610–12.

Heito. "Wetti's Vision." *Visio Wettini*. Ed. Ernst Dümmler. *MGH Poetae* 2: 267–75.

Henryson, Robert. *Moral Fables*. Ed. and trans. George D. Gopen. Notre Dame, 1987.

Hervieux, Léopold. *Les Fabulistes latins depuis le siècle d'Auguste jusqu'à la fin du Moyen Age*. 2d ed. 5 vols. Paris, 1893–99.

Hesiod. *Works and Days*. Ed. and trans. Hugh G. Evelyn-White. *Hesiod, The Homeric Hymns and Homerica*. Loeb Classical Library. Cambridge, Mass., 1914. 2–65.

Honorius Augustodunensis. *Gemma Animae*. Ed. Migne, *PL* 172: 541–738.

Hrabanus Maurus. *Carmina*. Ed. Ernst Dümmler. *MGH Poetae* 2: 159–244.

————. "Cyprian's Supper." Ed. H. Hagen. "Eine Nachahmung von Cyprian's Gastmahl durch Hrabanus Maurus." *Zeitschrift für wissenschaftliche Theologie* 27 (1884): 165–79.

————. *De universo libri viginti duo*. Ed. *PL* 111: 9–614.

Hrotsvitha. *Opera*. Ed. Helena Homeyer. Munich, 1970.

Hymnus de natale innocentum. Ed. Ernst Dümmler. *MGH Poetae* 2: 246–47.

Isidore of Seville. *Allegoriae quaedam Scripturae Sacrae*. Ed. *PL* 83: 97–130.

————. *Etymologiae*. Ed. W. M. Lindsay. Oxford Classical Texts. 2 vols. Oxford, 1911.

Jean de Condé. *La Messe des oiseaux et le Dit des Jacobins et des fremeneurs*. Ed. Jacques Ribard. Paris, 1970.

Jerome. *Apologia aduersus libros Rufini*. Ed. *PL* 23: 397–456.

————. *Epistulae*. Ed. Isidor Hilberg. Corpus Scriptorum Ecclesiasticorum Latinorum 54. Vienna, 1905.

John Chrysostom. *Reparatio lapsi*. Ed. *Bibliotheca Casinensis seu Codicum Manuscriptorum* 3: "Florilegium." Monte Cassino, 1877. 389–411.

John of Capua. *Directorium humanae vitae*. Ed. Friedmar Geissler. *Beispiele der alten Weisen des Johann von Capua*. Deutsche Akademie der Wissenschaften zu Berlin, Institut für Orientforschung 52. Berlin, 1960.

John of Garland. *The* Parisiana Poetria *of John of Garland*. Ed. and trans. Traugott Lawler. Yale Studies in English 182. New Haven, Conn., 1974.

John the Deacon (Johannes Diaconus). *Versiculi de cena Cypriani*. Ed. Karl Strecker. *MGH Poetae* 4/2: 827–900.

John Scot Eriugena. *Carmina*. Ed. Ludwig Traube. *MGH Poetae* 3: 518–53.

Julian of Vézelay. *Sermon 19*. In *Sermons 17–27*. Ed. and trans. Damien Vorreux. Sources Chrétiennes 193. Paris, 1972. 2: 398–421.

"Learn, Lion." Incipit "Disce, leo supplex, apices sine murmure nostros." Ed. Karl Strecker. *MGH Poetae* 4/3: 1082–83.

Leo of Vercelli. *Carmina*. Ed. Karl Strecker. *MGH Poetae* 5: 476–89.

————. "Meter." *Metrum Leonis*. Incipit "Effuga regno." *Carmen 4*. Ed. Karl Strecker. *MGH Poetae* 5: 483–89.

————. *Epistulae*. Ed. Hermann Bloch. "Beiträge zur Geschichte des Bischofs Leo von Vercelli und seiner Zeit." *Neues Archiv* 22 (1879): 13–136.

————. Letters to and from Duke William V of Aquitaine. Ed. and trans. Frederick Behrends. *The Letters and Poems of Fulbert of Chartres*. Oxford Medieval Texts. Oxford, 1976. 198–203.

"The Little Hare Wept." Incipit "Flevit lepus parvulus." Ed. G. Scalia. "Il *Testamentum Asini* e il lamento della lepre. Redazioni nuove." *Studi Medievali* 3d ser. 3/1 (1962): 143–44.

"The Lombard and Snail." *De Lombardo et lumaca*. Incipit "Venerat ad segetes Lombardus, circuit illas." Ed. Magda Bonacina. *Commedie latine del XII e XIII secolo*. Pubblicazioni dell'Istituto de filologia classica e medievale dell'-Università de Genova 79. Genoa, 1983. 4: 95–135.

"The Louse." *De pediculo*. Incipit "In cute sudanti sub veste pediculus hesit." Ed. Frederick Walter Lenz. "[P. Ovidii Nasonis] De Pediculo Libellus." *Eranos: Acta philologica suecana* 53 (1955): 61–74 (here: 66).

Lucian. "The Fly." In *Lucian*. Ed. and trans. A. M. Harmon. Loeb Classical Library. New York, 1913. 1: 81–95.

Lydgate, John. "Debate of the Horse." Ed. Henry Noble MacCracken. *The Minor Poems of John Lydgate*. Early English Text Society 192. London, 1934. 2: 539–66.

Macrobius. *Commentarii in* Somnium Scipionis. Ed. Iacobus Willis. Leipzig, 1970.

————. *Commentary on the Dream of Scipio*. Trans. William Harris Stahl. Records of Civilization, Sources and Studies 48. New York, 1952.

Marie de France. *Fables*. Ed. and trans. Mary Lou Martin. Birmingham, Ala., 1984.

Marquis, Don. *archy and mehitabel*. Garden City, 1931.

MGH Poetae = Monumenta Germaniae Historica, Poetae Latini Medii Aevi, 1 (Berlin, 1881), ed. Ernst Dümmler; 2 (1884), ed. Ernst Dümmler; 3 (1886), ed. Ludwig Traube; 4, fascicle 1 (1899), ed. Paul von Winterfeld; 4, fascicles 2–3 (1923), ed. Karl Strecker; 5, fascicles 1–2 (1937–39), ed. Karl Strecker; 6, fascicle 1 (1951), ed. Karl Strecker.

Midrash Rabbah. Ed. and trans. H. Freedman and Maurice Simon. 13 in 10 vols. London, 1939.

"Multi sunt presbyteri qui ignorant, quare." Ed. *Analecta Hymnica* 33: 190–93, no. 213.

————. Ed. and trans. Olga Dobiache-Rojdesvensky. *Les Poésies des Goliards*. Les textes du Christianisme 9. Paris, 1931. 122–27.

"The Nanny Goat." *De capra*. Incipit "Ecussum cornu gemeret dum forte capella." Ed. Karl Strecker. *MGH Poetae* 4: 1080–81.

Neckham, Alexander. *De laudibus divinae sapientiae*. Ed. Thomas Wright. *De naturis rerum et de laudibus divinae sapientiae*. Rolls Series. London, 1863.

————. *Fables*. Ed. Léopold Hervieux. *Les Fabulistes latins*. 2d ed. Paris, 1893–99. 3: 462–67.

Nicolaus of Myra (the Sophist). "Progymnasmata." In: *Rhetores Graeci*. Ed. Leonard Spengel. Leipzig, 1856. 3: 449–98.

Nigel of Canterbury, also known as Nigel (de) Longchamp(s) and Nigel Wireker.

Epistola ad Willelmum. Ed. J. H. Mozley. *Medium Aevum* 39 (1970): 13–20.

———. *Speculum stultorum*. Ed. John H. Mozley and Robert R. Raymo. University of California English Studies 18. Berkeley and Los Angeles, 1960.

———. Trans. Karl Langosch. *"Narrenspiegel" oder Burnellus, der Esel, der einen längeren Schwanz haben wollt*. Insel-Bücherei 668. Leipzig, 1982.

———. Trans. J. H. Mozley. *A Mirror for Fools, or The Book of Burnel the Ass by Nigel Longchamp*. Oxford, 1961. Repr. Notre Dame, Ind. 1963.

———. Trans. Graydon W. Regenos. *The Book of Daun Burnel the Ass: Nigellus Wireker's Speculum Stultorum*. Austin, Texas, 1959.

———. *Tractatus contra curiales et officiales clericos*. Ed. André Boutemy. *Nigellus de Longchamp dit Wireker, Tractatus contra curiales et officiales clericos*. Université de Bruxelles, Travaux de la Faculté de Philosophie et Lettres 16. Paris, 1959.

Notker Balbulus. *Gesta Karoli Magni Imperatoris*. Ed. Hans F. Haefele. MGH Scriptores Rerum Germanicarum, N.S. 12. Berlin, 1962.

Odo of Cheriton, *Fabulae*. Ed. Hervieux 4: 171–255.

———. Trans. John C. Jacobs. Syracuse, 1985.

Orwell, George. "Author's Preface to the Ukrainian Edition of *Animal Farm*." *The Collected Essays, Journalism and Letters of George Orwell*. New York, 1968. 3: 402–6.

The Owl and the Nightingale. Ed. Eric Gerald Stanley. 2d ed. Manchester, 1972.

PL = Patrologiae Cursus Completus, Series Latina. Ed. J.-P. Migne. 222 vols. Paris, 1844–55; 1862–64.

Paulus Albarus. *Carmina*. Ed. Ernst Dümmler. *MGH Poetae* 3: 126–42.

Persius. *A. Persi Flacci et D. Iuni Iuvenalis Saturae*. Ed. W. V. Clausen. Oxford Classical Texts. Oxford, 1959.

Peter of Beauvais. *Pierre de Beauvais, Guillaume le Clerc, Richard de Fournival, Brunetto Latini, Corbechon: Bestiaires du Moyen Age*. Trans. Gabriel Bianciotto. Paris, 1980.

Peter the Venerable. *De miraculis libri duo*. Ed. *PL* 189: 851–954.

Phaedrus. *Fables*. Ed. and trans. Ben Edwin Perry. *Babrius and Phaedrus*. Loeb Classical Library. Cambridge, Mass., 1965.

Physiologus Latinus. Ed. Francis Carmody. *Physiologus Latinus. Editions préliminaires, versio B*. Paris, 1939.

———. Ed. Francis Carmody. "Physiologus Latinus, versio Y." The University of California Publications in Classical Philology 12 (1941): 95–134.

———. Trans. Michael J. Curley. Austin, 1979.

Plato, *Phaedo*. Trans. Hugh Tredennick. In: *The Collected Dialogues of Plato, Including the Letters*. Ed. Edith Hamilton and Huntington Cairns. Bollingen Series 71. Princeton, 1963. 40–98.

Poeta Astensis. *Novus Avianus*. Ed. Emil Grosse. Programm des Königlichen Friedrichs-Collegiums zu Königsberg. Kaliningrad, 1868.

Porphyrio, Pomponius. *Commentum in Horatium Flaccum*. Ed. Alfred Holder. Innsbruck, 1894.

"The Prose of the Ass." Incipit "Orientis partibus." Ed. E. K. Chambers. *The Mediaeval Stage*. 2 vols. Oxford, 1903. 2: 280–81.

————. Ed. and trans. Henry Copley Greene. "The Song of the Ass: *Orientis Partibus*, with special reference to *Edgerton MS. 2615.*" *Speculum* 6 (1931): 534–49.

Prudentius. Ed. and trans. H. J. Thomson. 2 vols. Loeb Classical Library. Cambridge, Mass., 1949–53.

Pseudo-Acro. *Scholia in Horatium Vetustiora*. Ed. Otto Keller. 2 vols. Leipzig, 1902–1904.

Pseudo-Aristotle. *History of Animals*. Book 10. Trans. Jonathan Barnes. *The Complete Works of Aristotle: The Revised Oxford Translation*. Ed. Jonathan Barnes. 2 vols. Bollingen Series 71/2. Princeton, 1984. 1: 984–93.

Pseudo–Hugh of St. Victor. *De bestiis et aliis rebus libri quatuor*. Ed. PL 177: 9–164.

"Quaerebat maerens matrem per prata vitellus." Ed. Neff 1908. 197.

Querolus. Ed. and trans. Willi Emrich. *Querolus oder die Geschichte vom Topf: Querolus sive Aulularia*. Schriften and Quellen der alten Welt 17. Berlin, 1965.

"Quid mihi caprigero cornuque minaris abunco." Ed. Karl Strecker. *MGH Poetae* 4/3: 1082.

Quintilian. *Institutio oratoria*. Ed. M. Winterbottom. 2 vols. Oxford Classical Texts. Oxford, 1970.

————. *The Institutio Oratoria of Quintilian*. Ed. and trans. H. E. Butler. Loeb Classical Library. 4 vols. London, 1921–22.

Le Roman de Renart le Contrefait. Ed. Gaston Raynaud and Henri Lemaître. 2 vols. Paris, 1914.

Le Roman de Renart: Première branche. Ed. Mario Roques. Les Classiques français du Moyen Age 78. Paris, 1948.

————. Trans. Patricia Terry. *Renard the Fox: The Misadventures of an Epic Hero*. Boston, 1983.

Romulus. Ed. Georg Thiele. *Der lateinische Äsop des Romulus und die Prosa-Fassungen des Phädrus*. Heidelberg, 1910.

"The Sad Calf." Incipit "Quaerebat maerens matrem per prata vitellus." Ed. Neff 1908. 197.

Schnur, Harry C., ed. *Lateinische Fabeln des Mittelalters*. Munich, 1979.

Second Shepherds' Play (Secunda Pastorum). Ed. A. C. Cawley. *The Wakefield Pageants in the Towneley Cycle*. Old and Middle English Texts Series 1. Manchester, England, 1958.

Sedulius. *Carmen paschale*. Ed. Johann Huemer. *Seduli opera omnia*. Corpus Scriptorum Ecclesiasticorum Latinorum 10. Vienna, 1885.

Sedulius Scottus, *Carmina*. Ed. Ernst Dümmler. *MGH Poetae* 3: 154–237.

————. *Carmen* 2.10. Incipit "Gloria nostra redit, clementia luxque serena." Ed. Ernst Dümmler. *MGH Poetae* 3: 178–79.

————. "The Ram." *De quodam verbece a cane discerpto*. Incipit "Cum deus altipotens animalia condidit orbis." *Carmen* 2.41. Ed. Ernst Dümmler. *MGH Poetae* 3: 204–7.

————. "The Ram." Trans. Edward Gerard Doyle. *Sedulius Scottus: "On Christian Rulers" and "The Poems."* Medieval and Renaissance Texts and Studies 17. Binghamton, N.Y., 1983. 140–43.

————. "The Ram." Ed. and trans. Reinhard Düchting. "Vom Hammel, den ein Hund gerissen." In: Schwab 1970. 114–21.

————. Ed. and trans. Godman. 292–301.

————. *Collectaneum miscellaneum*. Ed. Dean Simpson. Corpus Christianorum Continuatio Medievalis 67. Turnhout, 1988.

Semonides. Ed. and trans. Hugh Lloyd-Jones. *Females of the Species: Semonides on Women*. London, 1975.

Seneca, L. Annaeus. *Dialogorum libri duodecim*. Ed. L. D. Reynolds. Oxford Classical Texts. Oxford, 1977.

"The Sick Lion." Incipit "Aegrum fama fuit quondam iacuisse leonem." Ed. Neff 1908. 193–96.

————. Ed. and trans. Edwin H. Zeydel. In: *Ecbasis cuiusdam captivi: Escape of a Certain Captive*. University of North Carolina Studies in the Germanic Languages and Literatures 46. Chapel Hill, 1964. 97–101.

Simon of Saint-Bertin. *Gesta Abbatum Sancti Bertini Sithiensium*. Ed. O. Holder-Egger. MGH Scriptores 13. 600–663.

Statius. *P. Papini Stati Silvae*. Ed. John S. Phillimore. 2d ed. Oxford Classical Texts. Oxford, n.d.

"The Swan Lament." Incipit "Olim lacus colueram." *Carmina burana*. Vol. 1, part 2: "Die Liebeslieder." No. 130. Heidelberg, 1941. 215.

————. Trans. E. D. Blodgett and Roy Arthur Swanson. *The Love Songs of the Carmina Burana*. Garland Library of Medieval Literature Series B: 49. New York, 1987. 185.

————. Ed. and trans. George F. Whicher. *The Goliard Poets: Medieval Latin Songs and Satires*. 1949. Repr. Westport, Conn., 1979. 250–51.

————. Ed. and trans. Edwin H. Zeydel. *Vagabond Verse: Secular Latin Poems of the Middle Ages*. Detroit, 1966. 94–97.

"The Swan Sequence." Incipit "Clangam, filii." Ed. and trans. Dag Norberg. *Manuel pratique de latin médiéval*. Connaissance des Langues 4. Paris, 1968. 174–76.

————. Ed. and trans. Godman. 322–25.

Symphosius. *Aenigmata Symphosii*. Trans. Raymond Theodore Ohl. Ed. Fr. Glorie. *Variae collectiones aenigmatum Merovingicae aetatis*. Corpus Christianorum Series Latina 133A. Turnhout, 1968. 2: 611–721.

Tatwine. *Enigmata Tatuini*. Ed. Maria de Marco. *Tatuini opera omnia*. Corpus Christianorum Series Latina 133. Turnhout, 1968. 1: 165–208.

"Terence and His Mocker." *Terentius et delusor*. Incipit "Mitte recordari monimenta vetusta, Terenti." Ed. Karl Strecker. *MGH Poetae* 4/3: 1088–90.

"The Testament of the Ass." *Testamentum asini*. Ed. F. Novati. *Carmina Medii Aevi*. Florence, 1883. 71–80. Standard edition.

————. Ed. G. Scalia. "Il *Testamentum Asini* e il lamento della lepre. Redazioni nuove." *Studi Medievali* 3d ser. 3/1 (1962): 129–51. Edition of three other versions.

————. Trans. Paul von Winterfeld. *Deutsche Dichter des lateinischen Mittelalters in deutschen Versen*. Ed. Hermann Reich. Munich, 1913. 228.

"The Testament of the Piglet." *Testamentum Porcelli*. Ed. Barry Baldwin. *An Anthology of Later Latin Literature*. London Studies in Classical Philology 19. Amsterdam, 1987. 231–37.

———. Ed. and trans. Nikolaus Adalbert Bott. *Testamentum Porcelli. Text, Übersetzung und Kommentar*. Abhandlung zur Erlangung der Doktorwürde der Philosophischen Fakultät der Universität Zürich. Zürich, 1972.

Theobald. *Physiologus*. Ed. and trans. P. T. Eden. *Theobaldi "Physiologus."* Mittellateinische Studien und Texte 6. Leiden, 1972.

Theodore of Canterbury. *Penitential*. Ed. Paul Willem Finsterwalder. *Die Canones Theodori Cantuariensis und ihre Überlieferungsformen, Untersuchungen zu den Bußbüchern des 7., 8. und 9. Jahrhunderts*. Weimar, 1929.

Theodulf of Orléans. "The Battle of the Birds." *Carmen 72. De pugna avium*. Incipit "Hoc, Modoine, tibi Teudulfus dirigit exul." Lines 1–232. Ed. Dieter Schaller. "Philologische Untersuchungen zu den Gedichten Theodulfs von Orléans." *Deutsches Archiv für Erforschung des Mittelalters* 18 (1962): 43–51.

———. Lines 137–224. Ed. and trans. Schaller 1970a. 106–13.

———. Lines 131–90. Ed. and trans. Godman. 172–75.

———. "The Fox and Hen." *Carmen 50. De vulpecula involante gallinam*. Incipit "Est locus, hunc vocitant Carroph cognomine Galli." Ed. Ernst Dümmler. *MGH Poetae* 1: 550–51.

———. "What Do the Swans Do?" *Carmen 27*. Incipit "Quid cycni faciunt, resonant dum talia corvi." Ed. Ernst Dümmler. *MGH Poetae* 1: 490–93.

Thierry of St. Trond. "Weep, Dogs." Incipit "Flete, canes, si flere uacat, si flere ualetis." Ed. Jean Préaux. "Du *Culex* de Virgile à son pastiche par Thierry de Saint-Trond." In: *Présence de Virgile. Actes du Colloque des 9, 11 et 12 décembre 1976 (Paris E.N.S., Tours)*. Ed. Raymond Chevallier. Paris, 1979. 195–208 (here: 195–97).

Urban II, Pope. "Bull of 14 April 1096, to the Monastery of Montierneuf of Poitiers." In: *Analecta Juris Pontificis, dissertations sur différents sujets de droit canonique, liturgie et théologie*. 10th series, 5, part 2, no. 89, columns 546–48. Rome, 1869.

Venantius Fortunatus. *Opera Poetica*. Ed. Friedrich Leo. MGH Auctores Antiquissimi 4, part 1. Berlin, 1881.

Vergil. *P. Vergili Maronis opera*. Ed. R. A. B. Mynors, Oxford Classical Texts. Oxford, 1969.

Visio cuiusdam clerici de poenis Fulradi in purgatorio. Ed. K. Hampe. *Neues Archiv der Gesellschaft für Ältere Deutsche Geschichtskunde* 22 (1897): 628–33.

Visio cuiusdam pauperculae mulieris. Ed. Herbert Houben. "Visio cuiusdam pauperculae mulieris. Überlieferung und Herkunft eines frühmittelalterlichen Visiontextes (mit Neuedition)." *Zeitschrift für die Geschichte des Oberrheins* 124, N.F. 85 (1976): 31–42 (here: 37–40).

Vita sancti Ciarani episcopi de Saigir. Ed. Carolus Plummer. *Vitae Sanctorum Hiberniae*. Oxford, 1910. 1: 217–33.

Walahfrid Strabo. *Carmina*. Ed. Ernst Dümmler. *MGH Poetae* 2: 259–428.

———. "To Erluin." *Carmen* 19. *De quodam somnio ad Erluinum*. Incipit "Nox erat et magni alternis per climata caeli." Ed. Ernst Dümmler. *MGH Poetae* 2: 364–65.

———. "Wetti's Vision." *Visio Wettini*. Ed. and trans. David A. Traill. Lateinische Sprache und Literatur des Mittelalters 2. Bern, 1974.

———. *Visio Wettini*. Ed. and trans. Hermann Knittel. Sigmaringen, 1986.

Walter Map. *De nugis curialium. Courtiers' Trifles*. Ed. and trans. M. R. James, C. N. L. Brooke, and R. A. B. Mynors. Oxford Medieval Texts. Oxford, 1983.

Warner of Rouen. *Satire* 2. Incipit "Rotberto doctis fulgenti semper alumnis." Ed. Lucien Musset, "Le Satiriste Garnier et son milieu (Début du XIᵉ siècle)." *Revue du Moyen Age Latin* 10 (1954): 237–66 (here: 259–66).

William Fitz Stephen. *Norman London*. Trans. H. E. Butler. London, 1934. Repr. New York, 1990.

William of Blois. "The Quarrel of the Flea and Fly." *Pulicis et musce iurgia*. Incipit "Si quem ficta iuvant et verba moventia risum." Ed. and trans. Antonio Scolari. "I 'Versus de pulice et musca' de Guglielmo di Blois." *Studi medievali* 3d series 26 (1985): 373–404 (here: 393–404).

Winrich of Trier. "The Debate of the Sheep and Flax Plant." *Conflictus ovis et lini*. Incipit "Tempore quo campi linum solet herba vocari." Ed. Moriz Haupt. "Hermanni Contracti Conflictus ovis et lini." *Zeitschrift für deutsches Altertum* 11 (1859): 215–38.

"The Wolf." *De lupo*. Incipit "Sepe lupus quidam per pascua lata vagantes." Ed. Friedrich Walter Lenz. "Bemerkungen zu dem pseudo-ovidischen Gedicht *De lupo*." *Orpheus* 10 (1963): 21–32 (here: 25–28).

"The Wolf by Ovid." *Ouidius de lupo*. Incipit "Sepe lupus quidam per pascua lata uagantes." Ed. Voigt 1878. 62–71.

"The Wolf Goes to Hell." *Luparius descendens in Auernum*. Incipit "Forte lupus quidam per pascua lata uagantes." Ed. Voigt 1878. 72–80.

"The Wrangle of the Dwarf and Hare." *Altercatio nani et leporis*. Incipit "Musa, mihi ante alias predulcis amica sorores." Ed. Ernst Dümmler. "Lateinische Gedichte des neunten bis elften Jahrhunderts." *Neues Archiv der Gesellschaft für Ältere Deutsche Geschichtskunde* 10 (1885): 333–57 (here: 354–55).

Ysengrimus. Ed. Ernst Voigt. Halle a. S., 1884. Repr. Hildsheim, 1974.

———. Ed. and trans. Jill Mann. Mittellateinische Studien und Texte 12. Leiden, 1987.

Ysengrimus abbreviatus. Ed. Lieven van Acker. "L'Ysengrimus Abbreviatus." *Latomus* 25 (1966): 912–47.

SECONDARY SOURCES

Aarne, A., and Stith Thompson. 1961. *The Types of the Folk-Tale*. 2d ed. Folklore Fellows Communications 184. Helsinki.

Adams, J. N. 1982. *The Latin Sexual Vocabulary*. Baltimore.

Adrados, Francisco Rodríguez. 1984. "The Earliest Influences of Indian Fable on Medieval Latin Writings." *Classica et mediaevalia* 35: 243–63.

———. 1979. *Historia de la fábula greco-latina*. Vol. 1, parts 1–2. Madrid.

Ahl, Frederick M. 1982. "Amber, Avallon, and Apollo's Singing Swan." *American Journal of Philology* 103: 373–411.

Alford, Violet. 1978. *The Hobby Horse and Other Animal Masks.* Ed. Margaret Dean-Smith. London.

Allen, Mary. 1983. *Animals in American Literature.* Urbana.

The American Heritage Dictionary of the English Language. 1969. Ed. William Morris. Boston.

Amira, Karl von. 1891. "Thierstrafen und Thierprocesse." *Mitteilungen des Instituts für Österreichische Geschichtsforschung* 12/4: 545–601.

Arbesmann, Rudolph. 1979. "The *Cervuli* and *Anniculae* in Caesarius of Arles." *Traditio* 35: 89–119.

Archibald, Herbert T. 1902. "The Fable in Archilochus, Herodotus, Livy, and Horace." *Transactions of the American Philological Association* 33: lxxxviii–xc.

———. 1910. "The Fable in Horace." *Transactions of the American Philological Association* 41: xiv–xix.

Armstrong, Jean. 1985. *Animal Farm by George Orwell.* Macmillan Master Guides. Houndmills, U.K.

Arnott, W. Geoffrey. 1977. "Swan Songs." *Greece and Rome* 24: 149–53.

Aspects of the Medieval Animal Epic. Proceedings of the International Conference, Louvain, May 15–17, 1972. 1975. Ed. E. Rombauts and A. Welkenhuysen. Mediaevalia Louvaniensia Series 1, Studia 3. Louvain.

Atkins, J. W. H., ed. and trans. 1922. *The Owl and the Nightingale.* Cambridge. Repr. New York, 1971.

Axton, Richard. 1974. *European Drama of the Early Middle Ages.* London.

Bacchiega, Mario. 1983. *Papa Formoso (processo al cadavere).* Gli Antagonisti 6. Foggia.

Bächtold-Stäubli, Hanns, and Eduard Hoffmann-Krayer, eds. 1927–42. *Handwörterbuch des deutschen Aberglaubens.* 10 vols. Berlin and Leipzig.

Baird, J. L., and John R. Kane, eds. and trans. 1978. *Rossignol.* Kent, Ohio.

Bakhtin, Mikhail. 1968. *Rabelais and His World.* Trans. Hélène Iswolsky. Repr. Bloomington, 1984.

Barnouw, Adriaan J. 1967. *Reynard the Fox and Other Works of Mediaeval Netherlands Secular Literature.* Ed. E. Colledge. Leiden.

Bartelink, G. J. M. 1977. "Een thema uit de fabelliteratuur en het dierenepos in de Middeleeuwen." *Lampas* 10: 283–301.

Bartholomaeis, Vincenzo de. 1924. *Le Origini della poesia drammatica italiana.* Bologna.

Baumstark, Anton. 1957. *Nocturna laus.* Liturgiewissenschaftliche Quellen und Forschungen 32. Münster.

Benfey, Theodor. 1859. *Pantschatantra: Fünf Bücher indischer Fabeln, Märchen und Erzählungen.* 2 vols. Leipzig.

Bergmann, A. 1925. "Die Dichtung der Reichenau im Mittelalter." In: Beyerle 1925c. 2: 711–55.

Berkenhoff, Hans Albert. 1937. *Tierstrafe, Tierbannung und rechtsrituelle Tiertötung im Mittelalter.* Sammlung Heitz: Akademische Abhandlungen zur Kulturgeschichte, Reihe 7, Band 4. Strasbourg.

Bernhart, Joseph. 1961. *Die unbeweinte Kreatur. Reflexionen über das Tier.* Munich.

Bernt, Günter. 1968. *Das lateinische Epigramm im Übergang von der Spätantike zum frühen Mittelalter.* Münchener Beiträge zur Mediävistik und Renaissance-Forschung 2. Munich.

Berschin, W. 1975. "Sancta Gereonis columna. Zu *Ysengrimus* II 179ff. und IV 25f." In: *Aspects of the Medieval Animal Epic.* 105–12.

Bertini, Ferruccio. 1985. "Gli animali nella favolistica medievale dal *Romulus* al secolo XII." *L'Uomo di fronte al mondo animale nell'alto medioevo, 7–13 aprile 1983.* Settimane di studio del centro italiano di studi sull'alto medioevo 31. Spoleto. 2: 1031–51 (discussion 1053–56).

———. 1975. *Il monaco Ademaro e la sua raccolta di favole fedriane.* Genoa.

Best, Thomas W. 1983. *Reynard the Fox.* Twayne's World Authors Series 673. Boston.

Beudel, Paulus. 1911. *Qua ratione Graeci liberos docuerint, papyris, ostracis, tabulis in Aegypto inventis illustratur.* Monasterii Guestfalorum.

Beyer, Jürgen. 1969. *Schwank und Moral. Untersuchungen zum altfranzösischen Fabliau und verwandten Formen.* Studia romanica 16. Heidelberg.

Beyerle, Konrad. 1925a. "Das Reichenauer Verbrüderungsbuch als Quelle der Klostergeschichte." In: Beyerle 1925c. 2: 1107–217.

———. 1925b. "Zur Einführung in die Geschichte des Klosters. I. Von der Gründung bis zum Ende des Freiherrlichen Klosters (724–1427)." In: Beyerle 1925c. 1: 55–212.

———. 1925c. Ed. *Die Kultur der Reichenau: Erinnerungsschrift zur zwölfhundertsten Widerkehr des Gründungsjahres des Inselklosters 724–1924.* 2 vols. Munich.

Bianciotto, Gabriel. 1973. "Renart et son cheval." *Etudes de langue et de littérature du moyen âge offertes à Félix Lecoy par ses collègues, ses élèves et ses amis.* Paris. 27–42.

Bieler, Ludwig. 1963. *Ireland, Harbinger of the Middle Ages.* London.

Billerbeck, Margarethe. 1976. "Die Horaz-Zitate in der *Ecbasis cuiusdam captivi.*" *Mittellateinisches Jahrbuch* 11: 34–44.

Bischoff, Bernhard. 1966. "Ein Brief Julians von Toledo über Rhythmen, metrische Dichtung und Prosa." *Hermes* 87 (1959): 247–56. Repr. in: *Mittelalterliche Studien* 1.

———. 1966. "Elementarunterricht und Probationes Pennae in der ersten Hälfte des Mittelalters." In: *Classical and Mediaeval Studies in Honor of Edward Kennard Rand.* Ed. Leslie Webber Jones. New York, 1938. 9–20. Repr. in: Bernhard Bischoff. *Mittelalterliche Studien: Ausgewählte Aufsätze zur Schriftkunde und Literaturgeschichte.* Stuttgart. 1: 74–87.

———. 1967. "Eine Sammelhandschrift Walahfrid Strabos (Cod. Sangall. 878)." In: Bernhard Bischoff. *Mittelalterliche Studien: Ausgewählte Aufsätze zur Schriftkunde und Literaturegeschichte.* Stuttgart. 2: 34–51.

———. 1967. "Theodulf und der Ire Cadac-Andreas." In: Bernhard Bischoff, *Mittelalterliche Studien: Ausgewählte Aufsätze zur Schriftkunde und Literaturgeschichte.* Stuttgart. 2: 92–98.

Blackham, H. J. 1985. *The Fable as Literature.* London.

Blaise, Albert. 1954. *Dictionnaire latin-français des auteurs chrétiens.* Strasbourg. Repr. 1962 and 1975.

————. 1966. *Le Vocabulaire latin des principaux thèmes liturgiques*. Turnhout.

————. 1975. *Lexicon latinitatis medii aevi: Praesertim ad res ecclesiasticas investigandas pertinens*. Turnhout.

Bloch, Hermann. 1897. "Beiträge zur Geschichte des Bischofs Leo von Vercelli und seiner Zeit." *Neues Archiv* 22: 13–136.

————. 1902. "Zu den Gedichten Leo's von Vercelli." *Neues Archiv* 27: 752–54.

Boas, M. 1914. "De librorum Catonianorum historia atque compositione." *Mnemosyne* N.S. 42: 17–46.

Boglioni, Pierre. 1985. "Il Santo e gli animali nell'alto medioevo." In: *L'Uomo di fronte al mondo animale nell'alto medioevo. 7–13 aprile 1983*. 2 vols. Spoleto. 935–94.

Bone, Robert. 1975. *Down Home: A History of Afro-American Short Fiction from Its Beginnings to the End of the Harlem Renaissance*. New York.

Boutemy, André. "Pulicis et musce iurgia. Une œuvre retrouvée de Guillaume de Blois." *Latomus* 6 (1947): 133–47.

Brechter, Suso. 1941. *Die Quellen zur Angelsachsenmission Gregors des Grossen*. Beiträge zur Geschichte des alten Mönchtums und Benediktinerordens 22. Münster.

————. 1967. In: *La conversione al Cristianesimo nell'Europa dell'Alto Medioevo, 14–19 aprile*. Settimane di studio del Centro italiano di studi sull'alto medioevo 14. Spoleto. 191–215.

Brinkmann, Hennig. 1966. "Wege der epischen Dichtung im Mittelalter." In: *Studien zur Geschichte der deutschen Sprache und Literatur*. Düsseldorf. 2: 106–36.

Brockelmann, C. 1978. "Kalilah wa-Dimnah." In: *Encyclopedia of Islam*. 2d ed. Leiden and London. 4: 503–6.

Bruckner, Albert. 1938. *Scriptoria medii aevi helvetica*. Geneva.

Brugnoli, Giorgio. 1959a. "Cuculus: Nota di critica semantica." *Rivista di cultura classica e medioevale* 1: 64–78.

————. 1959b. "Ovidio e gli esiliati carolingi." *Atti del Convegno internazionale ovidiano, Sulmona, maggio 1958*. 2 vols. Rome. 2: 209–16.

Brunhölzl, Franz. 1961. Review of Michel's *Die Ecbasis . . . ein Werk Humberts*. *Zeitschrift für deutsche Philologie* 80: 100–01.

————. 1975. *Geschichte der lateinischen Literatur des Mittelalters*. Vol. 1. Munich.

Brunner-Traut, Emma. 1980. *Altägyptische Tiergeschichte und Fabel. Gestalt und Strahlkraft*. 6th ed. Darmstadt.

Budde, Rainer. 1970. "Die Statuen der Evangelisten Markus und Lukas in der Vierung des Domes zu Münster und ihre stilistische Nachfolge." *Wallraf-Richartz-Jahrbuch. Westdeutsches Jahrbuch für Kunstgeschichte* 32: 67–98.

Bulst, Walther. 1955–56. "Alchuuines *Ecloga de cuculo*." *Zeitschrift für deutsches Altertum und deutsche Literatur* 86: 193–96.

Cahier, Charles, and Arthur Martin. 1847–53. *Mélanges d'archéologie, d'histoire et de littérature*. 3 vols. Paris.

Carpenter, Rhys. 1946. *Folk Tale, Fiction, and Saga in the Homeric Epics*. Berkeley and Los Angeles.

Cawte, E. C. 1978. *Ritual Animal Disguise*. Cambridge.

Chailley, Jacques. 1960. *L'Ecole musicale de Saint-Martial de Limoges jusqu'à la fin du XIe siècle*. Paris.

Chambers, E. K. 1903. *The Mediaeval Stage*. 2 vols. Oxford.

Chambry, Emile, ed. 1927. *Esope: Fables*. Paris.

Charbonnier, Elisabeth. 1984a. "Manger et boire dans l'*Ysengrimus*." *Manger et boire au Moyen Age. Actes du colloque de Nice (15–17 octobre 1982)*. Vol. 1 "Aliments et Société." Publications de la Faculté des Lettres et Sciences Humaines de Nice, 1st series, no. 27. Paris. 405–14.

———. 1984b. "Un épisode original: La mort du loup dans le livre VII de l'*Ysengrimus*." In: *Epopée animale*; *Fable*; *Fabliau*. 133–39.

Chauvin, Victor. 1897. *Bibliographie des ouvrages arabes ou relatifs aux arabes publiés dans l'Europe chrétienne de 1810 à 1885*. 12 vols. Liège, 1892–1922. Vol. 2: *Kalîlah*.

Ciccarese, Maria Pia. 1987. *Visioni dell'aldilà in Occidente: Fonti, modelli, testi*. Biblioteca Patristica. Florence.

Clogan, Paul M. 1982. "Literary Genres in a Medieval Textbook." *Medievalia et Humanistica* 11: 199–209.

Clover, Carol J. 1980. "The Germanic Context of the Unferþ Episode." *Speculum* 55: 444–68.

Cohn, Hugo. 1910. *Tiernamen als Schimpfwörter*. Berlin.

Collins, S. T. 1950. "Sur quelques vers de Théodulfe." *Revue Bénédictine* 60: 214–18.

Colson, F. H., ed. 1924. *Institutionis oratoriae Liber I*. Cambridge.

Comerci, Giuseppe. 1979. *Realtà, morale e simboli nell' 'Ecbasis captivi.' Con un'appendice su critica nominativa dalla scena e difesa dei 'principes civitatis' in Cicerone*. Reggio Calabria.

———. 1980. *Parola e cultura nella significazione letteraria. Studio filo-semiologico di ecbasis, dall'antichità al medioevo*. Reggio Calabria.

Cooper, Helen. 1977. *Pastoral: Mediaeval into Renaissance*. Ipswich, Mass.

Courcelle, Pierre. 1944. "Quelques symboles funéraires du néo-platonisme latin. Le vol de Dédale—Ulysse et les Sirènes." *Revue des Etudes Anciennes* 46: 65–93.

———. 1974. "Tradition néo-platonicienne et tradition chrétienne des ailes de l'âme." In: *Problemi attuali di scienze e di cultura. Atti del convegno internazionale sul tema: Plotino e il Neoplatonismo in Oriente e in Occidente (Roma, 5–9 ottobre 1970)*. Accademia nazionale dei Lincei, year 371, part 198. Rome.

Craigie, William A. 1931. *A Dictionary of the Older Scottish Tongue from the Twelfth Century to the End of the Seventeenth*. Chicago.

Crusius, Otto. 1894. "Fabeln des Babrius auf Wachstafeln aus Palmyra." *Philologus* 53: 228–53.

Cumont, Franz. 1949. *Lux perpetua*. Paris.

Curletto, Silvio. 1989–90. "Temi e trasformazioni nella favola del leone malato e del lupo scorticato." *Sandalion* 12–13: 115–38.

Curtius, Ernst Robert. 1953. *European Literature and the Latin Middle Ages*. Trans. Willard R. Trask. Bollingen Series 36. 1953. Repr. 1973. Princeton.

Dähnhardt, Oskar. 1912. Editor. *Natursagen. Eine Sammlung naturdeutender Sagen, Märchen, Fabeln und Legenden*. Vol. 4: "Tiersagen," part 2. Ed. Oskar Dähnhardt and A. von Löwis of Menar. Leipzig and Berlin.

D'Ancona, Alessandro. 1874. *I precursori di Dante*. Florence.

Dargan, E. P. 1906. "Cock and Fox: A Critical Study of the History and Sources of the Mediaeval Fable." *Modern Philology* 4: 38–65.

Deanesly, Margaret, and Paul Grosjean. 1959. "The Canterbury Edition of the Answers of Pope Gregory I to St. Augustine." *Journal of Ecclesiastic History* 10: 1–49.

de Boor, Helmut. 1966. *Über Fabel und Bîspel*. Bayerische Akademie der Wissenschaften, philosophisch-historische Klasse, Sitzungsberichte. Heft 1.

de Boor, Helmut, and Richard Newald. 1953. *Geschichte der deutschen Literatur*. Munich.

De Lorenzi, Attilio. 1955. *Fedro*. Florence.

Decker, Heinrich. 1958. *Italia Romanica. Die hohe Kunst der romanischen Epoche im Italien*. Vienna.

Della Corte, Francesco. 1966. "Tre papiri favolistici latini." *Atti del'XI Congresso internazionale di papirologia, Milano 2–8 settembre 1965*. Milan. 542–50. Repr. 1973. In: *Opuscula*. Vol. 4. Genoa. 147–55.

Deschamps, Paul. 1947. *La sculpture française époque romane*. Paris.

Díaz y Díaz, Manuel C. 1976. "Sobre las series de voces de animales." *Latin Script and Letters A.D. 400–900: Festschrift Presented to Ludwig Bieler on the Occasion of his 70th birthday*. Ed. John J. O'Meara and Bernd Naumann. Leiden. 148–55.

Dickins, Bruce, and R. M. Wilson. 1951. *Early Middle English Texts*. London.

Diez, Erna, and Johannes B. Bauer. 1973. "Fuchs." *Jahrbuch für Antike und Christentum* 16: 168–78.

Dinzelbacher, Peter. 1978. "Die Visionen des Mittelalters. Ein geschichtlicher Umriß." *Zeitschrift für Religions- und Geistesgeschichte* 30: 116–28.

Doberstein, John W. 1940. "Luther and the Fables of Aesop." *The Lutheran Church Quarterly* 13: 64–74.

Dolbeau, François. 1980. "Une Vision adressé à Heito de Reichenau (m. 836) dans la chronique de Saint-Maixent." *Analecta Bollandiana* 98: 404.

Donatus, Mary. 1934. *Beasts and Birds in the Lives of the Early Irish Saints*. Ph.D. diss., University of Pennsylvania, Philadelphia.

Donovan, L. G. 1983. "*Ysengrimus* and the Early *Roman de Renard*." *Revue canadienne d'études néerlandaises*, special issue 4/1: 33–38.

Douglas, Mary. 1966. *Purity and Danger: An Analysis of the Concepts of Pollution and Taboo*. Repr. 1984. London.

Drabble, Margaret, ed. 1985. *The Oxford Companion to English Literature*. 5th ed. Oxford.

Dronke, Peter. 1965. "The Beginnings of the Sequence." *Beiträge zur Geschichte der deutschen Sprache und Literatur* 87: 43–73.

———. 1973. "The Rise of the Medieval Fabliau: Latin and Vernacular Evidence." *Romanische Forschungen* 85: 275–97.

———. 1974. *Fabula. Explorations into the Uses of Myth in Medieval Platonism*. Mittellateinische Studien und Texte 9. Leiden and Cologne.

Du Méril, M. Edélestand. 1854. *Poésies inédites du moyen âge précédées d'une histoire de la fable ésopique*. Paris. Repr. n.d. Bibliotheca musica bononiensis sezione 5, no. 4. Bologna.

Düchting, Reinhard. 1968. *Sedulius Scottus. Seine Dichtungen*. Munich.

———. 1970. "Vom Hammel, den ein Hund gerissen." In: *Das Tier in der Dichtung*. Ed. Ute Schwab. Heidelberg. 114–27.

Dumézil, Georges. 1929. *Le problème des centaures. Etudes de mythologie comparée indo-européenne*. Annales du Musée Guimet, Bibliothèque d'Etudes 41. Paris.

————. 1943. *Servius et la Fortune. Essai sur la fonction sociale de Louange et de Blâme et sur les éléments indo-européens du "cens" romain*. 2d ed. Paris.

Dümmler, Ernst. 1878. "V. Die Handschriftliche Ueberlieferung der lateinischen Dichtungen aus der Zeit der Karolinger. I." *Neues Archiv* 4: 87–159.

Dünninger, Eberhard. 1962. *Politische und geschichtliche Elemente in mittelalterlichen Jenseitsvisionen bis zum Ende des 13. Jahrhunderts*. Inaugural-Dissertation. Julius-Maximilians-Universität zu Würzburg.

Ebeling, Erich. 1927. *Die babylonische Fabel und ihre Bedeutung für die Literaturgeschichte*. Mitteilungen der Altorientalischen Gesellschaft 2, no. 3. Leipzig.

————. 1957. "Fabel." *Reallexikon der Assyriologie*. Ed. Erich Ebeling, Bruno Meissner, and Ernst Weidner. Berlin. 3: 1–2.

Ebert, Adolf. 1879 for 1878. "Theodulf und Raban." *Berichte über die Verhandlungen der Königlich Sächsischen Gesellschaft der Wissenschaften zu Leipzig, philologisch-historische Klasse* 30/2: 98–100.

————. 1880-89. *Allgemeine Geschichte der Literatur des Mittelalters im Abendlande*. 3 vols. Leipzig.

Ehrismann, Gustav. 1918-35. *Geschichte der deutschen Literatur, bis zum Ausgang des Mittelalters*. 2d ed. 2 vols. Munich, 1932.

Eisenhofer, Ludwig, and Joseph Lechner. 1961. *The Liturgy of the Roman Rite*. Trans. A. J. Peeler and E. F. Peeler. Ed. H. E. Winstone. Edinburgh.

Elliott, Robert C. 1960. *The Power of Satire. Magic, Ritual, Art*. Princeton.

Ellis Davidson, H. R. 1983. "Insults and Riddles in the Edda Poems." *Edda. A Collection of Essays*. Ed. Robert J. Glendinning and Haraldur Bessason. Manitoba. 25–46.

Epopée animale; Fable; Fabliau. Actes du IVe Colloque de la Société Internationale Renardienne. Evreux, 7–11 septembre 1981. 1984. Ed. Gabriel Bianciotto and Michel Salvat. Publications de l'Université de Rouen 83. Paris.

Erb, Ewald. 1964. *Geschichte der deutschen Literatur von den Anfängen bis 1160*. Volk und Wissen 19. Berlin.

Erb, Teja. 1971. "Pauper et dives im *Ysengrimus*." *Philologus* 115: 93–100.

Erdmann, Carl. 1941. "Konrad II. und Heinrich III. in der *Ecbasis captivi*." *Deutsches Archiv für Geschichte des Mittelalters* 4: 382–93.

Ermini, Filippo. 1938. *Medio Evo Latino. Studi e ricerche*. Rome.

Evans, E. P. 1906. *The Criminal Prosecution and Capital Punishment of Animals*. New York.

Falsett, H. J. 1960. *Irische Heilige und Tiere in mittelalterlichen lateinischen Legenden*. Ph.D. diss. Universität Bonn.

Faral, Edmond. 1923. "Le Roman de Renart." In: *Histoire de la littérature française*. Ed. Joseph Bédier and Paul Hazard. 2 vols. Paris. 1: 28–33.

Faust, Manfred. 1969. "Metaphorische Schimpfwörter." *Indogermanische Forschungen* 74: 54–125.

Fechter, Werner. 1969. "Die Zitate aus der antiken Dichtung in der *Ecbasis Captivi*." *Der altsprachliche Unterricht* 12/4: 5–30.

Filosa, C. 1952. *La favola e la letteratura esopiana in Italia dal medio evo ai nostri giorni*. Milan.

Finch, C. E. 1969. "Suetonius' catalogue of animal sounds in Codex Vat. Lat. 6018." *American Journal of Philology* 90: 459–63.

Fischer, Steven R. 1982. *The Complete Medieval Dreambook: A Multilingual, Alphabetical* Somnia Danielis *Collection*. Bern.

Fleckenstein, Josef. 1966. *Die Hofkapelle der deutschen Könige*. Schriften der Monumenta Germaniae historica (Deutsches Institut für Erforschung des Mittelalters) 16, no. 11. Stuttgart.

Flinn, John. 1977. *Le Roman de Renart dans la littérature française et dans les littératures étrangères au Moyen Age*. Paris.

Flusche, Michael. 1975. "Joel Chandler Harris and the Folklore of Slavery." *Journal of American Studies* 9: 347–63.

Forsyth, Ilene. 1976. "The Ganymede Capital at Vézelay." *Gesta: International Center of Medieval Art* 15: 241–46.

Foulet, Lucien. 1914. *Le Roman de Renard*. Bibliothèque de l'Ecole des Hautes Etudes, Sciences Historiques et Philologiques 211. Paris.

Franz, Adolph. 1909. *Die kirchlichen Benediktionen im Mittelalter*. 2 vols. Freiburg im Breisgau.

Freud, Sigmund, and D. E. Oppenheim. 1958. *Dreams in Folklore*. Trans. A. M. O. Richards. Ed. James Strachey. New York.

Fuiano, Michele, 1961. *La cultura a Napoli nell'alto Medioevo*. Naples.

Gaide, Françoise, ed. and trans. 1980. *Avianus, Fables*. Collection des Universités de France publiée sous le patronage de l'Association Guillaume Budé. Paris.

Garmonsway, G. N. 1959. "The Development of the Colloquy." *The Anglo-Saxons. Studies in Some Aspects of Their History and Culture Presented to Bruce Dickins*. Ed. Peter Clemoes. London. 248–61.

Gatti, Paolo. 1979. "Le favole del monaco Ademaro e la tradizione manoscritta del *Corpus* fedriano." *Sandalion* 2: 247–56.

Geertsom, A. van. 1962. "Bruno, de auteur van de *Ysengrimus*." *Verslagen en Mededelingen van de Koninklijke Vlaamse Academie voor Taal- en Letterkunde* Nieuwe Reeks 2, Aflevering 1: 5–73.

Gellinek-Schellekens, Josepha E. 1984. *The Voice of the Nightingale in Middle English Poems and Bird Debates*. New York.

Glauche, Günter. 1970. *Schullektüre im Mittelalter: Entstehung und Wandlungen des Lektürekanons bis 1200 nach den Quellen dargestellt*. Münchener Beiträge zur Mediävistik und Renaissance-Forschung 5. Munich.

Godman, Peter. 1985. *Poetry of the Carolingian Renaissance*. London.

Goldschmidt, Adolph. 1947. *An Early Manuscript of the Aesop Fables and Related Manuscripts*. Studies in Manuscript Illuminations 1. Princeton.

Gompf, Ludwig. 1973. "Die *Ecbasis cuiusdam captivi* und ihr Publikum." *Mittellateinisches Jahrbuch* 8: 30–42.

Gordon, Edmund I. 1958. "Sumerian Animal Proverbs and Fables. 'Collection Five.'" *Journal of Cuneiform Studies* 12: 1–21.

———, 1962. "Animals as Represented in the Sumerian Proverbs and Fables: A Preliminary Study." *Drevnii Mir. Sbornik Statei Akademiku Vasiliiu Vasil'evichu Struve*. Moscow. 226–49.

Gose, Elliott. 1988. *Mere Creatures: A Study of Modern Fantasy Tales for Children.* Toronto.

Gougaud, Louis. 1927. *Devotional and Ascetic Practices in the Middle Ages.* Trans. G. C. Bateman. London.

Graf, Adolf. 1920. *Die Grundlagen des Reineke Fuchs. Eine vergleichende Studie.* Folklore Fellows' Communications 38. Helsinki.

Graven, Jean. 1950. *Le Procès criminel du Roman de Renart: Etude du droit criminel féodal au XIIe siècle.* Geneva.

Grimm, Jacob. 1834. *Reinhart Fuchs.* Berlin.

Grubmüller, Klaus. 1977. *Meister Esopus. Untersuchungen zur Geschichte und Funktion der Fabel im Mittelalter.* Münchener Texte und Untersuchungen zur deutschen Literatur des Mittelalters 56. Zurich.

———. 1978. "Überlegungen zum Wahrheitsanspruch des *Physiologus* im Mittelalter." *Frühmittelalterliche Studien* 12: 160–77.

Gülich, Elisabeth. 1967. "Die Bedeutung der Tropologia in der *Ecbasis cuiusdam captivi.*" *Mittellateinisches Jahrbuch* 4: 72–90.

Gupta, R. D. 1975. "Indian Parallels of the Fox Story." In: *Aspects of the Medieval Animal Epic.* 241–49.

Gurevich, Aron. 1988. *Medieval Popular Culture: Problems of Belief and Perception.* Trans. János M. Bak and Paul A. Hollingsworth. Cambridge Studies in Oral and Literate Culture 14. Cambridge.

Hägg, Tomas. 1983. *The Novel in Antiquity.* Oxford.

Hammann, M. H. 1867–68. "Briques suisses ornées de bas-reliefs du treizième siècle." *Mémoires de l'Institut national genevois.* Vol. 12.

Hammond, N. G. L., and H. H. Scullard. 1970. *The Oxford Classical Dictionary.* 2d ed. Oxford.

Hanning, Robert W. 1977. *The Individual in Twelfth-Century Romance.* New Haven, Conn.

Hartig, Michael. 1925. "Die Klosterschule und ihre Männer." In: Beyerle 1925c. 2: 619–44.

Hauck, Albert. 1904–20. *Kirchengeschichte Deutschlands.* 4th ed. 5 vols. Leipzig.

Hauck, Karl. 1954. "Haus- und sippengebundene Literatur mittelalterlicher Adelsgeschlechter, von Adelssatiren des 11. und 12. Jahrhunderts aus erläutert." *Mitteilungen des Instituts für Österreichische Geschichtsforschung* 62: 121–45. Repr. 1961. In: *Geschichtsdenken und Geschichtsbild im Mittelalter.* Ed. W. Lammers. Wege der Forschung 21. Darmstadt. 165–99.

Hausrath, August. 1898. "Das Problem der äsopischen Fabel." *Neue Jahrbücher für das klassische Altertum* 1: 305–22.

———. 1937. "Germanische Märchenmotive in griechischen Tierfabeln: Ein Beitrag zur Vorgeschichte des Reinhart Fuchs." *Neue Jahrbücher für Wissenschaft und Jugendbildung* 13: 139–50.

Hélin, Maurice. 1951. "Recherche des sources et traditions littéraires chez les écrivains latins du moyen âge." *Mélanges Joseph de Ghellinck, S.J.* 2 vols. Gembloux. 2: 407–20.

———. 1967. "Notes sur l'*Ecbasis.*" *Latomus* 26: 787–99.

Henderson, Arnold Clayton. 1973. "Moralized Beasts: The Development of Medieval Fable and Bestiary, Particularly from the Twelfth through the Fifteenth

Centuries in England and France." Ph.D. diss., University of California, Berkeley.

———. 1978. "'Of heigh or lough estat': Medieval Fabulists as Social Critics." *Viator* 9: 265–90.

———. 1981. "Animal Fables as Vehicles of Social Protest and Satire: Twelfth Century to Henryson." In: *Third International Beast Epic, Fable and Fabliau Colloqium*, 160–73.

———. 1982. "Medieval Beasts and Modern Cages: The Making of Meaning in Fables and Bestiaries." *Publications of the Modern Language Association* 97: 40–49.

Hendrickson, Robert. 1983. *Animal Crackers: A Bestial Lexicon*. New York.

Henkel, Nikolaus. 1976. *Studien zum Physiologus im Mittelalter*. Hermaea: Germanistische Forschungen N.S. 38. Tübingen.

Herrlinger, Gerhard. 1930. *Totenklage um Tiere in der antiken Dichtung*. Tübingener Beiträge zur Altertumswissenschaft 8. Stuttgart.

Hesbert, René-Jean. 1986. "Le Bestiaire de Grégoire." In: *Grégoire le Grand. Chantilly: Centre culturel Les Fontaines 15–19 septembre 1982*. Ed. Jacques Fontaine, Robert Gillet, and Stan Pellistrandi. Paris. 455–66.

Hesseling, D. C. 1893. "On Waxen Tablets with Fables of Babrius (Tabulae ceratae Assendelftianae.)" *Journal of Hellenic Studies* 13: 293–314.

Hoffmann, Hartmut. 1958. "Poppo von Trier in der *Ecbasis cuiusdam captivi*?" *Archiv für Kulturgeschichte* 40: 289–315.

Holman, C. Hugh. 1972. *A Handbook to Literature, Based on the Original by William Flint Thrall and Addison Hibbard*. 3d ed. Indianapolis.

Holtz, Louis. 1981. *Donat et la tradition de l'enseignement grammatical: Etude sur l'Ars Donati et sa diffusion, IVe–IXe siècle, et édition critique*. Paris.

Howe, Nicholas. 1985. "Aldhelm's *Enigmata* and Isidorian Etymology." *Anglo-Saxon England* 14: 37–59.

Hume, Kathryn. 1975. "*The Owl and the Nightingale*." *The Poem and Its Critics*. Toronto.

Hunger, Herbert. 1966. "Die Schildkröte im Himmel (Stephanites und Ichnelates I, 40)." *Wiener Studien* 79: 260–63.

Hyde, Walter Woodburn. 1914–15. "The Prosecution and Punishment of Animals and Lifeless Things in the Middle Ages and Modern Times." *University of Pennsylvania Law Review* 64: 696–730.

Jackson, W. T. H. 1960. *The Literature of the Middle Ages*. New York.

Jacobs, Joseph. 1889. *The Fables of Aesop as first printed by William Caxton in 1484 with those of Avian, Alfonso and Poggio, now again edited and induced*. Vol. 1: "History of the Aesopic Fable." Repr. 1970. New York.

Jacquart, Danielle, and Claude Thomasset. 1988. *Sexuality and Medicine in the Middle Ages*. Trans. Matthew Adamson. Princeton.

Jarcho, Boris I. 1928. "Die Vorläufer des Golias." *Speculum* 3: 523–79.

Jauss, Hans Robert. 1959. *Untersuchungen zur mittelalterlichen Tierdichtung*. Beihefte zur Zeitschrift für romanische Philologie 100. Tübingen.

Johnston, Christopher. 1912. "Assyrian and Babylonian Beast Fables." *American Journal of Semitic Languages and Literatures* 28: 81–100.

Kaczynski, Bernice M., and Haijo Jan Westra. 1982. "Aesop in the Middle Ages:

The Transmission of the Sick Lion Fable and the Authorship of the St. Gall Version." *Mittellateinisches Jahrbuch* 17: 31–38.

———. 1988. "The Motif of the Hypocritical Wolf in Medieval Greek and Latin Animal Literature." In: *The Sacred Nectar of the Greeks: The Study of Greek in the West in the Early Middle Ages*. Ed. Michael W. Herren with Shirley Ann Brown. London. 105–41.

Kamphausen, Hans Joachim. 1975. *Traum und Vision in der lateinischen Poesie der Karolingerzeit*. Lateinische Sprache und Literatur des Mittelalters 4. Bern.

Keidel, Georg C. 1894. "Die Eselherz- (Hirschherz-, Eberherz-) fabel." *Zeitschrift für vergleichende Literaturgeschichte* N.S. 7: 264–67.

Keith-Falconer, Ion G. N. 1885. *Kalilah and Dimnah, or the Fables of Bidpai*. Cambridge. Repr. 1970. Amsterdam.

Kiessling, Nicolas. 1977. *The Incubus in English Literature: Provenance and Progeny*. n.p.: Washington State University Press.

Kindermann, Udo. 1980. "Ecbasis captivi." In: *Die deutsche Literatur des Mittelalters. Verfasserlexikon*. 2d ed. Ed. Kurt Ruh et al. Berlin. 2: 315–21.

Klauser, Theodor. 1953. *Der Ursprung der bischöflichen Insignien und Ehrenrechte*. 2d ed. Krefeld.

Klenner, Karl-Ernst. 1958. *Der Tierstimmen-Katalog als literarisches Phänomen*. Inaugural-Dissertation zur Erlangung des Doktorgrades der Philosophischen Fakultät der Westfälischen Wilhelms-Universität zu Münster. Münster in Westfalen.

Klingender, Francis. 1971. *Animals in Art and Thought to the End of the Middle Ages*. London.

Klopsch, Paul. 1973. "Carmen de Philomela." In: *Literatur und Sprache im europäischen Mittelalter: Festschrift für Karl Langosch zum 70. Geburtstag*. Ed. Alf Önnerfors, Johannes Rathofer, and Fritz Wagner. Darmstadt. 173–94.

Knapp, Fritz Peter. 1975a. "Materialischer Utilitarismus in der Maske der Satire: Magister Nivards *Ysengrimus*." *Mittellateinisches Jahrbuch* 10: 80–99.

———. 1975b. *Similitudo. Stil- und Erzählfunktion von Vergleich und Exempel in der lateinischen, französischen und deutschen Grossepik des Hochmittelalters*. Philologica Germanica 2. Vienna.

———. 1979a. *Das lateinische Tierepos*. Erträge der Forschung 121. Darmstadt: Wissenschaftliche Buchgesellschaft, 1979.

———. 1979b. "Das mittelalterliche Tierepos. Zur Genese und Definition einer grossepischen Literaturgattung." *Sprachkunst: Beiträge zur Literaturwissenschaft* 10 Jahressonderband: Komparatistik in Österreich. 53–68.

———. 1983. "Von der antiken Fabel zum Lateinischen Tierepos des Mittelalters." In: *La Fable*. Ed. Francisco R. Adrados. Entretiens sur l'antiquité classique 30. Vandoeuvres-Genève, 22–27 août 1983. 253–306.

Köhler, C. S. 1881. *Das Tierleben im Sprichwort der Griechen und Römer*. Leipzig.

Kramer, Samuel Noah 1981. *History Begins at Sumer*. Philadelphia.

Kratz, Dennis. 1976. "Aeneas or Christ? An Epic Parody by Sedulius Scottus." *The Classical World* 69 (1976): 319–23. Repr. 1980. In: *Mocking Epic. Waltharius, Alexandreis and the Problem of Christian Heroism*. Studia Humanitatis. Madrid.

———. "An Epic Parody by Theodulf of Orléans." (Unpublished paper, provided by author.)

Krohn, Kaarle. 1888. *Bär (Wolf) und Fuchs; eine nordische Tiermärchenkette*. Trans. Oscar Hackman. Helsingfors.

Künstle, K. "Die Theologie der Reichenau." In: Beyerle 1925c. 2: 703–10.

Küpplers, Jochen. 1977. *Die Fabeln Avians*. Habelts Dissertationsdrucke: Reihe Klassische Philologie 26. Bonn.

Lämke, Dora. 1937. *Mittelalterliche Tierfabeln und ihre Beziehungen zur bildenden Kunst in Deutschland*. Deutsches Werden: Greifswalder Forschungen zur deutschen Geistesgeschichte 14. Griefswald.

Langosch, Karl. 1960. Review of Michel's *Die Ecbasis . . . ein Werk Humberts*. *Historische Zeitschrift* 190: 195–96.

La Penna, A. 1961. "La morale della favola esopica come morale delle classi subalterne nell'antichità." *Società* 17: 459–537.

Lapidge, Michael. 1977. "The Authorship of the Adonic Verses *ad Fidolium* attributed to Columbanus." *Studi Medievali* 3d ser. 18, part 2: 249–314.

Lapôtre, Arthur. 1901. "Le *Souper* de Jean Diacre." *Mélanges d'Archéologie et d'Histoire* 21: 305–85. Repr. 1978. In: *Etudes sur la papauté au IX< siècle*. Torino. 439–519.

Lauchert, Friedrich. 1889. *Geschichte des* Physiologus. Strasbourg.

Lawler, Traugott, ed. 1974. *The "Parisiana Poetria" of John of Garland*. Yale Studies in English 182. New Haven.

Le Déaut, R. 1963. *La Nuit Pascale*. Analecta Biblia 22. Rome.

Le Goff, Jacques. 1984. *The Birth of Purgatory*. Trans. Arthur Goldhammer. Chicago.

Leach, Edmund. 1964. "Anthropological Aspects of Language: Animal Categories and Verbal Abuse." *New Directions in the Study of Language*. Ed. Eric H. Lenneberg. Cambridge, Mass. 21–63.

Leach, Maria. 1961. *God Had a Dog: Folklore of the Dog*. New Brunswick, N.J.

Lehmann, Paul. 1941–62. *Erforschung des Mittelalters: ausgewählte Abhandlungen und Aufsätze*. 5 vols. Vol. 1: Leipzig. Vols. 2–5: Stuttgart, 1959–62.

———. 1925. "Die mittelalterliche Bibliothek." In: Beyerle 1925c. 2: 645–56.

———. 1927. *Pseudo-antike Literatur des Mittelalters*. Studien der Bibliothek Warburg 13. Leipzig.

———. 1958. Review of Michel's *Die Ecbasis . . . ein Werk Humberts*. *Archiv für Erforschung des Mittelalters* 14: 256–58.

———. 1963. *Die Parodie im Mittelalter*. 2d ed. Stuttgart.

LeLièvre, F. J. 1954. "The Basis of Ancient Parody." *Greece and Rome* 23, 2d Series 1: 66–81.

Lenaghan, Robert T., ed. 1967. *Caxton's Aesop*. Cambridge, Mass.

Liver, Ricarda. 1971. "Cornomannia: Etymologisches und Religionsgeschichtliches zu einem stadtrömischen Fest des Mittelalters." *Vox Romanica* 30: 32–43.

———. 1982. "Der singende Schwan. Motivgeschichtliches zu einer Sequenz des 9. Jahrhunderts." *Museum Helveticum* 39: 146–56.

Looshorn. 1880. "Die lateinischen Übersetzungen des h. Johannes Chrysostomus im Mittelalter." *Zeitschrift für katholische Theologie* 4: 788–93.

Lot-Borodine, M. 1937. "L'Aridité ou *Siccitas* dans l'antiquité chrétienne." *Etudes carmélitaines mystiques et missionaires* 22: 191–205.

Lother, Helmut. 1929. *Der Pfau in der altchristlichen Kunst.* Studien über christliche Denkmäler 18. Leipzig.

Luria, S. 1934. "L'asino nella pelle del leone." *Rivista di filologia e d' istruzione classica* 12: 447–73.

Lyman, Darryl. 1983. *The Animal Things We Say.* Middle Village, N.Y.

Lynch, Joseph H. 1986. *Godparents and Kinship in Early Medieval Europe.* Princeton.

McCulloch, Florence. 1962–63. "The Funeral of Renart the Fox in a Walters Book of Hours." *Journal of the Walters Art Gallery* 25–26: 9–27.

MacCulloch, J. A. 1930. *The Harrowing of Hell.* Edinburgh.

McKane, William. 1970. *Proverbs: A New Approach.* London.

McNally, R. E. 1958. "The *Tres Linguae Sacrae* in Early Irish Biblical Exegesis." *Theological Studies* 19: 395–403.

Manitius, Karl. 1955. "Eine Gruppe von Handschriften des 12. Jahrhundert aus dem Trierer Kloster St. Eucharius-Matthias." *Forschungen und Fortschritte* 29: 317–19.

Manitius, Max. 1911–31. *Geschichte der lateinischen Literatur des Mittelalters.* 3 vols. Munich.

Mann, Jill. 1977. "*Luditur Illusor*: The Cartoon World of the *Ysengrimus.*" *Neophilologus* 61: 495–509.

———. 1984–85. "Proverbial Wisdom in the *Ysengrimus.*" *New Literary History* 16: 93–109.

———. 1986. "La favolistica latina." In: *Aspetti della letteratura latina nel secolo XIII.* Ed. Claudio Leonardi and Giovanni Orlandi. Quaderni del "Centro per il Collegamento degli Studi medievali e umanistici nell'Università di Perugia" 15. Perugia and Florence. 193–219.

———. 1988. "The *Roman de Renart* and the *Ysengrimus.*" In: *A la recherche du Roman de Renart: Kenneth Varty.* Ed. Kenneth Varty, R. Bellon, and others. 2 vols. New Alyth, Perthshire. 1: 135–62.

Manser, P. A., and Konrad Beyerle. "Aus dem liturgischen Leben der Reichenau." In: Beyerle 1925c. 1: 316–437.

Marcovich, M. 1971. "Voces animantium and Suetonius." *Ziva Antika. Antiquité vivante* 21: 399–416.

Marg, Walter. 1967. *Der Charakter in der Sprache der frühgriechischen Dichtung. Semonides-Homer-Pindar.* Libelli 117. Darmstadt.

Marrow, James. 1977. "Circumdederunt me canes multi. Christ's Tormentors in Northern European Art of the Late Middle Ages and Early Renaissance." *Art Bulletin* 59: 167–181.

Martin, Ernst. 1908. "Zur Geschichte der Tiersage im Mittelalter." *Untersuchungen und Quellen zur germanischen und romanischen Philologie Johann von Kelle dargebracht.* Vol. 1. Prager Deutsche Studien 8, no. 1. Prague.

Martínez Pizarro, Joaquín. 1976. "Studies on the function and context of the *Senna* in Early Germanic Narrative." Ph.D. diss., Harvard University, Cambridge, Mass.

Maxilimianus, P. 1954. "Philomena van John Pecham." *Neophilologus* 38: 206–17, 290–300.

Meissner, A. L. 1876. "Die bildlichen Darstellungen des Reineke Fuchs im Mittelalter." *Archiv für das Studium der neueren Sprachen und Literaturen* Jg. 30, Bd. 56: 265–80.

Ménabréa, Léon. 1846. *De l'origine, de la forme et de l'esprit des jugements rendus au moyen-âge contre les animaux.* Chambéry.

Menke, Hubertus. 1970. *Die Tiernamen in Van den Vos Reinaerde.* Beiträge zur Namenforschung, N.F. Beiheft 6. Heidelberg.

Meuli, Karl. 1932–33. "Maske, Maskereien." In: Bächtold-Stäubli. *Handwörterbuch des deutschen Aberglaubens.* 5: 1744–1852.

———. 1955. "Altrömische Maskenbrauch." *Museum Helveticum* 12: 206–35.

———. 1975. "Herkunft und Wesen der Fabel." In: Karl Meuli. *Gesammelte Schriften.* 2 vols. Ed. Thomas Gelzer. Basel. 2: 731–56.

Meyer-Lübke, W. 1935. *Romanisches etymologisches Wörterbuch.* 3d ed. Heidelberg.

Meyers, Jean. 1986. *L'Art de l'emprunt dans la poésie de Sedulius Scottus.* Bibliothèque de la Faculté de Philosophie et Lettres de l'Université de Liège 245. Paris.

Meyvaert, Paul. 1959. "Les *Responsiones* de S. Grégoire le Grand à S. Augustin de Cantorbéry." *Revue d'Histoire Ecclésiastique* 54: 879–94.

———. 1966. "A Metrical Calendar by Eugenius Vulgarius." *Analecta Bollandiana* 84: 349–77.

———. 1971. "Bede's Text of the *Libellus Responsionum* of Gregory the Great to Augustine of Canterbury." In: *England before the Conquest: Studies in Primary Sources Presented to Dorothy Whitelock.* Ed. Peter Clemoes and Kathleen Hughes. Cambridge. 15–33.

Michel, Anton. 1957. *Die* Ecbasis captivi per tropologiam, *ein Werk Humberts, des späteren Kardinals von Silva Candida.* Bayerische Akademie der Wissenschaften, philosophisch-historische Klasse, Sitzungsberichte 1957, Heft 1.

Mierlo, Joseph van. 1943a. "Het oudste Dierengedicht in de Letterkunde der Nederlanden." *Verslagen en Mededeelingen der Koninklijke Vlaamsche Academie voor Taal- en Letterkunde.* 13–31.

———. 1943b. "Het Vroegste Dierenepos in de Letterkunde der Nederlanden. *Isengrimus* van Magister Nivardus." *Verslagen en Mededeelingen der Koninklijke Vlaamsche Academie voor Taal-en Letterkunde.* Antwerpen. 281–335, 489–548.

Misch, Georg. 1931–69. *Geschichte der Autobiographie.* 3d ed. 7 vols. Leipzig, Berlin, Frankfurt am Main.

Mittellateinisches Wörterbuch bis zum ausgehenden 13. Jahrhundert. 1960–. Ed. Otto Prinz and Johannes Schneider. Munich.

Morenz, Siegfried. 1954. "Ägyptische Tierkriege und die Batrachomyomachie." *Neue Beiträge zur klassischen Altertumswissenschaft. Festschrift zum 60. Geburtstag von Bernhard Schweitzer.* Ed. Reinhard Lullies. Stuttgart. 87–94.

Morris, Colin. 1972. *The Discovery of the Individual 1050–1200.* Church History Outlines 5. London.

Mozley, J[ohn] H[enry]. 1965. Review of Zeydel's edition and translation of the *Ecbasis captivi. Medium Aevum* 34: 135–39.

Müllenhoff, Karl. 1875. "Über Reinhart Fuchs." *Zeitschrift für deutsches Alterthum* 18, N.S. 6: 1–9.

Müller, Michael. 1932. "Zur Frage nach der Echtheit und Abfassungszeit des *Res-*

ponsum b. Gregorii ad Augustinum episcopum." *Theologische Quartalschrift* 113: 94–118.

———. 1934. "Ein sexual-ethisches Problem der Scholastik." *Divus Thomas: Jahrbuch für Philosophie und spekulative Theologie,* 3d series 12: 442–97.

Mullin, Redmond. 1979. *Miracles and Magic: The Miracles and Spells of Saints and Witches.* London.

Murphy, James J. 1980. "The Teaching of Latin as a Second Language in the 12th Century." *Historiographia Linguistica* 7: 159–75.

Myres, John Linton. 1950. *The Structure of Stichomythia in Attic Tragedy.* London.

Nagy, Gregory. 1976. "Iambos. Typologies of Invective and Praise." *Arethusa* 9: 191–205.

Neff, Karl, ed. 1908. *Die Gedichte des Paulus Diaconus.* Quellen und Untersuchungen zur lateinischen Philologie des Mittelalters 3, no. 4. Munich.

Nikolasch, Franz. 1969. "Zur Ikonographie des Widders von Gen 22." *Vigiliae Christianae* 23: 197–223.

Nøjgaard, Morten. 1964–67. *La Fable antique.* 2 vols. Copenhagen.

———. 1979. "The Moralisation of the Fable: From Aesop to Romulus." In: *Medieval Narrative: A Symposium.* Ed. Hans Bekker-Nielsen, Peter Foote, Andreas Haarder, and Preben Meulengracht Sørensen. Odense. 31–43.

Norberg, Dag. 1988. *Les Vers latins iambiques et trochaïques au Moyen Age et leurs répliques rythmiques.* Kungl. Vitterhets Historie och Antikvitets Akademien, Filologiskt arkiv 35. Uppsala.

Norris, Margot. 1985. *Beasts of the Modern Imagination: Darwin, Nietzsche, Kafka, Ernst, and Lawrence.* Baltimore.

Nozaki, Kioyshi. 1961. *Kitsune, Japan's Fox of Mystery, Romance and Humor.* Tokyo.

Oexla, Otto Gerhard. 1970. "Le Monastère de Charroux au IXᵉ siècle." *Le Moyen Age* 76: 193–204.

Orlandi, Giovanni. 1973. Review of P. T. Eden, ed. *Theobaldi Physiologus. Studi medievali,* 3d series 14: 902–22.

———. 1985. "La Tradizione del *Physiologus* e i prodromi del bestiario latino." In: *L'Uomo di fronte al mondo animale nell'alto medioevo, 7–13 aprile 1983.* Settimane di studio del centro italiano di studi sull'alto medioevo 31. Spoleto. 2: 1057–106.

Otto, August. 1890. *Die Sprichwörter und sprichwörtlichen Redensarten der Römer.* Leipzig.

Oulmont, Charles. 1911. *Les Débats du clerc et du chevalier dans la littérature poétique du moyen âge.* Paris.

Oxford English Dictionary.

Oxford Latin Dictionary. 1968–82. Ed. P. G. W. Glare. Oxford.

Pangritz, Walter. 1963. *Das Tier in der Bibel.* Munich.

Panzer, Friedrich. 1906. "Der romanische Bilderfries am südlichen Choreingang des Freiburger Münsters und seine Deutung." *Freiburger Münsterblätter* 2: 1–34.

———. 1931. "Zur Tiersage." *Oberdeutsche Zeitschrift für Volkskunde* 5: 120–23.

Papademetriou, John-Theophanes A. 1983. "Some Aesopic Fables in Byzantium and the Latin West. Tradition, Diffusion, and Survival." *Illinois Classical Studies* 8/1: 122–36.

Paris, Gaston. 1910. "Le Roman de Renard." In: *Mélanges de littérature française du moyen âge*. Ed. Mario Roques. Paris.

Paris, Paulin. 1861. *Les Aventures de Maître Renard et d'Ysengrin, suivies de nouvelles recherches sur le Roman de Renart*. Paris.

Parks, Ward. 1990. *Verbal Dueling in Heroic Narrative: The Homeric and Old English Traditions*. Princeton, N.J.

Pascher, Joseph. 1963. *Das liturgische Jahr*. Munich.

Patch, Howard Rollin. 1950. *The Other World According to Descriptions in Medieval Literature*. Cambridge, Mass. Repr. 1980. New York.

Payer, Pierre J. 1984. *Sex and the Penitentials: The Development of a Sexual Code 550–1150*. Toronto.

Peeters, Leopold. 1971. "Zu *Ysengrimus*, Liber Secundus vv. 69–70: *Celebrant*." *Leuvense Bijdragen* 60: 105–14.

Peiper, R. 1876. Review of Voigt's edition of the *Ecbasis captivi*. *Anzeiger für deutsches Altertum und deutsche Literatur* 2/2: 87–114.

Perella, Nicolas James. 1969. *The Kiss Sacred and Profane*. Berkeley and Los Angeles.

Pérez Vidal, J. 1947. "Testamentos de bestias." *Revista de Dialectología y Tradiciones populares* 3: 524–50.

Perry, Ben Edwin. 1940. "The Origins of the Epimythium." *Transactions and Proceedings of the American Philological Association* 71: 391–419.

———. ed., 1952. *Aesopica*. One volume in an incomplete series. Urbana, Illinois.

———. 1959. "Fable." *Studium Generale* 12: 17–37.

———. 1960. "Some Traces of Lost Medieval Story-Books." In: *Humaniora: Essays in Literature, Folklore, Bibliography Honoring Archer Taylor on his Seventieth Birthday*. Ed. Wayland D. Hand and Gustave O. Arlt. Locust Valley, N.Y. 150–60.

———. 1962. "Demetrius of Phalerum and the Aesopic Fables." *Transactions and Proceedings of the American Philological Association* 93: 287–346.

———. ed., 1965. *Babrius and Phaedrus*. Loeb Classical Library. Cambridge, Mass.

Phillpotts, Bertha S. 1920. *The Elder Edda and Ancient Scandinavian Drama*. Cambridge.

Pierce, Frank. 1955. "Cervantes' Animal Fable." *Atlante* 3: 103–15.

Pintus, Giovanna Maria. 1985–86. "Storia di un simbolo: Il Gallo." *Sandalion* 8–9: 243–67.

Plöchl, Willibald. 1953–55. *Geschichte des Kirchenrechts*. 2 vols. Vienna.

Pop, Démètre. 1933. *La Défense du Pape Formose*. Paris.

Préaux, Jean G. 1947. "Thierry de Saint Trond, auteur de poème pseudo-ovidien *de Mirabilibus Mundi*." *Latomus* 6: 353–68.

———. 1978. "Du *Culex* de Virgile à son pastiche par Thierry de Saint-Trond." In: *Présence de Virgile. Actes du Colloque des 9, 11 et 12 décembre 1976 (Paris E.N.S., Tours)*. Ed. R. Chevallier. Paris. 195–208.

Provenzo, Eugene Francis, Jr. 1976. "Education and the Aesopic Tradition." Ph.D. diss., Washington University, Saint Louis, Missouri.

Puelma, Mario. 1972. "Sänger und König. Zum Verständnis von Hesiods Tierfabel." *Museum Helveticum* 29: 86–109.

Pugliarello, Mariarosaria. 1973. *Le Origini della favolistica classica*. Brescia.

Puntoni, Vittorio. 1912. *La Favola esopica dell'aquila e della testuggine*. Bologna.

Quintavalle, Arturo Carlo. 1974. *La Cattedrale di Parma e il romanico europeo*. Parma.

Raby, F. J. E. 1957. *A History of Secular Latin Poetry in the Middle Ages*. 2d ed. 2 vols. Oxford.

————. 1951. "Philomena praevia temporis amoeni." In: *Mélanges Joseph de Ghellinck, S.J.* 2 vols. Gembloux. 2: 435–48.

Radin, Paul. 1945. *The Trickster: A Study in American Indian Mythology*. New York.

Randall, L. M. C. 1962. "The Snail in Gothic Marginal Warfare." *Speculum* 37: 358–67.

Rathay, J. 1876. Review of Voigt's edition of the *Ecbasis captivi*. *Zeitschrift für die österreichischen Gymnasien* 27: 676–82.

Ratkowitsch, Christine. 1989. "Der Hammel Tityros—Versuch einer Deutung von c. 2, 41 des Sedulius Scottus." *Wiener Studien. Zeitschrift für klassische Philologie und Patristik* 102: 251–66.

Rawson, Jessica. 1977. *Animals in Art*. British Museum Publications. London.

Reich, Hermann. 1904. "Der Mann mit dem Eselskopf. Ein Mimodrama vom klassischen Altertum verfolgt bis auf Shakespeares Sommernachtstraum." Separat-Abdruck aus dem Jahrbuch der Deutschen Shakespeare-Gesellschaft 40. Weimar.

Reindel, Kurt. 1960. Review of Michel's *Die Ecbasis . . . ein Werk Humberts*. *Historisches Jahrbuch* 79: 348–53.

Reinle, Adolf. 1959. *Das Amt Willisau mit St. Urban*. Die Kunstdenkmäler der Schweiz: Die Kunstdenkmäler des Kantons Luzern 5. Basel.

Revue canadienne d'études néerlandaises: Canadian Journal of Netherlandic Studies. 1983. Special Issue 4/1: "Le *Roman de Renard*: On the Beast Epic." Ed. Haijo J. Westra.

Reynolds, L. D., and R. H. Rouse. 1983. "Caelius Aurelianus." In: *Texts and Transmission: A Survey of the Latin Classics*. Ed. L. D. Reynolds. Oxford. 32–35.

Ricci, M. L. 1963. "Motivi ed espressioni bibliche nel centone virgiliano *De Ecclesia*." *Studi italiani di filologia classica* 35: 161–85.

Rice, Winthrop Huntingdon. 1941. *The European Ancestry of Villon's Satirical Testaments*. Syracuse University Monographs 1. New York.

Righetti, Mario. 1959–69. *Manuale di storia liturgica*. 3d ed. 4 vols. Milan.

Roberts, Michael. 1985. *Biblical Epic and Rhetorical Paraphrase in Late Antiquity*. ARCA Classical and Medieval Texts, Papers and Monographs 16. Liverpool.

Robertson, D. W., Jr. 1951. "Some Medieval Literary Terminology, with Special Reference to Chrétien de Troyes." *Studies in Philology* 48: 669–92.

Röllig, Wolfgang. 1984. "Etana." In: *Enzyklopädie des Märchens: Handwörterbuch zur historischen und vergleichenden Erzählforschung*. Ed. Kurt Ranke. Berlin. 4: 494–99.

Rönsch, H. 1884. "Einiges zur Erläuterung der Caena Hrabani Mauri." *Zeitschrift für wissenschaftliche Theologie* 27: 344.

Rose, Valentin. 1892. *Die lateinischen Meerman-Handschriften des Sir Thomas Phillipps in der königlichen Bibliothek zu Berlin*. Berlin.

Ross, Werner. 1954. "Die *Ecbasis captivi* und die Anfänge der mittelalterlichen Tierdichtung." *Germanisch-Romanische Monatsschrift* 35: 266–82.

Rowland, Beryl. 1984. "The Relationship of St. Basil's *Hexaemeron* to the *Physiologus.*" In: *Epopée animale; Fable; Fabliau.* 489–98.

Rudolph, Conrad. 1990. *The "Things of Greater Importance": Bernard of Clairvaux's* Apologia *and the Medieval Attitude toward Art.* Philadelphia.

Rüegg, August. 1945. *Die Jenseitsvorstellungen vor Dante und die übrigen literarischen Voraussetzungen der "Divina Commedia".* 2 vols. Einsiedeln and Cologne.

Sauvage, André. 1975. *Etudes de thèmes animaliers dans la poésie latine: Le cheval-les oiseaux.* Collection Latomus 143. Brussels.

Savage, John J. 1949–51. "The Mediaeval Tradition of Cerberus." *Traditio* 7: 405–10.

Sbordone, Francesco. 1949. "La Tradizione manoscritta del *Physiologus* latino." *Athenæum* 27: 246–80.

Scalia, G. 1960. Review of Hoffmann's "Poppo von Trier." *Studi Medievali*, 3d series 3/1: 237–41.

Schaller, Dieter. 1960–61. Review of Jauss, *Untersuchungen. Anzeiger für deutsches Altertum und deutsche Literatur* 72: 68–76.

———. 1970a. "Lateinische Tierdichtung in frühkarolingischer Zeit." In: *Das Tier in der Dichtung.* Ed. Schwab. 91–113, 272–76.

———. 1970b. "Vortrags- und Zirkulardichtung am Hof Karls des Grossen." *Mittellateinisches Jahrbuch* 6: 14–36.

———. 1971a. "Der junge 'Rabe' am Hof Karls des Grossen (Theodulf carm. 27)." *Festschrift Bernhard Bischoff zu seinem 65. Geburtstag.* Ed. Johanne Autenrieth and Franz Brunhölzl. Stuttgart. 123–41.

———. 1971b. "Poetic Rivalries at the Court of Charlemagne." in: *Classical Influences on European Culture.* Ed. R. R. Bolgar. Cambridge. 151–57.

Schauenburg, Konrad. 1972. "Ganymed und Hahnenkämpfe auf römischen Sarkophagen." *Archäologischer Anzeiger* 501–16.

Scheidegger, Jean R. 1983. "Le Conflit des langues: Ecriture et fiction dans l'*Ysengrimus*." In: *Revue canadienne d'études néerlandaises*, Special Issue 4/1: 9–17.

Schirokauer, Arno. 1953. "Die Stellung Äsops in der Literatur des Mittelalters." in: *Festschrift für Wolfgang Stammler.* Berlin. 179–91. Repr. 1957. In Schirokauer. *Germanistische Studien.* Hamburg. 395–415. Trans. 1954. "The Place of Esop in Medieval Literature." *Library Chronicle of the University of Pennsylvania* 20: 5–16.

Schmidt, Paul Gerhard. 1974. "Das Zitat in der Vagantendichtung. Bakelfest und Vagantenstrophe *cum auctoritate.*" *Antike und Abendland* 20 (1974): 74–87. 1990. Trans. Peter Godman. "The Quotation in Goliardic Poetry: The Feast of Fools and the Goliardic Strophe *cum auctoritate.*" In: *Latin Poetry and the Classical Tradition: Essays in Medieval and Renaissance Literature.* Ed. Peter Godman and Oswyn Murray. Oxford.

Schneider, Johannes. 1966. "Zum Nachleben der römischen Satiriker in den mittellateinischen satirischen Dichtungen des deutschen Bereichs in der Zeit der Salier und Staufer." *Wissenschaftliche Zeitschrift der Universität Rostock* 15: Gesellschafts- und sprachwissenschaftliche Reihe 4/5: 517–24.

Schönfelder, Albert. 1929. "Textänderungen zu *Ysengrimus*." *Zeitschrift für deutsches Altertum und deutsche Literatur* 66: 50.

———. trans., 1955. *Isengrimus. Das flämische Tierepos aus dem Lateinischen ver-deutscht*. Niederdeutsche Studien 3. Münster.

Schouwink, Wilfried. 1984. "The Sow Salaura and Her Relatives in Medieval Literature and Art." In: *Epopée animale; Fable; Fabliau*. 509–24.

———. 1985. *Der wilde Eber in Gottes Weinberg: Zur Darstellung des Schweins in Literatur und Kunst des Mittelalters*. Sigmaringen.

Schreiner, Klaus. 1966. "*Discrimen veri ac falsi*. Ansätze und Formen der Kritik in der Heiligen- und Reliquienverehrung des Mittelalters." *Archiv für Kulturgeschichte* 48: 1–53.

Schumann, Otto. 1936. Review of Strecker's edition of the *Ecbasis captivi*. *Anzeiger für deutsches Altertum und deutsche Literatur* 55: 121–24.

———. 1979–83. *Lateinisches Hexameter-Lexikon. Dichterisches Formelgut von Ennius bis zum Archipoeta*. Monumenta Germaniae Historica Hilfsmittel 4. 6 vols. Munich.

Schüppert, Helga. 1972. *Kirchenkritik in der lateinischen Lyrik des 12. und 13. Jahrhunderts*. Medium Aevum: Philologische Studien 23. Munich.

Schütze, Gundolf. 1973. *Gesellschaftskritische Tendenzen in deutschen Tierfabeln des 13. bis 15. Jahrhunderts*. Europäische Hochschulschriften 3.24. Bern.

Schwab, Ute. 1969. "Gastmetaphorik und Hornarithmetik im *Ysengrimus*." *Studi Medievali* 3d series 10/2: 215–50.

———. ed., 1970. *Das Tier in der Dichtung*. Heidelberg.

———. 1981. "Zum Verständnis des Isaak-Opfers in literarischer und bildlicher Darstellung des Mittelalters." *Frühmittelalterliche Studien* 15: 435–94.

Schwarzbaum, Haim. 1969. "The Vision of Eternal Peace in the Animal Kingdom (Aa-Th 62)." *Fabula* 10: 107–31.

Schwed, John F. 1969. "The Mask of Friendship. Mumming as a Ritual of Social Relations." In: *Christmas Mummings in Newfoundland*. Ed. Herbert Halpert and G. M. Story. Toronto. 104–18.

Schwinge, Ernst-Richard. 1968. *Die Verwendung der Stichomythie in den Dramen des Euripides*. Bibliothek der klassischen Altertumswissenschaft. N.S. 2/17. Heidelberg.

Scobie, Alex. 1983. *Apuleius and Folklore: Toward a History of ML3045, AaTh567, 449A*. Folklore Society Mistletoe Series 17. London.

———. 1973. *More Essays on the Ancient Romance and Its Heritage*. Beiträge zur klassischen Philologie 46. Meisenheim am Glan.

Scolari, Antonio. 1985. "I 'Versus de pulice et musca' di Guglielmo di Blois." *Studi Medievali*, 3d series 26: 373–404.

Scott, Peter Dale. 1965. "Alcuin's *Versus de cuculo*: The Vision of Pastoral Friendship." *Studies in Philology* 62: 510–30.

See, Klaus von. 1964. "Skop und skald. Zur Auffassung des Dichters bei den Germanen." *Germanisch-Romanische Monatsschrift* N.S. 14: 1–14.

Seemann, Erich. 1923. *Hugo von Trimberg und die Fabeln seines Renners. Eine Untersuchung zur Geschichte der Tierfabel im Mittelalter*. Münchener Archiv für Philologie des Mittelalters und der Renaissance 6. Munich.

Seiler, Friedrich, 1877. Review of Voigt's edition of the *Ecbasis captivi*. *Zeitschrift für deutsche Philologie* 8: 362–74.

————. 1878. "Kleinigkeiten zur *Ecbasis captivi*." *Anzeiger für deutsches Altertum und deutsche Literatur* 4: 296–98.

Seroux d'Agincourt, J. B. L. G. 1823. *Histoire de l'art par les monuments, depuis sa décadence au IVᶜ siècle jusqu'à son renouvellement au XVIᶜ.* 6 vols. Paris.

Servaes, Franz-Wilhelm. 1974. "Typologie und mittellateinische Tierdichtung." *Der altsprachliche Unterricht* 17: 17–29.

Shippey, Thomas Alan. 1970. "Listening to the Nightingale." *Comparative Literature* 22: 46–60.

Sifakis, G. M. 1971. *Parabasis and Animal Choruses. A Contribution to the History of Attic Comedy.* London.

Singer, Samuel. 1944–47. *Sprichwörter des Mittelalters.* 3 vols. Bern.

Smolak, Kurt. 1980. "Der verbannte Dichter (Identifizierungen mit Ovid in Mittelalter und Neuzeit)." *Wiener Studien* 14: 158–91.

Sorrento, L. 1943. *Medievalia.* Brescia.

Spanke, Hans. 1931. "Zu den Gedichten Walthers von Châtillon." *Volkstum und Kultur der Romanen* 4: 197–220.

————. 1977. *Studien zu Sequenz, Lai und Leich.* Ed. Ursula Aarburg. Darmstadt.

Spicq, C. 1944. *Esquisse d'une histoire de l'exégèse latine au moyen âge.* Paris.

Spiegelberg, Wilhelm. 1912. *Demotische Texte auf Krügen.* Vol. 5. Leipzig.

Stäblein, Bruno. 1975. "Schriftbild der einstimmigen Musik." In: *Musikgeschichte in Bildern.* Ed. Heinrich Besseler and W. Bachmann. Vol. 3: "Musik des Mittelalters und der Renaissance," Lieferung 4. Leipzig.

————. 1962. "Die Schwanenklage. Zum Problem Lai-Planctus-Sequenz." In: *Festschrift für Karl Gustav Fellerer zum sechzigsten Geburtstag am 7. Juli 1962.* Ed. Heinrich Hüschen. Regensburg. 491–502.

Stammler, Wolfgang, and Hildegard Stammler. 1926. *Alte deutsche Tierfabeln.* Jena.

Steblin-Kamenskij, M. I. 1969. "On the Etymology of the Word Skáld." In: *Afmaelisrit Jóns Helgasonar, 30. júní 1969.* Reykjavik. 421–30.

Steinen, Wolfram von den. 1946. "Die Anfänge der Sequenzendichtung." *Zeitschrift für schweizerische Kirchengeschichte* 40: 190–212, 241–68; 41 (1947): 19–48, 122–62.

————. 1957–58. Review of Michel's *Die Ecbasis . . . ein Werk Humberts. Anzeiger für deutsches Altertum und deutsche Literatur* 70: 114–16.

Steinschneider, Moritz. 1908. *Rangstreit-Literatur. Ein Beitrag zur vergleichenden Literatur- und Kulturgeschichte.* Sitzungsberichte Wien 155, 4. Vienna.

Strecker, Karl. 1933. "Ecbasis captivi." In: *Die deutsche Literatur des Mittelalters: Verfasserlexikon.* Ed. Wolfgang Stammler. 4 vols. and additional volume. Berlin, 1933–55. 1: 484–90.

————. 1935. "Ecbasisfragen." *Historische Vierteljahrsschrift* 29: 491–508.

Strömbäck, Dag. 1948. "Cult Remnants in Icelandic Dramatic Dances." *Arv,* N.S. 4: 132–45.

————. 1955. "Icelandic Dramatic Dances and Their West European Background." *Universitet i Bergen Årbok 1955* Historisk-antikvarisk rekke no. 1: 92–99.

Suchomski, Joachim. 1975. *"Delectatio" und "utilitas." Ein Beitrag zum Verständnis mittelalterlicher komischer Literatur.* Bibliotheca Germanica 18. Bern.

Sudre, Léopold. 1892. *Les Sources du* Roman de Renart. Paris.

Surdel, Alain-Julien. 1984. "Pour une lecture plus 'clunisienne' de *l'Ecbasis cuiusdam captivi per tropologiam*." *Epopée animale; Fable; Fabliau*. 641–55.

———. 1989. "Divertissement pascal et latinité médiévale: *L'Ecbasis cuiusdam captivi per tropologiam*." In: *Reinardus: Yearbook of the International Reynard Society*. Ed. Brian Levy and Paul Wackers. Grave. 1/1: 154–66.

Sypher, Eleanor Kramer. 1973. "A Rhetorical Study of Nivardus of Ghent's *Ysengrimus*." Ph.D. diss., Columbia University.

Sypher, F. J., and Eleanor Sypher, trans. 1980. Ysengrimus *by Magister Nivardus*. New York.

Szövérffy, Joseph, ed. 1975. *Peter Abelard's* Hymnarius Paracletensis. 2 vols. Brookline, Mass.

———. 1970. *Weltliche Dichtungen des lateinischen Mittelalters: Ein Handbuch*. One volume in an incomplete series. Berlin.

Tardel, Hermann. 1926. "Die Testamentsidee als dichterisches Formmotiv I." *Niederdeutsche Zeitschrift für Volkskunde* 4/2: 72–84.

Taylor, Archer. 1948. *The Literary Riddle before 1600*. Berkeley and Los Angeles.

Thiel, Helmut van. 1971–72. *Der Eselroman*. 2 vols. Zetemata: Monographien zur klassischen Altertumswissenschaft 54: 1–2. Munich.

Thesaurus Linguae Latinae. Leipzig, 1900–.

Third International Beast Epic, Fable and Fabliau Colloquium. Münster 1979. Proceedings. 1981. Ed. Jan Goossens and Timothy Sodmann. Niederdeutsche Studien 30. Cologne.

Thompson, Stith. 1946. *The Folktale*. Repr. 1977. Berkeley.

———. 1955–58. *Motif-Index of Folk-Literature*. 2d ed. 6 vols. Bloomington, Ind.

Thornton, T. C. G. 1972. "Trees, Gibbets, and Crosses." *Journal of Theological Studies*, N.S. 23: 130–31.

Thurston, Herbert. 1904. *Lent and Holy Week*. New York.

Tobler, Adolf, and Erhard Lommatzsch, eds. *Altfranzösisches Wörterbuch*. Wiesbaden.

Toldo, Peter. 1908. "Leben und Wunder der Heiligen im Mittelalter, XVII. Tiere." *Studien zur vergleichenden Literaturgeschichte* 8: 18–48.

Torrance, Robert M. 1978. *The Comic Hero*. Cambridge, Mass.

Traube, Ludwig. 1911. "Einleitung in die lateinische Philologie des Mittelalters." Vol. 2. in: *Vorlesungen und Abhandlungen*. Ed. Paul Lehmann. 3 vols. Munich, 1909–20.

Trillitzsch, Winfried, ed. and trans. 1964. *Ecbasis cuiusdam captivi per tropologiam*. Leipzig.

Truc, G. 1912. "Les états mystiques négatifs (la tiédeur–l'acédia–la sécheresse." *Revue philosophique* 73: 610–28.

Tubach, Frederic C. 1969. *Index Exemplorum*. Folklore Fellows' Communications 204. Helsinki.

Ullmann, Walter. 1974. *A Short History of the Papacy*. London.

Väänänen, Veikko, ed. 1966–70. *Graffiti del Palatino*. 2 vols. Acta Instituti Romani Finlandiae 3–4. Helsinki.

Varty, Kenneth. 1967. *Reynard the Fox*. New York.

Vinay, Gustavo. 1949. "Contributo alla interpretazione della *Ecbasis captivi.*" *Convivium* 234–52.

———. 1952. "La commedia latina del secolo XII." *Studi Medievali* N.S. 18/2: 209–71.

Vinycomb, John. 1906. *Fictitious and Symbolic Creatures in Art, with Special Reference to Their Use in British Heraldry.* London.

Voigt, Ernst, ed. 1875. *Ecbasis captivi, das älteste Thierepos des Mittelalters.* Quellen und Forschungen zur Sprach- und Culturgeschichte der germanischen Völker 8. Strasbourg.

———. ed., 1878. *Kleinere lateinische Denkmäler der Thiersage.* Quellen und Forschungen 25. Strasbourg.

———. 1891. "Das erste Lesebuch des Triviums in den Kloster- und Stiftsschulen des Mittelalters (11–15 Jahrhundert)." *Mitteilungen der Gesellschaft für Deutsche Erziehung- und Schulgeschichte* 1: 42–53.

———. 1894. "Ein unbekanntes Lehrbuch der Metrik aus dem 11. Jahrhundert." *Mitteilungen der Gesellschaft für Deutsche Erziehungs- und Schulgeschichte* 4: 149–58.

Voretzsch, Carl. 1896. Review of Léonard Willems. *Zeitschrift für romanische Philologie* 20: 413–23.

Vyver, A., van de, and Charles Verlinden. 1933. "L'Auteur et la portée du *Conflictus ovis et lini.*" *Revue Belge de Philologie et d'Histoire* 11: 59–81.

Wackernagel, Wilhelm. 1848. "Der Wolf in der Schule." *Zeitschrift für deutsches Altertum* 6: 285–88.

———. 1873. "Von der Thiersage und den Dichtungen aus der Thiersage." In: *Kleinere Schriften.* Vol. 2: *Abhandlungen zur deutsche Litteraturgeschichte.* Leipzig. 3 vols. 1872–74. Repr. Osnabruck, 1966.

Waddell, Helen. 1934. *Beasts and Saints.* London.

Waley, A. trans. 1943. *Monkey.* By Wu Ch'êng-ên. New York.

Walther, Hans. 1920. *Das Streitgedicht in der lateinischen Literatur des Mittelalters.* Quellen and Untersuchungen zur Lateinischen Philologie des Mittelalters 5, no. 2, Munich. Repr. 1982. Hildesheim.

———. 1963–68. *Carmina Medii Aevi posterioris Latina.* Part 2, vols. 1–6: Proverbia Sententiaeque Latinitatis Medii Aevi. Göttingen.

Ward, Donald. 1973. "On the Poets and Poetry of the Indo-Europeans." *Journal of Indo-European Studies* 1: 127–44.

Ward, H. L. D. 1883–93. *Catalogue of Romances in the Department of Manuscripts in the British Museum.* 2 vols. London. 2: 586–740.

Warnke, K. 1900. "Die Quellen des Esope der Marie de France." In: *Forschungen zur romanischen Philologie. Festgabe für H. Suchier.* Halle. 161–284.

Watkins, Calvert, ed. 1985. *The American Heritage Dictionary of Indo-European Roots.* Boston.

Wattenbach, Wilhelm. 1896. *Das Schriftwesen im Mittelalter.* 3d ed. Leipzig.

Wattenbach, Wilhelm, and W. Levison. 1952–73. *Deutschlands Geschichtsquellen im Mittelalter. Vorzeit und Karolinger.* 5 vols. Weimar.

Wehrli, Max. 1969. "Vom Sinn des mittelalterlichen Tierepos." *Formen mittelalterlicher Erzählung: Aufsätze.* Zurich. 113–25.

338   Bibliography

Weicker, Georg. 1902. *Der Seelenvogel in der alten Literatur und Kunst*. Leipzig.

Weimann, Robert. 1967. *Shakespeare und die Tradition des Volkstheaters*. Berlin.

Weisbach, Werner. 1945. *Religiöse Reform und mittelalterliche Kunst*. Einsiedeln.

Wenzel, Siegfried. 1967. *The Sin of Sloth: Acedia*. Chapel Hill, N.C.

Werlich, Egon. 1967. "Der westgermanische Skop. Der Ursprung des Sänger-gestandes in semasiologischer und etymologischer Sicht." *Zeitschrift für deutsche Philologie* 86: 352–75.

Werner, Jakob. 1907. "Verse auf Papst Innocenz IV. und Kaiser Friedrich II." *Neues Archiv* 32: 602–4.

West, Martin Litchfield. 1974. *Studies in Greek Elegy and Iambus*. Untersuchungen zur antiken Literatur und Geschichte 14. Berlin.

Westra, Haijo J. 1989. "The Speech of Animals in the *Ysengrimus* and the Subversion of a Christian Hierarchy of Discourse." In: *Reinardus: Yearbook of the International Reynard Society*. Ed. Brian Levy and Paul Wackers. Grave. 1/1: 195–206.

Whitesell, Frederick R. 1947. "Fables in Mediaeval Exempla." *Journal of English and Germanic Philology* 46: 348–66.

Willems, Léonard. 1895. *Etude sur l'Ysengrinus*. Université de Gand: Recueil de Travaux Publiés par la Faculté de Philosophie et Lettres 13. Ghent.

Wilmore, Sylvia Bruce. 1974. *Swans of the World*. London.

Wilmotte, Maurice. 1918. "La Patrie du Waltharius." *Revue Historique* 127: 1–30.

———. 1937. "Un centon d'Horace au Xᵉ siècle." *Travaux de la Faculté de Philosophie et Lettres de l'Université de Bruxelles* 7: 255–65.

Wilson, R. M. 1970. *The Lost Literature of Medieval England*. 2d ed. London.

Winterbottom, Michael. 1967. "On the *Hisperica Famina*." *Celtica* 8: 126–39.

Winterfeld, Paul von. 1904. "Paulus diaconus oder Notker der Stammler?" *Neues Archiv der Gesellschaft für Ältere Deutsche Geschichtskunde* 29: 468–71.

Witke, Charles. 1970. *Latin Satire: The Structure of Persuasion*. Leiden.

Wittig, Kurt. 1958. *The Scottish Tradition in Literature*. Edinburgh.

Wolfe, Bernard. 1949. "Uncle Remus and the Malevolent Rabbit." *Commentary* 8: 31–41.

Wölke, Hansjörg. 1978. *Untersuchungen zur Batrachomyomachie*. Beiträge zur Klassischen Philologie 100. Meisenheim am Glan.

Wooller, Susan Jacqueline. 1976. "Lupus in Fabula: The Wolf in Medieval German Fables." Ph.D. diss., McGill University, Montreal.

Wright, Thomas. 1865. *A History of Caricature and Grotesque in Literature and Art*. London. Repr. 1968. New York.

Yates, Donald N. 1979. "The Cock-and-Fox Episodes of *Isengrimus*, Attributed to Simon of Ghent: A Literary and Historical Study." Ph.D. diss., University of North Carolina at Chapel Hill.

———. 1981. "Isengrimus *à clef*." In: *Third International Beast Epic, Fable and Fabliau Colloquium*. 517–36.

———. 1983. "Chanticleer's Latin Ancestors." *Chaucer Review* 18: 116–26.

———. 1984. "Parody in Isengrimus." In: *Epopée animale; Fable; Fabliau*. 701–8.

Yunck, John A. 1963. *The Lineage of Lady Meed: The Development of Mediaeval Venality Satire*. Publications in Mediaeval Studies 17. Notre Dame, Ind.

Zarncke, H. E. 1890. "Beiträge zur *Ecbasis captivi.*" *Berichte über die Verhandlungen der Königlich Sächsischen Gesellschaft der Wissenschaften, Leipzig, philologisch-historische Klasse* 42: 109–26.

Zellinger, J. 1925. "Das geköderte Leviathan im *Hortus deliciarum* des Herrad von Landsberg." *Historisches Jahrbuch* 45: 161–77.

Ziegler, Konrat, and Walther Sontheimer, eds. 1964–75. *Der kleine Pauly.* 5 vols. Munich.

Zimmerman, Albert, and Gudrun Vuillemin-Diez, eds. 1974. *Antiqui und Moderni. Traditionsbewusstein und Fortschrittsbewusstein im späten Mittelalter.* Miscellanea Mediaevalia 9. Berlin.

Ziolkowski, Jan. 1981. "Medieval Latin Beast Poetry: The Development from A.D. 750 to 1150." Ph.D. diss., Cambridge University.

———. 1983a. "Ne bu ne ba." *Neuphilologische Mitteilungen* 84: 287–90.

———. 1983b. "Sedulius Scottus's *De quodam verbece a cane discerpto.*" *Mediaevalia* 9: 1–24.

———. 1985a. "The Medieval Latin Beast Flyting." *Mittellateinisches Jahrbuch* 20: 49–65.

———. 1985b. "Quotations as Glosses: The Prologue of the *Ecbasis Captivi.*" *Res Publica Litterarum* 8: 281–90.

———. 1990a. "The Form and Spirit of Beast Fable." *Bestia: Yearbook of the Beast Fable Society* 2: 4–18.

———. 1990b. "Poultry and Predators in Two Poems From the Reign of Charlemagne." *Denver Quarterly* 24/3: 24–32.

———. 1990c. "Teaching Animals." *Bestia: Yearbook of the Beast Fable Society* 2: 30–40.

———. 1991. "Walahfrid's Poem about a Man Carried to Heaven by an Eagle: Parodic Vision or Serious *Illusio?*" *Poetica: An International Journal of Linguistic-Literary Studies* 34: 1–38.

Index of Subjects and First Lines

Numerals in italics refer to the texts translated in the appendices.

University of Pennsylvania Press
MIDDLE AGES SERIES
Edward Peters, General Editor

F. R. P. Akehurst, trans. *The* Coutumes de Beauvaisis *of Philippe de Beaumanoir.* 1992

Peter L. Allen. *The Art of Love: Amatory Fiction from Ovid to the* Romance of the Rose. 1992

David Anderson. *Before the Knight's Tale: Imitation of Classical Epic in Boccaccio's* Teseida. 1988

Benjamin Arnold. *Count and Bishop in Medieval Germany: A Study of Regional Power, 1100–1350.* 1991

Mark C. Bartusis. *The Late Byzantine Army: Arms and Society, 1204–1453.* 1992

J. M. W. Bean. *From Lord to Patron: Lordship in Late Medieval England.* 1990

Uta-Renate Blumenthal. *The Investiture Controversy: Church and Monarchy from the Ninth to the Twelfth Century.* 1988

Daniel Bornstein, trans. *Dino Compagni's* Chronicle *of Florence.* 1986

Betsy Bowden. *Chaucer Aloud: The Varieties of Textual Interpretation.* 1987

James William Brodman. *Ransoming Captives in Crusader Spain: The Order of Merced on the Christian-Islamic Frontier.* 1986

Kevin Brownlee and Sylvia Huot. *Rethinking the* Romance of the Rose*: Text, Image, Reception.* 1992

Otto Brunner (Howard Kaminsky and James Van Horn Melton, eds. and trans.). Land *and Lordship: Structures of Governance in Medieval Austria.* 1992

Robert I. Burns, S. J., ed. *Emperor of Culture: Alfonso X the Learned of Castile and His Thirteenth-Century Renaissance.* 1990

David Burr. *Olivi and Franciscan Poverty: The Origins of the* Usus Pauper *Controversy.* 1989

Thomas Cable. *The English Alliterative Tradition.* 1991

Anthony K. Cassell and Victoria Kirkham, eds. and trans. *Diana's Hunt/Caccia di Diana: Boccaccio's First Fiction.* 1991

Brigitte Cazelles. *The Lady as Saint: A Collection of French Hagiographic Romances of the Thirteenth Century.* 1991

Karen Cherewatuk and Ulrike Wiethaus. *Dear Sister: Medieval Women and the Epistolary Genre.* 1993

Anne L. Clark. *Elisabeth of Schönau: A Twelfth-Century Visionary.* 1992

Willene B. Clark and Meradith T. McMunn, eds. *Beasts and Birds of the Middle Ages: The Bestiary and Its Legacy.* 1989

Richard C. Dales. *The Scientific Achievement of the Middle Ages.* 1973

Charles T. Davis. *Dante's Italy and Other Essays.* 1984

Katherine Fischer Drew, trans. *The Burgundian Code.* 1972.

Katherine Fischer Drew, trans. *The Laws of the Salian Franks.* 1991

Katherine Fischer Drew, trans. *The Lombard Laws.* 1973

Nancy Edwards. *The Archaeology of Early Medieval Ireland.* 1990

Margaret J. Ehrhart. *The Judgment of the Trojan Prince Paris in Medieval Literature.* 1987

Richard K. Emmerson and Ronald B. Herzman. *The Apocalyptic Imagination in Medieval Literature.* 1992

Felipe Fernández-Armesto. *Before Columbus: Exploration and Colonization from the Mediterranean to the Atlantic, 1229–1492.* 1987

R. D. Fulk. *A History of Old English Meter.* 1992

Patrick J. Geary. *Aristocracy in Provence: The Rhône Basin at the Dawn of the Carolingian Age.* 1985

Peter Heath. *Allegory and Philosophy in Avicenna (Ibn Sînâ), with a Translation of the Book of the Prophet Muhammad's Ascent to Heaven.* 1992

J. N. Hillgarth, ed. *Christianity and Paganism, 350–750: The Conversion of Western Europe.* 1986

Richard C. Hoffman. *Land, Liberties, and Lordship in a Late Medieval Countryside: Agrarian Structures and Change in the Duchy of Wrocław.* 1990

Robert Hollander. *Boccaccio's Last Fiction: Il Corbaccio.* 1988

Edward B. Irving, Jr. *Rereading* Beowulf. 1989

C. Stephen Jaeger. *The Origins of Courtliness: Civilizing Trends and the Formation of Courtly Ideals, 939–1210.* 1985

William Chester Jordan. *The French Monarchy and the Jews: From Philip Augustus to the Last Capetians.* 1989

William Chester Jordan. *From Servitude to Freedom: Manumission in the Sénonais in the Thirteenth Century.* 1986

Ellen E. Kittell. *From* Ad Hoc *to Routine: A Case Study in Medieval Bureaucracy.* 1991

Alan C. Kors and Edward Peters, eds. *Witchcraft in Europe, 1100–1700: A Documentary History.* 1972

Barbara M. Kreutz. *Before the Normans: Southern Italy in the Ninth and Tenth Centuries.* 1992

E. Ann Matter. *The Voice of My Beloved: The Song of Songs in Western Medieval Christianity.* 1990

María Rosa Menocal. *The Arabic Role in Medieval Literary History.* 1987

A. J. Minnis. *Medieval Theory of Authorship.* 1988

Lawrence Nees. *A Tainted Mantle: Hercules and the Classical Tradition at the Carolingian Court.* 1991

Lynn H. Nelson, trans. *The Chronicle of San Juan de la Peña: A Fourteenth-Century Official History of the Crown of Aragon.* 1991

Charlotte A. Newman. *The Anglo-Norman Nobility in the Reign of Henry I: The Second Generation.* 1988

Joseph F. O'Callaghan. *The Cortes of Castile-León, 1188–1350.* 1989

William D. Paden, ed. *The Voice of the Trobairitz: Perspectives on the Women Trobadours.* 1989

Edward Peters. *The Magician, the Witch, and the Law.* 1982

Edward Peters, ed. *Christian Society and the Crusades, 1198–1229: Sources in Translation, including The Capture of Damietta by Oliver of Paderborn.* 1971

Edward Peters, ed. *The First Crusade*: The Chronicle of Fulcher of Chartres *and Other Source Materials.* 1971

Edward Peters, ed. *Heresy and Authority in Medieval Europe.* 1980

James M. Powell. *Albertanus of Brescia: The Pursuit of Happiness in the Early Thirteenth Century.* 1992

James M. Powell. *Anatomy of a Crusade, 1213–1221.* 1986

Michael Resler, trans. Erec *by Hartmann von Aue.* 1987

Pierre Riché (Michael Idomir Allen, trans.). *The Carolingians: A Family Who Forged Europe.* 1993

Pierre Riché (Jo Ann McNamara, trans.). *Daily Life in the World of Charlemagne.* 1978

Jonathan Riley-Smith. *The First Crusade and the Idea of Crusading.* 1986

Joel T. Rosenthal. *Patriarchy and Families of Privilege in Fifteenth-Century England.* 1991

Steven D. Sargent, ed. and trans. *On the Threshold of Exact Science: Selected Writings of Anneliese Maier on Late Medieval Natural Philosophy.* 1982

Sarah Stanbury. *Seeing the* Gawain-*Poet: Description and the Act of Perception.* 1992

Thomas C. Stillinger. *The Song of Troilus: Lyric Authority in the Medieval Book.* 1992

Susan Mosher Stuard. *A State of Deference: Ragusa/Dubrovnik in the Medieval Centuries.* 1992

Susan Mosher Stuard, ed. *Women in Medieval History and Historiography.* 1987

Susan Mosher Stuard, ed. *Women in Medieval Society.* 1976

Jonathan Sumption. *The Hundred Years War: Trial by Battle.* 1992

Ronald E. Surtz. *The Guitar of God: Gender, Power, and Authority in the Visionary World of Mother Juana de la Cruz (1481–1534).* 1990

Patricia Terry, trans. *Poems of the Elder Edda.* 1990

Hugh M. Thomas. *Vassals, Heiresses, Crusaders, and Thugs: The Gentry of Angevin Yorkshire, 1154–1216.* 1993

Frank Tobin. *Meister Eckhart: Thought and Language.* 1986

Ralph V. Turner. *Men Raised from the Dust: Administrative Service and Upward Mobility in Angevin England.* 1988

Harry Turtledove, trans. *The* Chronicle *of Theophanes: An English Translation of Anni Mundi 6095–6305 (A.D. 602–813).* 1982

Mary F. Wack. *Lovesickness in the Middle Ages: The* Viaticum *and Its Commentaries.* 1990

Benedicta Ward. *Miracles and the Medieval Mind: Theory, Record, and Event, 1000–1215.* 1982

Suzanne Fonay Wemple. *Women in Frankish Society: Marriage and the Cloister, 500–900.* 1981

Jan M. Ziolkowski. *Talking Animals: Medieval Latin Beast Poetry, 750–1150.* 1993

Jan M. Ziolkowski is Professor of Medieval Latin and of Comparative Literature at Harvard University.

This book has been set in Linotron Galliard. Galliard was designed for Mergenthaler in 1978 by Matthew Carter. Galliard retains many of the features of a sixteenth-century typeface cut by Robert Granjon but has some modifications that give it a more contemporary look.

Printed on acid-free paper.